REASC

FOR WHAT HAPPENS TO YOU
IN YOUR LIFE
&
YOUR AFTERLIFE

REVEALED BY SPEAKERS
IN THE AFTERLIFE

R. Craig Hogan

Greater Reality Publications
http://greaterreality.com

Contact:

Greater Reality Publications
23 Payne Place, Normal, IL 61761
http://greaterreality.com
800 690-4232
Email: info@greaterreality.com
Order copies: http://orders.greaterreality.com

ISBN 0-9802111-3-1
ISBN-13 978-0-9802111-3-9

Contents

The Four Books

This book is one of four in a series explaining what we know today about the nature of reality, why we know we continue to live after the body dies, our purpose in this life, what happens in pre-birth planning, why we have the experiences we have during this life, and what happens when we leave to live in the life after this life. The books contain explanations of important truths:

1. Your Mind is not produced by or contained in your brain. Your Mind doesn't need a body or a brain.

2. Your Mind is an individual expression of the Universal Intelligence all people are part of—we are all one Mind.

3. Our one Universal Intelligence creates the world we live in.

4. We plan our lives before coming to earth.

5. The purposes of our lives are to learn lessons, grow in love and compassion, and live together with love, peace, and joy.

6. Our individual Minds continue to live after the body ceases to function.

The first two truths are explained in the first book, *Your Eternal Self: Science Discovers the Afterlife*, developed and updated from the book *Your Eternal Self*. It contains the evidence that your Mind is not in your brain, we are one Mind, and you continue to live after the body dies.

The second book, *Reasons for What Happens to You in Your Life and Your Afterlife: Revealed by Speakers in the Afterlife*, explains information from residents of the life after this life about what happens to a person through the major stages of life: deciding to enter Earth School; planning the Earth School experience; learning to succeed in

Earth School; growing in love, compassion, and understanding; graduating; and living in the life after the Earth School life.

The third book, *There Is Nothing but Mind and Experiences,* explains that the Universal Intelligence is the basis of reality and we are individual expressions of it. In it you will learn why we know this is true and what it means for your life in Earth School.

The last book, *Answers to Life's Enduring Questions: From Science Discoveries and Afterlife Revelations,* is an easy-to-read summary of the contents of the other three books, meant for people who want the perspectives but not the detailed explanations and evidence.

Preface

We are not human beings having a spiritual experience.
We are spiritual beings having a human experience.

~ Pierre Teilhard de Chardin

      We are enrolled in Earth School because it provides experiences that result in happiness and sadness, challenges and triumphs, ecstasy and misery, success and failure, cherishing and losing, joy and grief. We call this life Earth School because we entered this unique world of our own free will to love, learn lessons, and be happy. If we are not loving and being loved, learning lessons and helping others learn lessons, and being happy and at peace, then we still have much to learn. That isn't to say we're a failure if we feel unloved, have difficulty loving others, are giving up rather than learning from challenges, or are often depressed and unhappy. Every one of us is learning at the level in which we're able to learn at this time in our eternal lives. We're A+ students at the head of our class. There is no failure or judgment.

      We can choose to be loved and abundantly love others, to be filled with peace and contentment, to confront challenges with confidence and learn from our triumphs, and to be joyous nearly all the time. We can use our free will to create the lives we want to live. We just have to know who we are in eternity, have confidence that we can triumph over adversities and learn from the struggles, and use our free will to make changes in our lives and understanding of experiences that will bring us love, peace, and joy.

      I wrote this book because there is widespread ignorance and misinformation about our place in eternity, the purpose of our lives in Earth School, and what our lives will be like after we graduate. People are taught we must meet certain standards to be worthy of love, that we must live separated from most people out of wariness, that challenges and disasters are beyond our control so we are helpless victims, that we need specific things and people in our lives to be happy, and that to be contented the world and people around us must change because we're dependent on things and people for our happiness. These are all lies that are preventing people from living loving, peaceful, joyful lives.

The most important and difficult task in our lives in Earth School is to reject these lies and give up on trying to find happiness in anything we call me or mine. When we have swept our Minds clean, we can furnish our lives with the knowledge and beliefs that will allow us to learn life's lessons while always being loving, peaceful, and joyful.

Most people don't know why we're here, why our lives have suffering and tragedies, what we can do to live joy-filled lives, and what to expect after we graduate from this life. Most people drift through life without a clear sense of purpose or understanding that they are creating their lives and can change themselves to live in love, peace, and joy. They feel they are victims of a cold, uncaring universe. They are not. They have the ability and resources to create lives filled with happiness, fulfillment, and optimism about the future. They just don't know how to use the ability and resources.

I also wrote this book because most people don't know what has happened to their loved ones who are no longer seen in this life, and they fear what will become of themselves when their bodies die. People visit the cemetery looking down at the ground or up at the mausoleum and grieve as though their loved ones were there, buried in the ground or cold and lifeless in the crypt. They feel unease about how their loved ones are faring, and they fear for their own destiny. Many people sense their loved ones live on in another form, but they don't understand the realities of what happens when someone is no longer using a body in this world. They have been taught erroneous myths: that people not living in bodies are vaporous apparitions or have merged into the Universal Intelligence or have reincarnated so they're not even the same person they were.

This book will reassure you that your loved ones who preceded you to the next stage of life are living contented, fulfilled lives today, and you will do the same. You can communicate with them when you want to. You can have continuing, loving relationships with them while you are still in Earth School. They will come to your graduation from this life and sit patiently waiting for you to come off the stage into their embrace. Every person you have loved and every pet you ever owned will be there to greet you. The graduation ceremony will be a celebration.

I wrote this book to tell you what we know today about our purpose in this life, why this life is as it is, what happens in the transition from this life, and how people live in the life after this life. It will clear up misconceptions for you and give you reassurance that your loved ones are living a full life as healthy, happy individuals who have just moved to another country. I want this book to give you comfort, reassurance, and joy that you will live on after you stop using the body, and you will have joyous reunions with all those who have preceded you.

Love, peace, and joy,
Craig

A Note about Personal Pronouns

In the past, masculine pronouns ("he," "his," "him") were used to refer to a person when the gender wasn't specified. With the movement to remove gender discrimination in language usage, writers were forced to use clumsy alternatives such as "(s)he" and "he/she" for the personal pronoun that refers to one person. Those were never satisfactory. To get around the problem, some writers alternate between feminine and masculine pronouns throughout the document. That also is distracting and unsatisfactory.

However, languages always take care of themselves. They evolve to fit society's requirements. In today's English, people are substituting plural pronouns for singular in their speaking and writing, as in "Each plant supervisor must monitor their employees carefully." The result is quite satisfying. While some grammarians resist the movement, organizations are sanctioning this use of plural pronouns. In 2016, the American Dialect Society agreed "they" and "their" can be used as singular pronouns.[1]

Since that is the most satisfactory solution for avoiding the issue of sexism in language, this book uses plural pronouns for singular ones freely.

Afterlife Research and Education Website Links

Additional readings and links with valuable information about the subjects of the chapters are on the website at www.earthschoolanswers.com.

There Is Nothing but Mind and Experiences

You will understand the concepts in this book better if you read *There Is Nothing but Mind and Experiences.* You will see references throughout this book to Mind, experiences, the Universal Intelligence, the Earth School Mind, and other concepts explained in *There Is Nothing but Mind and Experiences.*

1

Why We Know These Explanations Are True

Today, for the first time in humankind's history, technology is allowing us to record and disseminate messages from people living in the life after this life. We have vast libraries of their descriptions of what happens before we enter Earth School, what our lives can be like if we wake up to our true nature and learn how to have a change of heart and Mind, what transpires during the transition from this life to the next, and evidence people live on after the body no longer functions. The communications with vast numbers of people now living in the life after this life are proof these communicators we have called "deceased" are very much alive. We have many recordings of spouses and children, who left Earth School years before, speaking casually to their loved ones still on this side of life, as though they were sitting at the breakfast table talking about everyday events.

These many accounts of the life after this life have an extremely high level of corroboration with each other. AfterlifeData.com is the largest database of afterlife descriptions and analyses on the Internet, containing a large collection of spirit communications describing the next stage of life. The results of the research comparing accounts of the nature of the afterlife in the AfterlifeData.com archives show 94.4 percent agreement on 265 very specific afterlife topic areas.[2] The corroborated evidence is undeniable. We know we live on after our bodies cease to function. The information in this book is taken from these corroborated descriptions.

Following are some of the communications we're having commonly now that are teaching us about the afterlife.

Near-death experiences: According to a Gallup poll in 1992, 13 million Americans, 5 percent of the population, have had near-death experiences (NDEs).[3] The same poll found that 774 NDEs are experienced every day in the United States. A survey in Germany found 4 percent of the population had experienced an NDE.[4] Their accounts provide corroborated descriptions of characteristics of the next stage of life viewed from the experiencers' vantage point overlooking the next life from the edge of this life.

After-death communications: A broad range of studies of after-death communications have shown that around 40 percent of people say they have had an after-death communication experience, with the percentage as high as 70 or 80 percent for widows.[5] Many books have been written by people who have learned to communicate with their loved ones no longer on the earth realm. Amazon.com lists 40,000 books involving the afterlife. The accounts of the communications are detailed and agree in their descriptions of the life after this life.

Induced After-Death Communication and Repair & Reattachment Grief Therapy: From 70 to 98 percent (depending on the environment) of patients who undergo Induced After-Death Communication (IADC™) or Repair & Reattachment Grief Therapy insist they experienced an after-death communication with the person for whom they are grieving. Thousands of people have now had these experiences.[6] The reports people provide to their psychotherapists during these counseling sessions have added to our understanding of the life after this life. The people's loved ones describe their life there, the nature of life in general, the events during their transition from the earth realm, and a wide range of other information about this life and the next.

Mental medium communications: Over the last two centuries, thousands of mediums have had communication with people who have transitioned to the next life, with the results of the medium readings being verified by the family members. The shelves of bookstores are now crowded with books containing mediums' accounts of the readings and what the sessions have taught them about the afterlife.

Carefully controlled research has demonstrated that mental mediums communicate with people living in the life after this life. Researchers from the University of Arizona conducted experiments to see whether the mediums are communicating with people's loved ones. Between 77 and 85 percent of the facts the mediums described, without knowing or seeing the sitter, were accurate.[7]

Other researchers from the Windbridge Research Center used a quintuple-blind protocol in which the researchers, the sitters, and the mediums knew nothing about each other. The findings were that the readings had similar rates of accuracy.[8]

Donna Smith-Moncrieffe, director of the research organization Metaphysics Research, found that 73 percent of readings in her double-blind research met "the high-level evidence standard."[9]

These reports have provided insights into the life after this life that are consistent across time, geography, and cultures.

Direct voice and materialization medium communications: A number of direct-voice and physical mediums have enabled people in the life after this life to speak to assembled groups. Direct-voice mediums and materialization mediums have held carefully controlled séances in which unmistakable voices of those in spirit are heard. Thousands of their sessions now exist and are available in audio recordings, such as those of David Thompson[10] and Leslie Flint.[11] They have provided the clearest descriptions of the afterlife. To listen to some recordings, link to www.earthschoolanswers.com/reunions/.

Family member communications with loved ones: Anyone can communicate with loved ones living in the next life. Many people have taught themselves how to communicate with their husbands, wives, siblings, and children using meditation, pendulums, and other means. They have shared what they have learned in a large number of books that provide a rich source of information about the next life.

In all, we now have a vast amount of information from the citizens of the life after this life. This storehouse of knowledge has given us an understanding of pre-birth events, mental and spiritual growth during this life, what happens to someone when the body dies, what life is like on the next planes of life, and what those in the next stage of life advise for us who are still on the earth.

In this book, you will see citations that reference books containing valid, reliable communication with people living in the life after this life.

Recommended Video with Examples Proving the Reality of the Life after This Life

Videos containing audio clips of speakers in the life after this life, descriptions by people who have had afterlife communications, and communication by people who have learned to have their own afterlife communication experiences are available at www.earthschoolanswers.com/proof/.

Recommended Sources of Information about Life after This Life

These books containing statements by people living in the life after this life are among the sources used for this book:

~ Miles Allen's *The Realities of Heaven: Fifty Spirits Describe Your Future Home*[12]

~ Stafford Betty's *The Afterlife Unveiled*[13]

~ Anthony Borgia's *The World Unseen*,[14] which includes *Life in the World Unseen, More About Life in the World Unseen,* and *Here and Hereafter*

~ Riley Heagerty's *The Hereafter: Firsthand Reports from the Frontiers of the Afterlife* [15]

~ Robert Crookall's *The Supreme Adventure: Analyses of Psychic Communications*[16]

~ Rob Schwartz's *Your Soul's Plan*[17] and *Your Soul's Gift*[18]

~ Mike Tymn's *The Afterlife Revealed: What Happens After We Die*[19]

Many other books containing records of people's communication from the life after this life are included in the bibliography.

In addition, the Leslie Flint recordings are a treasure trove of recordings of people living in the life after this life speaking through direct-voice medium Leslie Flint about their transitions, the period after their transitions, and their lives in the life after this life. The recordings are available to listen to on the Leslie Flint Education Trust's website at www.leslieflint.com.

2

What Is Earth School?

Everything we experience during our lives from birth to our transition at the death of the body is Earth School. Before our entry into Earth School, our Higher Selves and Souls wanted to have specific experiences that would help us grow in wisdom, love, and compassion and feel the range of emotions resulting from Earth School experiences. We chose to participate with other Souls in Earth School experiences in the twentieth and twenty-first centuries because this is the realm and the time affording experiences through which we can learn and grow.

Earth School consists of accessible experiences from the Universal Intelligence. The fact that earth is a world of experiences doesn't mean it isn't substantial—it is. Matter and energy are the fabric of Earth School. But the threads and weave of the fabric are entirely the Universal Intelligence.

Some suggest that this experiential world is an illusion, called "maya" in Buddhism and Hinduism. Life is not an illusion in the sense of being a hallucination. However, the basis of matter and energy is different from the commonly held belief that matter and energy exist independent of the Universal Intelligence. The matter and energy that seem to make up Earth School are only experiences accessed by our Minds, which are individual manifestations of the Universal Intelligence. Read *There Is Nothing but Mind and Experiences*[20] to find out why we know that is true.

The Universal Intelligence Is Making Available Earth School Experiences That Perfectly Suit Us

Our eternal selves are having experiences made available uniquely for us in a realm we call earth. This realm is perfectly designed to allow us to thrive and achieve our goals. In the cold, dead universe described by materialist scientists, such a realm would not be possible.

Roger Penrose, mathematical physicist and Nobel Laureate in physics, claims that in order for a physical world to produce a universe that even very roughly looks like ours, its initial conditions at the big bang must have been fine-tuned with a precision of one to $10^{10^{123}}$, which would be the largest number ever conceived.[21] A universe of matter and energy apart from consciousness, with monstrous galaxies and a plethora of stars, is impossible.

Stephen Hawking, the theoretical physicist who was director of research at the Centre for Theoretical Cosmology at the University of Cambridge, wrote, "The remarkable fact is that the values of these numbers [the constants of physics] seem to have been very finely adjusted to make possible the development of life."[22]

Michael Turner, an astrophysicist at the University of Chicago Fermi Lab, wrote, "The precision is as if one could throw a dart across the entire universe and hit a bull's-eye one millimeter in diameter on the other side."[23]

The characteristics of a perfectly tuned universe the scientists are amazed to see are the scenery for our experiences in Earth School. This seemingly impossible realm has the evidence of such fine-tuning because it is being provided for us uniquely. It fits perfectly.

There Is No Universe of Matter and Energy Apart from Us

There is no universe made of matter and energy that exists whether we are here or not. The earth is not just the third rock from the sun, born in the chaos of collisions of planetoids composed of stardust. Earth is not an accident in time created 4.5 billion years ago that will expire in fire in another 4.8 billion years. We individuals on earth are not soft rocks, flukes of nature that haltingly evolved from accidents in a primordial soup of protein molecules through dumb chance. Instead, Earth School, the universe, and all that ever was or ever will be is experiences in the Universal Intelligence that we participate in as individuals. The sole purpose of Earth School is to give us opportunities to love, learn, and be happy.

Max Planck, the theoretical physicist who originated quantum theory and won the Nobel Prize in Physics in 1918, wrote,

> I regard consciousness as fundamental. I regard matter as derivative from consciousness. We cannot get behind consciousness. Everything that we talk about, everything that we regard as existing, postulates consciousness.[24]

A well-known researcher of Spiritualism and mediumship, Riley Heagerty presents a quote by a "spirit communicator" about matter and consciousness:

> There is one universal being, present in all parts of the universe, whose purposes are benevolent. Mind does not proceed from matter nor matter from mind, but both are qualities with that being. You are part of that being.[25]

We as expressions of the Universal Intelligence have the primary role in creating and sustaining Earth School. R. C. Henry, professor of physics and astronomy at Johns Hopkins University, wrote,

> A fundamental conclusion of the new physics also acknowledges that the observer creates the reality. As observers, we are personally involved with the creation of our own reality. Physicists are being forced to admit that the universe is a "mental" construction.[26]

There is nothing but the Universal Intelligence, and we are Earth School Minds who are individuated members of the Universal Intelligence.

Even quantum physics, looking at reality from a materialistic perspective, now agrees we create the reality we experience when we attend to it. Anton Zeilinger, the Austrian quantum physicist, writes,

We know that it is wrong to assume that the features of a system which we observe exist prior to our measurement. What we perceive as reality now depends on our earlier decision on what to measure; which is a very deep message about the nature of reality and about our role in the Universe. We are not just passive observers looking at the stage and watching things.[27]

Some people call this reality a "vibration," which suggests a physical realm that vibrates. Our Earth School Minds do not vibrate, and there is no realm outside of the Universal Intelligence. It is better to think of the varieties of reality as attunements to the experiences in each reality. My Earth School Mind receives its individuality as an expression of the Universal Intelligence by being attuned to Earth School experiences. So does your Earth School Mind. Because we're attuned to the same set of experiences, we are able to act together.

Tim Gray, speaking from the life after this life to medium August Goforth, explains the same understanding:

And, August, I also now see that the dense bodies of humans on earth prevent them from usually directly feeling the experience of simultaneously interacting realities, which is going on always, no matter what plane they are on—at least on your plane and the one I'm on. The concept of vibration is used a lot for the ongoing life experience of all beings on all planes of existence. I see the word "vibration" a lot in many of the books you read, and I hear it communicated in many contexts around me here. I've become more aware that it's not simple but a very complex, mysterious something. I didn't realize any of this on my own, since my understanding of it was very limited as a human on earth. I was like a newborn baby when I got here, and still am in most ways.[28]

Instead of thinking of Earth School as a vibration, it is better to think of it as being like a dream that has all the sensory characteristics we experience and does not end by waking until the end of the Earth School experiences. It is solid and real, with the experiences of matter and energy.

These Experiences Have Causes, Effects, and Continuity

To love, learn lessons, and experience happiness, Earth School has causes, effects, and continuity. This is the billiard-ball world where one thing seems to cause another. We act and what is acted upon reacts. We know when we enter a room and experience the sight of a chair that someone has had the experience of placing a chair there. Chairs don't appear without cause and effect; someone placed the chair there. The Universal Intelligence provides the experiences that maintain our sense that what we experience was caused by experiences that preceded them.

These experiences are accessible to us so we feel we have a stable environment we all share. Without continuity, we would not feel safe and stable. We would not be able to plan and make decisions about the future. Having a past with experiences from which we learn and having a future to provide potentials for growing in love and wisdom are necessary for our success in Earth School.

Continuity allows us to exercise our free will to manipulate the environment in Earth School to achieve our goals. We know because of our past experiences that we can anticipate success in planning for future experiences. We know how to change our choices to make desirable future experiences materialize because of the continuity we expect from Earth School.

Our life experiences come to us because of our collective expectation that the world will be as it is from day to day and that as we make changes to the world, the experiences become available from our common Universal Intelligence. We don't think about the process; we don't ask for everyday experiences. The experiences come as a natural flow, just as a flower unfolds from a bud without the bud's asking to become a flower.

We Were Reared to Expect the Earth School Experiences

These experiences that come to our minds are what we all learned to expect from childhood. We expect weather, houses, trees, peaches, and the people we know because we were reared to expect them as we grew in our early days in Earth School. Those who came before us experienced them, and now the Universal Intelligence continues to give all of us these experiences because we newcomers learned to expect them. We are perpetuating the Earth School realm by expecting these experiences. The Universal Intelligence gives us what we expect just as it gives us the memory of a person's face when we ask to experience it in our Minds. If we didn't have the continuity in our experiences of the world, we would feel "out of our minds." We would be severely stressed because we could not feel the world is safe and predictable.

When we walk together into a room, we experience a room drawn from experiences in the Universal Intelligence because we intended to walk into the same room. I am accessing the experiences of the room and you are accessing the experiences of the room. We each access our own set of experiences. They are similar because the experiences have accumulated from our past experiences with the room, so there is continuity in what we each experience. However, there is no room outside of us. All these experiences are accessible by our Minds from the Universal Intelligence.

Who Created Earth School?

The question must be in the present tense: "Who is providing the experiences of Earth School?" The past tense is appropriate only for a universe made of matter and energy outside of us. There is no world outside of our Minds that was created and now exists somewhere in space. There are only the experiences we have in the point of now that are accessible from the Universal Intelligence.

Who determines the experiences we have in Earth School? We do. We are having the experiences because we want and expect them. We are experiencing an Earth School available to us because of our expectations and plans for the Earth School experience. We are creating the Earth School experiences at a level much more fundamental than our sluggish day-to-day consciousness. At that deeper level, we are accessing the experiences because we as individuals and as a whole humanity expect them. The Universal Intelligence does provide the scenery for the drama of our lives, such as flowers, forests, rivers, weather, and all of Mother Nature, but we continue to experience them because we grew up experiencing them. These experiences we call reality are not in a physical reality in space. We form them into reality.

Most of these experiences have been experienced over time by all the people who have had experiences in Earth School. Then they created new experiences that became available to people's Minds in the Universal Intelligence.

We chose to attune ourselves to the experiences available in the Universal Intelligence for the twentieth and twenty-first centuries in Earth School. We access the experiences attuned to this time and place because we grew into the common experiences of Earth School from childhood. We could have grown up as Inuit Eskimos, ancient Egyptians, or pygmy tribespeople in the Congo basin. We would have accessed different experiences with different people who had the same experiences drawn from the Universal Intelligence.

Out of the billions and billions of experiences we could have, drawn from all times and all realms in the cosmos, we are accessing the narrow sliver that fits with our brief lives in Earth School. Every experience that ever was or ever will be is accessible to us because we are the Universal Intelligence taking on roles as individuals in Earth School. However, our Minds stay in character and access only those experiences that give us continuity, stability, and cause and effect in our narrow sliver of Earth School. We don't realize we are accessing the right experiences, and we usually don't ask for them. As we play our roles in Earth School, our lives unfold as we access the right experiences to make what I call "myself" in what I experience as Earth School.

Amy Johnson, a British aviator who left Earth School in 1941, spoke from the life after this life in a Leslie Flint session in 1971 describing the way in which humanity has created the cosmos as it is. You can listen to Amy Johnson speaking these words and more about how humankind has created the environment at www.earthschoolanswers.com/amy/.

> I don't think it was ever intended that anyone should have been born imperfect either mentally or physically. I think this is what man himself has created over eons of time and although one doesn't like the old adage about the sins of the fathers falling on

the children, because it all sounds so unjust and very unfair, but then again, if one sees more clearly that one is the product of other people in every sense. I mean mentally, physically and every way—not just of one's parents either.

Because when you realize you're all sharing the same spirit and that you're all brought into being in the material sense in the same way, that you're all sort of linked up and that after all is said and done, I don't think that if … it can be anything else. If generations of people think wrongly, then they're bound to recreate and create wrongly, you know, and they're bound to be imperfections because you cannot think wrong without acting wrong, and the physical conditions of the past must catch up with the present and the future.[29]

We are one with the physical realm and are creating a world that is shaped by the spiritual beings we have grown to be. All of us, together, are bearing fruit from the trees we are, every moment of our lives. Together, our world has available for us only the fruit we have all created. If we live in a world of fear, self-absorption, tragedy, suffering, disease, conflict, and violence, it is because we are creating it, moment by moment. If we live in a world of love, compassion, joy, and other-centeredness, it is because we are creating it.

Seven Ways We Create Our Reality

We create the reality of Earth School in seven ways:

1. We planned the general framework of our lives in Earth School before our births. The Universal Intelligence is giving us the general circumstances of what we planned. However, we have free will to reject any part of the plan if we so decide.

2. We have control over our responses to experiences. We can change the programming we received in childhood to create our own, unique interpretations of experiences and responses. We can interpret other people as being loving and lovable (although flawed), and our experiences as

opportunities for happiness. We have the opportunity to control our interpretations.

3. We make ourselves happy or miserable by choosing to dwell on happy or miserable thoughts. The reality we create in Earth School can be one in which we see love, peace, and joy in all things or we see rejection, discord, and unhappiness. What we choose to see in what we experience results in our emotional reactions.

4. We create our body experience. At a very deep level, we change our body experiences by our expectations. We make ourselves sick and fatigued or energetic and healthy. Read the full explanation in *There Is Nothing but Mind and Experiences*.[30]

5. We create the life we decide to live with what we intentionally put in it. If we fill our lives with people, things, and experiences embodying fear, competition, manipulation, self-absorption, anger, and violence, our world will feel like it's filled with fearful, competitive, manipulative, angry, self-absorbed, violent people and we will live in the miserable, dysfunctional world we've created. Living in atmospheres with negativity is like swimming through polluted water.

   On the other hand, if we fill our lives with people, things, and experiences embodying love, peace, and joy, our lives will be more loving, peaceful, and joyful. We will be loving, peaceful, and joyful with others and they will reciprocate. We create that atmosphere.

6. We are also creating reality as a collective. If humankind evolves to have only love, joy, and peace with each other, everything in Earth School will show the influence of those glorious sentiments. The stress illnesses will disappear. Violence will be no more. People will care for one another eagerly so there will be no misery or suffering. These positive characteristics of living together will come about because we will be creating a new, glorious reality and

eradicating a reality filled with hatred, unhappiness, self-absorption, and discord.

7. The Universal Intelligence is giving us the matter and energy at the fundamental level of the Earth School world because of what we have learned to expect in the world. This realm is available to us through the Universal Intelligence as the perfect environment in which to love, learn lessons, and be happy—to fulfill our purposes in Earth School. Since we have been reared in Earth School as it is, the Universal Intelligence gives us continuity by maintaining the experiences we have of the Earth School environment. We don't have to ask for it—the Universal Intelligence gives it to us without our realizing it. And so, we perpetuate the Earth School environment because we now expect it, including diseases.

Those experiences we all access can be changed by our collective minds, even the experience of mountains, but we will not come to the point of changing the experience of the Rocky Mountains. We instead accept the experiences we have in Earth School, manipulate experiences in it, and love, learn, and enjoy life within the experiences.

Yeshua bar Yosef, a great teacher whose name evolved into the English "Jesus," is reported to have said, "Truly, I tell you, if anyone says to this mountain, 'Go, throw yourself into the sea,' and does not doubt in their heart but believes that what they say will happen, it will be done for them" (Mark 11:23 NIV). Scholars have suggested this is a metaphor of sorts, but in his wisdom, Yeshua meant that literally. We create our reality. Because we create the scenery collectively, we can't do something that violates others' experiences. The mountain will remain there. However, it is our deeply felt experience of the mountain together that gives us a mountain. If we all expected the mountain to cast itself into the sea, it would be so. Yeshua meant that literally.

Our Fellowship in Earth School Is Important

Our fellowship with each other is very important. Thus our shared experiences are critical to our time in Earth School. They unify us. We are like a family or a team with the same goals and the same activities. We are in this together. We who enrolled together, including our Soul group, are comrades in this experience. Siblings with the same biological parents are closer to each other than any other people because they share the same genetic makeup. In the same way, we are brothers and sisters with those currently enrolled in Earth School. We agreed to have these experiences with each other. We are attuned to the same narrow set of experiences out of the billions and billions of experiences available in the Universal Intelligence. We are creating this reality together by our expectations for what this reality must contain. Out of the untold masses of people and entities living on the millions of planes and spheres with their own realities, only we are so closely bonded in this Earth School because we are attuned to the same vast set of experiences.

We Are Responsible for Changing Humankind

An important responsibility we have in Earth School is to evolve humankind. Humankind is in the situation it is in today because all the individuals, including you and me, are creating this Earth School as it is. If we want this time on Earth to be filled with love, joy, and peace, we must create a loving, joyful, peaceful world. It may seem that we individuals have little power over the other seven or eight billion people on the planet, but all the people are individuals changing themselves and thereby changing the world. When we change, society will change. When society changes, all of us will live in the paradise that is Earth School imbued with love, peace, and joy. We have a responsibility to change society.

When we change society, those who enter Earth School after us will not have to abandon so much of their childhood teaching. Children will be well on their way to achieving higher levels of love, compassion, peace, and brotherhood because society will have given them interpretations, beliefs, and mores that they agree as adults are loving, compassionate, and other-centered.

Why Does Earth School Have Laws of Physics?

We discover consistencies about matter and energy we call laws of physics, but they are only experiences in our Minds that are expressions of the Universal Intelligence. The Earth School environment has what Tom Campbell calls "rule sets" we must adhere to.[31] If we jump off a high cliff, we will be dashed on the rocks below. Eating high-calorie foods will result in our gaining weight. We must travel through space by our conscious effort to go from Paris to New York. We experience the arrow of time, from past to present to future. All the characteristics of Earth School are part of the environment created for us that will enable us to love, learn lessons, and have happy lives. We call these rule sets laws of physics or natural laws.

The rule set is unique to Earth School. Most of the rules don't apply in other realms. In the realm of life that most people enter after graduating from Earth School, which the Theosophists called "Summerland," jumping off a cliff will not result in our dashing ourselves on the rocks below. We won't need to worry about gaining weight; in fact, we won't need to eat at all. There is the perception of space as there is in Earth School, but when someone wants to visit a library a thousand miles of earth space away, that person simply intends to be there and instantly is standing before the stacks of books. Space is in our perception, not in a world outside of us.

Time also is in our perception. The residents of the life after this life say there is a "time of sorts" because there are sequences and people have memories of experiences. However, they do not observe time as we do. There are no clocks, and no one refers to "o'clock" (meaning "of the clock") when deciding when to meet. They simply have the commonly held thought when it is time to meet. They gain a sense of earth time when they receive our thoughts about holidays and celebrations. Our preoccupation with time in Earth School is part of the Earth School experience, not a condition of the cosmos.

The rule sets for Earth School give us consistency, consequences for actions, and clear, predictable structure for daily life. We need that stability to function. Humankind then imposes other sets of rules on us that are not part of the rule set. We must not take someone else's stuff against their will. We may "own" things, but the ownership is entirely by assent of those around us. We may not drive a car without a license. All of the rules society imposes add to the rules that are the rule sets for Earth School.

Will Earth School End?

> Some say the world will end in fire,
> Some say in ice.
> From what I've tasted of desire
> I hold with those who favor fire.
> But if it had to perish twice,
> I think I know enough of hate
> To say that for destruction ice
> Is also great
> And would suffice.
>
> ~ *Robert Frost*

Materialists, believing the universe is an accident in time independent of us, assume the universe began from a tiny singularity at the big bang and will eventually either collapse back into a singularity, so it ends in fire, or will continue expanding until the energy is dissipated, so it ends in ice, figuratively.

However, the universe is only experiences we individual manifestations of the Universal Intelligence have. It never "began" in the sense of being created. Instead, people started having experiences that are Earth School experiences.

The "universe" is experiences we are accessing in our awareness from moment to moment. The universe doesn't "exist" in the sense of being matter, energy, and forces separate from people with separate people living in it. As long as there are people attuned to Earth School, they will continue to have Earth School experiences. Nothing can harm the individuals in the Universal Intelligence. If people stop having Earth School experiences, it will be because we are all attuned to other realms. If we decide to tune into Earth School again, we will continue with the experiences we're having, but there will still be no realm of matter and energy that exists apart from individuals.

We are having experiences in Earth School to love, learn lessons, and enjoy the experience. Earth School will not end in fire or ice. People will continue to experience an Earth School as long as it fits with people's goals for their lives.

Why Are There Beginnings and Endings?

Beginnings and endings seem like the natural order of things, but they are not. They are part of the Earth School experience. We experience things being created and annihilated. We have seasons with growth and destruction of the growth. We have birth experiences and death experiences. Earth School is the realm of change in which we experience beginnings and endings.

In the other realms of life, experiences change but do not end. People grow in mental and spiritual stature but do not experience a death. Flowers and animals flourish without dying. People transition to higher levels in their lives, but nothing dies. There are no ends, although there are transitions.

Why Are There Cruel and Violent People Here?

This period in Earth School's history is a crucible with all types of Earth School Minds. Some have planned lives in which they have no conscience: they are psychopaths. Some have chosen to be in a family and environment with great conflict, abuse, and violence. Others have chosen to be in a family and environment filled with love, regard, and sensitivity.

In Earth School, we interact with the entire range of people, from those who planned insensitive, violent lives to those who planned gentle, loving lives. We interact with different types of people from moment to moment. As a result, we have great challenges, a variety of models of kind, loving people, and a wide range of opportunities. We chose to enter Earth School knowing there are dangers, tragedies, and pain. We knew we would see maleficence, manipulation, greed, and inhumanity. But we also knew there would be the happiness of loving and being loved, feelings of happiness and delight, triumphs over challenges, ecstasy in learning and discovering, and great rewards. We knew this would be a time of discovery, advancements in spiritual wisdom and technological knowledge, and opportunities to love, grow, and enjoy life.

Do We Have Free Will to Choose as We Wish?

In this ever-changing realm that is Earth School, we have free will to choose what we want to become. We can thwart our life's plan by making choices that divert us from the path. However, our guides and Soul take steps to shepherd us toward the right path. Their guidance does not interfere with our free will. We can choose to live a life of personal growth in becoming more wise, peaceful, loving, and happy, or continuing to tolerate stunted growth, discord, discontent, and unhappiness.

The reactions that are loving and compassionate or cruel and insensitive come automatically from our subconscious repertoire of interpretations of experiences. However, we have the ability to examine and work at changing the automatic reactions so we are loving, compassionate, and other-centered. We can choose to live lives full of love, peace, and joy even though we started our lives with examples and teaching from the environment we grew up in that resulted in tendencies toward being self-absorbed, violent, cruel, insensitive, and unhappy.

We are exercising our free will when we challenge our beliefs and circumstances with the help of our guides, loved ones, and Soul. Their counsel does not interfere with our free will. It enhances our decisions. On the other hand, people who feel they need to maintain rigidly a belief system and lifestyle based on their early childhood in Earth School are not exercising their free will. They are prisoners of their childhoods, blindly following what comes from the subconscious formed by their parents and society.

We have free will to truncate our experience in Earth School by ending our lives. However, suicide and violence are not in any Soul's plan. These events are free-will choices people make that are not planned, although a person may choose to be born into violence-enhancing circumstances with a personality prone to committing violent acts.

The talented medium and teacher Suzanne Giesemann asked Sanaya, a collective of consciousness of Minds from a higher dimension that she channels, whether murder is in a Soul's plan. Sanaya answered, "The soul does not come back to murder. That is free will gone awry."[32]

She also received a clear message about rape and similar violent acts from a trusted person living in the next life:

> Suzanne, we come to love each other. Being thrown into a human body is like being thrown into the lion's den. What there is is the possibility of being put into soul groups with people in various stages of awakening. It just doesn't make sense. The soul comes to love. The soul comes from a place of love. You're not going to get your "get out of jail free" card if they know you're going to be a repeat offender. The soul comes to love, to be set free, not to go into bondage by raping or killing or maiming someone. Those are the lions and tigers and bears. Yes, the potential is there to do harm, and it's when a lower soul gets in with other lower souls that the free will does go awry.[33]

Rob Schwartz, author of *Your Soul's Plan* and *Your Soul's Gift*, describes insights he received about suicide through the mediums he worked with as he learned about Soul planning.

> In the Suicide chapter in my second book *Your Soul's Gift*, I share the story of Carolyn, whose only child Cameron suicided shortly after he graduated from high school. Carolyn and I had a channeling session in which we spoke with Jeshua (Jesus). Jeshua began by telling us that suicide is never planned prior to birth as a certainty, but it is planned as a possibility or sometimes as a high probability, as was the case with Cameron. In other words, Cameron knew that he was taking on so much in this lifetime that a suicide was likely. He was willing to take that risk, and his loved ones agreed before birth to accept that risk as well.[34]

When someone ends their life or there is a murder, the life plans of the others involved with the person may be affected. In that case, their Souls and guides work to change the circumstances in their Earth

School environments to shepherd the others back into alignment with their pre-birth plans. The person may still decline to accept the realignments.

We always have free will to thrive in Earth School as we follow our life's plan or thwart it, even to the point of exiting Earth School before our tasks have been accomplished.

Does Chance Exist?

Since we plan our lives before entering Earth School, some ask whether our lives are pre-determined. In other words, can things can happen by chance? The answer is that some things do happen by chance. Anabela Cardoso is a former Portuguese career diplomat who lives in Spain and publishes the *Instrumental Transcommunication Journal*. She reports that entities communicating from the Rio do Tempo (Timestream) station, which broadcasts voices from the other realms to earth, explain that chance does exist.

> This statement drives me to consider that perhaps only the most important events of each life are predetermined in a kind of compromise between the deterministic view of some Spiritualists and the random chance view of some materialists.[35]

Why Is There Time?

Time as we know it is part of the scenery in Earth School. Time in other realms is not quite the same as time in Earth School. People living in the life after this life say they don't have the sense of time we have in Earth School. There is no sun, so there are no years or days. There is no moon. There are no clocks. People don't count time. They do get a sense of time when they return to Earth School, and they receive our thoughts, so they know when birthdays and anniversaries are coming up. Otherwise, they don't keep track of what we call time.

As we have experiences in the now, the environment and circumstances change. Because the environment is different in one point of now from the previous now, we say there has been a time period over which the change occurred. Change results in a sense of time. Without change and the experiences we now have in our repertoire of experiences that we call memories, there would be no sense of time.

We have a sense of what we call the past because we can access memories of experiences we have had in Earth School. We construct what we believe will happen in the future from our memories of experiences that happened in the past that we project into the future. Our sense of time, in other words, is entirely in our Minds. If we had no memories of experiences, we would have no sense of time.

The experiences we say happened in the past that are now accessible are not stored in the brain—that is a primitive notion from the time when it was thought that Minds and memories were in brains. Instead, memories are experiences accessible from a vast field of experiences that includes everything ever experienced in Earth School and every thought anyone has had. We know that is true because people are able to access experiences using just the Mind: psychics are able to access thoughts and sensed experiences the psychic never experienced; remote viewers are able to experience objects thousands of miles away the remote viewers never experienced; past-life regression participants are able to access memories from lives other than their own. All these people access the experiences through the same procedure we use to access memories: they intend to bring the experiences into their awareness and the experiences come. Accessing experiences does not require that the experiences have been in what we call our past.

We have the ability to access experiences we have had more easily than experiences someone else has experienced or experiences of objects thousands of miles away we have not encountered. If we suddenly had access to the experiences that another person has had, we would feel we have a different past and would envision a different future. Time would be different, and we would be different people because our accumulation of memory experiences would have changed. We need the arrow of time from past to present to future in order to function and learn in Earth School.

Why Is There Space?

Experiences must be apparent in space. The experience of sight requires a sense of space. The experience of touch requires a non-touch when space intervenes between the toucher and touched. The experience of sound requires atmosphere between the sounding event and the ear experience. The experience of taste requires movement through space to having the mouth experience. Smell requires the experience of an odorous source that is acquired in space. However, they are all experiences. We could have the experiences without the intervening space, but that is not the way Earth School is set up. To have a body experience in Earth School that has experiences, we must have a sense of space.

However, our Minds and the Universal Intelligence do not require space. When we think of a waterfall, the image comes to mind, but there is no space in our Mind. We have the sense of space between us and the waterfall, but there is no space when we access the memory. Space isn't necessary. But the actual experience of the waterfall in Earth School requires that we have the sense that the waterfall is some distance from us to see the breadth of it. That is part of the waterfall experience.

When we sit in a theater watching a movie with gangsters speeding through the streets of Chicago, we sense the space the car is traveling through. But there is no space. There is only a two-dimensional screen. We don't have to transport Chicago to the theater to have our sense of space during the chase. Our Minds have the experience of the car and fill in the space before and after it. The experiences come without space or time. We add them.

We walk through space in Earth School and get into cars or planes to travel through space. But in the next stage of life, people think of being in a location and are instantly there. They can return to visit their families in Earth School by simply intending to be with them. Space has no bearing on their activities. On the other hand, because they are recent graduates of Earth School and still need and want a sense of space, they do navigate in space and see at a distance.

However, that is purely because their Minds are comfortable with space after having lived in Earth School with space.

What Earth School Is

Earth School is the set of experiences we have together as we grow in love and compassion, learn lessons, and enjoy the experience. The experiences are accessible from the Universal Intelligence based on our expectations we developed during our history in Earth School. There are beginnings and endings, cause and effect, continuity, time, and space. The crucible of Earth School has all manner of people so we can have varied challenges and experiences that will enable us to grow and become all we can become.

3

Why Did Our Souls Decide to Enroll Us in Earth School?

We enrolled in Earth School to have experiences that could enable us to evolve into being loving, peaceful, and joyful. We might wonder why the Universal Intelligence doesn't simply give us the end results—make us unconditionally loving, peaceful, and joyful on the spot, without going through the struggles of Earth School to change and grow. And why does the Universal Intelligence expect us imperfect, impatient, and impudent humans to experience growing into being loving, peaceful, joyful beings?

The answer is that only by living through experiences and growing from them can we develop in love, wisdom, and happiness. Without the unique experiences, we couldn't know what it is like to have Earth School's struggles, overcome them, and grow in wisdom and self-confidence because of the experiences. We couldn't know what it is like to grow from having mistrustful and cynical thoughts to having the comfortable feelings of trust and optimism, or to come from a feeling of being conditionally loved or rejected to the exuberant feeling of being loved and accepted with no conditions or expectations. Without experiencing the struggles and triumphs, we could not experience the growth away from self-absorption and insensitivity to being loving and other-centered, or the growth away from self-absorbed, unsatisfying greed and selfishness to the joy of helping others as they go through their own struggles.

We can realize why we enrolled in Earth School by understanding who we are at our lowest level of development and who we can become through Earth School experiences. We begin Earth School by being taught that loving others and feeling love from them must be conditional and tainted with mistrust and selfish expectations. Earth School teaches us an understanding of the nature of reality and our place in eternity that is fraught with misinformation, superstition, and ignorance. We mistrust others and feel we are absolutely separate. We have no confidence that we are loved and given guidance by unseen people and entities who dedicate themselves to our well-being. We accept depression, disappointment, and unhappiness as the way life must be—*c'est la vie.*

Through the unique experiences available in Earth School, we can have a change of heart and mind that overcomes those negative conceptions of who we and humanity are. We can learn to be unconditionally loving and enjoy the experience of living with others who love without expectation or judgment. We can learn to trust others and believe those we love would never judge, manipulate, or deceive us. We can learn that we are spiritual beings, manifestations of the Universal Intelligence that is the source of all creation. We can become confident that unseen arms enfold us in love and guide us into learning lessons and being confident that we are supported in every struggle we encounter. We can learn to be happy in our Earth School lives for the pure sake of being in this paradise of experiences, with no requirements or reasons necessary for our happiness.

These wonderful fruits of life in Earth School result from having unique experiences only Earth School can provide. The process of evolving away from ignorance and mistrust to love, peace, and joy must happen through experiencing challenges, losses, and disappointments, learning from them, and emerging with wisdom and changed sentiments of love and compassion. And only Earth School can offer the wonderful experiences that bring us joy and pleasure.

Only an experiential world can bring about the teaching to enable us to develop the deep-seated emotions of love and compassion.

What Are the Unique Reasons Our Souls and Higher Selves Decided to Enroll Us in Earth School?

Imagine someone is starting a new life with no memories of a life previous. This person loves music and is especially enthralled when listening to piano concertos. At the moment they begin this new life, they find themselves in a room with a piano, people who encourage one another to learn to play the piano well, and the world's most highly regarded piano teacher freely noodling on the piano. It would be very clear what the purpose of this person's life is. Playing the piano would give them bliss, and the opportunity to learn to play the piano is freely accessible to them.

In the same way, we have equally obvious evidence of our purposes for being in Earth School. We just need to look at what we have available in our Earth School lives and what brings us bliss.

Evidence of Purpose 1

People want desperately to be loved. Even the most apparently insensitive and cruel people have the deep-seated need to be accepted and loved by others. Gang bangers who kill rival gang members do so to be accepted by the gang. Some overly controlling spouses who eventually harm their partners do so because of an irrational fear they may lose their partner's love. When someone is shunned by others, the person is lonely and unhappy—dramatic feelings that result from the fact that feeling loved and accepted is such a deep-seated need. The need to feel loved is one of humankind's primary needs.

Findings show that babies who are deprived contact comfort, particularly during the first six months after they are born, grow up to be psychologically damaged. Given the importance of the need to be loved, it isn't surprising that most of us believe that a significant determinant of our happiness is whether we feel loved and cared for. In the surveys that I have conducted, people rate "having healthy relationships" as one of their top goals—on par with the goal of "leading a happy and fulfilling life."[36]

As a result, we know this truth about a purpose for enrolling in Earth School:

Experiencing the feeling of being loved is one of our purposes for being in Earth School.

Evidence of Purpose 2

We receive more love and appreciation when we show love for others and have a drive to satisfy their needs. When we give love, we are satisfying the need for love others in Earth School feel. For us to satisfy our need to be loved, we must have others in our lives who love us. Others must have a drive to satisfy our needs and love us if we are to be satisfied and loved.

> We know that the desire to love and care for others is hardwired and deep-seated because the fulfillment of this desire enhances our happiness levels. Expressing love or compassion for others benefits not just the recipient of affection, but also the person who delivers it.[37]

We know that we have access to the experiences of this world with a unique breadth of people that gives us perspectives and forces us to reconsider who we are and who they are at every moment. In this way, we are compelled to grow and change to continue to be happy. As we mature, we become more sensitive and loving. It is clear that Earth School has a direction for our growth—toward love for ourselves and for others.

The direction of our growth as a species is toward having greater love and concern for others. As spiritually backward as humankind is today, the world has actually grown steadily toward being more tolerant and compassionate. Humankind has grown from being dominated by autocratic governments to having a majority of democracies. Women gained equal rights with men in the U.S. in the twentieth century. At the same time, society determined that discrimination based on race, ethnicity, or religious creed is unacceptable. The movement is clearly toward a more humane humanity.

When all people are more concerned with others than themselves and give all they have to others without self-absorption or greed, then all people's needs will be satisfied because we will be taking care of others and being taken care of by others.

As a result, we know this truth:

Developing a nature that loves others and desires to express it is one of our purposes in being in Earth School.

Evidence of Purpose 3

Deep within us, we know that being compassionate is a pinnacle trait in humankind. We desire it from others toward us, admire people who are naturally compassionate, and feel joy when we see someone being compassionate to a person in need. The spiritual luminaries, such as Yeshua bar Yosef, Jesus, taught that compassion is one of the noblest traits a person can have. After saying we must love our neighbor as ourselves, Jesus illustrated who our neighbor is by telling the Parable of the Good Samaritan, a story of compassion. We show our love by being compassionate.

As a result, we know this truth:

Developing a compassionate nature is one of our reasons for being in Earth School.

Evidence of Purpose 4

We know that when all people have natures that are loving and compassionate, all people will live in love, peace, and joy. This earth realm will be the Heaven on earth described by luminaries such as

Yeshua bar Yosef, Jesus. To have that Heaven on earth, we must change our lives to be loving and compassionate. It is attainable. When all people have natures that are loving and compassionate, humankind will live in love, peace, and joy. It is in our future. Altruism and self-expansion result in more fulfilled lives:

> In a research project at my university, we studied the effects of different types of purpose and found that an altruistic and a "self-expansive" purpose were much more strongly associated with well-being. ... Altruism is much more fulfilling than self-accumulation because it connects us to other people and helps us to transcend a self-centered preoccupation with our own desires or worries. Altruism is also non-material, and therefore limitless. We don't need to compete against each other for kindness. A self-expansive purpose is so fulfilling because it gives us a sense of dynamic movement, with feelings of flow and accomplishment and meaning.[38]

As a result, we know this truth:

Helping humankind live together in love, peace, and joy is one of our purposes for being in Earth School.

Evidence of Purpose 5

As we live in Earth School, we become more capable, wiser, more knowledgeable, more tolerant, more trusting, and more the type of person we value. We feel these qualities are admirable. We want people around us who have these qualities, and we want these qualities in our own lives. The qualities come only through having experiences and learning that naturally result in deep-seated changes in who we are. We desire the changes.

As a result, we know this truth:

Learning lessons that give us more knowledge, wisdom, tolerance, trust, and other traits we desire is one of our purposes for being in Earth School.

Evidence of Purpose 6

Other people we love are also growing in love, compassion, and wisdom while enjoying Earth School's experiences. We know we feel fulfilled and loving when we are helping them grow and enjoy life. We also know that as we help them become all they can become, they are more capable and interested in reciprocating the love and aid we provide them. When other people must care for us because we are ill, disabled, or incapacitated, the caregivers grow in their capacity to love and serve. As a result, when we are the person being cared for, we are contributing to their development by planning before birth to live our lives with limitations.

As a result, we know this truth:

Helping others grow in love, compassion, and wisdom while they enjoy Earth School experiences is one of our purposes for being in Earth School.

Evidence of Purpose 7

People's greatest fear is the fear that at the death of the body, their Mind will die also. We want to live without fear of the future and the transition called death. We want to be confident that our destination after making the transition is comfortable and that we live on as the individuals we are while in Earth School.

As a result, we know this truth:

Learning that we are spiritual beings who do not die is one of our purposes for being in Earth School.

Evidence of Purpose 8

We live more fulfilled, satisfying lives when we accept and love ourselves, with all our failings and vulnerabilities. We feel confident to engage the world and allow others to engage us. Each day brings challenges, but we are up to every challenge. The results of some of these forays are not successful, but when we do not regard ourselves as failures, our daily challenges become proving grounds for our own capabilities. We know the importance and desirability of self-love and confidence in our happiness and contentment.

One of the signs of a healthy personality is spontaneity. People comfortable and confident in their sense of self speak openly without fear of the consequences and are open to what others say without feeling harmed or defensive about what they say. People bound up by fears and lack of self-confidence don't let others know who they really are, hide their true feelings, and become defensive if someone challenges them or their beliefs. They live wearing a mask, feeling inauthentic and misunderstood. People who can be open and spontaneous are happier.

As a result, we know this truth:

Learning to love ourselves and feel our own worth and competence are purposes for being in Earth School.

Evidence of Purpose 9

Our relationships are stronger and more fulfilling when we accept others for who they are, with all their failings, vulnerabilities, and differences from us. When we accept others without judgment, our relationships are fulfilling, and we have no strife with others. If we are judgmental, other people are offended and less able to love us. We want to participate with others in being peaceful, loving, and joyful so we have more peace, love, and joy in our lives.

As a result, we know this truth:

> Learning to accept others without judgment is one of our purposes for enrolling in Earth School.

Evidence of Purpose 10

Everyone desperately wants to be happy. This type of happiness is a lasting, pervasive feeling of well-being that has no reason for it—the person is just happy nearly all the time. The feeling of happiness is one of the fundamental emotions engendered by the Universal Intelligence. Happiness is not made of component parts such as subatomic particles. It cannot be contained, purchased, or given as a gift. The emotion results from our feeling of wellbeing and contentment. We crave it. People spend their whole lives trying to feel happy.

As a result, we know this truth:

> Growing to feel happy with no reason for it is one of our purposes for being in Earth School.

Evidence of Purpose 11

At some moments, our happiness rises into the stronger feeling of joy. Maslow called the feelings peak experiences.[39] Joy is an ecstatic feeling that punctuates our life with excitement and thrill. Earth School is a banquet of experiences that bring us abundant joy so enthralling that we want some experiences to never end. It is apparent that the Universal Intelligence creating Earth School for us is providing us with experiences that bring us joy.

As a result, we know this truth:

> Enjoying the pleasure of joyful experiences is one of our purposes for our being in Earth School.

Evidence of Purpose 12

People feel exhilaration at being competent and capable. Pianists, gymnasts, and athletes practice long hours to become better at what they do to feel the exhilaration of mastery. Physicians, accountants, counselors, welders, carpenters, and other specialists go through years of training to become adept in their areas of expertise. People have an inherent feeling of satisfaction and fulfillment when they have mastered skills and acquired knowledge.

As a result, we know this truth:

Feeling competent and capable in endeavors that bring us bliss is a purpose for being in Earth School.

Evidence of Purpose 13

People feel most secure and capable when they have the freedom to be self-determined, make their own decisions, and pursue their own goals regardless of the outcomes or censure by others. People are happiest when they have a strong sense of personal responsibility, feeling they are the masters of their fates. Regardless of the circumstances and social expectations in life, people are happiest when they feel confident in their positions and that, through their own initiative and industry, they will be successful. They feel most fulfilled when they make decisions on their own, regardless of pressures against them.

As a result, we know this truth:

Becoming self-determined, confident, independent, and capable of making choices is one of the reasons we enrolled in Earth School.

Evidence of Purpose 14

People enjoy their lives more when they have clear goals and a sense of purpose. People with clear goals and a sense of purpose work at achieving goals and experience success when they are attained. People who have no life goals and no sense of purpose feel life is hopeless and meaningless.

> But without a sense of purpose, we are more vulnerable to becoming depressed in response to negative events. We become more susceptible to psychological discord—to boredom, frustration and pessimism. We are more liable to feel the residual pain of trauma from the past (and traumatic past experiences in themselves have also been linked to addiction). Drugs and alcohol are therefore appealing as a way of escaping the psychological problems caused by a lack of purpose. But addiction can also be seen as an attempt to *find* a purpose.[40]

As a result, we know this truth:

Having clear goals and a sense of purpose is one of the purposes of being in Earth School.

Evidence of Purpose 15

Earth School contains sensual experiences—sex, eating, drinking, being touched, seeing magnificent art objects and scenes, hearing enthralling music, smelling pleasant smells, and feeling exhilaration. The experiences are accessible through the Universal Intelligence. They are inherent in our lives in Earth School and clearly to be enjoyed. They result in ecstatic feelings.

As a result, we know this truth:

Enjoying the sensual experiences available to us on earth is one of the reasons we enrolled in Earth School.

Evidence of Purpose 16

We are supported by the Universal Intelligence, guides, helpers, our Souls, loved ones living in the next stage of life, and individuals interested in us. There is a great investment in our individual development. Those who love us who are not of this earth make a concerted effort to help us be successful in all of these purposes for being in Earth School. To avail ourselves of the guidance and counsel they have to give to us, we must grow in our confidence that they exist and are providing us with direction and messages.

As a result, we know this truth:

Coming to trust the support and guidance given to us by guides, helpers, and loved ones in the life after this life is one of the reasons we are in Earth School.

We know that we are most fulfilled and happy when we are successful in achieving these purposes. In summary, the reasons we have enrolled in Earth School are to

- Experience the feeling of being loved
- Develop a nature that loves others and desires to express it
- Develop a compassionate nature
- Help humankind live together in love, peace, and joy
- Learn lessons that give us more knowledge, wisdom, tolerance, trust, and other traits we desire
- Helping others grow in love, compassion, and wisdom while they enjoy Earth School experiences
- Learn that we are spiritual beings who do not die
- Learn to love ourselves and feel our own worth and competence
- Learn to accept others without judgment
- Learn to feel happy with no reason for it
- Enjoy the pleasure of joyful experiences

- Feel competent and capable in endeavors that bring us bliss
- Become self-determined, confident, independent, and capable of making choices
- Have clear goals, striving to achieve them and enjoying the success
- Enjoy the sensual experiences available to us in Earth School
- Come to trust the support and guidance given to us by guides, helpers, and loved ones in the life after this life

Spirituality is engaging in efforts to fulfill these purposes. Spiritual practices enable us and others to fulfill them. When humankind is populated by people successfully fulfilling these purposes, we will live together in love, peace, and joy. Earth will be the Kingdom of Heaven Yeshua (Jesus) said is available to us now: "Have a change of heart and mind (a metanoia), for the Kingdom of Heaven is here now" (Matthew 4:17).

The reason our Souls chose to enroll us in Earth School is to fulfill these purposes for ourselves, for the others enrolled with us, and for humankind.

4

What Is the Current Environment of Earth School?

We have chosen to enter Earth School at this time because it has characteristics that will enable us to grow in love and compassion, develop wisdom, and enjoy the time we have here. These are the current characteristics of Earth School:

- Earth School is a mix of the most backward spiritual elements and more advanced. There are hostile, selfish people and loving, caring people. People can choose between being self-absorbed and self-serving and being other-centered and other-serving. As a result, in this realm people can grow from being self-absorbed to being loving and other-centered.

- However, Earth School is going through a monumental evolution. People are becoming more spiritual, loving, compassionate, and other-centered, even as cruelty, war, deception, self-absorption, and violence continue.

- In the next decades and centuries, humankind will evolve to have a peaceful, loving, joyful world. We have entered Earth School now knowing the changes will be happening. We decided to enroll in Earth School at this time to live through the changes and help make them happen.

We Live in "The Fear Ages"

We live with a plethora of fears all day, every day. Rob Schwartz includes this description of Earth School's condition today.

> During the course of my research, I came across a young man who in meditation contacted a future self, that is, an incarnation of his Soul at a future time. The future self told him that people of the future refer to this time on earth as "the fear ages." Consider the significance of this label. Of the almost infinite descriptors that might be applied to our age, they chose *fear*. Fear is a predominant emotion of our time.[41]

Earth School today has the most extensive, pervasive networks of communication in the history of humankind. In the eighteenth century, people would learn about life from the small circle in their geographical location, perhaps 100 acquaintances in a lifetime. They might hear someone read reports about events that happened in some other location, but most people had no interest in the "news," and those who did learned about a very small number of events outside of each individual's location. None of this information was as dramatic as video is today. It was all verbal. Very few people ever saw a murder. Today, the average child has seen 8,000 murders by age 10.[42] The portrayals are highly graphic and realistic.

Among the large numbers of events the media and entertainment could choose to present to people, they selectively present messages and experiences that induce fear, desire, greed, and basic negative human responses such as fear and rage. Politicians, news commentators, film producers, and companies that want to create an emotional reaction so people buy their products or services are intent on having all people feel fear, outrage, and separation from other groups so they can benefit from the panicked responses. The beneficiaries are those who receive money, position, or control when people tune in to their video presentations, elect them, or buy their products. They are motivated to make people feel fear, outrage, and separation by greed.

The result is an Earth School today dominated by fear, anxiety, and dissatisfaction with what people have in life. From childhood, people living in Earth School now have spent every day receiving a constant flow of these messages adeptly designed to make them fearful, anxious, suspicious, unsatisfied, and greedy. We are taught that sickness, violent tragedy, and death are just around the corner, and that what we have in our lives is inadequate—we must want and buy more.

Fear and greed are the dominant motivators in Earth School today. On an international level, we fear wars, nuclear annihilation, terrorism, economic collapse, asteroids, mass shootings, climate change, and pandemics because the media are preoccupied with presenting the most negative perspectives on them to entice people to tune in. It seems that uncontrollable riots are spreading across the world.

At the local level, we fear downturns in the economy, vandalism, burglary, crime, unexpected expenses, unbridled riots, and disturbances. The message is supported by the media intent on showing how the commonest of people in uneventful neighborhoods are vandalized and violently killed. The sensational news draws viewers.

On a personal level, we fear illness, medical bills, losing our jobs, failure, pain, loss of things we value, identity theft, being unloved, separation from people we love, and death. The media show us all the worst occurrences happening to normal, unsuspecting folks. And we are shown products and visions of wealthy individuals that breed dissatisfaction and frustration with our lives.

Politicians promulgate fear to herd people to their parties, which claim to be the safe ports. Climate alarmists show elementary children videos of dying polar bears and assure us that civilization will be wiped out in a few decades if we don't embrace their environmental and political agendas. Religions use fear of hell to keep parishioners coming to services and dropping money in the offering plate. Well-meaning medical organizations use fear to force people to change their lifestyles because they feel it is in people's best interests to frighten people into activities they feel are healthful.

Earth School today is a world of fear.

The state of fear people feel influences all of humankind. We are one consciousness creating this reality by our expectations for what the reality should be at a subconscious level. When we feel fear for any of a great variety of reasons, we create the world of fear. We pass that fear on to those around us, especially children. They then grow up in fear.

Suicide is the second leading cause of death for children, adolescents, and young adults age 15 to 24.[43] For every suicide, there are at least 100 suicide attempts.[44] The average feeling of happiness decreased for the Gen Z generation from an already low 2.15 on a three-point score in 2006 to 1.97 by 2017.[45] By 2016 and 2017, both adults and adolescents were reporting significantly less happiness than they had in the 2000s.[46] The Australian Youth Mental Health Report found that one in four young people ages 15 to 19 has experienced a "probable mental illness," meaning depression or anxiety or both.[47]

Mahatma Gandhi, speaking from spirit through Leslie Flint on June 21, 1961, explains these forces. You can hear Gandhi speaking these words from spirit at www.earthschoolanswers.com/Gandhi2/.

> It grieves us when we see how in your world there so much malice, so much hatred, so much intolerance, so much unhappiness, so much fear, so much doubt. Your world is full of fear: fear in its religious aspect, fear in its realization, as it feels, of the things that they know. ...
>
> There is much we want to release man from; above all, fear. Life in your world is full of fear. People fear so many things. ...
>
> We are very concerned with your world today. It does not get better, it gets worse. Much worse. It only needs a touch of a finger to set your world ablaze. This I do not think needs expressing too strongly. It is obvious. There is too much fear in the world.[48]

Fear results from the illusion that we are separate from one another, so we can treat each other badly and must fear others will treat us badly. We are taught we can take from others through deception, intimidation, and power. We don't see others as part of ourselves, whom we love at a deeper level below the thin surface of the greed. We fear others because we feel they will take from us and do bad things to us. This feeling of separation from others and fear is a root cause of the problems humankind is experiencing today. Albert Einstein described this truth.

> A human being is a part of the whole, called by us "Universe," a part limited in time and space. He experiences himself, his thoughts and feelings as something separate from the rest—a kind of optical illusion of consciousness. This delusion is a kind of prison for us, restricting us to our personal desires and affection for a few persons nearest to us. Our task must be to free ourselves from this prison by widening the circle of compassion to embrace all living creatures and the whole of nature in its beauty.[49]

However, living in a world of fear allows us to learn the folly of feeling fearful and to grow to reject fear and embrace love. Only in this world with its extremes resulting from fear can we triumph over fear by learning how to love. We have chosen to be in Earth School at this time because the triumph over fear is possible. We now just have to triumph.

In Earth School, Everything Is Constantly Changing

For us to have experiences that enable us to learn and grow, we must confront new experiences with new understanding and capabilities. Circumstances must change to give us new challenges. Things and people must come and go. Nothing is permanent. As we encounter changes that are challenging to us, we learn and grow through overcoming or adapting to the challenges.

If we do not meet the challenges, adapt to the changes, and stride into the future confidently, open to the change, we will be stuck in a world that no longer exists. We will feel ourselves to be aliens in the new world because we have not adjusted our Minds. Since the past is no longer available, we can inflict upon ourselves feelings of loss, depression, hopelessness, discontent, and anger toward the new world.

The world of an infant is different from the world of a 5-year-old, which is different from a 13-year-old's world, which is different from a 21-year-old's world, which is different from the world of a 60-year-old. In one period in Earth School, we live many different lives, with different perspectives, attitudes, expectations, personalities, repertoires of skills, and levels of love and compassion. We are continually living new lives as new people. Each new life within our Earth School life is ushered in by the ending of the previous life. In each new life, we face new experiences and challenges for us to deal with using our newly formed perspectives, attitudes, expectations, and personalities. It is not a law of the eternal cosmos that we should be born, live our lives, and graduate from the realm we are in. Those changes are created for the Earth School experience.

If things didn't change, we would never have the lives we have today. We wouldn't be challenged to adjust and grow. We would be stagnant and desperately unhappy with the emerging world in which we are strangers. Change is the necessary component of Earth School that allows us to mature and learn.

Is Earth School Evolving to Be Better?

Earth School is undergoing monumental changes now. In the West, Christianity and the church-state held power and controlled people's Minds until the twentieth century. The result was unspeakable cruelty and repression of individual thinking. Only the church's dogma was to be accepted as truth.

In the eighteenth through twentieth centuries, empirical science held sway. People were told their individual thoughts were irrelevant and naive. Truth was in the science books, and scientists were the priests. Individual development in matters of spirit was regarded as a waste of time. Society, schools, and institutions viewed the truths of objective science as important; an individual's beliefs and development of new beliefs were unimportant.

However, beginning with the last decades of the twentieth century, mass media allowed people to see other perspectives on reality. They began to experience through video media new and wonderful perspectives on life and the life after this life. Their eyes were opened. Masses of people began to experience a new sense of spirituality that had no name and no organization to give it identity.

While the church demonized communication with loved ones living in the life after this life, people have always had experiences showing their loved ones are alive and anxious to communicate. The warnings of the church and the general societal belief that there is no certainty of an afterlife are breaking down. Humankind is changing its nature. Children especially are more open to the greater reality and what we call psychic experiences. The most gifted of these children are called the "indigo children." John Leland, reporter for the *New York Times*, quotes the mother of an indigo child describing the change these indigo children are exemplifying:

> Our consciousness is changing, it's expanding, and the indigos are here to show us the way . . . We were much more connected with the creator before, and we're trying to get back to that connection.[50]

The Indigo Children: The New Kids Have Arrived[51] by Lee Carroll and Jan Tober has sold 250,000 copies since 1999. Hay House has sold 500,000 books on indigo children. The indigo child is a phenomenon in our world today foreshadowing the changes occurring in society.

Affiliation with religion is on the decline, but professed spirituality is increasing. A Pew research survey of American adults found that between 2012 and 2017, five short years, the number of adults who reported themselves to be "not religious" rose from 35 percent to 45 percent. However, the number of people who reported themselves to be "spiritual but not religious" rose from 19 percent to 27 percent during the same five-year period.[52]

Rob Schwartz interviewed a guide conveying messages through a woman whose Soul's plan he had been exploring. During the interview, the guide relayed the following message.

> The earth is currently moving up [in vibration] each day, and more Souls are rising to the occasion of living out of a higher thought form. Soon, there will not be room for those who do not

act for the good of all. The challenges you choose to learn may
no longer be appropriate to your Soul as you have chosen to
bring love and peace and light to the ones on your path. You
may enact changes for yourself and the good of all by always
seeing the best in all things and all beings and lifting them to
their highest good.[53]

Humankind is changing. We have come into this period of Earth
School's history to participate in the change.

What Could Earth School Eventually Become?

We did not choose to participate in the Earth School experiences
that will be available in the next centuries. In those later Earth School
periods, people will be more loving and other-centered. We are the
laborers laying the foundation for that glorious Earth School. As our
Minds grow, the conception of Earth School held by the participants
evolves. When the conception changes, the environment changes
because we are creating the Earth School environment through what
our Minds expect to be here.

As humankind grows to be more loving, compassionate, and
other-centered, the thoughts, feelings, and interactions of the people in
Earth School will become more loving, compassionate, and other-
centered. We will live together in love, peace, and joy.

The list below is what Earth School will be like then. We cannot
conceive of this reality now. It may seem like kum ba yah New Age
make-love-not-war talk, but we know from the nature of the life after
this life and the best of Earth School as it is today that these will be the
characteristics of this new Earth School. It will require that all of
humankind become loving and compassionate.

- People will take for granted that everyone lives on after
  the body dies and people will actively communicate with
  loved ones in the next stage of life easily and regularly.

- People will not seek fulfillment and happiness in things
  and activities. They will be most fulfilled when they
  make those around them satisfied and happy. They will

be devoting themselves to others with little thought of themselves. That doesn't mean they won't have needs and desires. However, the needs and desires won't result in their taking from others by bribing or threatening them; the others will give freely.

- People will live a minimalist life. There will be no wealth disparity because there will be no wealth.

- People will be more interested in helping others have their needs satisfied than having their own needs satisfied. Giving will be valued more highly than acquiring.

- There will be learning, but not schools where children are forced to learn facts. There will be gatherings of children in which they learn to become confident in themselves. Children will be encouraged to be all they can be with their unique abilities. There will be no required behaviors, expectations, judgment, report cards, or failure. They will grow from early childhood to take positions as valued, functioning members of the family and society who give what their talents can most easily, enjoyably, and successfully give to others at every age. They will learn to be loving and compassionate.

- Children and adults together will explore their inner selves and understand their psyches. No knowledge will be regarded as better or more valid than each person's self-discoveries. Humankind will continue to advance intellectually, but the inner person will always be valued more than the technological and manufacturing advancements.

- People will feel free to spend time on activities that may seem frivolous and unproductive, for years if they want to. Other people will encourage and support them.

- No work activities will be regarded more highly than any other. The person who prepares food will be held in as high esteem as the person who helps people heal.

- There will be no business owners and employees. Instead, all people will be working at the businesses to ensure they serve clients, consumers, and themselves. Some people will have the role of overseeing the entire business. Others will be doing more laborious tasks such as cleaning the business. Neither will be in a more senior position or held in higher esteem.

- There will be no money. Money is a means of giving someone something of value in return for their services or goods. People will freely, joyously give their services and goods without expecting something in return.

- There will be no need for fences, locks, guard dogs, surveillance cameras, and all the other things we need today to keep people from stealing what we call ours. No one will feel the need to steal. The owner will freely give whatever it is the person wants or help the person find another source if the owner wants to keep whatever the other person wants.

- "Mine" will be much less prominent. There will be much more "ours" or "everyone's."

- People will celebrate developing and becoming proficient through activities that now are regarded as competitive. Everyone will help others improve and become competent.

- There will be no wars or turmoil. People in more developed areas will strive to help those in areas that are less developed or have more undesirable living conditions.

- There will be no killing of people or animals for any reason.

- There will be no police or other entity that protects people from each other. People will not violate others' rights.

- There will be no insurance. When someone suffers a loss, all of society will rush to help the person recover.

These characteristics of a Heaven on earth seem unattainable. We look at them through twenty-first-century Earth School eyes. "I could never leave my doors unlocked. Someone would steal my things." "If we support people doing what they want, we'll have lazy bums we have to support." When all of humankind is loving, compassionate, and other-centered, these concerns we have now in Earth School will dissolve.

Are There Forces and Entities Dedicated to Promoting Humankind's Progress?

There are strong forces in the realms that intersect with the earth realm that are endeavoring to lift humankind out of the predicament in which we find ourselves. Mahatma Gandhi, speaking from spirit through Leslie Flint on June 21, 1961, explains these forces. You can hear Gandhi speaking these words from spirit at www.earthschoolanswers.com/Gandhi1/.

> It is our desire, all of we who come, that we shall, in time, break down these barriers that man has created in his foolishness. I am very concerned that you and others like you, should be the propagators of this great revelation which is so essential to the happiness and the welfare of the world.

> Today your world stands on the bridge, as it were, of destruction. Any time that bridge, which in itself is so unreliable, that it is doubtful if it will sustain the weight that is placed upon it. Because man himself, unconsciously and in some ways consciously, has brought into being such a condition of confusion, such a condition of hatred, of intolerance.

There is so much intolerance that is placed upon the world through man's foolishness. Unless something is done very soon, I can see that the weight of man's foolishness and ignorance, combined with his lack of spirituality, will destroy the very bridge that enables man to reach, in safety, the shore of peace and happiness.

We on this side, for a long time, have striven to build between our world and yours, a bridge—whereby man could climb to heights and find that peace which your world could give. We know that it is only in this truth, only in this realisation of communication, between the so-called dead and the living, that lies the salvation of your world.

All history repeats itself. History itself shows the very foundation of man's happiness, is in the knowledge and the realisation of the life that is to come. The earth life is but the training ground. It is but the school in which man must learn the lesson which will, in consequence, give him the opportunity to inherit the kingdom of the living Father.[54]

A man named Michael Fearon, formerly a biology master at Taunton School in the UK, who was killed in 1944 in World War II, spoke often to his mother during Leslie Flint sessions. Fearon describes the efforts by people on the other side to help humankind.[55] You can listen to Michael speaking these words at this link: www.earthschoolanswers.com/fearon1/.

We come to break down the barriers that lie between men. To break down the barriers that man has created by racial intolerance and hatred, by creed and by dogma. We come down that we might, in some measure, bring all peoples together as one family, under one God. We have a purpose and a mission.

We are not interested in powers and principalities. We are not interested in churches and in creeds and in dogmas. We are not interested in all the things that hold man to earth. We are interested in the things that make them free, that make them well and happy in spirit and in mind and in body.

We come that we might, in some measure, make your world a better place to live in for the people that follow after you that they be born free in their mind to live and to love and to learn and to understand the things that are of God. We have great purpose in coming, Mother.

We are not interested in the Church, we are not interested in institutions, as such. We are interested only in individuals; collectively and individually. We come to break down all the barriers that time and man has, in his ignorance, created. We know that we can do great things. But we know that we only do it when man's mind is freed from the shackles that bind him to the earth.

And in my opinion, creed and dogma are two of the most difficult things to rid them of. And that's one of our courses that we have to take to break down the stronghold of the Church. And the Church's foundation is still strong, even though it's toppling. We know that there is no strength in the Church, because there has never been true Spirituality in it.

Mrs. Fearon:
I agree with you, Mike. I get more help from you than from anybody. You know I thought perhaps, you know, it was my fault?

Michael:
No. I know that there's only one way to salvation, and that is by man's own desire for goodness within himself to be made manifest upon the earth. That man himself, within himself, has great strength, great strength of character, great strength of spirit. And that if he would look into himself and bring forth that which he finds, as Jesus did, nothing is impossible.

The Church will not do that for you. An individual must do it for himself, but we can show the way and we can give great help and aid to those who seek and strive. Once a man begins to seek and strive within himself for greater things, then we can help him greatly.

I know that there's much that we have to do. Sometimes it seems almost impossible to us to do it, but we can and we shall do it. For that which we are doing is not only our work, it is greater than ourselves, because we are but instruments of God. We do the work of God and we do it freely, we have no axe to grind. We do it because we love humanity, because we want to prevent humanity making the mistakes it has made over many years of the past. We want the truth to shine forth and make men free.[56]

Medium William Stainton Moses, receiving messages from a band of 49 entities communicating from the seventh or highest sphere, described the pervasive influence humankind is receiving.

Advanced spirits influence the thoughts, suggest ideas, furnish means of acquiring knowledge and of communicating it to mankind. The ways by which spirits so influence men are manifold. They have means that you know not of by which events are so arranged as to work out the end they have in view.[57]

Are Any of These Forces from Other Realms or Dimensions?

We know with certainty that there are spiritual beings living in other realms, sometimes described as other planets, spheres, realms, or dimensions. The Afterlife Research and Education Institute, Inc. (AREI) Circle of the Masters of Life is a physical mediumship circle developed by AREI. During the meetings, we have been told that people from other realms are in the team on the other side working with us. They have visited our circle because they are capable of entering our dimension of life unseen.

Sir Thomas Beecham, a British conductor who founded several British orchestras, came through in a Leslie Flint session in 1967 describing the fact that there are beings that have been endeavoring to help humankind. You can listen to him speaking these words at www.earthschoolanswers.com/beecham/.

> It's very distressing the way the world is now, we're very concerned about your world. My goodness me, and you know there are thousands of souls returning from the various worlds of the spirit. Now you take these UFOs as you term them. These entities that are reaching your world from different sources. You know that I have to explain this there is a reality in that. You mustn't think this is a lot of poppycock. There are entities on different planets who have the highest standard and attitude of life and condition of life and whose desire is to be of service and to help because there's a great fear, well not fear is not the word, great concern about the state of your world you know.[58]

Are There Forces and Entities Seeking to Retard Humankind's Progress?

There are forces and entities seeking to retard humankind's progress. Private Thomas Dowding, a 37-year-old British soldier killed on the battlefield in World War I, gave this description of evil thought forms through the mediumship of Wellesley Tudor Pole.

> "Hell is a thought region," Thomas Dowding communicated on March 17, 1917. "Evil dwells there and works out its purposes. The forces used to hold mankind down in the darkness of ignorance are generated in hell! It is not a place; it is a condition. The human race has created the condition."[59]

This thought region, he explains, "depends for its existence on human thoughts and feelings." People are there because they choose to be there, but "Release will come from within some day." When any person chooses to mature out of the condition, they rise from it immediately. [60]

AREI researchers experienced the impediments of similar entities determined to impede our progress toward helping humankind become more loving and compassionate. AREI had been successful in obtaining audio recordings of people living in the life after this life, but after two months, the recordings suddenly suffered from a decrease in quantity and quality. Medium Susanne Wilson learned from our guides that the problem was a group of entities who were thought forms that are created and nourished by hatred, violence, discord, and negativity in the earth realm. Susanne described them as having the features of lizards. AREI's recordings were threatening to these thought forms because the thought forms were created by the hostility, violence, and discord humanity was experiencing. If people learned from such recordings that we are eternal beings, one with each other, humankind would start to live in love, peace, and joy. These thought forms would disappear. However, they had a survival instinct. As a result, they were impeding the transmissions to ensure their survival. In cooperation with Susanne Wilson, AREI researchers sent angels of love to impede the entities' efforts. The mitigation was successful.

Imperator, the guide in the life after this life for William Stainton Moses, spoke through Moses and described the entities whose efforts are counter to humankind's advancement in love and peace:

> There is direct antagonism between [the spirits who want nothing to do with purification of humankind] and us, between the work which is for man's development and instruction, and their efforts to retard and thwart it. It is the old battle between what you call the good and the evil—between the progressive and the retrogressive. Into the ranks of that opposing army gravitate spirits of all degrees of malignity, wickedness, cunning, and deceit: those who are actively spurred on by hatred of light which an unenlightened spirit has, and those who are animated by supportiveness rather than by actual malice. It includes, in short, the undeveloped of every grade and class: spirits who are opposed, for infinitely varying reasons, to the organized attempt to lead men upward from darkness to light.[61]

Many people do not believe such entities exist. They believe them to be primitive, religious superstition. Imperator had something to say about the skepticism:

The idea that there is no such thing as evil, no antagonism to good, no banded company of adversaries who resist progress and truth, and fight against the dissemination of what advantages human humanity, is an open device of the evil ones for your bewilderment.[62]

We can resist the influences of these entities by remaining on a higher spiritual level in our daily lives, with more love, compassion, and wisdom. Eventually, these thought forms will be no more, banished by love.

Are There Unseen Entities Affecting Us?

Earth School is composed of experiences we are having. We have the experiences of sight, sound, touch, hearing, and tasting. We interact with people we can see and hear from. These experiences give us the feeling that is all there is to the world. However, we know that is not true. There are unseen entities that are also part of this world. They exert their influence upon us from their unseen conditions. They are all around us, all the time. Explanations of some of these entities follow.

Many beneficial entities are around us to help us.

As we go through our lives in Earth School, we are continually being given guidance and help from our Soul, guides, helpers, angels, and entities that have an interest in our well-being and development. We rarely realize we're being aided. We have inspirations or insights that suddenly come to us to solve problems or act. The guidance is sound, so we act upon it, not realizing its source. At times, the people around us in Earth School are influenced in ways that help us. All Souls, guides, helpers, and angels are working in concert to help us as we go through our years in Earth School. M. T. Shelhamer explains in *Life and Labor in the Spirit World.*

Others [spirits abiding here] find their work and pass a large part of their existence herein, in connection with the physical, in doing good, ministering to the spiritual necessities as well as laboring for the alleviation of the physical wants and sorrows of suffering humanity. And so you have a world within a world right here, and a double life pulsating, where you only perceive the expressions of the external; and those of you whose aspirations are holy, whose desire is to be of use in the world, who strive to do right, attract good spirits to your side; they come to gain magnetic strength from your lives, which enables them to resist the friction of material conditions while pursuing their labours for others, and at the same time they impart a blessing of peace to your souls. Often do you entertain unawares pure and silent guests, who watch you with their holy eyes and read your hearts with an erring precision.[63]

Ghosts can be just memories on the ether.

There are also visual experiences of entities we term "ghosts." These ghosts are described by those in the afterlife as being impressions on the memory of the "ether," the spiritual atmosphere surrounding earth. When emotional, traumatic events occur, the ether may retain a memory of the event. Later, sensitive people may be able to see the memory act out. These ethereal memories have no spirit attached to them, can move only in the ways the living person moved when the memory was created, cannot communicate, and are completely harmless. That is why hauntings often involve the same spirit seeming to perform actions repeatedly, with no communication between the apparitions and the witnesses. When the conditions between the earth's atmosphere and the ether are just right, the memories may play out like a movie so more than one living person witnesses them. That is what happens when people witness a battle scene being played out by what people call "ghosts." There is no living spirit there when the memory comes from the ether.

Harry Price, a British psychic researcher and author, transitioned from Earth School in 1948. He came through in a Leslie Flint session in 1963 to explain ghosts as memories on the ether. You can listen to the recording of this excerpt at www.earthschoolanswers.com/ether/.

First you have the ghost of an individual who is long since dead; that has no connection with the actual spirit of the person concerned. What I'm trying to say here is that you may have a very powerful thought force which may, by its very powers give the impression that the individual person or personality is there on the occasion of the haunting; and a lot of people, when they have seen what they term to be a ghost, are under the impression that they are seeing the apparition in outward shape and form of the individual who has long since been dead. What actually is happening there is that the individual concerned is not necessarily present. This is an astral projection upon the atmosphere which on certain occasions, usually because the atmosphere is conducive to it, manifests itself in shape or appearance. But this apparition has no power whatsoever, because the mentality of the mind of the individual—the ghost—is not there, is not present. In other words, it is a kind of a shell that is formed out of the ether under certain given conditions.[64]

Price makes the point that trying to eliminate such an astral projection upon the atmosphere is futile. There is no individual there to eliminate.

Some people will not leave earth, so they become earthbound.

There are myriad unseen people living in the Earth School environment without bodies called "earthbounds." Being still attuned to earth, they can walk, sit, ride, attend gatherings such as church services, and otherwise participate in earth activities unseen by people still living on earth. If they advanced to the next level, they would leave the earth realm and participate in that level's experiences and activities.

Kerry Pobanz, MA, author of *The Spirit-Person and the Spirit-World: An Otherdimensional Primer* and *Life in Eternity*, describes the reasons earthbounds stay on the earth realm:

Many psychic mediums and shamans explain that spirit persons generally become earthbound due to feeling shocked after a sudden traumatic death, because of false religious beliefs about the afterlife, or due to intense emotions of anger, fear, love, resentment, jealousy, guilt, remorse, etc. All of these are preoccupations which psychologically fixate a spirit person. As Baldwin notes, the earthbound spirit [EB] is frozen in the traumatic event or state of mind. This is because, to an overwhelming extent, the EB now indwells a place where time does not really exist and does not really pass. "It is a freeze frame, stop-action position." If a person dies, for instance, in the heat of hatred, then that state of mind continues after death, essentially unrelieved, and acts like a ball-and-chain to keep the spirit earthbound.[65]

As a result, the earthbound may be so totally immersed in the illusion, unable to see alternatives, that the person may stay in that state for centuries. Counselors and others continually work to try to get through to them, but since the earthbounds are still in the earth realm, they do not see or hear the counselors, just as people in Earth School do not see or hear guides or loved ones. Robert Crookall explains.

Such men are said to be so near to earth "conditions" that they are either unable to see discarnate "deliverers" who wish to assist them, or seeing them, regard them as "ghosts."[66]

Sometimes people living in Earth School called "rescuers" are able to help the earthbounds realize what has happened to them to open their perception to the counselors and loved ones who have been trying to reach them.

Earthbounds leave the Earth School attunement when they realize they are no longer in bodies or when they come to appreciate the benefits of going to the next focus of their eternal lives and give up on the reasons they tarried on earth. The transition from one attunement to another is entirely in the Mind and seamless. However, earthbounds have free will, so they may decide to stay in the Earth School environment as long as they want to stay. As a result, some earthbounds remain in that condition for hundreds and thousands of years.[67]

Earthbounds can be very frustrated at not being noticed.

As the earthbounds travel on earth, they can become very frustrated at not being seen or heard. French actor and singer Maurice Chevalier, speaking from the life after this life through Leslie Flint, describes trying to attract people's attention in the early period after his transition. You can listen to Chevalier speaking these words at www.earthschoolanswers.com/maurice/.

> You know, when I was very shortly after I died, I was a little bewilder about everything and I wandered up the Champs-Élysées and I was bumping into people and they didn't know. And I shout loud as I think. No one hear and I get very frustrated. And I sit at a café, and then a woman and a man come and sit down very near my table. And I look at them and I'm curious and they don't seem to know I am there. They have some café and they . . . they lift the cups to their lips, you know, and I think "Oh I would like for myself to have some," but it was not possible.

> No one hear my voice. I speak. I think. No one take notice. And then I get very cross and I kicked the tables and then I goes to the tables where the man and woman's sitting and I think now what can I do. I try. I shout. I kick the chair. I kick the man on his leg. He don't take no notice I get very cross and I think "What is all this?" I know . . . you know like I'm dead. That is I tell I understand I am dead but I don't know why these people don't know I'm dead. I want them to know I'm alive though I'm dead, you know.

> Oh I did many stupid things. I was up and down in what you call the elevator, and I got fed up with it . . . up and down, down and up, up and down. Peoples comes and stand right in front of me back of me and I breathe as I think on their neck and they don't take no notice. So one woman says "Oh what a cold breeze strucks me," and it was me.

> But you know it is all have to do with vibration. We are live on a different vibration according to our individual selves.[68]

Earthbounds may have unfinished business holding them to earth.

Some earthbounds stay in the Earth School environment because they have unfinished business. They could want to stay near a loved one who is ill or grieving. A soldier killed in battle described realizing his body and the bodies of his fellow soldiers were lying on the earth as they rose from it. He describes his anguish at thinking about his grieving wife:

> Soon there was a ray of light that grew brighter each moment and then a great concourse of men with kindly faces came and, with comforting words, told us not to fear—that we had made the great change, that the war for us was over. . . . I will not tell you of the sorrow that came with such realization, sorrow for the wife. Her great grief, when she learned what had happened, bound me to her condition. We sorrowed together. I could not progress [via the "second death"], out of the dream-like "Hades" into "Paradise" conditions, or find happiness, until time had healed her sorrow.[69]

The "second death" is the transitioning out of the Earth School environment into the environment of the life after this life. It would be better to call it the "second transition." There is no "death" involved. It is a simple transition.

Earthbounds may fear what comes next if they leave earth.

Some earthbounds accept the mythology of the church, so they are afraid if they leave the earth realm they may go to Purgatory or Hell. Neither exists.

Others who were materialists in their earth life are certain there is no life after the bodies dies, so they're afraid if they do something that shakes the balance of the position they are in, they will fall into the abyss of nothingness.

Earthbounds may be poltergeists.

Poltergeists can be earthbound people who are not able or willing to change their mental condition to allow themselves to leave

Earth School. They are almost always simply trying to attract attention and are frustrated that no one can see them or respond to their communication. As a result, they may bang on things, move things about if they can, and otherwise disrupt Earth School.

They are often immature spiritually and may have been violent or mischievous on earth. They continue their mischievous activities by staying in Earth School and influencing people who are susceptible because of their natural inclination toward the same sort of mischief, temporary weakening through drugs or alcohol, or opening themselves to influence by having some medium abilities but not being mature enough to keep the lower-level people from intruding.

In the below excerpt from the Harry Price session with Leslie Flint, Price describes poltergeists. You can listen to the recording of this excerpt at www.earthschoolanswers.com/polt/.

> Then of course you do have poltergeists which are invariably individuals who are earthbound who do, by the power of which they may have under the conditions which they exist in the particular place, able to use various things to attract attention. But usually you will find there is someone in that household— quite often a young person—who through the vitality and powers and psychic force makes it possible for them to become more material inasmuch that they can either if not be seen, they can use the power drawn from the individual in the household to move furniture or to throw things about. This is a deliberate attempt at communication; invariably not spiteful, very rarely spiteful, usually done in exasperation to attract attention to themselves, invariably because they wish something in that house to be discovered. … They realise that there is something they want to put right and until it is put right they do not feel they can leave the earth world—they cannot leave without this matter being settled. Usually a person is not earthbound for a very long time because after a time they are not able to get in touch, eventually they begin to realise the futility of trying to something in a material sense which often they realise is impossible, to attract the attention sufficiently to make it

possible what it is they wish to convey to be understood and they leave. But you do get the persistent types who will cling and will hold on and they will in consequence do everything in their power, particularly if they feel within themselves that it is absolutely essential that it should be attended to or done.[70]

A woman named Dorcas who came through in a Leslie Flint session described how she delighted in scaring people. You can hear Dorcas explaining what she did in more detail at www.earthschoolanswers.com/dorcas/.

> I was quite happy being Earthbound. I enjoyed watching other people and seeing what they were up to and keeping my eye open, you know?

> Aye, and I used to cause a bit of mischief at times too. I used to play pranks. I used to do all sorts of things. I used to get quite a great deal of fun and pleasure out of that; opening and shutting doors, and throwing coal and all sorts of things, breaking mirrors, and frightening people. . . .

> I made them know I was around, and they used to say, "that's old Dorcas here again" and they took it for granted, and they no worried so very much about it either. After a time when they were no more frightened of me, I got a bit fed up with that, and I decided to, to quit.[71]

Earthbound people stay on earth to participate in earth activities.

Other earthbound people remain in the Earth School environment to continue practicing the rituals they practiced while in bodies, such as religious practices. Dr. David Hossack, a noted American physician, spoke from spirit about these types of earthbounds.

> In the lowest of the spheres, that is, in the earth-bound spheres sectarian strife and religious movement are just as strenuous among the people as they were before these persons left the physical body. That state of transition is but little removed from the physical, for, while the majority there no they have left the

body, others have such an imperfect appreciation of the change, or have led such immoral lives that they are not conscious of the fact. Here the dogmas of orthodoxy are dominant, and the old religious teachings are promulgated, and the priesthood still holds power. One would think that an individual having passed through the portal called death and finding nothing as he had been taught, or as he had believed, would give up the old notions and try to comprehend the economy of the natural law under which he continued to live; but, strange as it may seem, many even then cling to the old beliefs as if in fear, as if to doubt we're sacrilege, and in many ways excuse their failure to find what they expected. They go into your churches and mingle with other people, a great invisible host, here the same old teachings, say the same creeds and continue in the same mental attitude until some condition is brought upon them that guides them into the avenue of knowledge, and as time goes on, one by one they break the shackles about their mentalities and by progression, through individual efforts, become inhabitants of the first spirit sphere. Everyday matters are no different in our sphere than in your sphere. You do not progress and obtain knowledge and advancements until you break away from the old beliefs and creeds. Neither do those out of the body in that earth-bound condition.[72]

Harry Price spoke about the earthbounds in the Leslie Flint session. He explained that they were materialistic in their earth life and cannot bear to give up on the things they loved on earth. You can listen to Price speaking this text at www.earthschoolanswers.com/earthbound/.

Well, of course there are these cases of individuals who are earthbound because of ignorance and because they are held so much down by material thoughts within themselves. I mean they are so much materialists in life that they cannot fail to be, although in a sense apart from the earth materialists do and they cling to those things they know and those conditions that they like and most of the time they live in a kind of illusionary world.

They seem to have such pleasure and fun and happiness of a kind out of making other people do the kind of things that they like doing. In other words of course, they sometimes impinge themselves on individuals in your world and use them often for their own ends, and that of course is bad and could in some instances be dangerous.[73]

Earthbounds may stay on earth to influence people.

Imperator, the control or guide for medium William Stainton Moses, describes in detail how people who will not leave the earth environment because of their attachment to the materialistic experiences on earth influence the weak and vulnerable to carry out acts through which they receive vicarious pleasure:

This tendency of bodily sin to reproduce itself is one of the most fearful and terrible of the consequences of conscious gross transgression of nature's laws. The spirit has found all its pleasure in bodily gratifications, and lo! when the body is dead, the spirit still hovers round the scene of its former gratifications, and lives over and over again the bodily life in vices of those whom it lures to sin. Round the gin-shops of your cities, dens of vice, haunted by miserable besotted wretches, lost to self-respect and sense of shame, hover the spirits who in the flesh were lovers of drunkenness and debauchery. They lived the drunkard's life in the body; they live it over again now, and gloat with fiendish glee over the downward course of the spirit whom they are leagued to ruin. Could you but see how in spots where the vicious congregate the dark spirits throng, you would know something of the mystery of evil. It is the influence of these debased spirits which tends so much to aggravate the difficulty of retracing last steps, which makes the dissent of Avernus [hell] so easy, the return so toilsome. The slopes of Avernus are dotted with spirits hurrying to their destination, sinking with mad haste to ruin. Each is the center of a knot of malignant spirits, who find their joy in wrecking souls and dragging them down to their own miserable level.[74]

Angry, hostile, and violent people staying in the Earth School environment will actively influence people in Earth School who are angry, hostile, and violent. They enjoy the vicarious experiences that result. They cannot control them or make them do anything against their will, but when a person is in a weakened condition, such as being drunk, they are more easily influenced by these earthbound people. This example is from someone in spirit who came through to medium Elsa Barker Patch, describing a scene at a bar.

> A young man with restless eyes and a troubled face . . . was leaning on the bar, drinking a glass of some soul-destroying compound. And close to him, taller than he and bending over him, with its repulsive, bloated, ghastly face pressed close to his, as if to smell his whiskey-tainted breath, was one of the most horrible astral beings I have seen in this world since I came out. The hands of the creature . . . were clutching the young man's form, one long and naked arm was around his shoulders, the other around his hips. It was literally sucking the liquor-soaked life of its victim, absorbing him, using him, in the successful attempt to enjoy vicariously the passion which death had intensified.

> But was that a creature in hell? you ask. Yes, for I could look into its mind and see its sufferings. For ever (the words "for ever" may be used of that which seems endless) this entity was doomed to crave and crave and never to be satisfied. And the young man who leaned on the bar in that gilded palace of gin was filled with a nameless horror and sought to leave the place; but the arms of the thing that was now his master clutched him tighter and tighter, the sodden, vaporous cheek was pressed closer to his, the desire of the vampire creature aroused an answering desire in its victim, and the young man demanded under the glass.[75]

Lutheran minister, theologian, and professor Alvin D. Mattson spoke from spirit through medium Margaret Flavell describing the reasons people become earthbound.

[earthbounds] stay near the earth to be near alcoholics or drug addicts who are still in the physical body, in order to participate vicariously in the sensations which alcohol and drugs give. They can be helped in the world beyond to clear their astral bodies of these cravings so they, too, may go on and progress. However this is a long and tedious process.[76]

These earthbounds who have not progressed can have such an influence over someone mentally or physically weak that it seems the person is possessed, but people can only be influenced, not possessed. In a Leslie Flint session, Charles Drayton Thomas, a Methodist minister before his transition, explained.

Undeveloped souls are not devils in any other sense than a bad man on earth may be termed "a devil," no such unprogressed person has power over us or over you. Evil thoughts and habits might invite such a one but, even so, he cannot control you further than you may choose to act in accordance with his suggestions.[77]

People who are earthbound often are unable to make connections other than to the people still living on earth. As a result, they usually "attach" themselves to someone. Kerry Pobanz, author of *The Spirit-Person and the Spirit-World: An Otherdimensional Primer* and *Life in Eternity*, explains.

While it is true that other notable writers/practitioners have addressed certain realities of earthbound spirits—e.g., Emanuel Swedenborg in *The Universal Human*, Carl Wickland in *Thirty Years Among the Dead* and, more recently, Edith Fiore in *The Unquiet Dead*, etc., none clearly grasped the fundamental truth discovered by Baldwin and Dae Mo Nim: that these emotionally bewildered spirits do not just float about in some featureless void after death but almost always attach themselves to people on earth. Stated more broadly, literally millions and millions of deceased human beings have opted, as spirits, and for many different reasons, to attach themselves to the physical bodies of people on earth. Needless to say, this is an extremely unnatural, distorted state of affairs, especially when one considers that the experience of "death" should rightfully carry a person into the next higher dimension of life.[78]

William J. Baldwin, PhD, DM, author of *Healing Lost Souls*, explains the reasons earthbounds may attach themselves to people.

> Once earthbound or, that is, unable to make a correct and rightful transition into the Light, the vast majority of [earthbounds] EBs seek out attachment to someone on earth. Baldwin and Modi offer the following useful list of reasons why EBs are motivated to attach themselves.

1. Newly deceased spirits retain their appetite for certain drugs and try to satisfy their addictions via attachment to users.

2. EBs become attached via the influence of other previously attached EBs (the phenomenon of "nesting" …)

3. EBs may be drawn to attach via benevolent, self-serving or malevolent motivations or, seemingly, some attachments may be completely random.

4. An EB attaches because it has unfinished business with the host, or others.

5. EBs attach because they are magnetically drawn to the host's strong emotions, e.g., anger, grief, repressed negativity, etc.

6. EBs attach because the host's stress has made the host susceptible, or because host has made itself susceptible through alcohol and drugs.

7. EBs attach because the host has become vulnerable through surgery, blood transfusions, organ transplant, accident trauma, falls, etc.

8. EBs may attach during sexual intercourse, and especially through the trauma of sexual abuse, rape, incest, etc.

9. EBs can attach during funerals if welcomed by a grieving person.

10. EBs often attach to sympathetic people in hospitals and
    nursing homes.[79]

Earthbound influences cause what is mistakenly called mental illness.

Some in the next realms of life have also said clearly that these
earthbound spirits are the cause of many cases diagnosed as psychosis,
paranoia, depression, addiction, manic depression, criminal behavior,
and phobias. They cannot "possess" a person, but people who are
sensitive to the other realms of life and easily influenced can become
the focus of earthbound spirits who wish to use them to have vicarious
experiences.

Elizabeth Fry, a leader in the movement during the eighteenth
century to reform prisons in the UK to make them more humane,
especially for children, explained the effects of earthbounds on people
in a Leslie Flint session. You can listen to her speak at
www.earthschoolanswers.com/fry1/.

I'm quite sure that many of the people in mental hospitals in
your world are under the influence of earthbound spirits and,
um, I think it is a great tragedy that this subject, this whole
subject is not better understood, uh, among those in the medical
profession. Because a lot of these cases are definitely obsession
and there's a great field, uh, for research, a great field there for
discovery, a great opportunity for people to work in that
particular field where people are suffering from mental
disorders.

Because a lot of these so-called disorders are not illnesses, in the
sense that you understand the term. They are definitely cases of
obsession. And we on this side have many souls who work in
groups and bands who do endeavour to help and to relieve and
to take away, where possible, these influences.

But you must remember that they are so close to Earth, they are
so much of the Earth, but it sometimes is very difficult to do
very much about it.[80]

Dr. Carl A. Wickland, a member of the Chicago Medical Society and American Association for the Advancement of Science, and director of the National Psychological Institute of Los Angeles, described his experience with people afflicted by these influences.

> Spirit obsession is a fact—a perversion of a natural law—and is amply demonstrable. This has been proven hundreds of times by causing the supposed insanity or aberration to be temporarily transferred from the victim to a psychic sensitive who is trained for the purpose, and by this method ascertain the cause of the psychosis to be an ignorant or mischievous spirit, whose identity may frequently be verified.[81]

Today, there are psychiatrists who specialize in treating people who are being negatively influenced by entities. Among the most prominent are psychotherapist Dr. Edith Fiore, author of *The Unquiet Dead: A Psychologist Treats Spirit Possession*, and psychotherapist Dr. William Baldwin, author of several books, including *Spirit Releasement Therapy: A Technique Manual*.

Young children may be influenced by earthbounds.

Many young children have mediumistic ability because their Minds are in the state that is associated with meditation and creativity in adults, called the alpha state. As cell biologist Bruce Lipton explains, in the first seven years of a child's life, the child's Mind is in a receptive, learning state. This state registers in the body experience as theta or alpha brainwaves. In this theta or alpha state, children are open and naively receptive. They are being programmed to live successfully on earth.[82] Poltergeists are often associated with children and adolescents because this openness is the same as medium ability. The entities can draw from this energy to act in the physical realm.

If children use a device such as a Ouija board, they can hear from earthbound people who intentionally deceive them. In those cases, the lower-level spirits can provide misleading and disruptive messages. In no circumstances, however, can a lower-level spirit possess someone.

Negative Thought Forms Affect Us Individually

In the Earth School environment there are unseen influences or forces that have an effect on people. I hesitate to call them "beings" or "entities." They have no personality as such. However, they have motives and perform actions that may disrupt people's lives. They are described as "thought forms" that are creations from the accumulation of negative thoughts. Thoughts have much more power than people realize.

George Wehner, a trance medium, was able to see in gatherings these thought forms he calls "elementals."

> I always have noticed in such gatherings, that a dull, reddish mist emanates from the sitters and hangs low in the room. Sometimes I have seen appear in this mist the eager faces of elementals, creatures not human, but with a human semblance. I have, on occasion, refused to sit when I have seen these things before going into trance.[83]

Later in his book he mentions the elementals again.

> Frequently I have seen degraded souls who were obsessing earth-people. Not only one, but often several of these obsessing entities clinging to their victims with the tenacity of leeches. And not always are these entities human, but sometimes elementals and elementaries. Especially have I seen them surround drunkards, dope fiends, and gamblers.[84]

Annie Besant and Charles Webster Leadbeater wrote *Thought-Forms*, a book describing the emotions, thoughts, and actions forms may take. Besant described them as "ensouled thought forms" and "destructive elementals."[85]

The True Nature of Earth School

Earth School is not made up of matter and energy apart from the Universal Intelligence. It did not come into existence 4.4 billion years ago and will not be incinerated when the sun expands and burns it to a crisp in 5 billion years. That is all just part of the story resulting in playing out causes and effects in a realm that exists only as now experiences in the Universal Intelligence for our Earth School Minds' benefit.

The current environment of Earth School is a realm of experiences with time, space, continuity, cause and effect, and beginnings and endings that Earth School Minds may choose to experience. It is a crucible, with self-centered, insensitive people and loving, giving, other-centered people. The environment allows us to make choices among the options to be more selfish or more giving. In that way, we can grow to become loving, compassionate, and other-centered while we enjoy all the experiences available in Earth School today.

5

Why Is There Evil and Suffering in Earth School?

Earth School is a crucible of negative and positive energies. Since we're here together now, it's apparent that we wanted to love, learn, and have experiences in this troubled environment. There are reasons for Earth School's level of what are regarded as evil and suffering. In this chapter, I explain evil and suffering in Earth School.

Why Is There Evil in the World?

We regard some act or person as evil when that person causes others mental or physical suffering, including murder, mass killing, ethnic cleansing, genocide, enslavement, kidnapping, torture, rape, destroying a person's spirit, and inducing fear. Volcanoes are not evil. Tigers are not evil. Even viruses and bacteria are not evil. They all cause suffering, but they have no intent to do harm. Evil is only in what people do to each other.

We regard actions as evil when someone chooses to cause others to suffer. We do not regard a toddler's destructive act as evil because the child is not making free-will choices as an adult does. In a trial, a judge determines whether the perpetrator is capable of understanding their actions before sentencing, regardless of the offense, because we assume a person unable to make free-will choices cannot be held accountable for their actions. This person's actions that harm others are not deemed evil. We do not regard the action of causing a car accident that results in injury or death as evil. The accident didn't result from a free-will choice to cause injury or death.

As a result, we can say that we regard the free-will choice to cause suffering as evil.

However, what people regard as evil differs dramatically among ages and cultures. We judge people and activities as evil depending on the mores of the group we belong to. In India, more than 5,000 brides are killed annually because their dowries are considered insufficient.[86] The families don't see this as evil. In Nigeria, the Yoruba people once saw the birth of twins as evil because they believed it meant the woman had engaged in sex with two men around the time of conception.[87] The God of the Old Testament ordered 160 killing sprees with a specific enumeration of 2.8 million deaths. Satan, on the other hand, was responsible for only 10 deaths.[88] We do not call the God of the Old Testament evil, but we do call the Satan figure evil. What people regard as evil is very much dependent on the people's belief system.

All of the following activities many regard as evil are acceptable in the United States today:

~ Inflicting pain on animals for sport

~ Using fear, deception, and falsehoods to maintain personal dominance and power over powerless people

~ Training people to murder by instilling blind obedience to commands to kill

~ Building devices that will kill and maim millions of people and animals in a single stroke

~ Invading a country and killing nearly 300,000 of its inhabitants

~ Incinerating 250,000 men, women, and children in an instant by obliterating an entire city

~ Executing people because society doesn't like their actions

We know these activities by their common names: hunting, politics, military development, Iraq war, bombing of Hiroshima and Nagasaki, and capital punishment.

People in the United States do not regard these activities as evil, but they inflict more harm on others than most of the actions regarded as evil in the world today. Actions in themselves are not evil. When people use their free will to perform acts that harm others, we regard the free-will choice as evil if it violates society's mores. The question is not "Why is there evil in the world?"; the question is "Why do people choose to perform actions that harm other people?"

The answer to the question "Why is there evil in the world" is that there is no evil in the world. There are only people who perform actions that harm other people physically or psychologically. If we are to eradicate the actions we regard as evil, we must help all people grow to be loving, compassionate, other-centered, sensitive to others, and unwilling to harm others physically or psychologically. For that to happen, the false sense of separation among people must fall away. We are not separate; we are one Mind with each other in the Universal Intelligence. Only the shell we take on to act in Earth School is separate from other people's shells. We, the Souls taking on separate bodies, are one Mind. When people come to realize that truth, there will be no more activities or people we would call evil.

Why Is There Suffering in the World?

A perennial question people ask as they try to understand our lives in Earth School is "Why is there so much suffering in the world?" The answers to the question are in understanding what suffering is and how suffering happens. There is suffering in the world, but its causes and outcomes are not what people believe them to be.

Some of this explanation is based on the Holmes and Rahe Stress Scale, also called the Social Readjustment Rating Scale. Thomas Holmes and Richard Rahe surveyed 5,000 medical students, asking them to rate on a scale of 1 to 100 the impact on their lives of 43 stressful events.[89] The result was the Stress Scale. You can learn more about it and link to the resulting stress test at www.earthschoolanswers.com/stress/.

When the stressors affect people strongly, we call it "suffering." I add a list of other stressors after these explanations of the stressors on the Holmes and Rahe scale.

Suffering Resulting from a Loved One's Transition

The most prominent reason people suffer to the point of becoming ill as reported in the Holmes and Rahe Stress Scale is because of a loved one's transition from Earth School. Three of the most stressful events on the scale are separations when a loved one transitions before we do. The average ranking for distress on the Holmes and Rahe Stress Scale is to the left of each.

1 Death of spouse

5 Death of close family member

17 Death of a close friend

When people talk about suffering from death, they usually refer to widespread atrocities that kill millions. An estimated total of 6 million Jews were killed in the holocaust. In total, Hitler was responsible for 11 to 12 million noncombatant deaths.[90] Estimates are 35 to 45 million died in Mao's Great Leap Famine. As many as 20 million died in Stalin's Russia.[91] Millions died from genocide in Cambodia, Rwanda, Bosnia, and Raipur.[92] A flu epidemic in 1918 killed 30 million people worldwide. Every minute, 25 people die from diseases borne by unclean water. Every hour, 300 people die from malaria.[93]

Seeing these numbers gives a distorted view of the exit from Earth School. The number of people that transition because of events makes no difference to an understanding of suffering. Suffering is individual. All of the phenomena in Earth School have relevance only for each of us as we experience life, love, and learn lessons. Evaluating the severity of suffering by the number of people experiencing it is not appropriate. Instead, we must understand the transition from this life for each individual.

Suffering from a loved one's transition from earth will cause sadness, but should not cause suffering.

We feel great sadness that a loved one has graduated from Earth School ahead of us. However the sadness does not have to result in debilitating or long-term suffering. The transition from Earth School results in suffering only if we believe the following:

~ The person may be gone forever, lost in the abyss of eternity.

~ We will never have contact with the person again.

~ The person is in some other existence we cannot reach or understand and may be unhappy or in dire circumstances.

~ The person is in the ground or in a mausoleum.

If we hold any of these beliefs, we certainly will feel great sadness and grief—we will make ourselves suffer. We miss having the person in the same condition they were in, with us. We want to have the same interactions and experiences, with instant, easy, undeniable contact. Believing the loved one is lost forever or is somewhere in an existence we can't contact and there will never be a reunion is ignorance that causes suffering. When we know our loved ones who have graduated have gone on to live in another location for a while but we can communicate with them and we will soon be with them, we will realize there is no need for such deep grief. In a short time, we will have a reunion and continue our lives together. Our loved ones are healthy, happy, and accessible, and we can communicate with them.

We bring suffering on ourselves as a result of ignorance about the transition from Earth School. We can reduce the suffering by changing our understanding. We do not die.

These are the truths about the transition from Earth School:

1. The loved one who has transitioned has changed form, but is still with us.

2. The loved one is happy, enjoying life, and growing, just as if they had gone off to live an exciting life in another country.

3. The loved one is accessible to communicate. The person still in Earth School just has to be willing to take the time to learn how to communicate.

4. In a very short time, there will be a wonderful reunion when all are in the same realm, living fulfilling lives together.

5. The exit was part of pre-birth planning by the person, the family, and all others involved.

Why does the body have to die?

Death is just a transition into the next stage of life, like going from infancy to childhood, childhood to adolescence, adolescence to young adulthood, and young adulthood to maturity. The next stage is a natural transition into the next stage of life.

However, the transition is different from the gradual changes we experience in Earth School. The reason is that somehow we must have a situation in which the body ceases to function so the transition can occur. Everything in Earth School has a reason for it. There are causes and effects. As a result, the body must be shed for some reason: old age, illness, accident, homicide, suicide, or other such event.

However, leaving the body behind is like getting on the plane to go to a new country to live for a few years until our family can come there and all live together. If someone we love gets on a plane to go to the new country, we don't grieve as if we will never see them again. We don't go on Sundays to the airport and put flowers at the TSA gate where we last saw our loved one.

In the same way, if we realize our loved one was never a body, but did put on a body overcoat for a period of time, we can feel joy and comfort knowing our loved one is alive, healthy, happy, and waiting at the arrival gate for us to come through when we make our own trip to that destination.

Why would the Souls of a family plan an early exit for a child?

There are many reasons the Souls of a family and the child's Soul plan a child's exit from Earth School. For the family planning the child's brief life before their entry into Earth School, the planned exit is not traumatic. While outside of Earth School with full understanding of what will happen, all see Earth School as a short time in eternity in which to learn lessons. The early exit is part of the lessons being learned by the child, the parents, and others who are part of the child's circle. All agreed to it during pre-birth planning.

This is an excerpt from Rob Schwartz's book *Your Soul's Plan*, in which medium Deb DeBari channels the Higher Self of a woman named Valerie whose son transitioned at a young age. Rob begins by asking Valerie's Higher Self, through Deb, a question.

> [Rob] "For what other reasons do Souls plan before birth to experience the loss of a loved one, particularly at a young age, perhaps from what we might consider to be unnatural causes?"
>
> [Deb states Valerie's Higher Self's answer.] "You are assuming that we are the only one that makes this decision. Think of the boy, the child. What if he decided that he was going to have an abbreviated life, wanted the benefits of having Valerie as the mother-personality for the time he was on earth, and she agreed? Sometimes, short lives are chosen when a Soul wishes to accelerate its growth. We ask you to know that there are no simple answers. All lives are interconnected. This is a basic spiritual tenet. So, to ask did A happen simply because of B— no, it happened because of B, B prime, C, and many other reasons. This is why planning is required before incarnation—to make sure that the life weavings benefit all for the lessons they wish to learn."[94]

Eventually, humankind will not grieve and suffer when a loved one transitions from earth.

When humankind matures in our understanding of life and the transition called death, the feeling of suffering resulting from a loved one's transition will disappear. A loved one's transitioning before us will result in sadness because the person is no long available in the body we knew, in the same realm we are in, but we will realize how natural and normal the transition is, and that soon we will again be on the same plane together. Death should not result in suffering.

Suffering from Losses

Eleven other stressors on the Holmes and Rahe Stress Scale result from life changes that cause some loss. People's lives change because something they have become accustomed to, relied upon, loved, or valued has been forcibly removed from their lives:

2 Divorce
3 Marital separation
4 Jail term
8 Fired at work
10 Retirement
11 Change in health of family member
13 Sex difficulties
16 Negative change in financial state
21 Foreclosure of mortgage or loan
23 Son or daughter leaving home
28 Negative change in living conditions

Suffering from Life-Change Stresses

The largest group of stressors is from changes in people's lives causing stress.

7 Marriage
9 Marital reconciliation
12 Pregnancy
14 Gain of new family member
15 Business readjustment
18 Change to a different line of work
19 Change in number of arguments with spouse
20 A large mortgage or loan
22 Change in responsibilities at work
24 Trouble with in-laws
25 Outstanding personal achievement
29 Revision of personal habits
30 Trouble with boss
31 Change in work hours or conditions
32 Change in residence

33 Change in school/college
34 Change in recreation
35 Change in church activities
36 Change in social activities
37 A moderate loan or mortgage
38 Change in sleeping habits
39 Change in number of family get-togethers
40 Change in eating habits
41 Vacation
42 Christmas
43 Minor violations of the law

Changes in life circumstances cause suffering when the person is fearful of the change, has difficulty adjusting, and is stuck in yearning for the past condition.

Losses and life changes do not have to result in suffering.

A person chooses to suffer when losses and life changes occur, but the suffering is not in the changes; it is in the person's reactions to the changes. If we cling to things and what was, we will inevitably suffer when the things disappear and what was is no more. We will continually fear that we may lose what we have and be extremely controlling to be sure we continue to have it. If we make ourselves feel uncomfortable when life changes and we lose what was, the discomfort may be suffering, but we are making ourselves suffer.

The Buddhists describe the reason for suffering as clinging to things I call "me" or "mine." When we must have something in our lives to be happy, we suffer when that thing is taken away, we suffer because we worry it might be taken away, and we suffer when we want it and can't have it. The Sanskrit word for this type of suffering is *duhka*.

The problem with feelings of happiness that come when we don't have what we desire is that the happiness is dependent on having something or avoiding something. Feeling happy because we have gotten something or have eliminated something is just another form of unhappiness. As long as we invest our happiness in having or avoiding things, we will be miserable because we can't always have what we want or avoid what we don't want. The result is a life filled with unfulfilled desires, fears, and squandering everything of ourselves and those around us to get what we want or avoid what we don't want. That is not lasting happiness.

The strongly negative, stressful feelings come from the beliefs we must have certain things and avoid other things to be happy. These beliefs are the programming that formed our psyches in the first seven years of our lives and are being reinforced by the unrelenting pressure of a society that requires us to grow up to be good consumers, desire possessions, base our lives on earning the money to buy the possessions, and believe we cannot be happy or successful or healthy without them.

The key to not feeling suffering from losses is to realize nothing in Earth School is of any value except our love, compassion, and feelings of peace and joy with people, especially those we love. Everything else is disposable. When we realize we are in a temporary period of life, that nothing is permanent, and that clinging to things will cause unhappiness because things will go away, then we can adapt to changes and look forward to the new world we are entering. We can close the door on what we had and look forward to what will be. If we continue to look backward, yearning for what was, we will be discontented with life and feel hopeless. We will make ourselves suffer.

Accepting changes as they occur, with the confidence that, in the end, we are cared for, results in little or no stress and unhappiness when changes and losses occur. As people grow to be other-centered, we will increasingly support one another during times of change and stress. Our guides and loved ones are supporting us, rejoicing with our triumphs, and aiding us in this process. They will help us adapt to these changes and find joy in what comes to us. We must learn to regularly communicate with them and learn how to receive their counsel.

Suffering from life changes is not a necessary characteristic of Earth School.

Suffering from People Harming Other People

Another category of stressors not on the Holmes and Rahe Stress Scale is traumatic life events and conditions from people harming other people.

~ Adult rape

~ Childhood sexual abuse and rape

~ Violence resulting in bodily harm

~ Witnessing the murder of a loved one

~ Witnessing or being the victim of atrocities

~ Witnessing or being the victim of domestic violence

~ Physical abuse

~ Emotional maltreatment

~ Neglect causing bodily and mental anguish

~ Serious accident

~ Natural and manmade disasters

~ Removal from a secure environment, as in a home or family

These traumatic experiences can be devastating. The victim relives the experiences in memories triggered throughout the person's lifetime. When the person re-experiences the traumatic memories, the trauma has the same effect as the trauma that resulted from the original experience. The emotional reactions are the same, even though the experiences are only remembered, not re-lived. To the Mind, the re-experience has the same impact as the original trauma. Each re-experience causes a new memory experience itself, so the traumatic memory experience remains at a high probability of being triggered by some experience during the Earth School day. Suffering continues.

Suffering from people harming others will be eradicated.

The suffering people cause for other people is not necessary in our lives. It is what people do to other people, not something inflicted on people by a god or the structure of Earth School. People will no longer harm other people when humankind awakens to the realization that we are spiritual beings, one with each other, who can live together in greater love, peace, and joy through kind, compassionate acts. The dysfunctional motives and actions people have learned from their childhoods in today's spiritually backward society will fall away.

We can change humankind, but it will take time. We must keep our focus on the goal and move people within our sphere of influence ahead toward being loving, peaceful, and joyful at every opportunity. Eventually, when enough people are moving humankind forward, we will see the traumatic events and resulting suffering from them disappear.

Suffering inflicted by people on others is not woven into the fabric of Earth School. We are inflicting it upon ourselves. It is a temporary condition that will be eradicated as humankind evolves.

Suffering from Starvation

One prominent event viewed as suffering in the world is starvation. Every 5 seconds a child dies of starvation.[95] The U.N. estimates 793 million people are today starving around the world.[96]

Perhaps the worst image of suffering is the photograph of a starving child in the Sudan trying to get milk from his starving mother's breast, but she has no milk because she herself is starving. The mother will watch her child die slowly and then will die herself.

Suffering from starvation is inflicted on people by other people.

It may seem that suffering is an integral, permanent characteristic of Earth School because it is so widespread, but it is only widespread because people are inflicting it on other people. Conflict, violence, poverty, and starvation are primarily caused by religious conflict, ethnic cleansing, and the desire to control resources and accumulate personal wealth. In *The Human Condition,* Howard Buffet explains.

> Sixty percent of hunger in Africa is caused by conflict, and it's the nastiest conflict you can imagine. The average time a person spends in a refugee camp is 17 years. You've ruined two generations of lives in that time—parents who have been driven

from their homes and livelihoods, and kids who never get an education.[97]

There is starvation from economics and environmental catastrophes, but most results from people causing starvation. To alleviate suffering in the Earth School realm, we must have societies that have evolved away from corruption, greed, fear, and violence into love, compassion, and other-centeredness. While that may seem to be an unattainable goal, it is not. The movement toward love, peace, and other-centeredness is unrelenting, just as the eventual understanding that the earth is not the center of the universe was an inevitable truth humankind would necessarily come to eventually.

Poverty could be eliminated if the wealthy countries were willing to divert a small amount of their wealth to eliminating it.

Jeffrey Sachs, one of the world's leading experts on economic development and the fight against poverty, stated, "The cost to end poverty is $175 billion per year for 20 years. This yearly amount is less than 1 percent of the combined income of the richest countries in the world."[98] That figure is only 19 percent of the United States military budget in 2021.

Global hunger could be eliminated by 2030 if the wealthy nations devoted $33 billion a year to its eradication.[99] That is only 3.5 percent of the United States annual military budget.

Poverty and starvation are inflicted on people by other people and could be alleviated by people. The world doesn't cause suffering from starvation.

Suffering from starvation may be freely chosen in pre-birth planning.

As terrible as the situation is, the starving mother watching her child die from starvation could have entered Earth School to be a martyr whose circumstances could stir people to have compassion and the drive to help alleviate the suffering. The possibility is not as preposterous as it sounds. A long list of people in Earth School have chosen starvation as their path. Jain monks have a practice called Sallekhana in which the person fasts to death. The practice has been observed by men, women, and even royalty. Each year, up to 500 followers of Jainism starve themselves to death.[100] In the 1981 Irish hunger strike, ten republican prisoners in Northern Ireland chose to starve themselves to death.[101]

In the example of a starving child in the Sudan trying to get milk from his starving mother's breast, the woman starving and watching her child starve and the child planned their lives before beginning the Earth School experience. During the planning, she would have had the clear perspective that the Earth School experiences would be only temporary, and she would be choosing them of her own free will. She had some reason for choosing to starve and watch her child starve. Just as people now living on earth are choosing to starve themselves, she may have accepted the fate of starving as part of her Earth School experience.

We must not judge why a person is going through the experiences they have chosen to go through. We chose to have experiences at this time in Earth School because we need something this period gives us. It could be that we felt the need for what we call suffering. It could be that we felt the need to experience love and compassion for people experiencing suffering. Or it could be that humankind needs to grow through realizing there is widespread suffering. We enter Earth School when we can co-create a reality with these circumstances. We chose this time.

Suffering from Illness

Debilitating illnesses, especially neurodegenerative diseases such as Alzheimer's, Lou Gehrig's disease (amyotrophic lateral sclerosis), multiple sclerosis, muscular dystrophy, Parkinson's disease, motor neurone disease, and other diseases, cause suffering because the person loses mental or physical capacities over time, often succumbing to the disease.

We bring much illness on ourselves.

Disease is humbling. It reminds us we are a community, dependent on one another, and that our period in Earth School is short. Disease continues to teach people not to be so tied to the objects in

Earth School, but to focus on what is important in life: our love, peace, and joy with each other.

However, we create the diseases that inflict us. Our attitudes, beliefs, and frame of mind create disease. Bruce Lipton, a cell biologist on the faculty in the Department of Anatomy at the University of Wisconsin School of Medicine and author of *Biology of Belief*, explains.

> If an individual's mind holds a "belief" that they anticipate expressing a specific disease, it can actually precipitate that illness, and even death itself. Does that imply we are *consciously* creating illness? Absolutely not! Disease-inducing negative thoughts, recognized as the *nocebo effect*, operate unconsciously and are almost always related to self-critical and disempowering beliefs acquired from parents, family, and even doctors, before the age of seven. Such beliefs downloaded into the subconscious mind control 95% or more of our cognitive activity and our resulting life experiences.[102]

> If you are programmed to believe you are weak, then you become weak. If you are programmed to believe you're going to get cancer, you're going to get cancer. Because the genes caused it? No. The chemistry from this belief caused it. What's freedom all about? The freedom is freedom from fear. Fear of what? Death? Health issues? Poverty? I say, as long as they hold that fear over you by definition you are powerless because the fear is something you can't overcome and therefore you will give everything to those people who promised you health or salvation. I'm going, "What a waste of your life and your money because when you fell in love, when you got healthy instantaneously just by being in love, that was a personal experience. I say, "Wait a minute. My life sucks but I can change it." It's like, "Yes. You can change it but you have to understand you have been programmed and until you get out of the program, the program wants your life." You can get out of the program because you can reprogram.[103]

In another place, Dr. Lipton explains, "Disharmony is expressed as disease. ... we are creating our illnesses because of the stresses that we live under and our attitudes and beliefs of victim and pressures and the Darwinian belief of survival of the fittest and a competition for life."[104] We are creating the disease in ourselves that people call "suffering."

View a video of Dr. Lipton describing how our thoughts create illness at www.earthschoolanswers.com/lipton/.

Elizabeth Blackburn, winner of a Nobel Prize in medicine, explains that chronic stress, negative thoughts, and pessimism shorten our lives. They damage our body, hasten our aging, and wreck our immune system. She explains that the deleterious effects are from the "telomere effect." Telomeres are the chromosomes located inside the cell's nucleus, which contains our genes and genetic information. In her book, *The Telomere Effect: A Revolutionary Approach to Living Younger, Healthier, Longer,* Blackburn explains that negativity, hostility, pessimism, and a lack of presence were proven to shorten longevity and lead to accelerated aging.[105] We shorten our lives by our beliefs and state of mind.

A study by Sheldon Cohen at Carnegie Mellon University found that people who are happy, lively, or calm, or exhibit other positive emotions, are less likely to become ill when they are exposed to a cold virus than those who report few of these emotions. When they do come down with a cold, happy people report fewer symptoms than would be expected from objective measures of their illness.[106]

One example of the change that happens to the body experience when a person understands that thoughts create illness is the case of Anita Moorjani in her book, *Dying to Be Me.* Moorjani had terminal lymphoma that had metastasized throughout her body. Her body functions were shutting down and she went into a coma that all expected would be the end of her life. She had a near-death experience. During her experience, she learned that the stresses of her life were responsible for the cancer. She had been stressed by difficulties with her Indian upbringing and living in Hong Kong with a completely different culture. During the near-death experience, Anita was told that she could decide whether to return to her body or not. She elected to return.

When she awoke, she had complete understanding of what had caused the cancer and that she had the power to heal herself. Within two weeks, 70 percent of the cancer completely disappeared. In five weeks all of the cancer had disappeared. She states that the reason for the cure is that she came back with an understanding that the cancer resulted from stress and conflict in her life and that we have control over healing in our bodies.[107] Her state of mind had eliminated the cancer.

What we call suffering from disease is resulting in large part from our belief systems and lifestyles.

The body experience changes from psychological suggestion.

Another reason we know our Minds bring illness to the body experience is that our body experience changes from psychological suggestion. Accounts in the literature describe people's physiologies changing when they are given the suggestion that something is true about their bodies. When a person's interpretations of experiences or beliefs change, the body experiences may change to match. What we call bodily suffering results, in large part, from what we are creating in our body experience.

In one study, reported in the *American Journal of Psychiatry*, a combat veteran was placed into a hypnotic trance. He was then told he was back in combat and a shell had just exploded, dropping a small particle of molten shell fragment on his hand. When he came out of the trance, the veteran complained of a pain in his hand as though he had a cigarette burn. Four hours later, a full blister about one centimeter in diameter had appeared on his hand, just as though a small particle of molten shell fragment had landed there. Of course, none had. His beliefs and expectations changed the experience of his body.

On the day after the burn had healed, he was again taken into a hypnotic trance and told his right hand was perfectly normal, but his left hand was anesthetized and drained of blood. When he was brought out of the hypnotic trance, a needle prick to a finger on his right hand caused him to wince, and he bled. A finger on his left hand was pricked. He felt nothing and no blood emerged from the wound.[108]

The beliefs resulting from interpretations changed the combat veteran's body experience. The body experience is in the Mind, as are all experiences, not in a world outside of the person. There are no bodies in worlds outside of the Mind. Since the body experience is in the Mind, changes in beliefs and expectations can result in changes in the body experience. In this instance, the person believed he had a burn and believed he had no blood in his anesthetized left hand, so his body experiences fit his beliefs and expectations.

Body experiences change from the placebo effect.

In the placebo effect, a person can be convinced something is true and the body experiences will reflect whatever the suggestion is.

In a Baylor School of Medicine study reported in the *New England Journal of Medicine,* patients with severe and debilitating knee pain were divided into three groups. Surgeons shaved the damaged cartilage in the knees of Group 1 patients. Surgeons flushed out the knee joints of Group 2 patients. Group 3 patients received a fake surgery: surgeons made incisions and bandaged the knees, but performed no surgery. The three groups had no knowledge of which procedure had happened to them.

All three groups went through the same rehab process. The result was that the placebo group improved as much as the other two groups that had surgery. The authors concluded the following:

> The new findings could transform the treatment of osteoarthritis. "This study has important policy implications," remarks lead investigator Nelda Wray of the Houston VA Medical Center and Baylor College of Medicine. "We have shown that the entire driving force behind this billion dollar industry is the placebo effect. The health care industry should rethink how to test whether surgical procedures, done purely for the relief of subjective symptoms, are more efficacious than a placebo."[109]

In another example of beliefs affecting the body experience, psychologist Dr. Bruno Klopfer describes a patient named Mr. Wright with an advanced lymph-node cancer called lymphosarcoma. Wright's neck, armpits, chest, abdomen, and groin were filled with tumors the size of oranges, and his spleen and liver were so enlarged that two quarts of milky fluid had to be drained out of his chest every day.

Mr. Wright learned about a drug called Krebiozen that was being used to treat this specific type of cancer. He begged his physician, Dr. West, to give him the drug. Dr. West reluctantly injected him with Krebiozen. Ten days after the first dose of Krebiozen, Mr. Wright left the hospital cancer free.

Two months later, Mr. Wright chanced upon a copy of a study reporting that Krebiozen was a fraud; it is worthless for the treatment of cancer. Upon reading it, his cancer quickly returned in full force.

Dr. West knew his patient was failing, so he tried an experiment. He announced to Mr. Wright that he was giving him a new variant of Krebiozen called "ultra-pure Krebiozen." Actually, he injected Mr. Wright with harmless saline solution. Sure enough, the tumors melted away and the fluid in his chest disappeared. He was once again cancer free.

A short time later, the American Medical Association announced that without a doubt, Krebiozen was utterly worthless. Mr. Wright saw the study and his cancer returned. He died two days later.[110]

Mr. Wright's interpretations of the experience of being injected with Krebiozen changed him physiologically. Such is the power of our beliefs and expectations resulting from our interpretations of experiences.

If humankind had the confidence that our lives are eternal, we are loved, and we are cared for by unseen hands, people would feel contented, happy, and confident they do not have diseases. Suffering from disease would be greatly reduced or eradicated.

The bodies of people with dissociative identity disorder (multiple personality disorder) change when they change personalities.

People's beliefs and expectations create their reality. Physiological changes occur when people with multiple personality disorder (now called dissociative identity disorder) believe they are another personality with a different physiology.

Dr. Pamela J. Maraldo describes the result of her research into the changes that result when a dissociative identity disorder patient changes personalities:

By changing personalities, a drunk person can instantly become sober, and different personalities within someone with multiple personality disorder also respond differently to various drugs. Braun records a case in which five milligrams of Valium sedated one personality, while 100 milligrams had little or no effect on another. Often one or more personalities of a multiple are children. While an adult personality is in the fore and takes an adult dose of medicine, they are fine, but if one of the child personalities abruptly takes over, they may overdose.

With a change of personalities in multiples, scars appear and disappear; burn marks and cysts do the same. The "multiple" can change from being right-handed to being left-handed with ease and agility. Visual acuity can differ so that some multiples have to carry two or three different pairs of glasses. One personality can be color-blind and the other not. Even eye color can change. Speech pathologist Christy Ludlow has found that "the voice pattern for each of a multiple's personalities is different, a feat that requires such a deep physiological change that even the most accomplished actor cannot alter his voice enough to distinguish his voice pattern."

. . . . Robert A. Phillips, Jr., a psychologist, reports that he has even seen tumors appear and disappear.

Multiples tend to heal faster. For example, there are several cases on record of third-degree burns healing with amazing rapidity. Most incredible of all, at least one researcher, Dr. Cornelia Wilbur, the therapist whose pioneering treatment of Sybil Dorsett (of the book and movie *Sybil*) is convinced that multiples do not age as fast as other people.[111]

Sybil was a psychiatric patient of Dr. Wilbur who had dissociative identity disorder with 16 distinct personalities that emerged over 40 years. One of her personalities was diabetic, while another was not. Sybil's blood sugar levels would be normal when she was in her non-diabetic personality, but when she shifted into her diabetic alter ego, her blood sugars immediately rose and all medical evidence demonstrated she was diabetic. When her personality reverted to the non-diabetic counterpart, her blood sugars immediately normalized.[112]

Dr. Francine Howland, a Yale psychiatrist specializing in treating dissociative identity disorder, describes a patient who showed up at an appointment with one eye swollen shut from a wasp sting. Dr. Howland called an ophthalmologist to treat the patient, but as they were waiting for the ophthalmologist to arrive, the patient changed to another personality and the pain and swelling quickly ended. When the ophthalmologist arrived, he confirmed that there were no signs of the wasp string or other trauma to the eye. When the patient returned home, the personality that suffered the wasp sting came back and the pain and swelling returned with a vengeance. The patient went to the ophthalmologist and was treated. The ophthalmologist attested to the fact that the patient indeed had an eye swollen shut from a wasp sting. He was perplexed and had no explanation for the strange phenomenon.[113]

The patient's Mind was creating the physical experiences.

Psychiatrist Bennett Braun, author of *The Treatment of Multiple Personality Disorders,* describes a patient named Timmy who had multiple personalities. One personality who was allergic to orange juice would break out in blistering hives shortly after drinking it. However, when he changed to another personality who was not allergic to orange juice, he was able to drink it uneventfully. If the allergic personality was in the midst of an allergy attack and shifted back to the non-allergic personality, the hives would disappear instantly.[114]

The people with dissociative personality disorder change the sets of beliefs and expectations that come to them when they change personalities. The experiences, such as drinking orange juice, remain the same. However, the beliefs and expectations result in changes in the body experience. Mind cannot change matter, so the material body must be made of Mind stuff. That means Earth School is made of Mind and experiences only. Matter and energy are just Mind stuff.

We are affecting our body experiences every day. What we believe deeply, without reservation, about our body experience is what the body experience becomes. The literature on healing attests to the fact that the body experience can become what we want it to become. Our belief makes us whole. This is another demonstration that what people term suffering from disease is, at least in most cases, a result of what people are doing to themselves and others.

Disease is not a permanent characteristic of Earth School.

Humankind is creating disease in Earth School because of our self-absorption, greed, insensitivity, and cruelty. We are told by people living in the life after this life that there will continue to be disease as long as humankind is lacking in love, compassion, and sensitivity. When all people are loving, compassionate, and sensitive, disease will disappear.

In this excerpt from Rob Schwartz's book *Your Soul's Plan,* medium Glenna Dietrich channels an angel who spoke about humankind's experience of the AIDS virus. Rob speaks first. The angel replies through Glenna.

[Rob speaks.] "What else is important to understand about the experience of AIDS?"

[The angel responds through Glenna.] "It is a plague of your time," replied the Angel, "that points to a pattern of self-hatred among humankind, a combination of centuries and generations of movement away from Spirit, movement away from light, and a belief in the self as the body and separate from ALL THAT IS."

[Rob] "Is it accurate then to say that AIDS is healing humanity?"

"That is correct," said the Angel.[115]

Disease is one of the trials people have come to Earth School at this time to triumph over and learn from. When humankind becomes loving and compassionate, disease will disappear. It will no longer be needed.

In a Leslie Flint session, Arthur Conan Doyle spoke of humankind's creation of disease. You can listen to Doyle speaking these words from spirit at www.earthschoolanswers.com/disease/.

When we see the misery of your world, when we see innumerable peoples who suffer, often unnecessarily—because much of your sickness and illness and disease is brought about by man himself by his wrong thinking, by his wrong living.[116]

In another Leslie Flint session, Flint's spirit companion Mickey spoke from the next stage of life about humankind's being responsible for its condition. You can listen to Mickey speaking these words from spirit in the second clip at www.earthschoolanswers.com/disease/.

Why do you have wars? Man creates them. People always say, "Why does God permit this?" He lets you get on with it. You see, God's got nothing to do with it; man creates his own happiness or unhappiness and it may be the unhappiness that's come into your life, is created by people around and about you. It's not necessarily of your doing, but everyone is an individual and the vibrations that they begin to feel can sometimes be disruptive.

You suffer from yourselves, because of your attitudes and your way of thinking. You create all the unhappiness and the misery as it enters your world, even disease, you know. I could go into depth on that, all the terrible things that happen in your world, in some shape or form, invariably are brought about by man. Of course, there are natural things, like earthquakes and things, which are not man's creation, but then again he goes on disturbing nature.[117]

In a third Leslie Flint session, Charles Drayton Thomas spoke about the fact that humankind has created disease. You can listen to Thomas speaking these words from spirit in the third clip at www.earthschoolanswers.com/disease/.

Oh, there's no doubt about it—that if people were to think healthily, they would live healthily.

But, man has created disease over centuries of time by wrong thinking and wrong living and has made it so, that all sorts of illnesses and, uh … varying, uh … kinds of, um … sickness enter into his physical body and, of course, in his mind. It starts with the mind and this is something which is very solid and very real.

Everything that is of the mind has, in a sense, while on earth, got a physical counterpart. It's a reaction to these thoughts. Brings in its wake all sorts of problems.[118]

While there is still disease in the world, a loving, compassionate humankind will make people's lives more comfortable. And the thought of transitioning from a debilitating disease will not have the impact it has when a materialistic belief system predominates. The person will look forward to the next stage of life when they are healthy and vibrant.

Eventually, when humankind is loving, peaceful, and joyful, disease will no longer be the force it is today.

Psychological Suffering

Some people experience suffering caused by mental conditions and illness such as

~ Chronic depression

~ Feelings of hopelessness

~ Bi-polar disorder

~ Anxiety disorders

~ Psychotic disorders

These mental conditions are part of the Earth School environment created by our collective minds, as illnesses are. When our Minds are in harmony and we live together in love, peace, and joy, these illnesses will fall away.

Most of the mental illnesses are created by the influence of entities intent upon controlling people still living on earth. Dr. Carl Wickland, who was chief psychiatrist at the National Psychopathic Institute of Chicago, became convinced that many of his patients suffering from mental illness had unseen entities attached to them that influenced them in their addictions, proclivities toward antisocial behavior, alcoholism, madness, and even murder.

> Spirit obsession is a fact—a perversion of a natural law—and is amply demonstrable. This has been proven hundreds of times by causing the supposed insanity or aberration to be temporarily transferred from the victim to a psychic sensitive who is trained for the purpose, and by this method ascertain the cause of the psychosis to be an ignorant or mischievous spirit, whose identity may frequently be verified.[119]

Wickland and his medium wife set up a rescue circle in which they communicated with lost souls who had transitioned away from the body but were unaware of their transition and often were in denial due to dogmatic religious or atheist beliefs.

Imperator, the guide of medium William Stainton Moses, described the influence of these attachments through Moses.

> "The drunkard retains his own thirst, but exaggerated," Imperator told William Stainton Moses, "aggravated by the impossibility of shaking it. It burns within him, the unquenched desire, and urges him to frequent the house the haunts of his own vices, and to drive wretches like himself to further degradation. " Imperator explained that such spirits hover around other drunkards and feed off them while further influencing them in their negative addiction.[120]

As with the other sources of suffering in Earth School, these mental illnesses are in large measure the result of humankind's condition. When people become more loving, compassionate, and kind, these negative entities will have no ability to influence people. They are able to influence only people who are already predisposed to drunkenness, mind-altering drugs, angry outbursts, crime, and arson. When society has matured away from the negative influences, there will no longer be easy prey for the entities. They, in fact, will no longer exist because they are created and sustained by negative emotions. There will also be fewer earthbounds to make mischief because people making the transition from the earth realm will have stronger spiritual grounding and an understanding of our nature as one Mind with one another.

People with mental illnesses will also be accepted and cared for more readily as humankind changes to be more compassionate and other-centered. The result will be that mental illness will not be so debilitating or cause such stress and unhappiness. We can alleviate suffering from mental illness.

Suffering from Accidents That Cause Painful Injuries or Loss of Function

The sixth stressor on the Holmes and Rahe Stress Scale is "personal injury or illness." It seems unfair that someone must live a life disabled by an accident or illness. Everyone, it seems, should be able to live a full, healthy life with no disabilities. However, suffering because of the loss of abilities results from interpretations of the experience, not from the disabilities. We will experience little or no suffering if we understand that the accident or illness and disability were part of careful planning by the person in the accident, the family, and all others involved. Everyone agreed to this event and the results before beginning the Earth School experience. All knew there would be limitations on life because of disabilities but chose to have the accident or illness out of love for each other, for reasons that may be unclear, but which we can be reassured are for everyone's benefit.

Rob Schwartz, in *Your Soul's Plan*, describes the life plan that resulted in a man named Jason becoming disabled from an accident.

> Jason's life blueprint calls for him to serve others through his relationships. In part, his service takes the form of teaching. . . . Jason planned a catastrophic accident to teach that a paralyzed body does not indicate a paralyzed mind, that a person remains whole even when the body does not. In part, Jason serves others by allowing others to serve him. Severe accidents are often planned because they provide opportunities for us to express and thus know ourselves more deeply as compassion, empathy, and forgiveness, including self-forgiveness for any anger felt toward the person who experienced the accident. All our virtues

of our Souls that cannot be expressed or known in the same way in the non-physical realm, where physical disability does not exist. Too, Jason's service takes the form of direct action. Recently, he began a new career as an independent living specialist, helping others who have been injured in accidents to adjust. Though the information he dispenses is valuable, his greatest impact is energetic. In his new life, he shows others the way by his spirit. He inspires them to do and to feel. He is of service. He is the Soul who planned this life, and he is living it, bravely, just as he planned.[121]

People also have the choice of accepting the disabilities with optimism and happiness, realizing we *have* abilities rather than being *defined by* the disabilities. Optimism and happiness depend on the person's beliefs and attitudes, not the nature of the disability. Having a disability does not mean the person must suffer.

Pain Causes Suffering

Pain is a unique form of suffering everyone experiences. Pain is the way the body has of telling us something is wrong and must be attended to. However, pain can overextend its function and leave the person in great discomfort or agony. Debilitating pain is probably the worst form of suffering because it is constantly present and may have no remedy.

Some pain most likely will be present even when humankind changes to live in harmony. However, most pain does not have to dominate a person's life and create suffering. Pain is experiences in the Mind, not in a body. The Mind feels pain and attributes it to something happening in the body, but the pain is only in the Mind. Pain, like emotions, is irreducible, meaning we cannot dissect it to tell what it is made of. We can only say, "I feel pain" or "That hurts." Pain is an experience.

The use of hypnosis to eliminate pain demonstrates that pain is an experience in the Mind, not a sensation in a body. Psychologists Guy Montgomery, PhD, Katherine DuHamel, PhD, and William Redd, PhD, analyzed 18 published studies on the use of hypnosis to manage pain.

The analysis showed that 75 percent of clinical and experimental participants with different types of pain obtained substantial pain relief from hypnotic techniques.[122] Affecting the Mind's experience of pain reduces pain.

According to the Arthritis Foundation, "Studies show that more than 75% of people with arthritis and related diseases experience significant pain relief using hypnosis."[123]

Professional hypnotherapist and psychotherapist Alex Lenkei hypnotized himself before an 83-minute procedure in which the base of his thumb was removed and some joints were fused to alleviate his suffering from arthritis in the hand. The doctors used a chisel, a hammer, and a medical saw to break his bone, remove the arthritic joint, and attach a tendon to the thumb. Lenkei remarked, "I didn't feel anything at all. There was no pain, just very deep relaxation. I was aware of everything that was going on in the (surgical) theater. I was aware of the consultant tugging and pulling during the operation. But there was no pain."[124]

Lenkei had altered his Mind's acceptance of the pain experience. If pain were in a body, it could not be controlled through hypnosis. The pain experience is in the Mind.

Pain does not have to result in suffering in most people. It can be mitigated, and the diseases that cause pain will become less prevalent when humankind changes to live in love, peace, and joy.

Changing Interpretations of Experiences Reduces the Feelings of Suffering

As a result of our childhood experiences and our life planning, we have deep-seated interpretations of experiences over which we make ourselves suffer. The interpretations arise automatically from our subconscious when experiences come into our point of now awareness. If these interpretations are of the type that result in fear, anxiety, anguish, grief, and other such negative emotions, we will feel suffering. If the interpretations are of the type that result in calm, peace, love, excitement, and other such positive emotions, we will feel contented and happy.

When we change the negative interpretations, we immediately feel happier. When we quit a job that made us miserable, we smile broadly and feel a weight has been lifted from our shoulders. When the anticipated rejection and anger we believe we will experience from a family member doesn't happen, we feel relief and happiness. When we learn the biopsy shows no cancerous cells, we feel ecstatic. The natural order is that when the interpretations are positive, we feel happy. Happiness, peace, and satisfaction are at the basis of our being.

We are not destined to perpetuate suffering. We cannot control the interpretations that come to mind immediately. However, we have free will, so we can change the interpretations over time so the same experiences bring us peace and feelings of love rather than anguish. Growing to diminish or eliminate the suffering is part of the Earth School experience.

Suffering Is Relative: We Make Ourselves Suffer

We must realize that what we call suffering is something we do to ourselves. We make ourselves suffer.

Suffering comes and goes. If it were inherent in the universe, it would be a constant feeling everyone has. However, one person in a circumstance may suffer from the events while another feels an impact that is much less disturbing. One person may feel suffering when a loved one transitions from Earth School, while another may be very sad, but realize the loved one has just changed form and is still present; there will be a wonderful reunion when both are in the same realm. Suffering isn't the same for all people or for all time in each person. Whether there is a feeling of suffering depends on the person's interpretation of the event, and it changes over time. It is all completely personal.

Whether the incidents continue to have the emotional impact of suffering or whether the person learns from the trauma and goes on to use the learning to live a fuller life depends on the person and the person's support system. The interpretations and emotional impact of the traumatic memories can be changed. Our free will makes the change possible. The changes may be difficult and take time, but the important understanding is that the changes can be made so the person lives a full, happy life. Traumatic life events and situations do not need to result in repeated suffering when images and thoughts of the trauma come to mind after the incidents.

An example of changing the impact of trauma is the success of a psychotherapy procedure called eye movement desensitization and reprocessing (EMDR). In one study, the procedure had a 77 percent success rate in reducing the trauma from post-traumatic stress disorder.[125] Traumatic images and thoughts can be reduced or eliminated.

The traumatic images and thoughts can trigger the person's feeling of great unhappiness or suffering. However, the individual's reactions to these stressors are still entirely in the Mind, not in the event. No event, no matter how horrendous, causes suffering. We make ourselves suffer over the event.

We must find life and joy in what we now have and what is now happening. No change can cause unhappiness and suffering if we are confident in who we are and assured that our lives have purpose. Every change is an opportunity to learn lessons and have a more fulfilled life. We just have to find out what the opportunity is.

We Chose to Have the Events We're Experiencing

We planned our lives before our births in intimate cooperation with the others who are now in Earth School with us. We chose a family to be born into, birth defects, inborn tendencies to have mental disorders, circumstances of our early childhood, stature, and all the other personal characteristics and events of our lives. We carefully planned our lives in dialogue with the others who would be in our lives so we could set up the circumstances most likely to enable us to learn the lessons we decided we need to learn.

We may have chosen circumstances and events that seem unfair and are tragic. However, we did so knowing only these extremes could help us learn the lessons we decided we want to learn. Our Souls plan lives with incidents we regard as suffering for many reasons. We and those we are planning to live with in our time in Earth School may decide we will have suffering so someone involved can respond with compassion to learn how to be compassionate.

Suffering is never a punishment. There is no punishment in the Universal Intelligence that is the source of creation. Suffering is always so we can learn lessons, help others learn lessons, or help humankind grow in love, compassion, and understanding.

Medium Staci Wells channeled the Soul of a woman named Doris who had breast cancer. Doris's Soul describes Doris's choice to have the breast cancer:

> All is choice. All is perception. This is not to say that the personality has no right to feel fear or grief, but all that is given, even the most difficult, has within it profound seeds of understanding and beauty. The experience of breast cancer may heighten the senses, may bring people into the life that would not have been there had they remained healthy, may perhaps awaken talent and strength they did not know they had. If one sees cancer as a cruelty, then one cannot overcome. One is already defeated. If one can look at the cancer in a neutral fashion the way one can look at fire positively or negatively or neutrally, one is better equipped to hear the lesson that is being articulated. Illness is a dis-ease. It is a final manifestation of emotional or mental difficulties. It is simply another layer of learning.

> There is no fault involved. There is no punishment. This is no sign of lack of love on the part of God, your guide, or your Angels. This is part of the human existence, as are the need for sleep, hot, and cold. As humanity learns to express itself on a higher vibrational level, illness will no longer serve a purpose and therefore will diminish.[126]

The Souls of the families of children with disabilities and the children's Souls have chosen the disabilities to help one another learn lessons they decided they wanted to learn in Earth School before they were born. In this example from Rob Schwartz's book, Rob explains the planning for two boys in one family to have mental disabilities:

> They [the parents] are all silent heroes. Bradley and Ryan [the disabled children] may or may not achieve in ways that society

will reward or recognize, yet their accomplishments will be great. Jennifer's [the mother] patience and compassion may not earn accolades, but her contribution is profound. Far from the world of competition and conquests, neither seeking nor garnering fame or praise, millions of handicapped children and their parents lead lives in which their courage is tested and reaffirmed daily with dignity and grace.

These are lives of quiet magnificence. [127]

In another poignant excerpt from Rob Schwartz's book, medium Staci Wells channels her guide explaining why a woman named Penelope was born deaf:

"One," he began as he enumerated his points. "One's inner experience is just as real, if not more so, than the outer world. Two. Deafness enables some people to focus on their goals in a better way. Three. Deafness is not a handicap. It is an opportunity. It provides a subtle shift in focus that is necessary for personal and profound spiritual growth. Deafness is not one's fault. It is a choice. Like every other choice, it provides the opportunity to experience life in exactly the way that is needed for one's purpose. And sometimes there is a need to balance that which has been done by the Soul. There have been Souls who have been cut or who have cut off the ears or limbs of others, who feel the need to punish themselves by incarnating and experiencing deafness, the loss of use of a limb, or disfiguring disabilities. Other times there is a need for the Soul to experience inner harmony. When the Soul is sensitive to the extent that Penelope's is, outer forces, sounds, and energies can present challenges to achieving inner harmony. In Penelope's case, it was her Soul's desire to exclude any sound that would remind her of the atrocities experienced in the earlier incarnation. Remember that to let go of fear is one of the greatest challenges you experience as humans. Penelope is still working on this challenge." [128]

Suffering Is Not a Necessary Part of Earth School

Our lives were not intended to have suffering. We should be living lives full of love, peace, joy, optimism for the future, and good health. When events occur that disrupt our lives, we should be able to adjust to them, secure in knowing we are spiritual beings living through temporary circumstances so we can learn lessons, and that we are supported by those around us who have learned to be other-centered and unconditionally loving.

Suffering is not a necessary condition of life in Earth School.

Humankind Can Bring About a World in Which There Is No Suffering

All of these forms of suffering result from ignorance about the transition called "death," clinging to things, unwillingness to adapt to and thrive with change, people harming other people, and an attitude toward events that creates the suffering. Earth School will eventually evolve to the point at which there are none of the forms of suffering because of changes of heart and mind among all its citizens. In this Heaven on earth where people ensure others do not suffer, there will be no violence to create suffering. Grief when a loved one leaves Earth School will be replaced by sadness at the separation with confidence that the transition is just a temporary separation and the loved one is available now to communicate. Living life with disabilities will not be suffering because all others will value and love the person, mitigating the shortcomings from the disability by satisfying the person's needs. The person with a disability will focus on their abilities, not the disabilities, and will lead fulfilled lives. People will not mistreat each other. Employees and management will treat each other with love, kindness, and respect. Everyone will be happy, content, and satisfied in their jobs.

The only suffering that will remain is pain in all of its forms. Pain is a necessary part of the human condition to warn us of a problem with the body experience. When the body is broken, the pain can become intolerable. Pain will remain in the Heaven on earth, but even great pain can be less stressful when people are intent on taking care of each other's needs. And the severity of the pain will be diminished by the positive affect people will feel, just as in hypnosis someone can have invasive surgery without feeling the pain.

In other words, we know that suffering is not a necessary part of the Earth School experience. It is prominent in the Earth School experience now because humankind has not yet evolved to be loving, compassionate, and other-centered. We do it to ourselves.

We chose to be in Earth School at this time because society, our families of origin, and the others we live with all would create and experience suffering as a natural course of living at this time. Within this suffering, we knew we would be able to learn the lessons we planned to learn.

6

Our Higher Self Decides to Love, Learn Lessons, and Enjoy Earth's Experiences

The Universal Intelligence is the basis of all reality. The Higher Selves in this all-encompassing Universal Intelligence are continually evolving and maturing. To be able to have a wide range of experiences that evolve an increasingly wise, knowledgeable, loving Higher Self, individuals must enter one of the millions of realms where the individual Minds are able to have experiences that allow them to learn lessons, love, feel the joy of being loved, and enjoy experiences.

The experiences and the growth from the experiences can come only in an environment in which the individuals have childhoods that prepare them for their lives, changes in circumstances that bring challenges to overcome and learn from, people who are self-absorbed and insensitive as well as people who are loving and other-centered, and the free will to decide to become what we desire to be.

The Higher Self has many individual selves that have graduated from Earth School and other realms. Each has had unique experiences that have added to our Higher Selves' wisdom, love, and compassion. The lives were planned carefully by the Higher Self, guides, and the individuals' Souls to bring needed understanding and experiences.

Our Higher Selves knew that only through experiences can individuals love, feel loved, and become more loving and compassionate. The more individuals learn to love and be compassionate, the happier and more fulfilled they are. In the process of loving and learning, people progress in ways they could not progress without the challenges and successes that come through experiences. A being could not be created that had the qualities resulting from growing through experiences. People can only achieve the growth by living through the experiences.

There are three primary reasons the Higher Self decides to bring an individual into an experiential realm:

- To learn, grow, and enjoy experiences
- To help others learn, grow, and enjoy experiences
- To help humankind evolve in wisdom and love

The individual may be part of a Soul group that includes individual parts of other Higher Selves. Michael Newton reports that the Soul groups have between three and twenty-five members. [129]

These are examples of life lessons that Souls and Higher Selves can learn only by being in circumstances in which experiences create challenges and resources that result in learning the lessons.

- Learning to love someone who is distant and cruel

- Learning how to be humble even when the person is gifted or financially advantaged

- Learning how to dedicate a life to a person who is disabled

- Learning to trust in the face of tragedy and loss

- Learning how to help others feel strong and good about themselves

- Learning how to find joy in a life that is impoverished

- Learning that possessions are not as important as love and relationships

- Learning how to be tolerant of intolerable people

- Learning how to be attuned to other people's feelings

The Higher Self decides to put a new individual into the situation of having experiences by accepting the limitations of a narrow life circumstance, rather like falling asleep and dreaming. In the dream, the individual has vivid, real experiences, with sights, sounds, touches, smells, and tastes, but there is no world outside of the dream that results in the sensed experiences. All of it happens in the Universal Intelligence.

The Higher Self now needs a school in which the individual will enroll.

7

Our Higher Self Selects Earth School

We have chosen to have experiences in Earth School with other individuals because Earth School in the twentieth and twenty-first centuries has the circumstances our Higher Selves, guides, and Soul knew we need to experience love, learn lessons, and enjoy the experience. The earth realm now is a crucible, with people at all levels of spiritual maturity, from violent, cruel individuals to loving, compassionate, other-centered people. Our presence shows we carefully selected this period in Earth School to attune to.

Could We Choose to Be in Some Other Realm?

The speakers from the life after this life tell us there are millions of other environments described as realms, spheres, and planets. An individual could choose to enter any of them for growth experiences. Arthur Ford, speaking from spirit through Ruth Montgomery, explains.

There are countless other souls who have developed while on other planets throughout the firmament . . . some more primitive and some more advanced, but all our souls with the pulse of God within.[130]

Medium Emily French reported that an individual living in the life after this life agreed.

> There are millions of worlds inhabited by human beings in that space you called the sky. Don't for a moment think that yours is the only world, and that God made the universe for you alone.[131]

Mickey, Leslie Flint's sprit companion who is living in the life after this life, describes the fact that there are other spheres and planes onto which people could incarnate. You can listen to Mickey speaking these words at www.earthschoolanswers.com/mickey3/.

> You see this is another thing. People always seem to assume that peoples who live on other planets or in other worlds, that they probably almost certainly must have lived on earth. As if the earth is the only breeding ground of … you know this is, uh, actually your world in time itself, if you must have time, is only a baby. There are worlds that have been in being for untold billions upon billions and eons and eons of time. And some of these are highly evolved states of being where peoples, not quite as you are, have assimilated such experience, far beyond your wildest dreams.[132]

Psychic medium Lenora Huett reported the statement by an individual living in the life after this life describing other sentient life forms.

> There are many [other types of beings] which would be recognizable to you and many which would not be recognizable, for their form is so completely different from that which you recognize. But even at that, they have a mentality of form.[133]

These "other forms" are spiritual beings just as we are. They are attuning to another school with different life forms. We could have chosen to live lives in one of those other spheres, accepting as natural and normal bodies, environments, and life experiences quite different from our Earth School bodies, environments, and life experiences.

Some of the other realms are inhabited by beings who were once at the level we are today in Earth School, but have developed far beyond humankind's current state. Mary Blount White, the blind medium who communicated through automatic writing with her brother Harry Blount in the life after this life, recorded this statement from him:

> [I was] taken to several other planets inhabited by beings who were once just people like us. [134]

On the question of whether other planets such as Mars or Venus might have life forms now, Henry Thibault wrote about other etheric zones or dimensions that are in the planets' environments but not visible or detectable by human senses.

> It is likely that there is no physical life as we understand it on these other material planets, but their etheric zones are peopled by spiritual beings of many kinds. [135]

A man named John Grant, speaking through direct-voice medium Leslie Flint, spoke of people living on other planets who will soon make contact with people on earth. There are also invisible worlds that generally are of a higher order of advancement. You can listen to this recording of John Grant speaking at www.earthschoolanswers.com/grant/.

> But in some shape or form, there is a manifestation of many forms of life in and around the Earth, reaching up and outwards to the varying other worlds, upon which certain worlds, entities do live of a much higher order than man himself—and these too, from certain spheres or planets, have at varying times made contact with Earth. But they have been denied, to a certain extent, the opportunity to converse with man.

> I am not suggesting here that there have not been isolated instances of souls from other planets, who have not, in some way or other, manifested themselves mentally . . . uh, there are contacts that have been made of a mental nature and, in

consequence, appearances of individual souls from other planets have manifested.

But, generally speaking, for a very long time there have been manifestations around the Earth of mentalities from other planets who are concerned, very much concerned, at the motives of man and the experiments of man and the effect that certain things could have—not only in the immediate future, but at a later date upon your world in particular and, to some extent, on astral worlds around the Earth, invisible to the human eye.

You see, man assumes anything that is visible is a real thing … uh, the moon it is a reality because it is visible, it is tangible and soon he'll be landing upon it and … as indeed are other worlds, of which as yet knows nothing.

But these are the so-called visible worlds, but the invisible worlds; these are invariably, though not always, the more highly evolved worlds. These are the worlds of the mind and of the spirit and these are the worlds which man has not seen and cannot see, because he is of a different substance and a different composition. But it is with the mind and the spirit that many of these things will eventually come into being and be harnessed— these forces, these powers—and man will become aware of them. This is what we hope.[136]

Our Higher Selves could have chosen any of the other realms for the experiences that would achieve our goals for the Higher Self's development. We chose Earth School in the twenty-first century because of the circumstances that will allow us to live a blissful life; love others, ourselves, and the Universal Intelligence; learn lessons; help others learn lessons; and help humanity evolve.

Why Did We Choose to Be in Earth School at This Time?

You and I chose to be enrolled in Earth School at this time. Our Souls developed our life plans even before our conception, knowing what would be happening in the evolution of humankind on earth in the twentieth and twenty-first centuries. We wanted to indulge in the richness of experiences available in Earth School now to learn the lessons we have come to learn; grow in love, compassion, and wisdom; and happily enjoy life's experiences. So we planned lives to live in Earth School and attuned our Minds to the Earth School environment.

We knew we were entering a time in Earth School's history filled with danger, tragedy, self-absorption, greed, wars, political upheavals, loss, and disease. We knew there would be people who are cruel, greedy, hostile, and violent, as well as people who are loving, other-centered, and giving. We wanted to live our lives with the struggles inherent in life in Earth School today.

We have chosen to be in Earth School because it is perfectly suitable for us to engage in the activities we know will result in the learning we want to have. The combination of required characteristics is unique to each individual. One may need the stresses of a family experiencing war or violent revolution. Another might need the fertile environment of a city such as New York in a bustling business environment. Any period in Earth School's history and any realm or sphere among the millions available could have been chosen.

Rob Schwartz presents a planning session described by the Soul of a woman named Doris channeling her own Oversoul as Rob asked questions. The Oversoul is the group of Souls we are. Our Soul is one individual Soul in the group. This excerpt begins with Rob's question.

"How and why did you choose the United States at this time?"

[Doris's Oversoul responds through Doris.] "It was coordination with other Souls. Because that was a part of our planning that had flexibility, we agreed with the United States. With the teaching aspect of what this Soul is being asked to do, the United States is a logical choice, having more freedom and a greater physical sphere of influence than many other countries. This Soul tends to be placed in countries that are at the forefront of a given period. For instance, The German officer was part of the end of the German empire. An English Knight was a player at the time of the War of the Roses, which changed domestic lines. There are other lives which are less at the forefront. The one immediately before this one was a relatively innocuous life in the United States in Chicago. Soul is meant to play a larger role. It is to our and its advantage to place itself where there is the highest degree of world attention."

"But you could have selected Atlantis, ancient Egypt, or the United States in the year 3000."

"Yes."

"Could you also have selected in different physical planets?"

"Yes, but we are finding that this Soul works extremely well in the bipedal human form, and therefore earth is a favorite school building."[137]

What is very interesting is the implication that Souls are in quadrupedal or perhaps sexapedal forms!

We have chosen to have experiences in Earth School because the crucible of different types of people and levels of spiritual growth in the twentieth and twenty-first centuries has the circumstances our Higher Selves, guides, and Soul knew we need to experience love, learn lessons, and enjoy the experience.

8

Our Souls Plan Our Earth School Experience

Our Souls planned the contents of our Earth School experience before we developed in Earth School. The planning was quite detailed, involving other people, guides, our Souls, and sometimes higher-order beings. This chapter explains the pre-birth planning process. Much of this chapter is taken from Rob Schwartz's *Your Soul's Plan*[138] and *Your Soul's Gift*.[139] I recommend highly that you read the books to understand how we plan our lives and the involvement of all parties in the planning.

When we realize we planned our lives in collaboration with people who love us, supported by the Universal Intelligence that is love, we can see our life's dramas differently. After researching and writing *Your Soul's Plan*, Rob Schwartz wrote this wonderful statement about how realizing we have planned our lives changes the way in which we live our lives.

And where I've judged, I now see a divine order to and in everything. Where I've seen flaw, I now see perfection—the perfection of lives unfolding just as we planned them. Such unfolding is evident not only in our challenges, but also in the most minute, seemingly insignificant aspects of life. Each leaf that falls from a tree, each blade of grass that bends in the wind.

... Nothing happens by chance, and all is in divine order. Always.

I have realized too that each of us has a divine purpose, a reason for being here that includes but goes well beyond our own learning. That is, we plan life challenges not only to remember who we really are, but also to share ourselves, our unique essence, with one another.[140]

Pre-Birth Planning

Our lives are carefully planned. They are not sequences of accidents in time. We chose the family of origin, mental and physical capabilities and limitations, events that would shape our minds and allow us to learn the lessons we chose to learn, and the potential exit points when we would graduate.

We have done the planning in dialogue with the others who will be in our sphere of contacts and influence in our lives, and with our guides, Souls, and higher-order beings whose role is to do as much as possible to ensure we learn the lessons and have the experiences we planned to have.

We are then immersed in the Earth School experience, playing the roles we determined we would play without knowledge of the planning or the roles others have chosen to take in our lives or our nature as eternal beings having a physical experience. Once we are in Earth School, we continue through the life experience until completion, with little or no knowledge of the choices we made before enrolling. We are reared in Earth School to take on all of Earth School's positive and negative characteristics so we can face the events we have chosen to face and learn from them.

However, we are also the Soul that is not constrained by the Earth School Mind. Our Souls are knowledgeable about who we are in eternity, the lessons we have set about learning, the events we have planned, and the others who have chosen to enroll in Earth School with us to learn lessons and help us learn our lessons.

It's difficult for us to conceptualize the Higher Self, Soul, and Earth School Mind. They are all one. We must resist having an image of them as separate entities, like three individuals standing on different levels. We must see them only as different functions within the one Universal Intelligence that are relevant to each of us.

Our Higher Self, Soul, and Earth School Mind are roles within the one Universal Intelligence. Each is a function that is relevant to our individual self. Each has a unique set of skills and knowledge, but all are one. The Earth School Mind doesn't know everything the Soul knows. The Soul is dedicated to the individual we are, so it functions differently from the Higher Self that has many Souls and Minds in its repertoire.

In the same way, we who are in Earth School are all one, even though we have different bodies, personalities, genders, and all the rest of what makes it seem we are separate. Everything in our cosmos is only Mind and experiences in the Universal Intelligence. We have experiences accessible from the Universal Intelligence that are unique to each of us, but we are the one Universal Intelligence engaged in different roles.

We have free will in Earth School. As we live our lives, we may choose not to have the experiences and not to learn the lessons we had planned before being born. However, we are not set into motion in life by those who have done the planning and let go to fend for ourselves. We are continually given guidance and insights by our Soul, the Souls of the others who are with us in Earth School, our guides, helpers, and loved ones concerned that we have a satisfying, fruitful Earth School experience.

We can often understand the life lessons we have set out to learn by looking at the circumstances of our lives and the struggles we are experiencing. What are the great struggles for me? What does it seem I must learn to lead a happy, fulfilled life in the face of these struggles? What does it seem others can learn from their struggles if I help them?

Everything in our lives is happening for a purpose, but our lives are not predestined. Every event has been planned or will be incorporated into our life's plan by circumstances that follow the event. If someone else changes their plan in ways that affect our plan, our guides, Soul, and others will inspire us into different actions to help us return to the process of learning the lessons we want to learn and being happy.

Every event and every challenge is an opportunity to grow in self-understanding that our Souls and guides take advantage of.

How Our Souls Plan for Us to Learn Lessons

Our Souls plan the experiences that will enable us to learn lessons with the group of beings functioning as a planning group. The composition of the group changes as people are added for specific activities. The group comprises Souls who will have Earth School experiences with us, guides available to come into the discussions as necessary to give the planning group help, our Souls, and occasionally, higher-level Ascended Masters, but they limit their involvement because the planning must be completed on the level of the Souls who will enroll us in Earth School.

Our Souls plan our lives first by deciding on the circumstances of our lives. We choose our families, friends and colleagues, physical and mental capabilities and limitations, gender, neighborhoods and home environment, prosperity or lack of prosperity, schools, careers, addictions, and other conditions of life. Our Souls then plan life events that will help us confront challenges and have learning experiences that will enable us to learn the lessons we have chosen to learn.

The plans do not include horrendous actions and violence. Suzanne Giesemann received this message from a person living in the next stage of life:

> I will tell you that you do plan your parents and your siblings and your race and your sex. That sort of thing, because of the opportunities [they provide]. Why would you choose to come back and do something that's completely against the nature of God if these things happen naturally as a result of people who haven't yet awakened doing stupid, human things. ... Rape and murder are human behaviors from souls who get so caught up in the story they forget their original assignment. And that is to get down here and learn how to love. That's like having a

teacher tell you to go into that math class and add 2 plus 2 until you get 5.[141]

Staci Wells, the medium working with Rob Schwartz, author of *Your Soul's Plan* and *Your Soul's Gift*, describes the planning as being done on boards whose contents have the appearance of flow charts and cells. The planning group sits in a room talking about what the Soul is interested in learning and how each entity can participate. They explore life-event alternatives and the results that might come from choosing each alternative. They evaluate what might happen in the person's life if a life-event occurs and how that will affect the learning and other events in the person's life. The learning experiences are planned with great care.[142]

The Primary Challenge

The planning group plans events and circumstances with great challenges the person must deal with and overcome. The challenges are intended to help the person learn the lessons the Soul and others want the person to learn. The greatest challenges were chosen because of the great lessons the person wanted to learn. The person may not be able to triumph over the challenges the first time they encounter them. The person's Soul and guides may alter upcoming events during the person's life in Earth School to present the challenges again. However, as with everything in our eternal lives, we have free will. We may choose not to go through the struggle of overcoming the challenges. There is no judgment for not confronting and learning from them.

Most people have a primary challenge that dominated their thoughts and plans in the pre-birth planning. It may be learning compassion, humility, trust, other-centeredness, sensitivity, or other positive learning. If a person's life seems to be dominated by challenges and growth in an area, that likely is the area of the primary challenge. The individual will feel guidance about the circumstances in which the primary challenge appears. Growth will happen each time the person faces the challenge.

Because it is so profound, the area of the primary challenge is the area of life that may not be successfully addressed. However, even when the challenge does not result in the desired outcomes, some learning has occurred.

Viewing the Alternatives During the Planning

The planning group is able to see the alternative paths the person may take during the Earth School experience. The experiences are not pre-destined. The person has free will and may choose a path not in the pre-birth planning. The planning includes contingencies for these detours. And the person's Soul and guides are engaged in working with the person every moment of the lifetime, so when detours occur, the person can be guided through influences and circumstances to choose an alternate path that will arrive at the desired learning.

Learning Lessons through Opposites

One of the foremost ways the planning group plans for the events to teach the desired lessons is through opposites. The Soul will plan for the person to be in circumstances and experiences characterized by the opposite of what they want to learn so they can experience that opposite condition and learn to value and appreciate the missing sentiment the Soul and Higher Self want to understand more fully. For example, a Soul that wants to understand humility may have the individual born into a family that is arrogant because of its wealth and position. In that circumstance, the person is able to become offended by the family's treatment of employees and others, thereby realizing the importance of being humble rather than arrogant. That person may then choose to lead a humble life without wealth and position.

Siddharta Gautama, the Buddha, is reported to have been a prince who learned that his position and wealth could not provide lasting happiness or protection from suffering. He left his wealthy conditions to discover a state of mind that was free from disturbing emotions and full of compassion. His successful learning has become the teachings of Buddhism. He spent his life teaching people how they could reach the same state.

Edward VIII, king of England for one year, abdicated the throne to marry Wallace Simpson, an American commoner. The day after his abdication, he announced in a radio broadcast to his subjects, "I have found it impossible to carry the heavy burden of responsibility and to discharge my duties as king as I would wish to do without the help and support of the woman I love. The decision I have made has been mine and mine alone ... The other person most nearly concerned has tried up to the last to persuade me to take a different course."[143] In his pre-birth planning, he had set his life's path to have position, power, and wealth. In that position, he saw how empty his life would be without the woman he had come to love. He learned to follow his heart and act against the entreaties of those around him, giving up his position and power. That decision was in his life's plan.

This is an example from Rob Schwartz's *Your Soul's Plan*:

For instance, a deeply compassionate Soul who wishes to know herself as compassion may choose to incarnate into a highly dysfunctional family. As she is treated with a lack of compassion, she comes to appreciate compassion more deeply. It is the absence of something that best teaches its value and meaning. A lack of compassion in the outer world forces her to turn inward, where she remembers her own compassion. The contrast between the lack of compassion in the physical world and her inner compassion provides her with a more profound understanding of compassion and, therefore, herself. From the perspective of the Soul, the pain inherent in this learning process is temporary and brief, but the resultant wisdom is literally eternal.[144]

All Involved Willingly Join as Partners in the Individual's Earth School Experience

Since all in the planning group will be playing parts in each other's Earth School experience, there is lively discussion about the plans for each Soul's life and the effect planned events will have on each person involved. Throughout all the deliberations, all realize that "Life is based on love and service. There is nothing else."[145]

Some life plans the planning group prepares for a person have lessons that benefit the entire group. They all participate, all share the struggles, and all experience the learning.

Some members may take on the personalities, motivations, and inborn tendencies that make them more unruly, insensitive, cruel, and disliked. During the planning process they are greatly affected by the roles they must plan and want to make sure those on whom they will inflict the negativity are willing to allow it. All know everything that will happen will be in love. In Earth School, we must realize that those who seem most insensitive and cruel, who may have antisocial personalities and impoverished consciences, have chosen to take on those roles out of love for the people most affected during the Earth School experience.

Some in the life planning agree to take on lives that are less for their own learning than to be part of the learning someone else is experiencing. In eternity, delaying personal growth is just for an instant, and even then, there are lessons to be learned. They may in fact lead lives in which they are reviled and otherwise have negative experiences. They are willing to go through those experiences for the love of the others who are learning lessons from the relationship.

In Rob Schwartz's book, Doris, who has breast cancer, is able to channel her own Oversoul, or Higher Self. Doris suffered abuse by her alcoholic mother. This is Rob's summary of Doris's life planning and the outworking of her life:

> When we plan our lives, we choose to "work" with other Souls whom we love very much and who love us. … Doris's mother knew before birth there would be painful conflict with her child. Only a Soul who truly loved Doris and was committed to Doris's evolution would agree to bear the brunt of her anger. In this way our greatest tormentors are often those with whom we share the most love when in spirit. When this lifetime is complete, Doris will thank her mother for the growth she fostered, and Doris's mother will thank her for the opportunity to have been of service. Gratitude towards those who have most challenged us—and thus most stimulated our evolution—is a

Soul-level perspective we can adopt while still in body. When we make that choice, we remove blame from our lives. Without blame, forgiveness becomes possible, and with forgiveness comes healing.

As [medium Staci Wells] pointed out, Doris's mother agreed to defer some of her growth to help Doris. It is common for Souls to put their learning aside to be of service to others. From the level of the personality, it is difficult to imagine that some of those who "mistreat" us are actually engaged in a form of service. It may be even more difficult to see that the so-called mistreatment entails sacrifice on their parts. These concepts which are so familiar to us before birth are forgotten when we incarnate. To remember them is to know self more profoundly and in ways that are not possible without a physical incarnation.[146]

Plans by People Who Want to Be of Service to Humankind

Some people have chosen to enter Earth School because the planning group realizes humankind needs the special messages and abilities the person will bring to all in their circle of influence and beyond. Their personal life lessons are less important for that lifetime than performing activities that will have an impact on others. Because they are bringing messages that may not be popular, they may experience trials and have to overcome obstacles. In some circumstances, an entire Soul group may enter Earth School to have an effect on humankind.

Plans to Enter Earth School with a Soul Group

Richard Martini, producer of films about the afterlife, describes the results of his research into Soul groups.

People under deep hypnosis claim (and that's the thousands of cases of Dr. Helen Wambach and Michael Newton and the 45 I've filmed) that we all have "soul groups" that we incarnate with. They average 3–25 people per group—almost like a classroom—and those people are often the ones you meet where you "feel like you've known them forever." They claim that some family members "may be part of our soul group" but that some may not. They may be with "affiliated groups" that we interact with in various lifetimes, but aren't always connected to. They also claim the members of our soul group may surprise us—it's generally people who've had some kind of dramatic effect on your lifetime. (Could be a person you only met once, or was a teacher, or someone you'd least suspect.) They claim that after your lifetime, you return "home" (their word) where you work out your next adventure with the guidance of your loved ones. You can say "no" to coming back—you're not forced to by anyone—but people claim they generally "come back to help their loved ones with their journeys." So there's that—no one comes alone, no one is alone, and no one leaves alone.[147]

Planning Arrangements for Life Circumstances to Be Intentionally Interrupted

The life planning includes arrangements that are interrupted, such as marriage, career, talents, skills, and other circumstances or abilities that profoundly affect the person. These circumstances might be termination by divorce, loss of a job, injury to an athlete, or loss of a skill. The circumstances or abilities may have served their purposes and are no longer necessary, or the change may be part of the learning process. The Soul may be moving on to another circumstance that will teach other lessons.

Tragedies as Part of Life Plans

Tragedies are part of the life planning. During the planning, the Souls involved in the tragedies are careful to plan them so the person has much guidance and support during the traumatic time. The lessons will be difficult, but the person will be given all the support necessary to learn from the adversity, including help from guides and others who are entering Earth School with the Soul.

People's Plans to Be of Service to Others

People who want to learn how to be of service to others may pair with people who want to experience the limitations resulting in the need for care and feel hopeful and secure when they are taken care of by others. The person serving may be a parent caring for a person who is a disabled child. The disabilities and their severity are planned. Both will achieve their life goals by cooperating in the Earth School experience.

Medium Staci Wells's spirit guide spoke about the reasons Souls choose to be disabled or to care for disabled children:

> "Handicaps are chosen by Souls because it gives them opportunities they would not normally have," replied the spirit guide. "Sometimes it gives Souls a different way to learn the same lesson they've been working on [in previous lives]. Often, it is [chosen as] a challenge to the caretaker to show compassion, mercy, and love. Souls choose to honor other Souls by making themselves the vehicle through which they can be born. They choose to care for those Souls by allowing them, the handicapped children, to live this life as they wished — less involved in the ordinary, everyday functions of life. It is a unique opportunity for the handicapped child, and it is an opportunity for the parent to show love. These agreements are made out of love." [148]

Plans That Include Less or More Structure

Some Souls choose less structure. They want the person entering Earth School to have more latitude in making choices during the person's Earth School experiences. We are always guided and helped by our Souls, guides, helpers, and loved ones, so we're not left to fend for ourselves entirely. Our lives will achieve our goals even when we have less structure in them. If one choice doesn't work, we will be guided to make other choices. In the end, however, we always make our own choices. We always have free will.

For those people who choose a less structured life experience, others in the group who enroll in Earth School with them may take on the role of educator, parent, or counselor to help them through the experience.

Other Souls planning the Earth School experience may want their individual selves in Earth School to have more of a rigid structure, and may choose a circumstance such as a disability that cannot be altered. They believe the person needs the rigidity to ensure the person learns the lessons set out in the plan.

People's Souls Plan for the Person to Experience Afflictions and Unfortunate Circumstances

We can see afflictions and unfortunate circumstances as the challenges our Souls have chosen. Illnesses such as AIDS, cancer, ALS, dementia, Alzheimer's, and the disabling results of accidents, are all chosen for some reason. For all of them, the person can meet the challenge and live a life that is rich and full. The afflictions and unfortunate circumstances don't create hopelessness, sadness, and despondence. Those are states of mind. The Soul that has chosen for the person to have a debilitating disease or mental condition has done so to learn some lesson. The person must understand the debilitating condition in this way and overcome its challenges to be happy in Earth School.

The person who is ill and the people caring for the person who is ill all have challenges that, if met successfully, will result in spiritual and mental strength. Those strengths will carry on and will raise the stature of humankind by that measure. The Soul and Higher Self will be enriched by the triumphs when the person with the afflictions learns to live a full life in love, peace, and joy. In pre-birth planning, during the life struggles, and after the transition, the person, the person's Soul, and the others involved all see the wisdom and necessity of the illness. The Earth School experience is short compared to the length of our eternal lives, but the lessons learned will have an impact on the Higher Self's and the Soul's learning.

The Life Plan Includes Events Because the Person Wants to Enjoy the Experience

The planning also includes events the Souls would like to experience because of their desire to have rich, fulfilling lives. Our time in Earth School is not just to learn lessons. We are to enjoy all the exciting opportunities and new experiences Earth School has to offer.

The Life Plan Includes Exit Points

The life plan includes exit points. Rob Schwartz's sources explain that there are "always three or four or five possibilities. No one has just one exit door."[149]

Violence, Murder, and Suicide Are Not Planned

Violence, murder, and suicide are not part of pre-birth planning. The individual may have taken on the characteristics that might make them prone to violence, such as an antisocial personality or psychopathology. The life circumstances might be such that they would lead the person to be more likely to commit violent acts, such as the circumstances of being abused and traumatized in childhood. However, the decision to murder or take one's own life is a free-will choice the person makes that is outside of the pre-birth plan.

The talented medium and teacher Suzanne Giesemann describes the message she received from William James, the father of American psychology, who is part of the collective in the life after this life called Sanaya.

> The soul takes on the experience of human life for the experience it will provide to the soul. Do not think in human terms; that is a bottom-up perspective. Humans know good and evil because you are immersed in this dualistic environment from day one. Think, if you must think, better said "feel" and "know," from the soul's perspective. What is the soul? A spark of the Divine. Its source is unified, nondualistic. Yes, the soul enters into a human body for the lessons the dualism will provide, but from the soul's perspective, it does so to practice

being more of a SOUL [his emphasis], not to practice being more of a HUMAN.

You can only have this perspective if you see from the higher perspective. Do you see, do you feel? The soul enters into human form knowing it will encounter challenges and difficulties and beings who have not awakened at all. Is this not challenge enough? Through these interactions, the soul must work to shine through, not to practice being human. You, the human, are an extension of the Soul. You did not choose to do evil. You chose to remember your Divine nature. See the world as the Soul sees it, and you will no longer make choices of a human nature.

If a human planned his or her life on earth, he might plan to be a murderer. You are thinking as a human script writer would sit at a table and plan a life. But Souls are not human. Souls are above the human condition. Souls see the landscape into which they will be descending and choose circumstances that will allow them to grow by exposing their presence as a Soul. You are here in human form to allow the light of the Soul to burst forth. It does not do so through murder, rape, and mayhem. It does so by urging the human away from these choices. Contrast is inherent in the human condition of ignorance. It need not be planned. Trust us in this. It is not punishment to take on a human form. The free will choices made by mankind are punishment enough. [150]

The others involved in the life also know there is a chance this Soul may become violent. They take on their roles in this Earth School experience accepting that possibility, in love, because they know the Soul must learn the lessons they have chosen, including learning how to reduce violent tendencies and learn to love freely.

For a full, clear explanation of the issues involved in suicides, read Mike Tymn's Appendix C in *The Afterlife Revealed: What Happens after We Die*. [151]

9

Our Souls Attune Us to Earth School

We must rid ourselves of the duality conception of a physical "out there" and a mental "in here." They result in a sense of separateness between the world of experiences and the Earth School Mind, a conception that is at the root of all of humankind's problems.

There is no "out there" in a separate physical realm of matter and energy with separate bodies. We are not separate Minds or spirits that "enter" Earth School, and "enter" a separate body. Instead, our Minds, which are individuated manifestations of the Universal Intelligence, become attuned to Earth School experiences at this time in its history. As we live our Earth School lives, the Universal Intelligence gives us the experiences comprising Earth School during this time. Others living with us in Earth School are receiving the same experiences, so we are all aware of a common Earth School, including the experiences of our bodies.

We do not enter Earth School or enter a body. We simply begin having the experiences of Earth School and the experiences of a body made available by the Universal Intelligence. The Polish composer and virtuoso pianist Frédéric Chopin, coming through from his life from the next life in a Leslie Flint session explains. You can hear Chopin

speaking this message and some additional words at
www.earthschoolanswers.com/chopin/.

> There's no such thing as a spirit inhabiting a body: that is
> another fallacy of the fools that try to explain things. We don't
> actually inhabit the body, in the sense that some people seem to
> think, that we are **in** the body in the same sense that people
> think that when a person dies we sort of, creep out of it. . . .

> Well, it's not like that. You cannot explain it in that way. What
> one must remember is that there is an etheric body (which is a
> duplicate of the material body) which is animated by the spirit,
> which has no body in the same sense. And that is not
> necessarily inside the physical body, but it is an animating
> force which is behind the etheric body and the material body.

> And when the physical body dies, the etheric body still retains
> its shape and form and it is that part of Man that is recognized
> as an individual. And it is that part which people communicate
> with. … The whole point is that there's too much talk about
> bodies. These bodies are merely vehicles in their expression of
> the mentality and the mind and the spirit … the vitality and the
> life … the vitalizing force which is life itself.[152]

During the whole time, we, our Soul, our Higher Self, and all of
Earth School are one in the Universal Intelligence. No part of us
"incarnates" somewhere outside of the Universal Intelligence with a
spark or piece of who we are remaining with the Higher Self. Our
Souls and Earth School Minds are individual manifestations of the one
Universal Intelligence. We have simply attuned ourselves to the Earth
School experiences others are having.

The Universal Intelligence, Higher Self or Oversoul, Soul, and Earth School Mind

The Universal Intelligence, Higher Self or Oversoul, Soul, and
Earth School Mind are all one. It is as though the Universal Intelligence
was dreaming the Higher Selves who were dreaming the numerous
Souls and Minds living in Earth School. All are the dream of the

Universal Intelligence. We are individuals in all those dreams. But these dreams have substance and real individuals interacting in real events. We as individuals continue our lives through eternity.

After years of pondering the enigma of how God is related to the substance of a physical world, the quantum physicist Amit Goswami came to an epiphany that explained the relationship fully: "There is nothing but God. There is nothing but God."[153] There is nothing but the Universal Intelligence.

What Is the Universal Intelligence?

We must give up on the Anglo Saxon term "God." The word has too many connotations created by the West's saturation with the Judeo-Christian religions. Foremost is the assumption that there is a personality or being with the range of human emotions that creates a world separate from himself (masculine pronoun). There is nothing but the Universal Intelligence. I do not use "Universal Mind" because "Mind" suggests a person with personality and human traits. Instead, the Universal Intelligence is the ground of being, the source, that manifests in what we call matter and energy. Everything is the Universal Intelligence in different forms, including all experiences and our Earth School Minds.

When people experience the Universal Intelligence in near-death experiences without the overlay of the Earth School Mind, they feel a pervasive, unfathomable love they have never experienced before. We know that the Universal Intelligence is characterized by unconditional, profound love.

We needn't try to define the Universal Intelligence further. Understanding it further is beyond the horizon of our ability to understand. For our lives, we can be content to realize that everything ever experienced and able to be experienced by humankind, in the past and future, anywhere in any universe, is the Universal Intelligence. And we are wholly that. There is nothing but Mind and experiences. They are the basis of our reality.

The authors of a blog titled "Why a Mental Universe Is the 'Real' Reality" describe the inscrutable nature of the Universal Intelligence. The authors are Deepak Chopra, MD, a board-certified physician, Means Kafatos, PhD, a professor of computational physics, Bernardo Kastrup, PhD, computer engineer with specialization in artificial intelligence, and Rudolph Tanzi, PhD, professor of neurology. They describe the Universal Intelligence that is the basis of all reality.

> Therefore, every theory of nature needs to grant at least one fundamental aspect of reality that cannot be explained, but in terms of which everything else should be explainable. For physicalists, this fundamental aspect of reality is, depending on the particular theory, a set of basic subatomic particles, superstrings, hyper-dimensional membranes, etc. But under the view that the universe is mental, the universal mind itself is the sole fundamental aspect of reality.

> As such, the universal mind cannot be explained, and does not need to be explained in terms of anything else. It simply is. Everything else, in turn, needs to be explained in terms of the behavior—excitations, modulations, vibrations, movements, or whatever other metaphor is most suitable—of the universal mind.[154]

What Is the Higher Self or Oversoul?

Within the one Universal Intelligence are innumerable Higher Selves. We are the Higher Self allowing part of ourselves we call an individual Mind to have Earth School experiences. It is like we're experiencing a movie. While we are in Earth School experiencing the movie, feeling ourselves to be the characters in the movie, we are still the Higher Self sitting in the audience enjoying the movie. We are both the actor and the spectator. We've just voluntarily decided we will allow ourselves to have the Earth School experiences so we can learn lessons and enjoy the experiences.

We are able to interrupt the movie by relaxing ourselves out of the focus on this experience and coming back into who we really are as expressions of the Higher Self. The actor and the spectator experience the one Self we always are. We are still attuned to Earth School, so when we come back from the relaxation we continue in the Earth School experience.

The Higher Selves comprise many Earth School Minds. When we talk of "incarnating," there is no "re-incarnating," meaning an Earth School Mind comes back to Earth School. We remain individuals after we have developed in Earth School, forever. Instead, many Earth School Minds that are aspects of a single Higher Self have come into Earth School and had experiences the Higher Self benefits from. Reincarnation is explained more fully later in this book.

An analogy will help you conceptualize the Higher Self and Earth School Minds. Imagine you are 75 years old looking through a picture album of your life. You see a picture of yourself as an infant, then as a 5-year-old, then as a pre-pubescent 12-year-old, then as an adolescent, then as a 25-year-old, then a 40-year-old, then as a 60-year-old, and finally as a 75-year-old. As you look at the pictures, you remark, "That's me when I was an infant. That's me when I was 5 years old. That's me when I was 25 years old." In all cases, you know every one of those people was you. They now make up who you are as a 75-year-old.

But they were all very different. Your body and Mind as an infant were quite different from your body and Mind as a 5-year-old, and greatly different from you as a 25-year-old or a 75-year-old. From birth to 24 months, you didn't know that an object existed if you couldn't see it. It disappeared when it left your sight and a new object appeared when you saw the object again. From age 2 to age 7, your thinking was based on intuition and experience, with little logic. You couldn't grasp cause and effect, time, and comparison. From ages 7 to 11 you developed your mental abilities but couldn't think abstractly or hypothetically. It wasn't until your mid 20s that your Mind was able to analyze problems that have no right answers, such as moral dilemmas. Not until after your mid-20s were you able to see yourself as an actor on the stage of life and evaluate how satisfied you or your employers, partners, and others were with your performance and their impact.[155]

As adults today, we can't understand ourselves as we were as infants, adolescents, and young adults. At each age, you were living a unique life with a unique body and a Mind you can't understand now. When you think back to things you did as a 5-year-old or 16-year-old or 25-year-old, you can hardly believe that was you. You cannot now understand the Minds that were you, but they were wholly you. Today, as a 75-year-old, the Minds of these very different individuals make up your Mind.

The Higher Self is like you as the 75-year-old. The Higher Self has many Earth School Minds that make up the Higher Self. Each is just a different aspect of the Higher Self. The difference between the analogy and your Higher Self is that every one of those individuals that make up the Higher Self still lives on as an individual. Each continues growing to higher spiritual and mental levels. But these individuals still all comprise the Higher Self.

Many people report profoundly moving experiences in communications with their Higher Selves, but we must remember that this communication is not with a separate entity. It is relaxing into a dialogue within ourselves like the one we have when we're reviewing alternatives to make a decision; the speaker and listener are one. The Higher Self knows the plan the Earth School Mind in Earth School is living out and was involved in developing the plan.

What Is the Soul?

The Soul is each person's link between the Higher Self and the Earth School Mind. The Soul is wholly dedicated to the Earth School Mind and experiences what the Earth School Mind is experiencing. The Soul is healthy, lucid, and intelligent, even though the Mind in Earth School may be limited by mental or physical disabilities or by being a fetus with no mental capacities in Earth School yet. Two examples of people communicating with their Souls follow.

Sonia Rinaldi, the Brazilian instrumental transcommunication researcher, has recorded the words articulated by the Soul of an unborn child speaking maturely about her condition. You can listen to the recording at www.earthschoolanswers.com/unborn/. The questions and answers are in Brazilian Portuguese.

Sonia has also recorded the words articulated by the Soul of an autistic girl who was unable to speak in this life. Her Soul speaks clearly, fluently, and confidently. You can listen to the recording at www.earthschoolanswers.com/autistic/.

Dr. Allan Botkin, the originator of the Induced After-Death Communication psychotherapy method helped a father enter the state of Mind in which he was able to communicate with the Higher Self of his mentally disabled son suffering from microencephalopathy, which left him with the mind of a six-year-old and unable to speak. In Dr. Botkin's induction, the father experienced his son speaking clearly and intelligently as he communicated with the boy's Soul. The father said, "He's thanking me for being such a wonderful father to him. He says, 'I'm here to look after you.' … Jason told me I shouldn't feel bad about his medical condition because it allows him to experience both worlds at the same time."[156]

The Soul is the unchanging awareness that is always present as experiences come and are replaced in the now point of awareness. The Soul is the gateway between the Universal Intelligence and the now point of the Earth School Mind.

The Soul takes an active role in helping the Earth School Mind achieve its goals in Earth School. It gives gentle guidance and can work with guides to inspire the Earth School Mind during Earth School experiences.

What Is the Relationship of the Universal Intelligence to Our Higher Selves, Souls, and Earth School Minds?

The authors of the blog "Why a Mental Universe Is the 'Real' Reality," cited earlier, write about the Mind's relationship to the Universal Intelligence.

> Our seemingly separate human Minds are dissociated personalities of this universal mind, akin to the multiple personalities of a person with Dissociative Identity Disorder [formerly multiple personality disorder]. The ideas and emotions experienced by the universal mind—within which we are all immersed—are presented to us in the form of the empirical world we see, hear, touch, taste and smell.[157]

The Earth School Mind is an individuated expression of the Higher Self having experiences provided by the Universal Intelligence. We are always the Higher Self, the Soul, and the Mind as expressions

of the Universal Intelligence. Our Souls and associated Earth School
Minds are attuned voluntarily to the lives we are experiencing in Earth
School; other Souls and Earth School Minds that are part of our Higher
Selves are having other experiences by being attuned to other
circumstances.

Medium Corbie Mitleid channeled the Soul of a woman named
Valerie during Rob Schwartz's research. This is her description of the
relationship of the Earth School Mind to the Soul:

> "The [Earth School] personality is created by the Soul, the
> Higher Self," Valerie's Soul added. "The personality is the
> illusion that is required on earth in this space-time to learn the
> lessons. For without a body and without time, there are lessons
> that cannot be learned."

> Now that the subject was raised, it seemed a good time for me
> [Rob] to explore the distinction between personality and Soul.

> "My understanding of the personality," I said, "is that it
> consists of a permanent eternal core that survives death and
> reunites with the Soul after death, as well as certain temporary
> traits that exist only during the lifetime."

> "That is accurate."

> "So, when a personality dies in a particular lifetime—say, when
> Valerie dies in this lifetime—then her permanent core will be
> reunited with you?"

> "At this point it is not separate. Do not consider reuniting, for
> that betokens a separation. There is never any separation. What
> the personality feels [after death], when it feels as one with God
> and the Higher Self, is simply the brushing away of cobwebs
> that obscured its view, but it does not mean that it has not been
> connected."[158]

Our Souls are always integral with our Earth School Minds and
both are individuated facets of our Higher Selves.

What Is the Earth School Mind?

The Earth School Mind has been called the body/Mind because it includes the reactions and senses of the body as well as the characteristics we normally associate with a Mind. However, the distinction is misleading. Instead of a body and Mind as separate entities, we must speak only of the Earth School Mind. There is no body to include as a component. Instead, we have a body experience in the Earth School Mind. I explain why here.

Today, as you read this, you are the Mind in Earth School, a unique focus generated for you by your Higher Self. You never separate from the Higher Self to enroll in Earth School. You may have heard the description that we have a part of us that remains in spirit while we are in Earth School. That suggests a separation between spirit and us as individuals because there is some part of us that is spirit that remains in the separated spirit. There is no separation. You are the Higher Self providing a focus of part of yourself to function in Earth School, with the rules and circumstances of Earth School. Your Soul is that aspect of the Higher Self that has agreed that you, a wholly part of the Higher Self, would be reared in Earth School with limitations. You are 100 percent the perfect Soul and 100 percent your Higher Self, but you have accepted the role of your Earth School personality with limitations that makes you an Earth School person.

It is much like your daily activities. You go to work and are a dental assistant. You go home and are a mother or father of a toddler. You attend a meeting of new mothers or fathers and are a meeting attender. You play different roles, so it seems you are three people. But you are not. You are one person playing three roles. In the same way, you are wholly your Higher Self, wholly your soul, and wholly your Earth School self. You're just having unique focuses and characteristics at each level.

The concept of our being Earth School Minds that are focuses in the Higher Self created by the Universal Intelligence is rather like the concept of being a character in a play. When you are playing a character, you are always you, but you have allowed yourself to take on the characteristics of the person you are playing. You could be a player in many different plays, with different characters, but you are always you. That is the way the Higher Self has Earth School Minds with their unique focuses. We as our Higher Self choose to take on a role. The difference between us as players in a play and Earth School Minds in the Higher Self is that when we develop as Minds in Earth School, we continue to be the Minds after graduating from Earth School.

Having a Higher Self with a number of focuses that are Earth School Minds is much like being in a dream. When you are in a dream, you are creating the characters and you are creating your own dream actor. You create the scenery and the drama in your dream. You play it out with vigor, joy, anxiety, frustration, and the gamut of emotions. But the whole time, you are yourself just having a night's sleep. Your dream self is never separate from you, and you are creating other characters who are in the dream that are not separate from you. The scenery is not separate from you. The drama and emotions are not separate from you. They are all part of you; they're part of your dream.

Tomorrow night, you'll have another dream with another set of characters and scenery. They are part of you as well. The characters in your first dream are not reincarnated as characters in your second dream. They are different but are all you.

In the same way, you are an Earth School Mind who is wholly the Higher Self. You are the Higher Self playing your part as an Earth School Mind in Earth School. You will continue to be an individual after you graduate and go on to other schools and experiences. You as an individual do not "re-incarnate." More individuals wholly part of your Higher Self individuate to have experiences on any of millions of other planes and spheres, including Earth School. You will stay yourself.

Unlike your dream in which you create the characters, in Earth School the other participants are also having their own experiences, rather like being in their own dreams. There is no outside world that exists independent of us. Instead, the Universal Intelligence is giving us the same experiences, the same dream, so it seems like there is a world outside of us. But it is just that Earth School is the scenery, continuity of events, and experiences that are the same for all of us Earth School Minds. We are in the same dream.

There is nothing but Mind and the experiences Mind has that are the creation of the Universal Intelligence. We have the experience of a body, but there is no body outside of our Earth School Mind. The body is just a complex set of experiences we call a body.

The Body and the Fetus

The body is always just a body experience, not some object. Until a person has body experiences after the experience of birth, the fetus is merely a potential body experience. The Soul never "enters" the fetus. That is a conception based in materialism. There is no material world. There is only Mind and experiences. There is no material fetus for the immaterial Mind to enter. Instead of the notion of entering a physical body, we must realize the Mind has body experiences. There is never a time when we enter a body.

The commonly used term for beginning Earth School experiences is to "incarnate." We must abandon this common term for beginning our Earth School experiences. We don't incarnate in the sense of becoming objects on an earth globe made of matter and energy that is apart from the Universal Intelligence. Instead we are Souls that attune our Minds to the commonly held story of Earth School at this time to have experiences.

"Earth plane" is also not an appropriate phrase. It suggests a material world that is independent of the Universal Intelligence. It is better to talk about attuning to the experiences others are having. When our Souls have our Earth School Minds attune to the experiences others are having at this time in Earth School, the Universal Intelligence gives us experiences we have together: chairs, rivers, a sun, weather, and all the other experiences we have in the Earth School Mind. There is no physical plane with physical chairs, rivers, a sun, and weather that exists when no one is there. All of the experiences are happening in our Earth School Minds that are unique attunements of the Universal Intelligence. The pre-birth planners and Soul could have attuned our Minds to a million other realms, but we have chosen to attune to this one together.

We begin Earth School when the Soul turns its focus to the story being played out in Earth School that is in the Minds of all of the current participants. The Earth School Mind then begins to develop. We fit into the Earth School environment by sharing in the conceptions, presumptions, and sensory experiences people already in Earth School have, available from the Universal Intelligence. We don't think about it or make it happen. The commonly held understanding among all who are in Earth School about the environment shapes our perception of Earth School. The common environment, conceptions, presumptions and sensory experiences are accessible by each of us through the Universal Intelligence. We share the same dream.

The Mind then develops from nothing into the person who can make free will choices to grow to become more wise, loving, compassionate, and other-centered. However, the Earth School Mind will have all the characteristics determined in pre-birth planning, such as physical characteristics, disabilities, and mental capabilities. The pre-birth planning comes to fruition as the person's Mind develops. However, none of the disabilities and limitations affect the Soul, which is always whole and mentally capable.

We start as Earth School Minds that are *tabula rasas*, blank slates, and grow to learn how to navigate in Earth School. At the moment when we have our first experience, we can say we have entered Earth School. It is a matter of a state of Mind.

Do We Reincarnate into Earth School?

Reincarnation is misunderstood. It doesn't mean someone keeps coming back to Earth School to learn lessons. We are told repeatedly by sources in the next life that we as individuals retain our individuality when we graduate from Earth School. All our experiences are part of the Higher Self's evolution, and we continue to grow in wisdom, love, and compassion for others after transition. Other individuals of the Higher Self attune to Earth School instead. The Higher Self and we learn from the experiences of these other people. We will then be able to re-experience what they have experienced as part of our learning.

However, in our pre-birth planning, another life in the Higher Self may be the basis for the life we plan. We may want to learn something not fully learned in that previous life or counter some actions in that other life during our life or in some other way want our life to augment or continue something of the other life. We come into Earth School as our unique self, and that individual continues to live in the life after this life as their unique self, but the lives are intertwined because of the desire among us in the Higher Self to have experiences based on that other life.

The clearest explanation of the concept of reincarnation is in Mike Tymn's *The Afterlife Revealed: What Happens after We Die*, Appendix B.[159]

Mike cites the afterlife researcher Frederick Myers, speaking in the life after this life through Geraldine Cummins, who explains about the individuals in the "group Soul."

> When I was on earth, I belonged to a group-soul, but its branches and the spirit—which might be compared to the roots—were in the invisible," Myers, one of the pioneers of psychical research before his death in 1901, communicated. "Now, if you would understand psychic evolution, this group-soul must be studied and understood. For instance, it explains many of the difficulties that people will assure you can be removed only by the doctrine of reincarnation. You may think my statement frivolous, but the fact that we do appear on earth to be paying for the sins of another life is, in a certain sense, true. It is our life and yet not our life. In other words, a soul belonging to the group of which I am a part lived that previous life which built up for me the framework of my earthly life, lived it before I passed through the gates of birth."

> Myers further explained that the group soul might contain 20 souls, 100, or 1,000. "The number varies," he said. "It is different for each man but what the Buddhists would call the karma I had brought with me from a previous life is, very frequently, not that of my life, but of the life of a soul that preceded me by many years on earth and left me the pattern

which made my life. I, too, wove a pattern for another of my group during my earthly career."

Myers added that the Buddhists' idea of rebirth, of man's continual return to earth, is but a half truth . "And often half the truth is more inaccurate than an entire misstatement. I shall not live again on earth, but a new soul, one who will join our group, will shortly enter into the pattern or karma I have woven for him on earth."[160]

Myers uses the same words "pattern" and "framework" others have used to refer to the association of one individual with another in the Higher Self. This affiliation between an individual and other individuals in the group Soul or Higher Self is where past life accounts come from. Someone in this life is re-experiencing another life that is affiliated with the person. Aspects of that other person are part of the individual currently in Earth School.

This pattern is described by a woman named Doris in Rob Schwartz's *Your Soul's Plan* as being a "plan" for a person's life constructed from parts of other lives, like a collage. This is her response about the individuals in the Oversoul. Rob begins with a question.

"You've used the word *we* several times," I said. "Who is 'we'?"

"We are an Oversoul. We encompass all personalities. The personalities do not die. They are a part of the great chorus. We leaf through them together with our guides as we plan a life as a painting in three dimensions, a collage."[161]

Doris's Oversoul later refers to Doris as a "Soul fragment," meaning that this Earth School individual is part of the larger Oversoul. During pre-birth planning, the planning group "leafs through" the various individuals who are part of the Oversoul or Higher Self to decide whether to learn new lessons based on previous learning or bring previous learning into the new Earth School experience. That is how an individual who has a past-life regression experiences a link with other individuals who have lived in Earth School.

Doris's Oversoul then explains what happens after the individual graduates from Earth School. Rob begins with a question.

"What happens after Doris's life is over?" I asked. "Is it correct to say that her energy will be reunited with you, and yet at the same time she will retain her individuality?" Based upon other conversations with spirit, this was my understanding.

"Yes. Certain aspects of the personality do dissolve upon transition, but the closer one comes [while in the body] to one's true Soul the more easily the personality is retrained."

"Then is it ever correct to say that one person was another person in a previous life?"

"There are fragments of the Soul which moved from one personality to another. For instance, in [Doris's] body, there is a substantial fragment of that Soul spark which was placed in the body of a male German soldier 90 years ago."[162]

That "Soul spark" is the affiliation of another Soul with the person now in Earth School that is experienced as a past life.

Rob then asks about whether more than one individual from the Oversoul can be living in Earth School or in any of the other millions of realms at the same time. Rob begins with a question.

"How many physical incarnations do you have at this time?"

"On this plane, there are two."

This revelation made me wonder how many lives her Soul was living on non-physical dimensions. "How many are on other planes?" I asked.

"An infinite number. They are born and die, grow and fade, as nexus points are reached."

"How much of your time, if I may use the word, is devoted to overseeing the two personalities on earth and guiding them?"

"There is always contact. The thread is always there with love and compassion, but the personality is there to better its own information and bring it back." [163]

Medium Craig Hamilton-Parker had the same response when he asked his guide, Taratha, about what he calls the "overself," which I have been referring to as the "Higher Self" or "Oversoul." This is his account:

> My own spirit guide, Taratha, has spoken about the primal form, which we attain once we have become fully integrated into the afterlife. As far as I understand, this is what others have called the "overself" the highest aspect of our consciousness. Taratha has also told my circle that only a fraction of our self incarnates on the earth at any one time. We are like a many-faceted diamond of which only one surface is in this world at any one time. The primal self is the core personality that has lived many times before and who is fully aware of the purpose of its existence in past lives, this life, and the lives to come.
>
> It is the real you. [164]

The real you is the Higher Self, Oversoul, or Overself. However, once our Soul has decided to come into Earth School, our Earth School Mind develops. We as the individual Minds have our own, distinct identities along with our Souls that are together part of the Higher Self. We continue to live our individual lives and grow in love, wisdom, and compassion as we enjoy the next periods of our lives.

What Happens to Unborn Children Not Carried to Term or Stillborn Children?

The hotly debated topic of abortion is based on faulty understanding of who we are in eternity. We have body experiences, not a body that is a physical object in a physical universe separate from the Universal Intelligence. There is only Mind and experiences in the

Universal Intelligence. We experience seeing a foot or feeling a wart or having a headache. What we call the body is just body experiences.

The Soul that will dedicate itself to having an Earth School Mind is involved in the conception and development of the fetus body experience from before the conception occurs. The planning has already gone on. The Higher Self has arranged for the Soul to attune to Earth School as an Earth School Mind. However, if the fetus body experience is no longer viable, for whatever reason, the Higher Self does not devote the Soul and Mind to that fetus. That just means no Mind has experiences in that potential for body experiences that we call the fetus. The Higher Self, Soul, and other members of the planning group simply find another family suitable to the Soul's plan.

Nothing can harm the Soul. When a fetus is aborted, it is just that no Earth School Mind is having experiences using the body experience of this fetus. Nothing is "killed" when the fetus doesn't come to term.

However, a mother's love for the individual who would grow into a person with the body experience of a fetus that is aborted or stillborn is a loving inspiration that results in the individual's being born in the life after this life and growing up there. The love is for the individual, not the experience of flesh that is a fetus. That individual is alive, available to communicate, and anticipating a loving reunion with the mother and others when they go on to the next stage of life.

Annie Nanji, speaking to her husband Dr. Dinshaw Nanji from spirit in Leslie Flint sessions, describes her two children, Sybil and Peter, whom she didn't realize would be in the life after this life because they were miscarriages. The children were born into the next life and grew to young adulthood. Below is a portion of Annie's account of discovering in the life after this life that she had two children. You can listen to Annie speaking at www.earthschoolanswers.com/children/.

> **Dr. Nanji:** And how long was it before you come in contact with Sybil and Peter?
>
> **Annie:** Well that was almost immediate, but the point is, I know it sounds strange now, but I could not realize at first, that

there could be any children. Because I thought to myself, this is impossible. I mean, it was not that I did not accept, in a way, but I thought well, you know, how can this be?

Dr. Nanji: But you knew there were miscarriages ?

Flint coughs.

Annie: Yes I know, but you must remember that when I was on your side, like most people, everybody, you don't think of children under those circumstances. And when I arrived here, they were here and...of course, I was happy to be with them, to know of them.

Dr. Nanji: But did the children know that you were their mama?

Annie: Yes. You see this is very strange. They knew of course that we were connected, that I was their mama. But I never had any children as far as I was concerned.

You can hear a man named Alf Pritchett who came through in a Leslie Flint session to describe his reunion with a sister who passed away as a newborn years before he was born: www.earthschoolanswers.com/alf2/. She had grown up in the next stage of life.

10

We Learn to Function in Earth School

We enter Earth School as newborns with Minds that are *tabula rasas*, blank slates. Infants are unable to function in the Earth School environment, so they must be cared for. The reason people in Earth School begin with blank slates is that we must develop the Earth School Mind that will enable us to function in the unique Earth School environment. The language, skills, attitudes, values, taboos, loves, fears, obedience to authority, allegiance to a religion, norms for acceptable behavior, prejudices, morality, and all the rest of what we learn as children become the repertoire we draw upon as we go through our daily lives in Earth School. The most important acquisition for psychological and spiritual growth is interpretations of experiences. "Interpretations" come to our Minds from our subconscious immediately and automatically when we have an experience. The experience occurs; the individual interprets the experience; sentiments and strategies for behavior arise from the interpretations.

Negative sentiments such as disdain, repulsion, aversion, and contempt, and positive sentiments such as compassion, sympathy, and love are embodied in the interpretations people give to experiences, not the experiences themselves. These interpretations came from our families of origin, schools, religious organizations, peer group, and society in general.

Bruce Lipton, PhD, a cell biologist in the University of Wisconsin Medical School and author of *Biology of Belief*, explains.

Give me a child for the first seven years,
and I'll give you the man

Many of you are familiar with this quote attributed to Saint Ignatius of Loyola (1491-1556), the Spanish priest who founded of the Society of Jesus, known as the Jesuits.

The emphasis of this quote is the recognition that a child's experiences and programming through age seven are the primary factors that determine the character of an individual's life. This insight from nearly 500 years ago now has a scientific foundation in regards to the role of conscious and subconscious minds and their influence on epigenetics.[165]

In the first seven years of a child's life, the child's Mind is in a receptive, learning state. This state registers in the body experience as theta or alpha brainwaves. In this theta or alpha state, children are open and naively receptive. They are being programmed. After childhood, the person transitions into a more focused, closed state that is characterized by beta brainwaves. The open, receptive state is then subjugated to the reasoning, focused state of adulthood. Psychics and mediums enter the alpha and theta states to receive psychic insights and messages, but children are in the state all the time for the first seven years.

The purpose of this unusually receptive state is so the child's Mind can be molded into the Mind the person will need to function successfully in Earth School in preparation for learning life lessons and growing in love and compassion. After the child has acquired the knowledge, sentiments, attitudes, and interpretations of life experiences during these early years, the child is ready to embark upon making decisions as an adult, especially decisions about how to change what the child learned during the first seven years to make the person into all they can be in this period of life in Earth School.

Bruce Lipton estimates that 95 percent of what governs our lives is the programming from childhood rising from the subconscious.[166] You can see a video of Bruce Lipton explaining this at www.earthschoolanswers.com/bruce/.

Later in life, experiences give rise to the interpretations we learned as children that arise unbidden from the 95 percent of our Minds governed by the subconscious programming we received as children. The negative or positive emotions naturally follow, even if the interpretations are not valid in the situations. These interpretations arise immediately from the subconscious with the experience. When we describe the contents of these interpretations, we must use words, but the interpretations come in nanoseconds, as entire packets, without words.

So a child learns love can be withdrawn at any time for offending a parent. That will result in programming that will stay with the child into adulthood, making the adult fearful of doing things that offend people for fear of losing their love. A little boy tells Mom he's going to sell lemonade. Mom looks at him scornfully and says, "That's ridiculous. You couldn't sell anything." After repeated statements that he is incompetent, the child will be programmed during the highly receptive years to believe he is by nature incompetent.

When the adult this little boy becomes must take over running a project in his company, the interpretation that will immediately come to the adult's mind will be the child's interpretation of the experience in a child's world that no longer exists. It is now in the programming that is 95 percent of his reaction to experiences. In that instant after hearing the offer to take over the project, he will feel fearful and unsure of himself. He won't know that the fear comes from programming he received as a child. His fear will just make him resist accepting the offer. He will then use a child's strategy to eliminate the uncomfortable negative feelings: he will not accept leadership of the project, just as he didn't open the lemonade stand to avoid failure.

He may even have what is called an introjection of Mom, meaning he has a little Mom in him repeating the message in his subconscious in a split second: "You couldn't sell anything." The message isn't in words; it is in a sentiment or conviction that flashes across his Mind. The interpretation that comes to him is the same interpretation he had when he was a child. The strategy for dealing with it is the same strategy he used as a child.

We spend our receptive, naïve childhoods being programmed with interpretations that some experiences may bring us physical harm, loss of something of value, a withdrawal of love, shunning and ostracism, and diminishing of our feeling of self-worth and self-esteem. We feel fear, unhappiness, and other negative emotions when similar experiences occur because of these interpretations. The experiences have no innate interpretations or emotions. We overlay the interpretations and feel the resulting emotions. When the interpretations of a set of experiences are negative, we work to avoid these experiences. As adults, we're living lives using interpretations formed in a child's mind that fit a child's world. We didn't create them or select the interpretations of experiences we wanted to have. They were imprinted on our Minds as though they had been recorded on an audio recorder or hard drive. They have become part of us in their entirety without being evaluated.

We may also have positive programming that gives us feelings of self-worth, self-esteem, confidence, and feelings of being loved. We receive them during childhood in the same way we receive the negative programming.

Some people base their entire lives on the programming from those first seven years. Every time an experience comes to them, the programming takes over and gives them the responses and resulting emotions. They use the childhood interpretations of experiences and the childhood strategies for coping throughout the rest of their lives. At worst, listening to the negative teachings may result in actions that are not successful and may be counterproductive.

Early Earth School Experiences Teach People to Fear

During those early years, people develop Minds full of fears, anxieties, and worries. The fears a child feels that they aren't loved, don't belong, and are otherwise inadequate aren't a part of natural maturation as becoming taller and growing facial hair are. The fears are taught by the people who rear the child. Today, as we go through our days, we create realities based on the childhood interpretations of experiences that result in fear, anxiety, worry, and frustration.

A 2017 survey of 1,200 Americans[167] by Christopher Bader, PhD, professor of sociology at Chapman University, found that people have a remarkable number of fears.

List of Fears	% Afraid or Very Afraid
1. Corrupt government officials	74.5
2. American Healthcare Act/Trumpcare	55.3
3. Pollution of oceans, rivers and lakes	53.1
4. Pollution of drinking water	60.7
5. Not having enough money for the future	50.2
6. High medical bills	48.4
7. The US will be involved in another world war	48.4
8. Global warming and climate change	48
9. North Korea using weapons	47.5
10. Air pollution	44.9
11. Economic/financial collapse	44.4
12. Extinction of plant and animal species	43.5
13. Terrorist attack	43.3
14. Identity theft	41.9
15. Biological warfare	41.8
16. Credit card fraud	40.3
17. People I love dying	39.7
18. People I love becoming seriously ill	39.1
19. Cyber-terrorism	39.1
20. Widespread civil unrest	39.1
21. Nuclear weapons attack	39
22. Terrorism	38.8
23. Government restrictions on firearms and ammunition	38.6
24. Government tracking of personal data	37.4
25. Corporate tracking of personal data	36.7

26. Oil spills	36.2
27. The collapse of the electrical grid	35.7
28. Being hit by a drunk driver	35.5
29. The Affordable Care Act/ Obamacare	33.9
30. Pandemic or a major epidemic	32.8
31. Being unemployed	30.7
32. Nuclear accident/meltdown	30.3
33. Losing my data, photos or other important documents in a disaster	29.0
34. Heights	28.2
35. Random mass shooting	28.1
36. Government use of drones within the US	27.2
37. Devastating drought	26.6
38. Break-ins	26.2
39. Becoming seriously ill	25.7
40. Theft of property	25.4
41. Sharks	25.4
42. Computers replacing people in the workforce	25.3
43. Devastating tornado	24.3
44. Reptiles (snakes, lizards, etc.)	23.6
45. Devastating earthquake	22.6
46. Devastating hurricane	21.4
47. Racial/hate crime	20.9
48. Dying	20.3

There are only two inborn fears: fear of loud noises and fear of falling.[168] All the rest of these fears are from interpretations of experiences taught by word or example during childhood in Earth School.

Children Today Are Taught Primitive Superstitions About Life and the Life After This Life

Unfortunately, the family of origin, school, religious organizations, and society in general teach primitive, destructive superstitions about our place in eternity and the life after this life. Children are taught these myths:

- Our loved ones who have "passed away" are buried in the ground or are stone cold dead in a mausoleum. To visit them, we must go to the cemetery and stare at the ground, but we can't talk to them. They're dead.

- We don't know where we go after the body stops functioning. It's a great mystery no one has the answer to. Religions have only the most primitive, vague references to an afterlife that offer no insights into the realm we enter after the body stops functioning.

- Acquiring things is the most important goal in life. During their early Earth School experiences, children are taught the only goal in life is to buy bigger, better, more expensive, more opulent things. Children are inculcated with the belief they must get good grades and go to college so they can get a good job and make money so they can become successful consumers. That's their life's goal. Adults work long hours and take extra jobs so they can earn more money, buy more things, and pay the loans incurred from buying more than they could afford on their available income.

- The ultimate goal for people who are successful in life is the infinite pursuit of infinite wealth. What we have acquired is never enough.

- Schools are places where children are taught to be obedient, memorize facts in the schoolbooks, and get good grades. Children are told nothing of value comes from looking within to discover insights. In school, children are taught to memorize facts in canonized books, not to explore personal paths and dreams.

- We must obey the authorities instead of partnering with them. Society places great value on the rule of law, not the desire to do of our own free will what is in the spirit of the laws.

- Children who are uninterested in or incapable of learning the school lessons are failures, even if they have talents in areas other than the schoolwork.

- We have no control of our lives. We are victims of fate in a world that makes us unhappy and miserable.

- People must not "waste time." Everyone must be productive. Doing nothing regarded as productive is frowned upon.

- Occupations are in a caste system. Doctors and lawyers are doing important work and are revered as demi-gods. House spouses are not really working. Fast-food workers are losers. People who are not working are worthless burdens on society.

- Some people own companies and can tell the people who actually do the productive work that results in revenue whether they can work, how much they receive, under what conditions they will work, when to work, when to eat, and how to work. Companies are a feudal system, not a democracy. The individual owners aren't doing the work, but they receive vastly more money than the workers who are producing what the company sells.

- People must guard the things they call "mine." They must cling to them to keep others from taking them away. They will not give away the things they call "mine" unless they don't care about the things anymore.

- Life is a competition. You must win against other people by beating them. Celebrate winning with trophies and accolades; prove losing is not tolerable by giving nothing to the losers except notations of failure and firing the coach.

- War is honorable. Schools teach that wars are necessary, highly regarded state activities. People in the wars are heroes. The deaths and ruined lives from post-traumatic stress disorder and physical disabilities created by war are not part of the teaching.

- Killing animals is great sport.

- Government killing of people in wars and executions is acceptable.

- We must strive to make our own way in life using solely the training and skills we receive in school and work activities. We're on our own. There are no insights from any other source coming into our Minds. The ideas of guides, angels, and helpers giving us insights is woo-woo nonsense.

- We must have insurance to cover losses because other people are not going to help people recover what they lose.

As long as people continue to live based on these erroneous beliefs taught in childhood that arise from the subconscious, they will not be able to grow into the unique people they were destined to become. They will remain ineffectual duplicates of the people who influenced them in childhood. They will be filled with fear and feelings of inadequacy.

As children in Earth School, we begin our lives with spiritual and mental deficits.

11

We Must Cast off Early Earth School Teaching

When I was a child, I talked like a child, I thought like a child, I reasoned like a child. When I became a man, I put the ways of childhood behind me. For now we see only a reflection as in a mirror; then we shall see face to face. Now I know in part; then I shall know fully, even as I am fully known. (The Apostle Paul, I Corinthians 13: 4-13, NIV)

The infant and child must learn to function successfully by internalizing capabilities as they are modelled and taught by the family of origin, religious and educational institutions, and society. When we emerged from childhood, we were equipped to make the decisions and perform the actions that would enable us to function in Earth School so we could learn lessons, grow in love, compassion, and wisdom, and enjoy the Earth School experiences. However, after learning the basic functions for life in Earth School, we were not unique individuals making our own decisions about who we were and who we wanted to be. Our functioning was based on what our family of origin, religious and educational institutions, and society programmed us to be. We were living someone else's life.

At some point, we became sufficiently mature to begin achieving the goals we came into Earth School to accomplish. We planned our lives carefully before our birth to learn the lessons we have come to learn; grow in love, compassion, and wisdom; enjoy life's experiences in comfort and happiness; help others as they learn, grow, and enjoy life; and help humanity evolve toward becoming loving, peaceful, and joyful. To achieve these pre-birth planning goals, each of us must use our free will to evaluate and accept or discard many things we learned in childhood so we can discover who we are and change ourselves to suit the person we have decided we want to be.

This chapter explains that we must abandon Earth School's early teachings to grow into the person we planned to become before beginning our experience in Earth School.

How Successful Is What Children Are Learning in Childhood?

The childhood learning from teaching, example lifestyles of adults, and sanctions from parents, school, religious organizations, and society molds children into adults who feel they are victims in a cold, insensitive world that has no purpose or meaning. The result is the pandemic of loneliness, self-absorption, unhappiness, despondence, depression, and suicide today.

A study found that narcissism in college students rose from the late 1970s to 2010, while feelings of empathy declined.[169] Twice as many Americans reported being lonely in 2020 as in 2018. Only 14 percent of adults say they're very happy.[170] The average feeling of happiness decreased for the Gen Z generation from an already low 2.15 on a three-point score in 2006 to 1.97 by 2017.[171] By 2016-17, both adults and adolescents were reporting significantly less happiness than they had in the 2000s.[172]

A 2018 study by Cigna found that 46 percent of U.S. adults sometimes or always feel lonely, and 47 percent "feel left out." Nearly half of Americans say they have no meaningful in-person social interactions daily.[173] A nationwide survey of Britons by the BBC found that 33 percent often or very often feel lonely. Nearly half of those over 65 consider the television or a pet as their main source of company. And 42 percent of Millennial women in the UK are more afraid of loneliness than a cancer diagnosis. In Japan, more than half a million people under 40 haven't left their house or interacted with anyone for at least six months.[174]

Kay Hymowitz, researcher and author about family issues, poverty, and cultural change in America, writes,

> Loneliness, public-health experts tell us, is killing as many people as obesity and smoking. … Germans are lonely, the bon vivant French are lonely, and even the Scandinavians—the happiest people in the world, according to the UN's World Happiness Report—are lonely, too. British prime minister Theresa May recently appointed a "Minister of Loneliness." … Japan [is] now in the throes of an epidemic of kodokushi, roughly translated as "lonely deaths." Local Japanese papers regularly publish stories about kinless elderly whose deaths go unnoticed until the telltale smell of maggot-eaten flesh alerts neighbors.[175]

The problem of unhappiness among people is growing in severity. A study by Cigna found a nearly 13 percent increase in loneliness between 2018 and 2020.[176] In 1990, 8 percent of Americans said they were at the lowest level of happiness on the survey, "not too happy." By 2018, the figure had jumped to 13 percent.[177] The "2019 World Happiness Report" states that in the early 1990s the average rating people gave for their happiness was only 2.28 on a three-point scale from 1 ("not too happy") to 3 ("very happy"). However, there has been a significant decline in feelings of happiness from then to 2019 when Americans rated their happiness on average as a 2.18, meaning they were feeling a lukewarm "pretty happy."[178]

What children are learning is resulting in lonely, unhappy, fearful adults who have little understanding of why they are alive, why things are happening in this life, and what living will be like in the life after this life.

A Great Source of Insecurity Is the Fear of Death

Surveys reveal that most people have some fear of the natural transition called "death." A 2019 survey by Statista Research found that

42 percent said they are somewhat afraid or very afraid of dying, 27 percent were not very afraid, and only 25 percent were not at all afraid.[179] We can assume that those who were afraid of dying or were "not very afraid" were not convinced they would continue to live after the death transition.

People receive no solace from the mythology they learned from childhood about the next stage of life. A 2011 Roper poll[180] found that

~ 67 percent of those surveyed still believe the Hell myth

~ 78 percent believe Heaven is a place where people exist only as spirits, with no physical substance

~ 85 percent believe God's love will be the center of the next stage of life

~ 32 percent believe people in the next stage of life are the same age as when they transitioned

~ 7 percent believe there will be total darkness

~ 4 percent believe life in the next stage of life will be boring

People also grieve for their loved ones who have left earth before them. The 2011 Roper poll revealed people's ignorance about being able to communicate with loved ones living in the next stage of life. Only 21 percent believed people can hear from or communicate mentally with someone living in the next stage of life.[181]

We Are Creating Our Worlds

What children are being taught in Earth School is failing humankind. We must realize that we are creating the world that is bringing us hopelessness and misery. Society, our families of origin, and organizations such as schools and religions teach children to believe they are flotsam and jetsam, bobbing about in an unsympathetic sea that flings them onto the rocks of suffering and misery. They are taught to see themselves as victims in a cold, mindless world they cannot control or appeal to.

The primary change in perspective we must make as we cast off Earth School's mistaken teachings is to realize we are creating our world. If we are miserable, it is because we are making ourselves miserable. Misery is not imposed on us. We can deny misery and make ourselves happy. Happiness is freely available when we realize we are not victims and can change our lives to be what we want our lives to be.

Two people have the experience of losing the use of their legs to a neurological disease. The experience is the same for both. One person curses god for inflicting this disease on them and feels their life is over. They spend their days being miserable, feeling cheated by fate, and anesthetizing themselves with alcohol and drugs. They feel this life is all they're allotted in eternity, and now it's wasted. They vigorously defend their right to be miserable.

The other person finds new interests they can pursue, learns to adjust to the new constraints, and is thankful for the abilities they have. They join a basketball team for people who have lost the use of their legs. They are upbeat and happy, realizing they will learn lessons from this experience and looking forward to the life after this life when they will understand why they have chosen disabilities for this life. There, they will have the use of all their limbs.

Each person has created a reality from the circumstances. One goes through life miserable and feeling victimized; the other goes through life happily, looking forward to newly found capabilities.

In childhood, people learn to feel they are victims with no ability to influence the content or quality of their lives. They are taught that we are allotted only this life, and if we are not healthy and capable, our lives are wasted.

For us to advance from the mythologies and untruths taught in childhood to become the mentally and spiritually mature person we set out to become in Earth School, we must abandon the notion that we are not in control of our lives. We must realize we are creating our lives, our happiness or misery, and the person we want to be through our free will, self-assurance, and industry.

Silver Birch, the collective of higher beings speaking through Maurice Barbanell, said, "As awareness increases, the individual realizes that they possesses infinite possibilities, that the road to perfection is an endless one."[182] For us to become all we had set out to become in Earth School, we must realize that a universe of opportunities is open to us if we will be open and receptive, with the confidence and fortitude to overcome obstacles and accept them.

Timothy Gray, living in the life after this life, speaking through August Goforth, describes this realization.

I'm learning that Heaven is in the mind, and mind is the true reality, existing beneath the illusory environments of the self-damned mind. Perfection is not something to be attained; it is something to be realized, to awaken to. Oh, the incredible ecstasy of awakening to the realization that there is no end to awakening! There is no end to Heaven, continually unfolding and revealing itself as we awaken to ever increasing awareness of having our being in and as paradise.[183]

We Must Abandon Much of What We Were Taught in Childhood

We must abandon much of what we were taught in childhood because the teaching is responsible for our unhappiness, loneliness, and fears. The repertoire of memory experiences, interpretations, emotions, strategies, sentiments, and norms we acquired during our childhood create the reality we live in now. Reality is not outside of us, being inflicted upon us. We are creating lives full of either happiness, love, and peace or unhappiness, loneliness, disconnection, and discord.

We create our suffering, and we create our happiness. We keep the interpretations that cause negative emotions in our repertoire if we don't realize we can change them. We ascribe their effects to things outside of us, but they are entirely in our Minds. If we don't use our free will and courage to take control and change the interpretations, they will repeatedly affect us when we have experiences; we will feel like helpless victims. However, we are choosing to allow the interpretations to affect us. We are creating an unhappy reality.

As adults we can change our reality because we have free will. If we do not confront and change the interpretations of experiences we learned as we grew up, we will continue to live someone else's life.

Intellectually and physically, we will be adults, but emotionally and spiritually we will remain children.

To grow to have a fulfilled, successful, happy life, we must confront and change the interpretations of experiences we learned as children that have kept us prisoners of childhood. We must break out of prison.

We Must Give up on Finding Security, a Sense of Belonging, and an Identity in Things and People

We must abandon the models and teaching from our childhood that taught us we can be happy and fulfilled only if we acquire and hold onto things, activities, and affiliations that will give us the feeling we are secure, loved, and successful.

To lead healthy, happy lives and grow in our ability to love and show compassion, we must engage in the scary, painful activity of giving up on the need for things, activities, and affiliations so we can establish our own unique, new identity that will remain, strong, vibrant, and full of self-assurance as each of the things we had been investing our identity in inevitably pass away.

People who refuse to give up on the old conditions of their lives when the inevitable changes occur make themselves miserable. Carl Jung, the pioneering psychoanalyst, wrote,

> For when new conditions not provided for by the old conventions arise, then panic seizes the human being who has been held unconscious by routine, much as it seizes an animal, and with equally unpredictable results.[184]

The attachment to things, activities, and affiliations is referred to in Buddhism as *dukkha.* The result of *dukkha* is suffering. The solution to *dukkha* is to stop clinging and attaching. We must see that the things, activities, and affiliations we thought were important have no lasting value. They will not give us enduring happiness. In the end, striving for them, worrying about losing them, and inevitably losing them makes us miserable. When we stop clinging to things, activities, and affiliations, the craving for them will disappear on its own. We will be happy without a reason for it. The cessation of the suffering is *nirvana.*

This giving up on things, activities, and affiliations is what makes Buddhism different from other religious philosophies. While other religions seek to achieve some state of grace through hard work and active repudiation, Buddhism teaches that we are inherently joyful and that we will have happiness without a reason for it when we abandon our misguided belief that we *must* have specific things, activities, and affiliations to be happy. When we do so, we experience the essential Buddhahood that is within us all.

We also will enhance our relationships. As long as we feel that to be happy, life and the people around us must give us things we need to be happy, we are placing tremendous burdens on the people in our lives. Some will acquiesce and give us what we insist we need, but with a measure of resentment. Others will simply leave. When we place no demands on the people around us to feel and behave in ways that give us microbursts of happiness, they will feel freer around us, more interested in us, and happier being with us. They will love us for who we are.

We Must Cast off Religion

It's been said that every religion has a glimmer of the truth about spirituality. However, that isn't true. A religion is a rigid set of beliefs members must adhere to. All required sets of beliefs stultify the progress toward becoming the person we can become.

When we are seeking wisdom and models to help us learn to be more loving, peaceful, compassionate, and happy, we must evaluate a religion as we evaluate any organization or person.

- Does it encourage all people to come together in love, without discrimination, or does it separate people because of beliefs?

- Does it teach people to listen to the guidance and wisdom within them, given freely from many sources, or does it teach people all guidance and wisdom comes from sources outside of them?

- Does it teach people to be free, open, and questioning, or does it teach people to accept only one truth, believe in one set of dogma, and follow the rules set forth by one organization or individual?

- Does it teach people to grow spiritually by being actively loving, compassionate, and other-centered, or does it teach people that to be spiritual they must perform rituals unrelated to our relationships with others and the wisdom that is within?

- Does it teach that all people will enjoy a wonderful next stage of life, without judgment or condemnation, or does it teach that some people will be judged and condemned?

- Does it teach people to be happy as they are, with all their flaws, or does it teach people they are flawed and must behave as the organization or person dictates to atone for the flaws?

- Does it teach people each individual has direct access to the Universal Intelligence, or does it teach people they can come to the Universal Intelligence only through the organization or person?

Because of its rules for members, religions can stand in the way of having spiritual experiences and growing to be loving, compassionate, and other-centered. Carl Jung wrote, "Religion is a defense against the experience of God."[185]

Joseph Campbell, professor of literature at Sarah Lawrence College, who wrote and spoke extensively about mythology and religion, wrote,

You hold on to your own ideology, your own little manner of thinking, and when a larger experience of God approaches, an experience greater than you are prepared to receive, you take flight from it by clinging to the image in your mind. This is known as preserving your faith.[186]

The Dalai Lama, spiritual leader of Tibet, spoke about religion:

This is my simple religion. There is no need for temples; no need for complicated philosophy. Our own brain, our own heart is our temple; the philosophy is kindness.[187]

Yeshua bar Yosef (Jesus) is reported to have told his followers to go to God by themselves, in private, away from the synagogue, and not babble on, because the Universal Intelligence knows what they need before they use words to announce it.

> And when you pray, do not be like the hypocrites, for they love to pray standing in the synagogues and on the street corners to be seen by others. Truly I tell you, they have received their reward in full. But when you pray, go into your room, close the door and pray to your Father, who is unseen. Then your Father, who sees what is done in secret, will reward you. And when you pray, do not keep on babbling like pagans, for they think they will be heard because of their many words. Do not be like them, for your Father knows what you need before you ask him. (Matthew 6:5-8, NIV)

The Necessity of Abandoning Childhood Teaching Is a Common Tenet of Many Great Thinkers and Luminaries

The understanding that we must come to a point in our lives at which we abandon what we were taught in childhood and begin to form ourselves into the real, unique person we want to become is a common theme expressed by many great thinkers and luminaries.

Carl Jung taught that to mature spiritually and mentally, each individual must develop their own, unique personality by liberating themselves from all other ways.

> With the very decision to put his own way above all other ways he has already in large part fulfilled his liberating vocation. He has cancelled the validity of all other ways for himself. He has placed his law above all conventions.[188]

The great Indian sage Sri Nisargadatta Maharaj described the necessity of demolishing the learning from early Earth School.

> You have put so much energy into building a prison for yourself. Now spend as much on demolishing it. In fact, demolition is easy, for the false dissolves when it is discovered.[189]

Einstein wrote that to achieve peace of mind we must free ourselves from the illusion we learned as children that we are separate from each other.

> A human being is part of a whole, called by us the "Universe," a part limited in time and space. He experiences himself, his thoughts and feelings, as something separated from the rest—a kind of optical delusion of his consciousness. The striving to free oneself from this delusion is in the one issue of true religion. Not to nourish the delusion but to try to overcome it is the way to reach the attainable measure of peace of mind.[190]

Yeshua bar Yosef (Jesus) spoke repeatedly about the change people must undergo to enter the kingdom of God, a state of Mind he described as being available now. Yeshua is said to have taught that people must be reborn, but not reborn physically. To enter this state of mind, the kingdom of God, we must be reborn "of the spirit."[191]

Friedrich Nietzsche, in *Thus Spake Zarathustra*, describes the metamorphosis a person must go through to come into what he called "his own world." Zarathustra wrote that the spirit of a person begins as a camel, with a strong load-bearing spirit, welcoming the burdens of life by kneeling down to willingly take them on itself. That is the person molded by early Earth School experiences, accepting everything that was taught and every interaction, activity, sentiment, and norm society finds acceptable.

In the first metamorphosis, the spirit of the person grows to have the strength and capability of a lion, able to free itself from the burdens laid on in childhood to become lord of its own life. However, to advance to freedom, the lion must slay a great dragon named "Thou-shalt." The dragon is covered by thousands of golden, glittering scales, and on each scale is written "Thou-shalt." In confronting the dragon, the lion counters, "I will," proclaiming the person's desire and will to be free from the burdens acquired from childhood teaching.

In response, the dragon lays in the path of the lion's progress. The dragon speaks: "All values have already been created, and all created values do I represent. Verily, there shall be no 'I will' any more."

The lion slays the dragon of "Thou-Shalt." With the dragon embodying the burdens of "thou-shalt" gone, the person undergoes a second metamorphosis into the spirit of a child, but not a naïve, immature child. The new spirit of a child is open, exploring and willing to adopt new thoughts and beliefs that are notably different, suitable to the individual the person is becoming, and perhaps even unsanctioned. It is a new beginning. Zarathustra explains that in order to create the new person, "there is needed a holy Yea unto life: ITS OWN will, willeth now the spirit; HIS OWN world winneth the [spirit of the person].[192]

The analogy of becoming like a little child is the same one used by Yeshua: "Truly I tell you, unless you change and become like little children, you will never enter the kingdom of heaven. Therefore, whoever takes the lowly position of this child is the greatest in the kingdom of heaven" (Matthew 18:1-5, NIV). The word translated "change" is στραφῆτε (straphēte), meaning "turn strongly around" or "reverse." It is much stronger than simply "change."

What Are the Impediments to Being Open to Examining Our Childhood Teaching and Accepting Alternatives?

When we confront who we are, we must be willing to uncover our deep-seated beliefs and examine them as an observer, outside of ourselves, realizing we may uncover things we're uncomfortable with discovering that are impeding our mental and spiritual growth. That brings anxiety. People avoid the anxiety by not examining their beliefs objectively or by clinging to the codified set of beliefs of some person or organization, especially a religion. To become all we can be, we must face the anxiety by courageously examining our deeply entrenched beliefs, welcoming change, realizing that only through change can we fulfill our life's destiny.

We fear giving up on the beliefs because we feel we'll be out of control, as though we're speeding through life at 120 miles an hour and if we relax our grip on the steering wheel, something awful will happen. We control so we feel safe.

We must not allow fear to dominate our lives. Silver Birch, speaking through Maurice Barbanell, describes the consequences of allowing fear to dissuade us against making changes in our lives.

> Never allow fear to find a lodgment within your being. It is a negative quality which destroys, vitiates and saps. It impairs your judgment; it clouds your reason; it prevents you from seeing issues clearly. There is no problem that comes to any Soul which you are incapable of solving. There is no difficulty that you cannot conquer—if you would but allow the latent divinity to rise to the surface.
>
> The people in your world have, with very few exceptions, not yet begun to live. They are expressing only infinitesimal portions of the power which is resident within them. In supreme moments of crisis or emergency they call on that power and it gives them added strength, added courage, added wisdom.
>
> But that power can be tapped all the time. It can give you health to master disease, direction in times of uncertainty, guidance when you are perplexed, strength when you are weary and vision when you are blind. It is there for you to express it.[193]

We Must Not Expect Others to Change

All of the changes we make must be in ourselves. We must not expect others to change to match what we want by playing the victim card. We are a victim only if we are relying on someone else for our feeling of well-being. Victims are needy. Their needs require others to take care of them. If we are in a situation that is aversive to us, we must change our attitude toward the situation or get out of the situation. We are a victim only if we stay in a situation that results in our feeling we are a victim. We cannot wait for things and people around us to change for us to feel less victimized.

We Must Accept That Giving up on Childhood Earth School Teaching Will Affect Relationships

Relationships and groups have interactions, activities, sentiments, beliefs, and norms.[194] The system is stable when everyone agrees on and lives by the beliefs in these five areas. When someone in the system changes a belief about a characteristic interaction or activity or about a commonly held sentiment or norm everyone has tacitly agreed to, the system is disrupted. Eric Berne, in his groundbreaking work, *Games People Play: The Psychology of Human Relationships*, referred to changing the dynamics of the system as "foiling the system."[195]

When the system is foiled, those who want to continue playing by the old rules can become agitated. They may ostracize the person not willing to play by the rules of the game. The ways they react depend on the people involved, but it is likely the system will not change to fit the person's new conception. Instead, the system will try to change the person or excrete person from the system.

Expect that you may receive criticism when you display your unwillingness to continue with an activity, interaction, belief, sentiment, or norm. The dynamic of the group will change. You may end up leaving the group, either psychologically or physically.

We Must Learn to Stop Anesthetizing

The early teaching in our lives can bring great unhappiness, so people anesthetize themselves against the unhappiness through drugs, alcohol, sex, work, or even the meditation practice of allowing the feelings to arise and pushing them away. However, in the end, these are futile attempts to deal with the discomforts that come from living life based on the dysfunctional early teaching. The issues are still there when the anesthetic wears off. Only by facing the issues directly, rejecting what is causing the unhappiness, and considering alternative beliefs can the person discover what leads to happiness and make it part of daily life.

We Must Realize It Is a Gradual Process

When we are feeling something we want to explore, such as a trauma or disturbance, we must relax and go into it. For a disturbance, we can see the disturbance as an object, not who we are. We will do that in that moment, but the disturbing feelings will come back.

Our effort isn't to relieve ourselves of the disturbing feelings, although that will happen. It is to grow ourselves into realizing we are the "I" that is not in the Earth School Mind. We are the Soul that has an Earth School Mind having experiences. Over time, we will realize that more and more. The disturbing feelings will decrease more quickly. We can then condition ourselves to go to that state in which we see ourselves as the I that is greater than the Earth School Mind. We will enter it more quickly.

It takes time. There is no quick solution.

As People Change, Society Must Change

Society is the sentiments, beliefs, and norms held and enforced by groups of people. Just as we must abandon the teachings we acquired in childhood to become the person we wanted to become in our pre-birth planning, society must abandon its prevailing sentiments, beliefs, and norms to nurture an environment in which children are reared to be loving, compassionate, and other-centered.

In the ideal future world, people will not have to cast off the teachings from childhood in Earth School to grow into loving, compassionate, happy adults. When adults reexamine everything they were taught as children, they will find that they accept most or all of what they were taught. Only because society today is so spiritually backward is it necessary for adults to abandon what they were taught as children so they can find their path to spiritual maturity, love, peace, and joy in life.

The sentiments, beliefs, and norms in schools, governments, and workplaces are false paths to arrive at what everyone truly wants: to be happy and loved. Schools teach children to be obedient so they can get a good job and become successful consumers to perpetuate the system. Children are not taught to think for themselves and consider alternative systems. The children accept their roles and carry them into adulthood because they have been told doing so will give them fulfillment, a sense of belonging, and happiness. Just as individuals must give up on the teaching from childhood, society must give up on schools that teach children to be obedient consumers. Society must learn that children can be guided to feel fulfillment, a sense of belonging, and happiness in their own, unique paths.

The sentiments, beliefs, and norms in the workplace must change for people to feel fulfilled and happy. Today, people have jobs in workplaces that are feudal systems with serfs and lords of the manor: they own nothing in the business, are given a plot of office space in which to work, own nothing in their plot, give everything they produce to the lords of the manor (owners, shareholders), can make no choices about what they do with their lives in the workplace, can be banished from the workplace on a whim, and receive a small fraction of compensation for the work they produce. Society must give up on a system in which a small elite have all the ownership and power and employees have no power, influence, or ownership. Society must change so people own their organizations, profit from their work activities, and are able to make choices about the organization and their actions in it. They will find their sense of belonging and happiness in their roles in the organizations they share ownership in and endeavor to make successful.

The government in the United States is a plutocratic oligarchy owned and maintained by the wealthy elite. The privileged group in power bicker among themselves and fight to gain more power and wealth while diminishing others' influence and position. The people governed are not considered in the interplay among plutocrats and have little influence in the decisions made. As a result, government rewards greed, ruthlessness, deception, and manipulation. The government officers feel they must have power and wealth to be happy. The citizens feel powerless and downtrodden.

A 2017 survey of 1,200 Americans by Christopher Bader, PhD, professor of sociology at Chapman University, found that 74.5 percent of the people in the survey were afraid or very afraid because of the corruption of government officials.[196]

Society must give up on the plutocratic oligarchy and involve all the citizens in a democracy. Government officials must come to be more concerned about the people they represent than about themselves. They will find their love, sense of belonging, and happiness in serving others.

When society changes, children will be reared in an environment that will make them loving, peaceful, and joyful so they grow naturally into loving, peaceful, joyful adults.

12

We Learn Lessons and Grow in Love and Compassion

> The greatest revolution of our generation is the discovery that human beings, by changing the inner attitudes of their minds, can change the outer aspects of their lives.
>
> ~ William James

We enrolled in Earth School to learn lessons, grow in love, compassion, and wisdom, enjoy life's experiences in comfort and happiness, and help others as they learn, grow, and enjoy life. Our Souls planned an Earth School environment in which we would more likely accomplish those goals in concert with the others who would be involved.

We spent our early days in Earth School learning from our family of origin, religious and educational institutions, and society how to function in the Earth School environment, interpret experiences, and develop strategies to respond to experiences in preparation for going on to accomplish the goals our Souls established for us.

As we come into the maturity in which we are able to form ourselves into our unique individuals, we must abandon much of what we learned from our family of origin, religious and educational institutions, and society because they are teaching children to be fearful, self-absorbed, materialistic, greedy, insensitive, competitive, conditionally loving, and ignorant about our true nature. The early teachings are resulting in self-absorbed, lonely, unhappy, fearful adults who are ignorant about what happens when the body dies.

The next step in our development is to remake ourselves into loving, compassionate, wise people who are happy for no reason, know and love ourselves, love others, know who we are in eternity, and help others as they learn, grow, and enjoy life.

We Are in Control of Our Lives

We did not enroll in Earth School to allow life to happen to us. We are the masters of our lives, striving to achieve our goals in the face of daunting challenges. We can change who we are, what we feel, and how we react to life's challenges. We can choose to be happy and successful most of the time in Earth School. We can be loving, compassionate, and other-centered so we have cordial, loving relationships. We just have to grow into the new person we are becoming as we cast off the old person we were.

As we go through our daily life in Earth School, the circumstances change, confronting us with new experiences. Some are challenging and difficult. Some cause dramatic changes that we react to with fear, grief, and depression. Others are full of joy, fulfillment, and ecstatic feelings of love. The key to becoming successful and happy in all the circumstances is learning to persevere through the challenges and tragedies grounded in knowing who we are in eternity. Earth School teaches lessons that are sometimes hard, but we can hold our Minds in a dual perspective—living through life's circumstances while observing them from the perspective of our Soul, learning from them but not being wounded by them. We will be continually happy when we learn to view events, our interpretations of the events, and sentiments in our lives as curious little creatures we hold in our hands and view from all sides, probing with questions: "Who are you, little creature?" "Why do you affect me the way you do?" "Where did you come from?"

When we first encounter an experience and are affected by our interpretation of it, we will view it from one perspective with one interpretation. By looking at from other perspectives and interpretations, we can see it for what it is. When we are able to look down on our sentiments, beliefs, and interpretations of experiences from a perspective outside of our normal responses, we can change our lives to be more enjoyable and happy. We will reduce the worry, fear, and frustration that results from allowing ourselves to be deeply affected by our interpretations of events and people. We will see life as a great adventure in which to love, learn, and be happy. Nothing will be so threatening or egregious that it interferes with our peace. We will take life less seriously.

Every new challenge, adversity, loss, and misfortune becomes a new problem we set ourselves to solving, knowing we will prevail and return to the happy lives we are intended to live. With each success, we grow in maturity, strength, humility, and love for those who walked with us through the trying times. When we confidently confront the challenges without shrinking from them by withdrawing, imploring others to rescue us, or anesthetizing the emotions with chemicals, work, or other diversion, we move upward a step higher toward the summit of our lives.

There is no single path every person must follow. No sacred text, religion, guru, or psychotherapist can decide for us how we must navigate through Earth School. We will make decisions every day and adjust our course as the circumstances change. There is no student manual for Earth School.

As adults we can change our reality because we have free will. If we do not confront and change the interpretations of experiences we learned as we grew up, we will remain prisoners of childhood. Intellectually and physically, we will be adults, but emotionally, we will remain children.

To grow to have a fulfilled, successful, happy life, we must confront and change the sentiments, beliefs, norms, and interpretations of experiences we learned as children. We are in control of our lives.

By Changing Our Minds, We Change Our Being

As we grow and change the interpretations and view of life and our place in eternity we learned as children, we become a different person. We are changing ourselves at the molecular level. Molecules, like everything else in Earth School, are based in the Universal Intelligence and are continually changing and being renewed. Our new self is different at the molecular level from instant to instant, so when we triumph over life's challenges, show our love and compassion for others, and become confident in ourselves as eternal beings, we change the molecular structure of our being that is continually being renewed.

Dr. Bruce Lipton, author of Biology of Belief, describes how a person's Mind affects the body experience.

> ... a change in perception of an individual can change their biology, virtually immediately. ... You can change your genetic activity by how you change your response to the environment. The commonly held perception is that your genes are a blueprint of your life—this is totally false. The blueprint of your life is based on your perception, because your genes will change according to your perceptions via epigenetics. Rather than putting emphasis on genes controlling life, the emphasis is fully turned around to recognize your perceptions, via signal transduction, are translated into biological behavior. These factors control not only your behavior but also control your genetic activity.[197]

An article in the *Indian Journal of Psychiatry* explains the findings of a psychiatrist and two professors in a Department of Biochemistry and Nutrition about the effects of mental changes on our bodies.

> Perceptual shifts are the prerequisites for changing the belief and hence changing the biochemistry of our body favorably. Our innate desire and willingness to learn and grow lead to newer perceptions. When we consciously allow newer perceptions to enter the brain by seeking new experiences, learning new skills and changed perspectives, our body can respond in newer ways—this is the true secret of youth. Beliefs

(internal representations/interpretations) thus hold the magic wand of remarkable transformations in our biochemical profile. If you are chasing joy and peace all the time everywhere but exclaim exhausted, "Oh, it's to be found nowhere!", why not change your interpretation of NOWHERE to "NOW HERE"; just by introducing a gap, you change your awareness — that changes your belief and that changes your biochemistry in an instant! ...

Our beliefs provide the script to write or *re*-write the code of our reality.[198]

As we change our Minds to be loving and other-centered, our body experience becomes healthy, youthful, and vibrant. More love and compassion imbues our being. We feel more blissful, empathetic, loving, and compassionate as a natural outpouring from our being. We become love.

In so doing, we are aligning ourselves more closely with our Soul, which is always loving and compassionate. We are spending our days in Earth School using the skills and knowledge we learned in our early years to be successful in the Earth School environment, but we are transforming ourselves from that child into the loving, compassionate adult we planned to become before we were born.

Our loving thoughts and deeds affect the lives of people around us and the evolution of humankind. Thoughts and sentiments are energy. When we feel compassion, the energy infuses everything in our life and in the world around us. It is another measure of compassion in the vessel of love humanity is drinking from.

Those around us whose lives are dominated by negative thoughts and emotions such as fear will change at the molecular level as well, but the change will not be good. Their negative emotions will result in newly formed Minds and bodies from instant to instant that are diseased, stressed, and impaired. People around the negative person are of the same one Mind, so they feel the negative energy of the thoughts and emotions at the subconscious level. Negative energies create negative people and environments. Our environments are being created continually, so what is created is being influenced by the people living in them. When we are loving and compassionate, others become loving and compassionate, and the environment around us is imbued with the light and energy of love and compassion.

Emotions Are Our Indication of Our State in Earth School

Emotions tell us how we're doing in our Earth School experience. If we are happy, looking forward to the future, feeling a purpose in life, feeling content and confident, without anxiety or fear, then we are well along in our growth in Earth School. If we feel fearful, lost, hopeless, defensive, without worth or purpose, and without hope for the future, then we have work to do in Earth School. We weren't meant to live lives with those feelings.

Emotions are fundamental in life. They cannot be divided into component parts, and they are unique in their impact on us. We know them well but cannot define them. They can only be described as a feeling. The feeling of joy is different from the feeling of sadness. The feeling of love is different from the feeling or rejection. The feeling of anger is different from the feeling of gratitude. But we cannot define the feelings using words other than more feeling words.

Feelings are reflected in the body experience, as are pain, touch, sense of position, and sense of movement. When something is threatening, we have the body experiences of our stomach churning, pulse increasing, blood pressure increasing, and anxiety. We can have senses about the future through these bodily sensations and emotions. Our guides and loved ones will give us a feeling of vitality, contentment, and happiness when something is positive and helpful for us. If we have the feeling something has no life in it, gives us unease and a nagging foreboding, then we are being steered away from it.

Researchers have identified bodily chemical changes in the presence of specific emotions. The feeling of happiness is associated with dopamine, oxytocin, serotonin, and endorphins. The feeling of sadness is associated with less of these chemicals and perhaps the presence of other chemicals. However, the body experience of these chemicals does not mean the Mind is feeling happy because of the chemicals. The body shows signs of these chemicals because the Mind already is feeling happiness or sadness. The Mind is influencing the body, not the other way around.

One demonstration of that fact is that in a near-death experience, when the body is shut down, the experiencer describes feeling a rush of feelings of peacefulness and happiness or joy.[199] The feelings are occurring while the body is being traumatized.

Emotions are the indicators of our present status in Earth School. We are successful in Earth School when we are happy with no reason for the happiness and have little fear or agitation about our lives and our futures. If we are worried, fearful about the future, feeling hopeless, and depressed, it is because of ignorance about our purpose in this life and the prospects for life in the next.

We Are All Seeking Love, but Differ in How We Seek It

Two goals in life are to have love, regard, and respect for ourselves and have love, regard, and respect for others. We must have both.

The prominent motivation in our lives is to be loved. We come to Earth School in large part to learn how to love so we show love to others. They in turn reciprocate with love for us. Our Souls know how to love. The Universal Intelligence is pure love. However, when we enter Earth School we are reared from childhood to accept the sentiments, norms, and behaviors of the society. Our society today teaches dysfunctional ways of gaining the feelings of being loved and belonging.

We have lost much of the closeness and intimacy previous cultures had with each other, especially children. A study of primitive cultures demonstrates that peaceful cultures are more likely to have body bonding or affection bonding between mothers and children than violent cultures. The study concluded,

> Human physical affectional love which is mutually shared neutralizes power in human relationships and provides for the neurobiological and neuropsychological foundations for egalitarian, peaceful and harmonious behavior in human relationships. This is the only true antidote or "behavioral

vaccine" to the depression, alienation, anger/rage/violence and alcohol/drug abuse and addiction which afflicts and is destroying *homo sapiens*.[200]

When people cannot receive overt signs of love, they will find some way to receive the love they so desperately want and need. They may adopt counterproductive strategies to gain some semblance of a feeling of loving and belonging. The strategies may be violent and cruel, so they don't seem to have a component of the need for love, but at their roots they are socially unacceptable ways of trying to gain the feelings of being loved and belonging.

The individual who uses violence may be doing so because they are not having feelings of being loved and belonging or are very frightened of losing the feeling of love and belonging. Violence is often simply a dysfunctional attempt to satisfy the need for love and belonging.[201]

Other than problems of crime to support drug habits, even the most perverted of activities is often inspired by the pursuit of love and a sense of belonging.

- Among potential terrorists, the need for identity and need for belonging are common motives.[202] "Membership in a terrorist group provides a sense of identity or belonging for those personalities whose underlying sense of identity is flawed. Belonging to the terrorist group becomes … the most important component of their psychosocial identity."[203]

- The root of much of the world's violence is tensions resulting from the perpetrators' need for identity and a sense of belonging.[204]

- People who induce guilt in close interpersonal relations do so "to cause one's partner to exert himself or herself more to maintain the interpersonal relationship."[205]

- Fear of death is linked to fear of loneliness and separation from friends and family.[206]

- Criminals' social bonds to other criminals or to criminal groups foster crime. A need to belong attracts unattached young people to join violent gangs to give them a sense of belonging to and being wanted by a group.[207, 208, 209]

- Social relationships with juvenile delinquent peers are among the strongest independent predictors of juvenile delinquency, demonstrating that belongingness needs are important motivators among delinquents.[210]

- Going along with objectionable actions by fellow group members because of the need to be accepted by the group has been a central factor in group violence such as the atrocities committed by the Ku Klux Klan,[211] Nazi police guards,[212] and gang rape.[213]

- The need to be loved and feel a sense of belonging results in the controlling personality. "[A] personality with a strong need for control requires the social interest of other people and expects that other people will include him in their social groups and activities."[214]

- The father who kills his daughter in an honor killing wants the approval of those around him because he shows he is obedient to his religion: ". . . he or she has no choice but to seek validation or approval through killing to be re-included and recognized by the community and family."[215]

Much of the hostility and violence in our world today would be eradicated if people were reared to love and be other-centered so they are kind and compassionate to one another. The need in the hostile, violent person is the same as the need in the peaceful, loving person. Only the strategies for satisfying the need are different.

We Are Helping Humankind Grow

During our childhood years, our Earth School selves are formed by our families of origin, society, and organizations such as schools and religions. In our spiritually backward society today, children are taught they must excel over others, produce money so they can purchase things, keep their business to themselves, and gain money and things at the expense of others.

As a result, when the child moves into adulthood, they must cast off the teachings of childhood and become reborn. They must take the teachings from childhood one at a time, review them, and change them over time.

However, if our families of origin, society, and organizations were spiritually mature, the young adult would have less to cast off and would be much ahead in loving, learning lessons, and being happy. By changing ourselves and helping others to change, we are changing humanity. When humanity becomes more loving and compassionate, there will be less selfishness, greed, cruelty, and violence.

How We Learn and Grow in Earth School

People learn how to be more loving and compassionate, just as we learn the skills and perspectives we need to evolve from a child into an adult. The process takes time and requires the commitment and resources to change. At times these resources are thrust upon us, as in a near-death experience. Usually, however, we choose to access and use the resources. Over time, their influence changes our reactions to experiences and our nature.

We learn and grow as a result of three resources:

- Knowledge
- Experiences
- Guidance

Influence 1: Knowledge

People may be convinced of a truth by evidence. The evidence results in growth of the person as the revelation changes the range of beliefs and actions influenced by it. The person also finds that others they admire believe something. This growth is normal as we mature from children to adolescents to young adults to mature adults. At every transition, new knowledge changes us.

The key to growth in Earth School is having the resolve to change some interpretations, beliefs, mores, or behaviors. If the person has the resolve, they will seek knowledge to support the resolve. The result will be that the person will advance in knowledge and change their understanding about life and interpretations of behaviors.

If the person is satisfied with their current level of understanding, they will not seek the knowledge and will be less likely to change. Life's challenges provide the impetus to learn more so the person restores comfort, removes distress, and eliminates cognitive dissonance.

The dysfunctional ways of handling the challenges are to continue to be oppressed by them without seeking the knowledge to overcome them or anesthetizing the uncomfortable feelings with drugs, alcohol, work, sex, pastimes. or separation. When we face the challenges and unpleasant emotions and examine them from outside of ourselves, we can understand them and choose to make changes that will overcome the challenges and alleviate the negative emotions. If we try to flee from them, the challenges will continue to arise and the unpleasant emotions will continue to affect us.

We can learn about our place in eternity, the nature of the pre-life and afterlife periods of our normal human development, the nature of reality, and the evidence that we survive when the body dies by reading books, viewing videos, and participating in groups that explore this knowledge.

Each person has an ever-changing boggle point. The boggle point is where the person resists believing anything beyond the boggle point. Overcoming the inertia at the boggle point takes openness, evidence, and gradual change. Some materialists will believe anything about mind except that the mind is influenced by factors outside of the brain. That is their boggle point. People who believe the mind is influenced by factors outside of the brain may not be willing to believe the mind is not created by or housed in the brain. That is their boggle point. People who believe the mind is not created or housed in the brain may not be willing to believe there is nothing but mind and experiences, with no physical realm outside of the mind. That is their boggle point. We must be willing to explore reality beyond our boggle point, being open to any knowledge that presents itself.

The boggle points shift throughout a person's life. The person changes. What was formerly a boggle point is today a self-evident truth. Openness to knowledge and dedication to learning truth help the person grow beyond the boggle point.

Influence 2: Experience

A person in Earth School may have a life-changing experience, such as a near-death experience. Two of the results of a near-death experience are that the person views life differently and has no fear of the transition after the body dies. Similarly, people who have afterlife communications describe having different beliefs about life and the life after this life. The experience changes them.

A primary mission of the Afterlife Research and Education Institute is to enable people to have their own afterlife communication so they realize their loved one is alive and well, are convinced they will continue to live after the body dies, and view people and life differently. Other experiences such as being at a deathbed and seeing visions, sitting in a physical mediumship séance and having a person from the life after this life talk to the person and touch him or her, and having the experience of a full materialization of someone living in the life after this life are all experiences that change people's understanding of our place in eternity.

We can have the experiences by learning how to have afterlife communications, attending meetings with mental and physical mediums, learning methods of having out-of-body experiences through The Monroe Institute or other such institutes, learning to increase our intuition and psychic ability, and being involved in groups where members share their experiences that we can participate in vicariously. AREI offers a free online training program to help people learn how to have afterlife connections with loved ones: www.earthschoolanswers.com/selfguided/.

Influence 3: Guidance

We are continually receiving guidance from guides, helpers, loved ones, and the Universal Intelligence to help us during our time in

Earth School. Some of that guidance leads us to events and knowledge that change our belief systems. When we are open to the guidance and allow our lives to flow freely, we will be inspired to travel paths that will be in our best interests.

An important realization we must come to is that we have support and guidance available to us throughout our Earth School experience. We just have to learn how to receive it and be confident in the source and the wisdom of the guidance.

Conditions for Spiritual Development

These are the conditions for spiritual development:

1. Be open to examining our beliefs and assumptions about life and adopting new beliefs.

2. Realize we are spiritual beings having an Earth School experience.

3. Know we are expressions of the Universal Intelligence with all its qualities.

4. Realize our loved ones are alive and happy although living in another location.

5. Know we have control over who we are and what we feel.

6. Feel the desire to become a loving, compassionate, other-centered person

7. Know we can change our lives to be filled with love, peace, and joy.

8. Know how the person we want to become differs from who we are now.

9. Face negative feelings and understand them and the interpretations that give rise to them.

10. Learn to feel, hear, and trust the guidance from our loved ones, guides, and others.

11. Learn to act upon the guidance we're given.

12. Learn who we are and to love ourselves.

13. Learn to be a loving, compassionate, other-centered person.

14. Have periods of relaxation, separation from daily life, and meditation.

15. Learn to Understand Our Feelings

16. Fill our lives with experiences imbued with love, peace, and joy.

17. Learn to be happy with no reason for it.

18. Triumph and enjoy the success.

19. Help others as they learn, grow, and enjoy life.

I explain each of these conditions for spiritual development below.

Condition 1: Be open to examining our beliefs and assumptions about life and adopting new beliefs

The primary obstacle to freedom and growth is closed-mindedness. We must be open to all thoughts and beliefs, with no "anything but" sentiments: "I'll believe anything but...." The scientists who are materialists assert "I'll believe anything but the notion that the individual lives on after bodily death," "I'll believe anything but that there are psychic abilities," "I'll believe anything but the idea that mediums communicate with people living in the life after this life." Those are not scientific sentiments; they are the religious beliefs of materialism.

Only when the person is open to all thoughts and beliefs can growth happen naturally. An open mind that accesses reliable sources will always be filled with the truth, just as water finds its own level. Dame Alice Ellen Terry, the renowned Shakespearean actress, speaking from spirit through the direct-voice medium Leslie Flint, explains the need for an open mind. You can listen to Ellen Terry speaking these words at this link: www.earthschoolanswers.com/terry/.

And I think freedom of expression, freedom of realization, freedom of thought, is truly the spiritual lesson that comes to us all gradually and gives us that spiritual consciousness and awareness and truly creates and makes possible a spiritual life.

But it is the narrow confines of earth which prevent individuals from becoming spiritual beings. One must have complete and absolute freedom of expression in the highest sense, to be able to discard all that which is of the material, all that which holds one down, all that which prevents one from expressing and expanding. Anything which is inclined to prevent the human life from developing and growing and expressing on earth must be and is bad. Anything that stultifies, anything that in anyway makes it an impossible thing for the human being to have freedom of expression and thought must be and is bad.[216]

Condition 2: Realize we are spiritual beings having an Earth School experience

We were taught in childhood that there is only dead matter and energy, that people disappear after death or are in some vaporous state inaccessible to us, and that we will disappear also, so this life is all there is to existence. To begin to grow into the person we planned to become before our births, we must change those false perspectives to realize we are eternal spiritual beings having a temporary experience in Earth School. That realization is the beginning of our free will choice to change ourselves into a new person.

Some people come to that realization through an epiphany inspired by an experience, such as having communication with a loved one living in the life after this life. Others learn they have abilities they couldn't have if the world were as they were taught in childhood. Remote viewing is a common ability people have that shows the Mind is not in the brain and there is much more to life than they had been taught. The remote viewer closes their eyes and can receive visual, auditory, and tactile impressions of something thousands of miles away. My own remote viewing had an impact on me as I grew to realize my place in eternity. You can learn more about remote viewing at www.earthschoolanswers.com/rv/.

The most dramatic impact that results in a shift in perspective is a near-death experience. The result of a near-death experience is that the person suddenly loses fear of death, views life differently, has changed interpersonal relationships, and may have newly developed psychic or mediumistic abilities.

The realization we are eternal spiritual beings having a temporary experience in Earth School will become more widespread as the following occur:

- Methods of afterlife communication become easily available so many people have the experience of communicating with loved ones living in the next stage of life.

- Children grow up seeing adults communicating with loved ones in the next life so it is natural and commonplace.

- People meet regularly in groups to share what they have learned about how to communicate with loved ones and their experiences in communicating.

- The media become more open to sharing news and stories about the life after this life and help spread the understanding. News programs share advancements in afterlife communication and have features on people's experiences.

Whatever tragedy we might experience, our destiny is the next life where there are no tragedies, death, or losses. We must confidently progress through what we're experiencing, knowing we will come to the other side of it. While we're going through the experiences, we can welcome the valuable lessons we're learning and the bountiful love and compassion growing between us. Tragedies happen, but they are temporary conditions leading to new learning and opportunities.

In our journey to live loving, peaceful, joyful lives, the first step is to realize we all are spiritual beings having an experience in Earth School together.

Condition 3: Know we are expressions of the Universal Intelligence with all its qualities

We are the Universal Intelligence temporarily taking on the limitations of the Earth School experience. However, we retain our individuality throughout eternity.

Since we are the Universal Intelligence, we have all the qualities of the Universal Intelligence, although we have chosen to obscure them because of the role we have chosen to accept in Earth School. These are the qualities of the Universal Intelligence:

- All encompassing, including all things, thoughts, and experiences

- Loving all of creation without conditions or limitations on the love

- Peaceful, unperturbed

- Nonjudgmental, without censure or condemnation

- Affirming of all thoughts and beliefs as equally acceptable

- Compassionate

- Attentive and available to receive questions and provide answers

- Responsive without reservation

- Wise and omniscient

- Caring without discrimination

- Patient

- Creative

- Unwavering, steady, consistent in what is accessible as the physical environment, causes and effects, and what we regard as the laws of physics

We are the Universal Intelligence temporarily taking on roles in Earth School. We do not lose our identity as the Universal Intelligence. However, in Earth School, we are tasked with growing to have more of the qualities of the Universal Intelligence by rejecting the early teachings of Earth School that obscure the qualities of our Universal Intelligence nature. The more we remove the shell of the Earth School self, the more these qualities of the Universal Intelligence become our nature.

Because we are the Universal Intelligence, we have all the qualities of the Universal Intelligence listed above that have been kept in abeyance during our Earth School tenure. Our mission in Earth School is to remove the early Earth School teaching that has obscured these qualities of the Universal Intelligence that are our true nature. We will display

- Our access to all things, thoughts, and experiences

- Love of all creation without conditions or limitations

- Unperturbed peace

- Acceptance of all people, without judgment that some beliefs are "right" and others "wrong"; the ability to see people as individuals at a stage in their evolution toward being more like the Universal Intelligence that we all are evolving to become; the ability to evaluate beliefs, thoughts, and actions as fitting or not fitting with the Universal Intelligence's nature, but without judging the person

- Openness to hearing and considering all thoughts and beliefs

- Compassion

- Attentiveness to others and availability to receive questions and give answers

- Sensitivity and responsiveness to others' conditions and needs; caring

- Wisdom, knowledge, and steady growth in understanding

- Realization we are one with every person, creature, or thing, with no sense of separation

- Patience

- Creativity

- Authenticity without distortion, hiding, or being other than who we are

All of these qualities are characteristic of the Universal Intelligence, and so are qualities that can be characteristic of us even as we are taking on our limiting roles in Earth School. We simply must reject the false teachings of our early childhood in Earth School and strive to realize and accept the qualities of the Universal Intelligence that have always been at the basis of our nature, but which have been hidden by the limitations of our Earth School Minds.

Condition 4: Realize our loved ones are alive and happy, although living in another location

When we realize we are eternal beings having a physical experience, that our loved ones who have graduated before us are happy, healthy, and contented in their new lives, and that we will have a joyous reunion when we move to the same land where they are, we will view this life as a wonderful time to learn lessons and grow in love and compassion, knowing nothing seriously wrong is going to happen to us.

Our loved ones are available to communicate and anxious to have an ongoing relationship with us. When afterlife communication becomes commonplace—at the dinner table, during family gatherings, in quiet times devoted to communication, at celebrations of life after someone has transitioned from earth—people will take for granted that our loves ones are constantly communicating with us and that we will shortly be living in the same land with them. Society will change. People will lose their fear of bodily death and see that the others in their lives are sojourners with them during this exciting, challenging adventure we call Earth School. They will come to realize we have no reason to feel separation or hostility; we can spend our days in love, peace, and happiness with all people we meet.

Condition 5: Know we have control over who we are and what we feel

As children, we were taught by word and example that we are inert bits of flotsam and jetsam bobbing on the ocean of an unfeeling, cold, lifeless universe. We were taught to suppress our feelings and tough it out by accepting what comes to us as fate. We were taught others must change for us to be happy; we have no control over our happiness as long as others are not giving us what we want. We were taught to flee from adversities and negative emotions by denying them or anesthetizing them with pharmaceuticals, alcohol, and preoccupations such as work.

For us to grow spiritually, become all we can become, and live happy, fruitful lives, we must break the bonds of these beliefs that we are powerless victims of fate. We must come to know we are the masters of our fate. We have control over our lives. We make of our lives whatever we choose our lives to be.

When we have the wisdom and courage to face life's challenges, knowing we will emerge triumphant, and repeatedly are successful, we will become stronger, more willing to face challenges, and happier. We must realize we have the control of what we want our lives to be. We are creating our reality.

Thus, when we are clear about the person we want to be, we will have the power to mold ourselves into that person. We can fashion ourselves into people who are loving, peaceful, and joyful.

Condition 6: Feel the desire to become a loving, compassionate, other-centered person

> When one door of happiness closes, another opens. But often we look so long at the closed door that we do not see the one that has been opened for us.
>
> ~ Helen Keller

When people are faced with the evidence that they are spiritual beings, they must feel the need to change for the new belief to affect them. If they dismiss the new understanding out of fear of the unknown, doubt, or fear of censure, they will not allow the revelation to have an effect on their lives.

If they allow the conviction resulting from the new evidence to affect their lives, they will experience what the Swiss developmental psychologist Jean Piaget called a "horizontal décalage." In this process, a person embraces a new realization that thrusts vertically from the horizontal plane of beliefs and assumptions to give the person a new perspective on the plane below. The person then reexamines beliefs and assumptions on the horizontal plane of related beliefs and assumptions to adapt each to the newfound perspective.

The dissonance between what our new realization has taught us and what we still believe causes us to feel what Carl Jung called "neurotic sufferings." However, he explained that the uncomfortable feelings are actually curative. They result in new developments in the person's personality.

> It seemed to Jung that the meaning of [neurotic] sufferings might consist in their compelling a man to come to terms with the foundation of his being and with the world, and thereby to gain a better knowledge of his limits and possibilities ... Jung thus puts the emphasis on the perspective aspect, giving neurosis a positive meaning and not regarding it only as a burdensome illness. According to him, it can even act as a stimulus in the struggle for the developments of the personality and be, paradoxically, a curative factor.[217]

Jung wrote,

> We may think there is a safe road. But that would be the road of death. Then nothing happens any longer—at any rate, not the right things. Anyone who takes the safe road is as good as dead.[218]

The "safe road" is to reject the new realizations to maintain the old self that was molded by childhood teaching. The person who does not go through this period of change has, for all practical purposes, never lived.

Jolande Jacobi, the Swiss psychologist who worked with Carl Jung, wrote that what seems to be neurosis can be the impulse to set foot onto a new road that resolves the symptoms of neurosis, but if the person is "stuck" and does not change, the result can be the discomforts of neurosis.

> Any obstruction of the natural processes of development … or getting stuck on a level unsuited to one's age, takes its revenge, if not immediately, then later at the onset of the second half of life, in the form of serious crises, nervous breakdowns, and all manner of physical and psychic sufferings. Mostly they are accompanied by vague feelings of guilt, by tormenting pangs of conscience, often not understood, in face of which the individual is helpless. He knows he is not guilty of any bad deed, he has not given way to an illicit impulse, and yet he is plagued by uncertainty, discontent, despair, and above all by anxiety—a constant, indefinable anxiety. And in truth he must usually be pronounced "guilty." His guilt does not lie in the fact that he has a neurosis, but in the fact that, knowing he has one, he does nothing to set about curing it.[219]

"Curing it" requires changing sentiments, beliefs, assumptions, and perspectives.

Abraham Maslow spoke of the need for people to grow to become all they are capable of being. Maslow, the originator of the Maslow Hierarchy of Needs, described this goal of growing to realize one's full potential as "self-actualization." He wrote that self-actualization is becoming "the best version of oneself."

> This tendency might be phrased as the desire to become more and more what one is, to become everything that one is capable of becoming." He explained that the sources for satisfying the lowest level needs on his hierarchy are external to the person. The sources for becoming self-actualized are within the person.[220]

The healthiest, happiest, and most contented people are motivated by striving for new realizations in life. "If you plan on being anything less than you are capable of being," Maslow wrote, "you will probably be unhappy all the days of your life."[221]

The greatest obstacle is fear of giving up the familiar and moving forward into unchartered territories. However, we must grow through the fear into self-confidence and strength. Sri Nisargadatta Maharaj, the Hindu guru of nondualism and author of *I Am That*, wrote,

> There are always moments when one feels empty and estranged. Such moments are most desirable, for it means the Soul has cast its moorings and is sailing for distant places. This is detachment—when the old is over and the new has not yet come. If you are afraid, the state may be distressing, but there is really nothing to be afraid of. Remember the instruction: Whatever you come across—go beyond."[222]

Condition 7: Know we can change our lives to be filled with love, peace, and joy

Children are taught that life is hard and we must accept it as it comes to us. We must be miserable at work, in our family lives, in school, and in all areas of our lives. We must look forward to weekends and vacations as the only time we can be truly happy. To be happy at other times, we must have perfect people in our lives and all the possessions that will bring us happiness.

When we have an ending for the words "I could be happy if ..." then we are seeking happiness in something outside of ourselves. The world is not making us miserable. We are making ourselves miserable.

We must know that we can live lives filled with peace and happiness. We choose them. What comes to us may be filled with disappointment and adversity, but our responses to what comes creates the quality of our lives. We can be peaceful and happy if we see ourselves as spiritual beings having a temporary physical experience. Nothing that happens to us is of consequence. Nothing impedes us from having love, joy, and peace in our lives except ourselves.

Condition 8: Know how the person we want to become differs from who we are now

Most people go through their entire lives living from the repertoire of beliefs they gained from childhood, never thinking that what they learned in childhood could be mistaken or detrimental to them, and that they can change their interpretations of experiences so they live loves filled with love, peace, and joy.

When we come to value being loving, compassionate, and other-centered, we can begin the process of examining who we are now and how that differs from the person we want to be. We will discover that many things we thought were necessary to our lives are not necessary at all. We then can choose to replace the desire for them with the desire to love and be loved, to act out of compassion, and to see that others' needs are satisfied.

The Awakening Slave

Michelangelo created four sculptures called by scholars of the artist's work the "prisoners" or "slaves." They look incomplete because the sculptures have exquisite sculpted portions and raw, unsculpted stone in the remainder of the sculptures. Michelangelo deliberately left portions incomplete to represent the eternal struggle of human beings to free themselves from the materialistic impulses they learned in childhood and thus to become uniquely fashioned individuals.[223]

We don't know what will emerge from the block of marble we developed from childhood. In that block of marble, there is a person who will emerge when we go through the arduous task of chipping away at the matrix. We have a universe of possibilities before us. We are free to become anything we want to become.

Only by bringing the beliefs and assumptions we learned in childhood into conscious awareness can we examine, understand, and change them. Then we must be open to new beliefs and assumptions based on the person we have decided we want to be.

Condition 9: Face negative feelings and understand them and the interpretations that give rise to them

Experiences are just temporary events that do not affect us as manifestations of the Universal Intelligence. They are only challenges for us to confront, understand, and use to help us learn and grow. We needn't be burdened by them or preoccupied with them.

When we feel negative feelings in the presence of a real, remembered, or imagined experience, we must learn to draw the negative feelings close, looking at them as though they were a creature we are holding in the palm of our hand. Negative emotions feed on avoidance. Running from negative feelings or anesthetizing them just keeps them alive and strengthens them. The negative feelings will return with each real, remembered, or imagined experience that stimulates them.

Negative emotions manifest when a negative interpretation emerges from the subconscious in the presence of an experience. We must ask of these negative feelings and fears, "What is my interpretation of the experience that gives rise to this emotion?" "What is the trigger in this experience that gives rise to the interpretation?" "Is the interpretation valid?" "What do I feel I will lose as a result of this experience?" "What is the worst thing that could happen as a result of this experience, and is that so terrible?"

We can then decide whether to continue holding the interpretation or to dismiss it through understanding the experience differently. All interpretations have been created through learning, especially in childhood. All can be unlearned over overwritten by new interpretations.

Condition 10: Learn to feel, hear, and trust the guidance from loved ones, guides, and others

This new person we want to be will come into being when we are able to feel the guidance of our hearts. We must learn to feel and be confident in the good, warm feelings we have about things, people, and events. And we must learn to feel and be confident in the uneasy, disturbing, fearful feelings we have about other things, people, and events. The discernment in those feelings becomes part of our being. We learn to relax and relinquish intellectual control, allowing our hearts to guide us. There, our guides, helpers, Souls, and loved ones are wafting sentiments into our body experience so we experience the feelings of comfort or discomfort that match whether the experience is good for us or not. Does it feel right or not?

This is the same as conscience. We say something is right or good or wrong and bad. However, these are sentiments. They are not in the thing or experience, and they are not cerebral thoughts.

The talented medium and teacher Suzanne Giesemann describes a method of assessing the wisdom of an action or guidance by using what she calls the "heart test": "Is it hopeful and healing?"[224] If so, we are being given a message that we can accept the likely positive nature of the action or guidance. We must learn to quiet ourselves and feel the sentiment in our body experience. The more we can sense the sentiment, the more easily we will be able to receive guidance.

Suzanne suggests we then test the action or guidance with what she calls the "sign test." We can ask for a specific sign within the next few days that what we have been given is from those in the life after this life.[225] In my own case, as I was preparing to write *Your Eternal Self*, I received the message through my automatic writing that the psychic Greta Alexander, now in the life after this life, wanted to help me write the book. I asked her how I would know it was her. Using automatic or inspired writing, I scribbled down the words I heard: "Test me, test me." I wrote, "What will the headline be on MSNBC online in the next few days?" I scribbled her response, "Hugo Targets Cuba." I wasn't sure what that meant, but found out that there was a hurricane in the Atlantic named Hugo that was some days away from the Caribbean. I checked MSNBC each day, and three days later, the exact headline appeared: "Hugo Targets Cuba." I printed the screenshot and still have the printout.

That took three days, but I also have received validations within a couple of hours. One day I was communicating with my mother through automatic writing and asked her for a validation of something she had given to me. I scribbled her response, "Two will be absent." I had no idea what that meant. Two hours later, as we were preparing for our physical circle at my home, one of the circle members walked through the door saying, "Judy and Carol won't be here tonight." Two were absent.

Learn to trust your guides and the guidance of your heart. Consult your guides and ask the questions you want answers to. Come to be confident that you have guides who are working with you in your best interests. Listen to them.

Condition 11: Learn to act upon the guidance we're given

We are continually being given guidance from guides, helpers, people interested in us, and loved ones living in the life after this life. We act based on the guidance without realizing the beneficial thoughts and right decisions were inspired by others.

A notable Lutheran minister, theologian, and professor Alvin D. Mattson described through medium Margaret Flavell the influence those living in the life after this life have on those still on earth by telling about his father's activities in the life after this life helping the survivors of the great tidal wave that swallowed up 300,000 Bangladeshis during a cyclone in 1971.

> He gets in touch with them and gives them little impressions to make them realize that the sun is high and it's time they got things done. He is not dealing with them when their dead. He is dealing with those who are still living [on earth]. He has a fine group of associates with him who worked to help them in their sleep.[226]

We all have a primary guide and other guides who support us on special occasions. We also receive guidance from our Soul and Higher Self, people interested in us we don't know, and our loved ones living in the life after this life.

We can learn who our guides are, although that isn't necessary. We just need to rely on the validity of what our guides are saying to us as they help us navigate our way through our days in Earth School.

I recommend the CD by Susanne Wilson for meeting your guides: *Guidance Quest: Connect with Your Spirit Guide.*[227]

You can meet your guide by relaxing and asking to meet. You may have to do that repeatedly and regularly before the communication comes. The reason is that we must ourselves be in the right frame of mind, and virtually all of us were reared to be in an agitated frame of mind from morning to night. You increase likelihood of meeting your guides by using a guided method such as Susanne Wilson's, by meditating regularly, and by asking to meet before drifting off to sleep each night. The key is relaxing away from the noise of the daily world we're immersed in. Don't expect immediate results, although they may come. The meeting most likely will happen when you least expect it, perhaps months after you request it.

However, it isn't important that you meet your guides or have names for them. What is important is that you learn that you are supported and given guidance every day from guides, helpers, people interested in you, and your loved ones living in the life after this life.

Condition 12: Learn who we are and to love the person we find

Part of our spiritual development in Earth School is to learn who we are and learn to love that person. The interactions in childhood in Earth School today teach most children they are not lovable as they are. They must strive to be better because they aren't good enough. The focus is on getting good grades, being a good boy or girl, wearing the right clothes, and hanging out with the right people. They aren't good enough just being who they are.

Children are taught to be unempowered. They begin by being dependent on their parents and society to take care of them and provide basic needs. Most children never grow out of that stage. As adults they still expect life to take care of them. They get a job so they can receive a regular paycheck. They obediently do whatever the owners of the company tell them to do. They conform to their church, their family, and their community. They feel hopeless and powerless to be anything different. They feel life determines who they are and what becomes of them, so they are powerless and hopeless.

Children are taught that love is conditional. They are praised and smiled upon when they do what they're told, and scorned, punished, and rejected when they do what they're told not to do. We take that for granted. We would not expect to teach children to be content with who they are without encouraging them to be something better to receive an adult's admiration.

Schools are structured to teach some children they will continue to be successful only if they follow the rules given to them, so they are constantly fearful of losing their place in society that has given them an identity. Many children are taught they are incapable because they cannot excel in the school structure. They don't measure up. And every comment by a teacher or failure to perform in school and every report card drives that message into the child's psyche.

A study of self-esteem in girls found that 75 percent felt much pressure to please everyone. The same study showed that 74 percent of girls in grades 9 through 12 say they often feel stressed by the pressure.[228]

One estimate is that 85 percent of people suffer from low self-esteem.[229] A psychotherapist from India estimates that 90 percent of Indians have low self-esteem.[230]

Self-compassion is even more important than self-esteem. Self-compassion is not narcissism. It is being understanding and tolerant of who we are and what we do. Dr. Kristin Neff, associate professor of human development at the University of Texas at Austin, writes,

> Self-compassion involves being kind to ourselves when life goes awry or we notice something about ourselves we don't like, rather than being cold or harshly self-critical. It recognizes that the human condition is imperfect, so that we feel connected to others when we fail or suffer rather than feeling separate or isolated. It also involves mindfulness—the recognition and non-judgmental acceptance of painful emotions as they arise in the present moment. Rather than suppressing our pain or else making it into an exaggerated personal soap opera, we see ourselves and our situation clearly.

> … self-compassion is not based on positive judgments or evaluations, it is a way of relating to ourselves. People feel self-compassion because they are human beings, not because they are special and above average. It emphasizes interconnection

rather than separateness. This means that with self-compassion, you don't have to feel better than others to feel good about yourself. It also offers more emotional stability than self-esteem because it is always there for you—when you're on top of the world and when you fall flat on your face.[231]

When we feel low self-confidence and are being self-critical we must grow through those moments by looking at ourselves and the situations with compassion. Imagine you are in a distressing moment. Sit quietly and imagine yourself outside of yourself, as your Soul, detached from the situation. Stay in that position. Talk to yourself as your Soul and reassure yourself about your worth and that you are capable and loved. Your Soul is always calm, self-assured, and confident in the future. Your Soul knows that what you are living through is just a temporary period of discouragement you will grow from. Address yourself by name. Help yourself see the most positive characteristics of yourself and positive outcomes. Encourage yourself, because you have been through experiences like this in the past. You are capable and will be victorious in this situation as well.

Condition 13: Learn to be a loving, compassionate, other-centered person

When we know and value the person we want to be, we can examine our thoughts and behavior and compare them to the thoughts and behavior that are characteristic of the person we want to become. With that clear conception of the person we want to be, we can change thoughts and behaviors as they come to us or in a deliberate process of awakening.

We must put ourselves into situations in which we can learn to become the person we want to be. We learn to love by loving. When we put ourselves into a position to love another, we are feeding the love fire that is growing inside us. Those feelings can only come through interacting with others and showing love, whether it is reciprocated or not.

We must perform the actions of loving without concern for whether the sentiments have caught up with the actions. If we wait for the sentiments to initiate loving acts, our growth will be retarded and we will easily become discouraged when we don't seem to have the feelings that match the person we know we want to become.

Conversely, we must avoid situations in which we are not loving and compassionate or are being unloving and insensitive. Our lives must change. Common activities and the people involved in them may have to be removed or altered. To become loving, compassionate, other-centered people, we must be among others who are loving, compassionate, and other-centered and are themselves developing.

After we have realized the model of the person we want to become, we go through Piaget's "horizontal décalage," in which we apply the newfound worldview to a wide range of behaviors and assumptions across our lives, changing each in turn to match the new worldview. In that way we become new people.

During the horizontal décalage, we have episodes in which we encounter a belief we have had that is not compatible with the new self we now know we want to become. That is called "cognitive dissonance." To maintain mental stability and comfort, we adjust our Mind to fit the new realization so we gradually become the person we have decided we want to be.

The change from self-centered to other-centered will be gradual. It will come in small successes. The wonderful feeling of seeing joy and love in other people when we are joyful and loving develops more joy and love.

Condition 14: Have periods of relaxation, separation from daily life, and meditation

We are continually monitoring our navigation of the world. We sense something and respond. The responses come from what we call the subconscious, but actually that is the entirety of the Universal Intelligence. What we call conscious thinking is a grain of sand on the vast stretch of beach that is the Universal Intelligence. We bring information into that tiny area and consider it, ponderously. Meanwhile, dozens of experiences that result in sensitivity, activity, emotion, and motive are arising out of the subconscious.

The result is that 95 percent of our decisions, thinking, and activities are rising from sources other than the focal point of awareness. When we have an experience, our response is immediate, summoned from our subconscious. We have no control over the response that comes. The response has been nurtured over decades of our lives.

However, when we shut down the world of experiences, the Universal Intelligence is available to us in a process called mindfulness meditation or the relaxation response. It comes as naturally as opening a faucet that permits water to flow. The more a person learns to relax the world of experiences so that the content of the subconscious emerges, the more the person will receive illumination at all times, not just during relaxation.

Among people who have learned to allow the flow are concert pianists, professional baseball players, gymnasts, sculptors, stock exchange traders, skilled orators, and all others who must allow their skill experiences to flow from the subconscious at great speed.

The average person experiences the flow when doing some mundane work that shuts down the aware, active mind and allows the flow from the spigot of the subconscious. Sleep, doing mindless activities such as washing dishes, and losing oneself while driving all shut down the racket of the world so the spigot of the subconscious can flow into conscious awareness.

Meditation is the most disciplined, certain method of allowing the contents of the subconscious that is accessing the Universal Intelligence. When we're open, we are abandoning our role that we agreed to take before we entered Earth School and we are open to who we really are, the Soul, and all the resources of the Universal Intelligence. We have always been the Universal Intelligence, but have voluntarily accepted the limitations of Earth School to learn lessons, grow in love and compassion, and enjoy the experiences. When we relax our focus on Earth School, we sink back into our true nature as the Universal Intelligence we have always been. Meditation does that.

Guided meditations are ideal for beginners. They take the person through a procedure that relaxes and shifts focus away from the world. They have a definite start and ending. The activity of sitting and listening is easier to accomplish than deciding to sit for a period of time each day. After the habit has been formed, the person might meditate without aids.

Medical doctor Matthew Thorpe and dietician Rachael Link explain that regular meditation has the following personal benefits:[232]

- Reduces stress
- Controls anxiety
- Promotes emotional health
- Enhances self-awareness
- Lengthens attention span
- May reduce age-related memory loss
- Can generate kindness
- May help fight addictions
- Improves sleep
- Helps control pain
- Can decrease blood pressure

When we come into a state of Mind to feel peaceful, thoughtful, and mindful, we find happiness, joy, and contentment. We put the world aside and allow the eternal being we are to emerge. Medium Suzanne Giesemann writes about going within.

> How do you find peace? By going within. Certainly, it can be found outside of you, but not for long, for that is not the nature of the external world. There you may get shaken up a bit, tossed about by the waves, and that is as it should be. But when you grow weary of the learning experiences offered to you there on the surface, sink, sink, sink to the quiet waters within. You cannot stay there forever, either, nor does your soul want to, for it longs to stretch and grow. This is the nature of life: ongoing cycles of stretching, growth, rest, and regeneration. You see it in nature all around you. When you can see it and recognize it within yourself, you can find peace even within the duality. You are so very loved.[233]

Not everyone will come to a level of nondual awareness, but when we realize we are the eternal Soul, we can come to the point at which we see that we are one with everything. We are having body experiences, but we are not the body. We are in Earth School, but Earth School is just a play with scenery and characters where we can love, learn lessons, and enjoy the experience.

Meditation helps increase intuitive, psychic, and mediumistic abilities because the channel to the Universal Intelligence becomes strengthened.

Condition 15: Learn to understand our feelings

We must allow life to flow, accepting every experience and feeling, examining each curiously, especially negative feelings. If we repress a negative feeling, anesthetize it with alcohol, drugs, work, or other diversion, the feeling will continue to rise with the same effect it had. To reduce the effect and understand the experience and our reaction to it, we must examine the interpretation of the experience that resulted in the negative feeling. We must ask "What feeling are you?" "Why am I feeling as I do?" "What is the negative interpretation that gives rise to this feeling?" "Do I want to keep these negative interpretations and the accompanying feeling?"

Understanding the negative feeling doesn't mean it will go away immediately. However, negative feelings cannot stand being uncovered. When they are discovered and understood, they will gradually disintegrate into dust and disappear in the shadowy corners of a dimly remembered past.

We are creating the feelings. Life is not imposing them on us. We are choosing to make ourselves feel negative emotions over things that happen naturally in life.

To love ourselves, you must know ourselves. We must spend time each day in thoughtful mindfulness, going inward and experiencing deeply.

Condition 16: Fill our lives with experiences imbued with love, peace, and joy

We increase our happiness and raise our vitality by filling our lives with happy, peaceful, wise, other-centered activities and people. If we spend time alone or with unhappy, violent, puerile, self-absorbed people, we will inevitably be unhappy and unfulfilled in life. These people and the activities they engage in drag the spirit down and give it feelings of depression and hopelessness.

The primary source of negative, fearful sentiments today is the media. Among the top 20 fears people expressed in the survey cited early, 15 dominate the media: corrupt government officials, pollution of oceans, rivers and lakes, the US involved in another world war, global warming and climate change, North Korea using weapons, air pollution, economic/financial collapse, extinction of plant and animal species, terrorist attack, identity theft, credit card fraud, cyber-terrorism, and widespread civil unrest. We might assume these topics are in the news because they're newsworthy, but the steady drumbeat of negative news is wearing on our psyches. It is giving rise to a society living in fear.

We must, therefore, find our own balance. We would be better off ingesting modest portions of news media, with a more complete diet of uplifting YouTubes, movies, and discussions with like-minded people. In today's electronic world we have a smorgasbord of media from which we can choose the most positive, inspiring, illuminating selections available. If the fears in the previously cited list are brewing in the backs of our Minds, it likely is because of exposure to the news media. We can minimize or eliminate that unhealthy influence by having less exposure to it.

Instead, we must fill our lives with loving, peaceful, joyful activities, events, and people. If we can't find groups with such people, we must start them. Each group of people gathering to share what we know about our place in eternity and the uplifting experiences in life adds that number of people to the roster of happy, fulfilled, positive people. And it reduces the ranks of the lonely, hopeless, disconnected people.

A panel discussion hosted by the National Institute for Health Care Management revealed that

> As a force in shaping our health, medical care pales in comparison with the circumstances of the communities in which we live. Few aspects of community are more powerful than is

the degree of connectedness and social support for individuals.[234]

To have love, peace, and joy in our lives, we must fill them with loving, peaceful, joyful experiences and people.

Condition 17: Learn to be happy with no reason for it

Happiness is a state of mind that we find pleasurable. We feel good when we're happy. There is no underlying set of components for happy, and we can't define it as being either matter or energy. It is a state of Mind, and it feels great. We use forms of "to be" to describe it: "I am happy," "I was happy," "I will be happy." That means we identify our whole being with the feeling. We are the feeling.

We seek circumstances that will bring about the state of Mind. We rearrange our thoughts so our consideration of a subject brings feelings of happiness. We avoid circumstances that take away happiness. Our happiness is one of the symptoms of success in Earth School. We are successful when we feel happy.

We must also abandon much of what we were taught in childhood because the teaching is responsible for our unhappiness. We create our suffering, and we create our happiness. We keep the interpretations that cause negative emotions in our repertoire if we don't realize we can change them. We ascribe their effects to things outside of us, but they are entirely in our Minds. If we don't use our free will and courage to take control and change the interpretations, they will repeatedly affect us when we have experiences; we will feel like helpless victims. However, we are choosing to allow the interpretations to affect us. We are creating an unhappy reality.

We must learn what makes us happy. When we are happy, we have a surge of bliss in our body experience. The feeling is described as being endorphins activating opioid receptors in the brain that minimize discomfort and create feelings of euphoria and wellbeing, but the feeling is actually a state of Mind, not of the body. The body experiences follow the state of Mind. When we think of things that make us happy, we feel bliss. Then if we think of something that worries us or makes us unhappy, the bliss disappears. If we then think of something that makes you happy, the bliss returns. If we do that for a minute or two, alternating things that give us bliss and things that disturb us, we will learn the body experience of bliss and discomfort. We can use that to identify what we want our lives to be filled with— those things that bring us bliss. And we can learn that things that bring us discomfort must be minimized, or we must change our interpretations that cause discomfort.

We feel the same thing when we're doing something we don't enjoy, like taxes. At some point, we think of checking our favorite Facebook group or email. We feel a surge of bliss. We check the Facebook group or email and don't want to return to our taxes because if we do, the bliss will stop.

We can learn what brings us bliss at every moment of our day. If you have attention-deficit disorder, you'll find yourself shifting attention often because you're scanning for the surge of bliss. If something you're doing loses your interest, your Mind will go to something that gives you the surge of bliss and you'll pursue that. Because of the nearly endless options available in email, social media, and videos on demand, the Internet is a candy store for adults with attention deficit disorder.

Most of the time, we are reacting to experiences done to us. We don't stop to learn about why we are reacting in a particular way to the experiences. We must learn to be observers of who we are. We must learn to feel and know the feeling. What brings us joy? We should sit quietly and relive those moments. Feel what joy is like. What brings us sadness. Relive those moments. What does sadness feel like? What makes us angry? When we relive those moments, we learn what the negative emotions feel like.

When we identify what makes us joyful and what makes us uncomfortable, we can minimize the effects of feeling uncomfortable by taking on another perspective. We change our interpretations. We are an eternal being having a spiritual experience. All of the things that bring us discomfort are just passing scenery as we live our lives in Earth School. When we realize that, we will feel ourselves being blissful with no reason for it. Bliss will be our natural state.

We also will be happy most of the time with no reason for it when we abandon the childhood teaching that we must acquire and hold onto things, activities, and affiliations to be happy. Life in Earth School is continually changing. Things, activities, and affiliations will cease and new ones may take their place. There is a constant churn. If we are attached to the things, activities, and affiliations, we will regularly be frustrated and despondent when they go away. To be consistently happy with no reason for it, we must give up on needing anything outside of ourselves in our lives. We want to have them, and we are delighted when they're present, but we must not need them.

One of the goals of our Earth School experience is coming to realize fully that we are sufficient within ourselves, with no need for anything outside of us. When we realize that, we enjoy surges of bliss when we have something in our life that brings us joy and periods of sadness when those things leave, but the sadness is not consuming. We are happy and contented with ourselves with no requirement that something or somebody outside of us must be present to give us happiness.

Having said that, when someone we love graduates from Earth School before us, the loss of their presence will cause great unhappiness. The depth and duration of the worst of the grieving will be lessened by an understanding of the fact that the person lives on, just in another location, and is accessible. We can then realize that we cannot have the same type of relationship we had and grow into the new relationship rather than pining for what is no more.

Condition 18: Triumph and enjoy the success

We must learn to love being successful and everything it takes to become successful. The success raises the spirits of everyone around the person and ultimately all of humanity.

With each success, we must enjoy our triumph and reward ourselves. We must relive the fears, the struggle, our strength, and the triumph. Each success makes us wiser, more capable, and more loving. The successes are stored up in our coffers for us to enjoy often. They will also buy more courage and wisdom later when new challenges come into our lives. We are endeavoring to become spiritually wealthy.

Our success has raised humanity by that measure. We are contributing to evolving the heaven on earth that will be the destiny of those who enroll in Earth School after us. We are laying the foundation for what they will build.

Condition 19: Help others as they learn, grow, and enjoy life

During this time in Earth School, we not only learn, grow in spiritual maturity, and enjoy life, we help others do the same, and in the end, we help humanity to learn, grow spiritually, and enjoy this life in peace and brotherhood. When we grow to be loving, compassionate, and other-centered, we will naturally want to help others grow. Being active in helping others, then, will increase our learning, growth, and enjoyment of life.

13

We Communicate with Loved Ones, Guides, Our Souls, and Others

As we go through Earth School, we have continual contact with loved ones, guides, our Souls, loved ones who have graduated before us, and people interested in us. It is important for us to receive and respond to these communications because they continue the bonds in love and help us as we accomplish our life-plan goals in Earth School. We know we are loved and are not alone in Earth School, even if other people on earth aren't helpful.

Medium William Stead, communicating with an individual in the life after this life named Julia Ames, recorded this message.

> Your lives are open to the eyes of those invisible spirits who are permitted to see what you think and hear what you say. You are compassed about by a far greater company of witnesses than you can imagine. 235

We also are part of the spiritual growth of our loved ones who are continuing to learn and grow in their lives after this life. They are increasing in love, compassion, and other-centeredness by helping people still in Earth School.

Among those who regularly communicate with us are our loved ones who have graduated from Earth School before us, although most people are not aware of their efforts at communicating. This chapter explains why we know we can communicate freely with them and how to communicate.

Our Loves Ones Are Fine

The most important concern for most people is whether their loved ones who have transitioned are all right. I can say with great assurance that they're fine—in fact, they're joyous. Everyone who speaks from the next life describes their happiness at being without worries, healthy, feeling light as a feather, with a young body that has no aches and pains. They're delighted.

They're not worried about us unless we're grieving and unhappy. They only grieve if we're grieving. They now know the truth that we and they are eternal beings. We'll live our lives and transition into the life after this life where we'll reunite. But in the meantime, they know we must continue to learn lessons, and they know they can't interfere with our struggles; we have to work them out ourselves. They are happiest when we're happy.

They're busy learning and working. They have occupations and preoccupations, often what they wished they could have done on the earth realm but couldn't. They haven't forgotten us, but just as most of us leave our family members to go to work each day, those who are in the life after this life are busy. They aren't preoccupied with staying around us.

However, we may receive assistance from them in taking care of ourselves and learning our life lessons. We may have a sudden insight or a feeling of calm and peace in the midst of worrying or stress. Someone on the earth realm may contact us unexpectedly with a message we need to hear, or we may chance upon some information in a book or on television that helps us through a crisis. Any of these insights may have been brought to us by that person in the afterlife we wish we could hear from. The assistance may not be in the way we might expect or wish, but it assuredly comes to us.

They will often return to be with us when we think of them. They don't observe birthdays and anniversaries because there is no time as we know it in the life after this life. However, when we think of them or they know the family is getting together, they often will stand unseen among us. Our thoughts come to them in the life after this life and they respond by coming to be with us on special occasions, either by being in the Earth School environment or being with us Mind to Mind from wherever they are.

If our loved one was an infant or a child, that little one will be cared for and we will be reunited when we transition to the next realm of our lives.

Do People Who Have Graduated from Earth School Miss Us?

People living in the next stage of life are still able to come into Earth School's environment and interact with us. They also receive our thoughts. They are never disconnected. As a result, they don't have the same concerns we have in Earth School about what happens after the transition. They know how we're doing and know we'll have a reunion soon. However, they do say they miss the things they did in Earth School with their loved ones.

They are especially disturbed when they feel the grief of a loved one on earth.[236] Mike Swain, speaking to his father through a medium from the life after this life explained.

> Grieving, weeping and wishing for the soul of the departed person to return, are the worst things that you people can do to someone who has just died.[237]

They earnestly want us to communicate with them and think of them as being close by in thought and love, not separated and gone.

> "Judge Hatch"(in Elsa Barker's *Letters from a Living Dead Man*, Rider & Co. Ltd., 1914, p. 74), after saying, "Your thought of us can make us happy," continued: "Your forgetfulness of us can throw us back entirely upon ourselves." Myers, communicating through Geraldine Cummins said, "Only in forgetfulness, in the fading of love, is there negation of life". . . . Myers appealed to

mortals to think of their "departed" loved ones and to think of them as living. Many who "come through" urged their mortal friends and relatives to keep their memories "green" by carefully observing special occasions, such as birthdays and anniversaries.[238]

Pets Are Alive and Well

Pets are kept by family members until the owners transition to the next life, at which time the pet returns to the owner without question. Our love creates a bond with our pets on the earth realm, so the pets live on after the pets' bodies die. There are many descriptions of all a person's pets greeting their owners when the owners follow them to the next realm of life.

Our Loved Ones Are Communicating with Us

Our loved ones are alive and well, living in the next stage of life. In our spiritually backward culture today, people are not taught that loved ones are anxious to continue the bonds they have with us, that they are available at any time to communicate, and that we are receiving regular communication from them, especially in the months after their transition from Earth School. So people live their lives in Earth School grieving for someone who is standing right next to them in spirit. The grieving people receive only a small part of the valuable guidance available to people in Earth School and allow the conditions in Earth School to override the guidance that does come through at a subliminal level.

They come to us anytime we ask to speak with them, wherever they may be. The attention to us may be through Mind-to-Mind communication, or they may enter the Earth School environment to be with us. The residents of the life after this life describe attending celebrations such as weddings, birthday gatherings, and their own funerals. They receive our thoughts and emotions about the events and are anxious to participate.

The Primary Reason We Don't Get the Communication Is That We Don't Know How to Receive It

The primary reason people feel their loved ones are not communicating with them is that those in Earth School haven't learned to receive the communication we know comes to them. We are so overwhelmed by the constant din of the earth environment that the communication we're receiving doesn't rise into awareness from the subconscious, where every communication is being registered. When a message does come as a subtle feeling, knowledge, or understanding, we dismiss it as imagination.

A young man killed over Flanders in World War I in 1914 communicated to his mother from spirit through medium Gladys Osborne Leonard. He described his attempts to connect with his mother.

> A few days later I was told I was to be taken home to see you. I can't remember the exact details of that evening, as I was shaken with conflicting emotions which coursed through me—joy, and fear, and hope, and grief, and impatience, and almost despair of the unknown future into which I had plunged without you. I passed with the two friends who guided me through the astral plane to the earth. As we came nearer, the atmosphere became thicker and misty, and the houses and everything seemed indistinct. The view disappeared, and I found myself standing in your room at the foot of your bed. A terrible feeling of despair filled my heart, for I knew what I had been told was true: I was indeed dead.

> You were sitting up in bed in an agony of grief, the tears streaming down your face, repeating my name over and over again, and calling me, and saw me not. I had expected a cry of joy, but it never came. I bent forward and called as loudly as I could, "Mummy, I'm here; can't you see or hear me?" You made no reply. I went to your side and put my arms round you, and though you were not conscious of my presence I seemed to be able to soothe you, for you became calmer and lay down. I felt

as if I were fainting, and had no will to resist when my guides took me away back to the hospital. I felt, however, that your love was mine still; I could feel its power, I understood it and realized it better than ever before. It was a spiritual caress, and I felt it through every fiber of my body, and was full of thankfulness. I knew, too, that in all my life your love had never failed me, and that, even now, you would find a way, if it were possible, to bridge the gulf between us—you would never let me "drop out."[239]

However, we can learn to communicate by being able to accept their Mind-to-Mind communication. For example, the Repair & Reattachment Grief Therapy method used by psychotherapists is 98 percent successful in connecting clients with their loved ones.[240] The reason it is so successful is the love connection between the person on this side of life and the person living in the next life.

You can read more about the procedure and see videos of people who have had afterlife communication experiences using it at www.earthschoolanswers.com/rochelle/.

Communicating with Us Is Difficult

Although people can learn to communicate with loved ones Mind to Mind, people living in the next life generally don't know how to get through to us. The ability to communicate with us in the earth realm is not widespread among people in the life after this life. Just as few people on our side of life are mediums who can communicate with those in the life after this life, most people in the next life aren't adept at getting through to us. They do try to communicate, however. They don't leave and forget about us. They register our thoughts, feel our grief, celebrate our joys, and are otherwise with us in thought wherever they are.

Successful communication from the life after this life is so difficult that many living there do not believe such communication is possible. Jabez Hunt Nixon, a justice of the peace and medium, recorded this statement by a man living in the life after this life.

I was telling some [other] spirits about these seances here, how the spirits could here converse with people of earth, and one man told me that such talk as that and such an idea was all foolishness.[241]

A young man named Mike Swain transitioned in a head-on auto collision. Mike Tymn reports Swain's message conveyed through Mike's father, a medium, about the difficulty people in the life after this life have in communicating with us on earth.

Mike went on to explain that in order for him to communicate through the medium, he had to reduce his vibrations to their slowest rate. "This isn't easy, Dad. Some of it is downright painful. It's like putting on a straight-jacket. I have to constrict myself more and more, like the rabbit in *Alice in Wonderland*, until my vibrations are moving as slowly as yours." He went on to say that he had discovered that he was one of a few people who could so lower his vibrations, and that perhaps 95% of the souls there are unable to manifest at the earth level.[242]

Timothy Gary, speaking from spirit through the mediumship of August Goforth, explains the difficulty they have with communicating.

It's inaccurate to think that because I've made my transition to a risen state [the life after this life] I'm somehow ahead of the game and have greater abilities and powers than those still embodied on earth. Especially in the beginning of my new risen life, I was no more able to contact you than you were able to contact me. I had to first become aware that such a thing was possible, and then I had to struggle with believing it was possible, and then I had to work and study with great diligence to make it possible. Much of what I was told seemed unfeasible or beyond my capabilities. Even when I was informed that I had finally achieved mental contact with you, I still doubted it. I didn't have enough experience, and until I did I was acting on blind trust.[243]

Those in the life after this life can learn to be better at communicating. There are classes in how to communicate with people living in Earth School. William T. Stead, who perished on the Titanic, communicated through various mediums. He explained that to be able to make his presence known, he learned skills from mediums on his side of life.

> It was explained to him that he had to visualize himself among the people in the flesh and imagine that he *was* standing there in the flesh with a strong light thrown upon himself. "Hold the visualization very deliberately and in detail, and keep it fixed on my mind, that at that moment I was there and they were conscious of it," Stead described the process.[244]

To understand what it's like for them to endeavor to communicate to us, try this little experiment. We know from the research done by Rupert Sheldrake and others that people do have a sense of being stared at.[245] People subtly know when someone is looking at them. The next time you're in a line of people waiting for something, pick someone ahead of you in line who is not engaged in a task, just standing idly. Focus on their neck and imagine tickling them on the neck. After a few seconds, very occasionally, people will turn around and look back, and even brush their necks. They don't know why, though. The message came through to their minds at a subconscious level, but they didn't get the clear message that another person is imagining tickling their necks. They won't turn around and say, "Why are you imagining tickling my neck?" The message is there, because they respond to it, but it doesn't rise to the level of their conscious awareness.

William T. Stead described his effort to get a message through to a medium:

> He stood by the medium, concentrated his mind on a short sentence, and repeated it with much emphasis and deliberation until he could hear part of it spoken through the medium.[246]

Several on the other side have described working to influence people on earth to receive their communication. One person in the life after this life named Alfred Higgins described both giving a message to his wife directly and giving a message to a medium to give to his wife.

He said he told his guide that he was interested in seeing how she was doing and the two were instantly with her in her kitchen. You can hear the recording of this effort and two others at www.earthschoolanswers.com/higgins3/.

> The next thing I knew I was standing in our kitchen and I was watching my wife. She was standing over the sink peeling some potatoes and I thought, "Well, this is funny." So I thought, "Well I don't know, I wonder if she knows I'm here," and I called her name. She didn't say nothing. She didn't hear me, obviously.
>
> So my friend says, "She won't hear you, you know." So I says, "Well I don't know. What could I do?"
>
> So he says, "There's nothing you could do. But she may sense your presence. You never know. Let's just wait a little while."
>
> So I just stood there and I concentrated.
>
> He says to me, "Concentrate your thought on her. Just think hard, you know. Think as hard as you can. Think her name."
>
> And I did and all of a sudden she stood up and she dropped down the … dropped down the knife and the potato she was peeling and she looked round. Looked proper bewildered, she looked. She looked almost scared and I felt rather sorry in a way that I'd scared her, because I realized it must have been me trying to get at her, you know. Anyway, oh, she just flew out of that kitchen. She opened the door and then she sort of shut it again and then she sat down and then she put her head on the table and started to cry. And I felt awful about this. I thought, "Oh dear, now this is terrible."
>
> And he says to me, "Don't worry. She senses. She feels. She knows in herself. She doesn't understand yet, but she knows in herself that you're near her."
>
> So I says, "Well, if I'm going to make her miserable like this, there's not much point, is there?"

So he says, "Don't let that worry you. This often happens to people. They don't know with any certainty. They've never been told about life after death. They've never been told about the possibility of communication and all that sort of thing. But she'll come ... she senses ... she feels and she in herself, deep down inside, she knows."[247]

In another part of the session with Alfred Higgins, Higgins describes trying to get a friend in a tavern to realize he was there by focusing on saying the friend's name. He begins by describing how he went to the tavern by putting his hand in his guide's hand. You can listen to Higgins at www.earthschoolanswers.com/higgins4/.

So I thought, "Well, this is alright." So he put his hand out towards me. I thought, "Oh well, I suppose I put my hand in his again," see, so I did. The next thing I knew I was standing in the bar of this pub, see, and there were three of my old mates there. I went and stood up beside one and I remembered what I'd been told to do about the wife - to concentrate, think hard, you see. And he'd got this mug of beer up to his mouth and I was thinking to myself his name, see, and all of a sudden he plonked that down on the counter, you know. And he looked quite bewildered. He looked round, and then he said to his mates, my other two friends, he says, "That's funny. I felt sure I heard... I felt sure I heard ..."[248]

Loved ones trying to communicate can communicate through thoughts, Mind to Mind. They focus on our minds and try to get a message through. The messages always come to us at a subconscious level, but the subtle messages don't rise to the level at which we can become conscious of them. We're too preoccupied with life to quiet ourselves and let the thought messages bubble up from the subconscious into our aware mind.

Another reason it may seem they don't communicate with us is that they're not as worried about us as we are about them, unless we're grieving and unhappy. They now know the truth that we and they are eternal beings. We'll live our life and continue to the next stage of life where we'll reunite, but in the meantime, they know we need to continue to learn lessons and they know they can do very little to help us with our struggles; we must work them out ourselves. They're happy and they know we're fine as well. They're happiest when we're happy.

How Do I Know When They're with Me?

At times, we suddenly have a memory, perhaps of something we hadn't thought of for years. That's our Minds connecting with their Minds. They're thinking of that memory, or they're focusing on us and sending that memory to us. We must thank them for it and let the love we feel pour over us. It's them communicating Mind to Mind.

We must not worry whether it's them sending it to us. For one thing, if we are receptive, they may send many messages to us, so the odds are very good it's them. When we have the impression they're with us, even if they're not, they receive the impression and will come to us, either physically or Mind to Mind from wherever they are. We must accept all notions of messages as communications from them.

People expect some material signs or manifestations. They look for the feathers or coins or numbers that show their loved one is connecting with them. What they must realize is that when the feathers or coins or numbers come to them, it is because their loved one is with them at that moment, inspiring them to look at the floor where the feather is or the sidewalk where the coin is or the license plate that has the numbers. Most of the time, they are just directing our attention to what is already there, not creating whatever it is. As a result, when we have that physical phenomenon, they're like with us; communicate with them. That's what they want. The feathers or coins or numbers are not important. They are just the ringing of the phone. We must pick up and talk. Some suggest we should speak with the newly transitioned aloud as well as telepathically.[249]

However, at other times, they seem to be permitted to make electrical devices function strangely or butterflies come around or coins appear, and other manifestations. We don't know how they do that or why they're assisted in doing that from the other side, but the signs are certainly the indications of their presence.

Bill and Judy Guggenheim, in their classic book *Hello from Heaven!*, list 12 of these events loved ones living in the life after this life inspire us with:

1. Sensing a presence
2. Hearing a voice
3. Feeling a touch
4. Smelling a fragrance
5. Visual experiences such as mists or full figures
6. Images of the deceased
7. Twilight experiences
8. ADC [after death communication] experiences while asleep
9. Out-of-body ADCs
10. Telephone calls
11. Physical phenomena
12. Symbolic ADCs such as butterflies; rainbows; many species of birds and animals; flowers; and finding numerous kinds of objects, such as coins, feathers, and pictures

Our Loved Ones Are Available to Communicate with Us

Our loved ones are most likely not earthbound, meaning they're not still on earth without a body walking around, visiting places, staying with people, riding in cars with people, and otherwise staying on earth, just not seen. Often during the period right after someone has stopped using a body, that person may stay on earth for an extended time because they are worried about someone on earth who is grieving, have unfinished business they are concerned about finishing, or have a desire to continue enjoying some pastime they enjoyed while using a body and want to now have the experiences vicariously by influencing someone on the earth realm to engage in them. However, our loved ones likely have gone on to the life after this life where they are enjoying themselves and becoming accustomed to their new surroundings.

Even though they will have gone on to the life after this life, it's important for us to realize that our loved one is available to communicate. They may not be around us as much on the earth realm now, but wherever they are, our loved ones will come to us when we want to communicate. They don't ignore us or feel anything negative about us. If we're not getting a connection, it isn't because they've found someone else they like better or they're miffed at us or anything else that results in a separation. It's just that connecting is as difficult for them as it is for us. We just have to keep up the dialogue. We must not stop because we aren't getting the response we want or we feel they may not have come to us when we want to communicate. They will come to us and will work at communicating. We just have to find methods that will enable us to receive the communication and respond.

Is Anyone Not Available to Communicate?

They are always available to communicate with us. If a medium tells you the person you want to connect with isn't available, that means the medium wasn't able to connect. Good mediums have times when they're able to connect and times when connections just don't come through. That has nothing to do with our loved ones. They always come through to us when we ask them to.

No one reincarnates so they are not available. Reincarnation is misunderstood. The messages we're getting consistently from people living in the next stage of life is that after our transition, our Higher Self incarnates a new individual to learn lessons in Earth School. We are linked to that new individual. That is why we can have past-life regressions and people talk about living other lives with each other. Read more about reincarnation on pages 144 to 148.

Mental Mediums Communicate with People Living in the Life after This Life

Mental mediums are able to communicate Mind to Mind with people living in the life after this life because their minds allow the impressions and messages to bubble up from their subconscious to their conscious minds more easily than the average person. Everyone receives the same impressions and messages that come from the Universal Intelligence to the individual Mind. Most people are so focused on the earth environment that the impressions and messages cannot enter their conscious minds. The messages are lost. A medium is able to allow the impressions and messages to come through.

The person in spirit must impress the medium with information meaningful to the person being read. However, try as the person in spirit may, the medium may not receive information the person being read recognizes. A man named Claude, killed in World War I, described the difficulty with communication to his mother through medium Gladys Osborne Leonard. He mentions that the person in the life after this life must speak through a "control" who is adept at communication. The "sitter" he refers to is the person on earth being read.

> In communicating, the spirit message comes first from the spirit, who has to concentrate to give it to the control . . . who has to impress it on the medium's brain to such an extent that the nerves and muscles of the mouth and tongue of the medium will respond to the action of the brain, and will speak the message as it has been given. I often think it wonderful how much does come through, when one realizes the many difficulties. The bias of the medium's mind, impressions from the sitter's subconscious self, unconscious telepathy from other minds, and so forth, all have to be taken into consideration.[250]

Those speaking from the life after this life must impress their messages upon the medium. Words and names are difficult to get through to the medium. The medium's mind is most receptive to images, including those representing concepts. The person in spirit communicating through a medium may be communicating that an anniversary is coming up, so the medium's subconscious creates an image such as a bouquet of white flowers as a signal to the medium a special event is coming up. The medium may have a sign such as a bell or flashing light showing a message is correct, or a ring to show someone was just married. Each medium has their own unique set of symbols. The medium will say things such as "I'm seeing a single red rose. That's my symbol for 'I'm sorry.'" The person in spirit is communicating the concept; the symbol comes from the medium's subconscious to allow it to rise into awareness. The medium must convey the message by asking the person being read whether the image and associated message make sense. For a good medium, that isn't fishing for information. The medium really doesn't know specifically what the symbol is communicating and needs validation. At other times, however, the medium does see the person in spirit or experiences something that happened to the person. Mediums will take on the physical symptoms of some trauma as it happened to the person in spirit.

Words and numbers are difficult for the person in spirit to communicate because there are no experiential images in these symbols. Instead, the person must convey an image to the medium's mind, such as the medium's own twin sisters, to indicate there are twins in spirit or there are twins in the family still on earth. An image of the medium's mother may come to the medium, but the significance is that it's the mother of the sitter coming through. The medium wouldn't know who the woman is if the mother in spirit showed an image of herself, so the medium is shown an image that will bring "mother" to mind.

Thomas Stewart White wrote a book containing messages that came from the life after this life through his medium wife Betty White. Betty describes the problem with getting messages from her mind onto paper through automatic writing.

> She [Betty] constantly complained of the dilution caused by this transfer [of messages through automatic writing]. What reached the paper was, according to her, but an unsatisfactory payoff shadow of the actuality.[251]

Alfred Higgins, coming through in a Leslie Flint session, describes the problems with trying to get a message through to a medium. He had impressed on his wife through his thoughts to go to a Spiritualist church so he could get a message through the medium there. He had been killed when he fell from a ladder, so he tried to get the ladder through the medium to his wife. An excerpt follows. You can hear the entire explanation by Alfred Higgins at www.earthschoolanswers.com/higgins1/.

So I concentrated like mad on her [the medium], you know, and eventually she picked it up. . . . She got certain things that I was trying to get to her. I got her to talk about. She kept getting a ladder. Of course, she got it all bugger mixed up (excuse me). But she got it mixed up, you know.

She says, "I don't know, my dear, if you're going to have a bit of luck, but I see a ladder with you." And I thought, "For crying out loud, this is getting on fine, this is!"

Anyway, of course, the missus did realize that after a while I'd had this accident on a ladder. So my missus says, "Well, I do place the business of the ladder."

And, of course, the medium got it all confused. She says, "I think as how there's something going to be very good for you, my dear. I see you rising, going up this ladder towards success."[252]

In the rest of the clip, he eventually does get through to his wife.

Frederic W. H. Myers, a pioneer in psychical research, communicated through medium Geraldine Cummins using automatic writing. He provided this description of how those on the other side influence the medium in automatic writing.

"The inner Mind is very difficult to deal with from this side," Cummins recorded. "We impress it with our message. We never impress the brain of the medium directly. That is out of the question. But the inner Mind receives our message and sends it on to the brain. The brain is the mere mechanism. The inner Mind is like soft wax, it receives our thoughts, their whole content, but it must produce the words to clothe it."

Myers went on to explain that success in sending the thought through depends on the inner Mind of the automatist [medium doing automatic writing], which must contribute to the body of the message. "In other words, we send the thoughts and the words usually in which they must be framed, but the actual letters or spelling of the words is drawn from the medium's memory. Sometimes we only send the thoughts and the medium's unconscious Mind clothes them in words."

Myers also offered that when discarnate beings want to communicate through a sensitive, they must enter a dream or subjective state which detaches them from the memory of concrete facts in their past lives. "Further, if we communicate directly through the medium, though we often retain our personality, our manner of speech, we are frequently unable to communicate through the medium's hand."[253]

The people coming into the earth environment experience another set of difficulties. Those in spirit who have come through to individuals on earth all describe entering the earth environment as being like entering a deep, dark fog.[254] They must reduce the speed of their energy, often called a "vibration," to come into the lower earth energy.

Medium Betty White conveyed the following description of the difficulty of conveying messages between the two worlds conveyed from a group of discarnate beings calling themselves "the Invisibles."

The atmosphere of the two spheres is so diverse in quality that, in passing from one to the other, there is always a diminution of speed, so sudden and so marked that a shock is given to the stream of our thoughts, and there is produced, just on the borderline, some inevitable confusion.[255]

How to Pick a Qualified Medium

We must be careful to visit a medium who is qualified. Many call themselves mediums who are not. Most of the unqualified mediums don't realize people can actually communicate with people living on the life after this life, so they figure when they're faking their readings, that's what everyone does. However, it is unethical.

Insist on evidential mediumship. In evidential mediumship, the medium will give many facts that are indisputably true. In a reading during the Canyon Ranch experiments done by Gary Schwartz, John Edwards described a fact that was so unique and detailed that it was evidence the person's grandmother was coming through. The grandmother had one black and one white poodle that tore up a reception prepared for a wedding. John Edward was given that highly evidential information. Those are facts the person being read would say "yes" to. They are evidential.

Both the people living in the next life and the medium want us to know the person is coming through to communicate with us. Both will endeavor to give evidence to validate for us it is them. It isn't disrespectful to the person living in the next life when we ask for evidence. If we are genuinely connecting with them, they will be anxious to prove it. Expect real details no one could know in the early moments of the reading.

If the medium "fishes" for information, leave. When the person claiming to be a medium is "fishing" or doing a "cold reading," the medium makes general statements and asks for validation, such as "You have an older person who has passed." Haven't we all? Then the medium will say, "Is that right?" The person being read says, "Yes, my Aunt Gertie." The medium says, "It's a woman and her first name is 'Gertie.' I'm getting a very uncomfortable feeling in my chest." The person being read says, "She passed from a stroke." The medium says, "That's it. Yes, when the stroke hit she couldn't breathe. And there's someone close to her who passed." "That would be Uncle Don," the person being read would say. The medium would say, "I got the D in the name as a male but got 'Donald' or something like that." The person being read would say, "That's his name. Boy, you're good!"

If the medium gives you only generalized halo statements, such as "Your loved one is well and wishes you the best. She looks in on you," be suspicious. A true reading will have the person the medium is connecting with give details about the person: what she looked like, how she transitioned, what she used to do with you on earth, or special actions or unique characteristics that are definite evidence the person is coming through. To ensure you don't sign on with a false or mediocre medium, use only a certified medium. For lists of certified mediums, go to www.earthschoolanswers.com/connect/.

Physical and Materialization Mediumship Communication

Physical mediumship differs from mental mediumship. In physical mediumship people called "sitters" sit in a room together and phenomena happen in the room, experienced by all present. The sitters may experience movement of objects and furniture, raps, taps, lights, voices, and a great variety of other occurrences. The room may be entirely dark or there may be a red or blue light. Mediums usually sit in a confined space, such as a cabinet.

There usually is one physical medium in the room, although there may be more than one. In most cases of demonstrations of physical mediumship, mediums and sitters are tightly controlled. The mediums usually are strapped to a chair with zip ties connecting their arms and legs to the table arms and legs. Tape likely will be applied across their mouths. Sitters hold hands so everyone knows where each sitter is in the room. The energy the entities use to make things happen comes from this physical medium, the sitters, and those in spirit. There are teams of entities working with the physical medium to make the manifestations happen.

Some physical mediums exude ectoplasm from any orifice in their bodies. Ectoplasm is a substance that exudes from any orifice in the medium's body. It is said to originate in the pancreas and be a semi-fluid, light-colored bodily substance with epithelial cells that had the consistency of mucous.[256] Ectoplasm in photographs appears on the medium's body or around it, forms into long rods that lift objects, hands, faces, and other things during the seance. The substance is light sensitive, so most séances are held in low light or total darkness to allow ectoplasmic manifestations.

Some mediums exude no ectoplasm. Theirs is an energy force that causes things to happen in the room. Energy is still taken from the sitters and augmented by the spirit team.

During a séance, objects may be heard landing on the table or floor. The objects are called "apports." The apports may be any physical object: flowers, coins, statuettes, pendants, and other such objects. The teams involved say that the objects are things that were lost somewhere in the world, not taken from their owners.

A materialization medium is a physical medium, but the materialization medium has the additional capability of having people from the life after this life materialize in the room. The materialization medium exudes ectoplasm, which drapes around the entity's ethereal body so it can be seen and touched. The resulting materialized form has all the qualities of a body living on earth, including the feel of bones, warmth, the softness of tissue, and even the deformities the individual had when on Earth. The materialized entities hold conversations, sing, walk around the room, touch sitters, and may allow themselves to be video recorded or photographed using infrared light.

There are very few physical and materialization mediums. They are born with the ability; it cannot be learned by someone without the inborn talent.

You can listen to the recording of one séance in which a loved one materializes with materialization medium David Thompson and has a conversation with his loved one who was among the sitters. This is the link: www.earthschoolanswers.com/dt/.

Materializations in the Earth Environment

People living in the life after this life can materialize on earth (see Chapter 2 for examples). Elisabeth Kübler-Ross tells of her experience with Mrs. Schwartz, a patient who had transitioned from earth and appeared to her two years later in fully materialized form. She had a conversation with her and touched her. In all respects, Mrs. Schwartz was fully human in form and substance.[257] A friend of mine named Mike Thomson had the surprise of having his ex-wife's uncle suddenly appear in the seat next to him as he was driving alone. The uncle spoke to him, then disappeared. Mike learned several hours later that his ex-wife's uncle had transitioned out of his body at the moment he appeared to Mike. Raymond Moody, author of *Life after Life* and other books on near-death experiences and the life after this life tells of having his deceased grandmother walk into the room where he was sitting, chat with him about their lives together, and leave. Such stories are common.

Other Forms of Mediumship

There are other forms of mediumship that allow communication with people living in the life after this life.

Trance mediumship. In trance mediumship, the entities take over a medium's body and use the medium's vocal and physical organs to speak and gesture. The medium voluntarily allows it to happen. No entity can take over someone's body without the person's consent. The trances may be light trance, in which the medium is awake, or deep trance, in which the medium is unconscious.

Direct-voice mediumship. In direct-voice mediumship, the entities form voice boxes using ectoplasm from the medium's body and speak through the voice boxes. You can hear examples from the most famous direct-voice medium, Leslie Flint, at this link: www.earthschoolanswers.com/lf/.

Channeling. Channeling is different from trance mediumship. In channeling, the medium allows another entity, usually a higher-level being, to take over their voice mechanism and body to speak. The vocal quality notably changes during the channeling. The channeler is awake during the channeling, but may not recall what happened during the channeling.

Inspiration. Artists, writers, scientists, philosophers, speakers, and others who create information so revolutionary, insightful, or original that it seems to be coming from higher source are doing a form of channeling, but it is not apparent to them. They receive inspirations when in the deepest focus on their occupation or preoccupation. They describe it as being almost in a trance. They lose track of time and the inspired activity flows. At its strongest, the activity is a form of channeling.

Automatic Writing and Inspired Writing. In automatic writing, the medium's hand is taken over by someone in spirit who writes using the hand. A woman who experienced automatic writing named Margaret Cameron described the feeling of her hand being taken over as like holding a live bird wrapped in a handkerchief.[258] Geraldine Cummins, a housewife with only an eighth-grade education, wrote six highly acclaimed books in cooperation with a spirit using automatic writing. Geraldine would go into a dreamlike state and her hand would start writing. Her handwriting changed with each spirit that wrote through her.[259] Medium Stainton Moses describes his experiences with automatic writing.

> My right arm was seized about the middle of the forearm, and dashed violently up and down with a noise resembling that of a number of paviors at work. It was the most tremendous exhibition of 'unconscious muscular action' I ever saw. In vain I tried to stop it. I distinctly felt the grasps, soft and firm, round my arm, and though perfectly possessed of senses and volition, I was powerless to interfere, although my hand was disabled for some days by the bruising it then got. The object we soon found was to get up the force.[260]

The most complete description of automatic writing is Mike Tymn's "Automatic Writing" on his blog. You can link to it on this page: www.earthschoolanswers.com/aw/.

In inspired writing, the writer relaxes and writes the first words that come to them, scribbling them without regard to penmanship or legibility. The writer carries on a dialogue, writing the words as they come from both the writer and the person in spirit. The person in spirit is not controlling the writer's hand. Instead, that person is inspiring the thoughts that come into the person's mind.

Induced After-Death Communications

Dr. Allan Botkin, a psychotherapist formerly at a Chicago VA hospital, developed an afterlife communication procedure using eye-movement desensitization and reprocessing (EMDR), a psychotherapy method that is remarkably successful at reducing PTSD and other traumas. The patient most often experiences profound breakthroughs in understanding that reduce the impact of the trauma dramatically. To date, 30,000 psychotherapists have been trained to use it and it has been endorsed by many psychological and health organizations, including the American Psychological Association and United States Veterans Administration.

Dr. Botkin discovered that his patients grieving for someone who had left earth were having afterlife communication experiences while sitting in his office when he used the EMDR procedure. I co-authored a book with Dr. Botkin describing the therapy method and 84 cases in the book, *Induced After-Death Communication: A New Therapy for Grief and Trauma*. The method is 70 percent successful in helping clients have an afterlife communication that greatly diminishes the client's grief.

You can read more about the therapy method and view of video of people who have had the procedure at www.earthschoolanswers.com/iadc/.

Repair & Reattachment Grief Therapy

Rochelle Wright, a Washington state licensed psychotherapist, refined Dr. Botkin's method to produce a procedure called Repair & Reattachment Grief Therapy. It reduces or virtually eliminates the deep grief in which the grieving person is immersed. The method is 98 percent successful.

The communication unfolds naturally when a facilitator helps the person enter a state in which the connection occurs, guided by those in the life after this life. The facilitator does not lead or prompt the person. The procedure is 98 percent successful and reduces grief from a rating of 10 or higher on a 10-point scale of disturbance to scores of 0 to 3 in one session.[261]

I co-authored the book *Repair & Reattachment Grief Counseling* with Rochelle. You can read more about the procedure and see videos of people who have had afterlife communication experiences using the procedure at www.earthschoolanswers.com/rochelle/.

Self-Guided Afterlife Connections Demonstrate the Reality of the Life after this Life

Other validations that people are connecting with their loved ones living in the life after this life come during the Self-Guided Afterlife Connections procedure. I developed the Self-guided Afterlife Connections Procedure to allow people to have their own afterlife connections without the aid of a facilitator, medium, or psychotherapist.

The individual goes through eight stages of training in a free online program to learn how to self-hypnotize. The first two stages explain to the participants the need for confidence that the afterlife is a reality and their loved ones are available to communicate. The third takes them into a light hypnotic state through a guided meditation. During this stage, participants learn to allow unfoldment to occur in their minds without inhibiting it or trying to manipulate what happens. The next four stages contain inductions that guide the participant into having increasingly independent self-inductions. After the last stage, the participant is able to perform self-hypnosis and have a connection with a loved one in the life after this life at any time, without aids such as a narration or music.

The result is that 86 percent of participants who complete the training report having a successful connection. The connections contain many validations that participants are communicating with loved ones.

You can read more about the Self-Guided Afterlife Connections procedure at www.earthschoolanswers.com/selfguided/.

Instrumental Transcommunication

Instrumental TransCommunication (ITC) uses electronic equipment to record voices and images of people living in the life after this life. A variety of methods have been used since the early part of the twentieth century. Some have had remarkable results, demonstrating that people living in the life after this life are able to communicate if we can create the right conditions.

Starting in 1949, Marcello Bacci, of Italy, began receiving voices through a tube radio he had. Thousands of people came to his home to have conversations with their loved ones through Bacci's radio. The participants all attested to the fact that their loved ones were speaking to them through the radio.

In 1959, Friedrich Juergenson recorded voices of his mother and father accidentally while recording bird calls. Eight years later, Dr. Konstantin Raudive used Jurgenson's methods, ultimately recording tens of thousands of voices in a laboratory.

In 1979, George Meek and Bill O'Neill created a device called Spiricom that recorded over 20 hours of the voice of a deceased NASA scientist, Dr. Mueller, who helped Meek and O'Neill refine their instrument.

A variety of other methods successfully captured images and voices until today, when the primary researchers are Sonia Rinaldi, in Brazil, Sheri Perl in the U.S., Anabela Cardoso in Portugal, and Hans Otto Koenig in Germany. Each month, Sonia Rinaldi has given as many as 163 sessions of recordings of children in the life after this life for parents, with as many as 200 messages per session. The parents have validated that the voices in the recordings are their children. You can listen to recordings Sonia has made at www.earthschoolanswers.com/sonia/.

Sheri Perl's Prayer Registry allows parents whose children have passed to be part of a large group of other parents. Sheri has recorded the voices of children to give to the parents. They all agree the voices they hear are their children. You can listen to recordings Sheri has made at www.earthschoolanswers.com/sheri/.

Hans Otto König and Maria Wauters have developed devices that allow people to have voice contact with their loved ones living in the next life. The listeners validate that the recordings are of their loved ones. You can hear recordings made by König and Wauters at www.earthschoolanswers.com/hok/.

Anabela Cardoso, a career Portuguese diplomat, has been recording voices directly from radios since 1997. She authored *Electronic Voices: Contact with Another Dimension,* and *Electronic Contact with the Dead: What Do the Voices Tell Us?* Two videos of Anabela Cardoso explaining how to use ITC to record voices are at www.earthschoolanswers.com/cardoso/.

All of these recordings of images and voices are evidence that the people who are communicating are living on happily in the life after this life.

Communication in Dreams

Our loved ones in the life after this life communicate with us Mind to Mind, telepathically. Our minds are so preoccupied with sensory experiences and activities in Earth School that we most often are not able to have the messages they send bubble up from the subconscious into consciousness to understand and interpret them.

However, we are often able to receive their messages when our conscious minds are preoccupied, as in self-hypnotism, psychotherapy methods such as Eye-Movement Desensitization and Reprocessing, while performing mindless activities like cleaning or driving, or during sleep.

Sir William Barrett, communicating to his wife from spirit, urged her,

> "Get into the *habit* of opening your mind to me when you go to bed, and then you will find that I shall impress you with the right solution to your difficulties in the morning."[262]

You can enhance your likelihood of receiving and remembering messages from loved ones by asking them to communicate with you during sleep, when you are involuntarily relaxed. Keep a notebook by your bed and when you arise, immediately write your recollection of any dreams activities during the night. Don't be discouraged if you must do this every night for some time. It often takes a while for the communication to be possible.

Other Methods of Afterlife Communication

As humankind has learned the realities about this life and the life after this life, people are developing new ways of having afterlife communications with loved ones. Some of the other methods are in the book *Afterlife Communication: 16 Proven Methods, 84 True Accounts*, I edited that contains descriptions of 16 methods written by the presenters of a conference I developed. The methods in addition to those already described include meditation connections, aiding lost souls through out-of-body travel, pendulum communication, and the psychomanteum threshold room.[263]

There Are Special Facilities People in the Life after This Life Can Use to Communicate with People on Earth

Speakers from the life after this life describe "houses" they can go to in order to communicate.[264] The people there are adept at communicating or have the technology to facilitate the communication. We also know there are stations that have facilities to facilitate communication.

> There are stations on this plane where communication with the earth realm is possible. . . . The technique employed, I understand, is quite "special" and very difficult at first to follow, even by those who desire to use it. But there *are* Stations, there are Directors for this work, there are Administrators and (in a sense) Technicians to run them.[265]

In the Afterlife Research and Education Institute's research in instrumental transcommunication, we have learned that there are at least three stations in which communication is transmitted from entities to the earth, where their messages are recorded in voices. The three are the Brazilian Station, the North American Station, and the oldest, the Rio do Tempo or Timestream Station in Europe. Each has technology, technicians, and directors who successfully convey words to researchers on earth.

They See the Earth through Our Senses

Loved ones see the earth through our senses unless they come into the earth realm environment to visit us. They can attune to us in Earth School from wherever they are and receive the sensory impressions and thoughts we are receiving.

However, they do not peer in at us when we are engaged in activities we would rather they not witness. A. D. Mattson, Doctor of Sacred Theology while on earth, speaking from spirit through Margaret Flavell Tweddel explains.

> There is a privacy around all people on earth which cannot be violated. Those of us in the astral world are not allowed to go

around and see what is going on in a person's life unless we are called to do so by that person.[266]

Can I Get Help from My Loved Ones in the Next Realm?

We are often given help from our loved ones living in the next life. When we are in distress or need, our loved ones come to us from wherever they are. They are always in contact with us. They will give us urgings and intuitions that sometimes come into Conscious Awareness but most often people dismiss. However, if we are open to their communication, we will receive marvelous counsel about our lives.

To get help, we just have to ask for it. Yeshua bar Yosef, the sage of the Galilee, is purported to have said these words:

> Ask, and it shall be given you; seek, and ye shall find; knock, and it shall be opened unto you. For everyone that asketh receiveth; and he that seeketh findeth; and to him that knocketh it shall be opened. (Matthew 7:7-8, KJV)

The activity of giving words to your request is very important. It sets our frame of mind to being humble in asking and being open to the response. Our loved ones come to us when we have expressed our question or need.

Then we must be open to the response. The response will be the first thing that comes into our mind, before we have a chance to think. If we think about it, we will taint the response with our own answers. If we don't get the answer immediately, we must leave it alone, without trying to puzzle out some unusual feeling or words we seem to get. We may get the answer later or in some other way. We must be open to whatever comes, without analyzing or second guessing. The answer will be obvious.

They Are Not Omniscient

Our loved ones living in the life after this life are not omniscient or able to describe the future. Judge David Patterson Hatch, speaking with automatic writing through medium Elsa Barker, explained.

In this communion between the outer and inner worlds, you in the outer world our apt to think that we know everything. You expect us to prophesy like fortunetellers, and to keep you informed of what is passing on the other side of the globe. Sometimes we can; generally we cannot.[267]

The Sense of Presence Is a Real, Valid Sense

When a loved one comes into the earth environment to be with us, we may have a sense of their presence. That's a real sense as real as seeing or hearing. We must accept it and know it's a true sense. At that moment, we can stop and say "Hello." We can tell the person how we're feeling and how happy we are that they're with us. Then we can go on, or we can stop and have a brief dialogue.

Often, people describe feeling more of the sense of presence of someone in the first weeks or months after the transition, but then have less of a sense of their presence after that. The person likely has gone on to the next level of their spiritual development, leaving the earth realm. However, after they have gone on to the next planes of their lives, they are still available to communicate. They are only a thought away. When we think of our loved one, they receive the thought, wherever they are, and send warm thoughts to us and are available to communicate, although they may not come back to the earth realm at that moment. If we are having a problem, are depressed, are ill, or otherwise in distress, they will return to the earth realm to be with us at that time. They also will come to the earth realm just to look in on us. They will more often do that if we have regular times when we communicate with them and we keep up the active communication.

They regularly send warm feelings our way to let us know we're loved and they're present. And we will receive assistance from them in taking care of ourselves as we learn life lessons. We may have a sudden insight or a feeling of calm and peace in the midst of worrying. Someone may contact us unexpectedly with a message we needed to hear, or we may chance upon some information in a book or on television that helps us through a crisis. Any of these insights may have been brought to us by that person in the afterlife we wish we could hear from. They work to inspire us to look at the book or television, or they may inspire a friend to call us when we need the connection.

One person came to the realization that the periods of spontaneous grief weren't just random moments of sadness: "I realized I was not missing her; I was FEELING her." The sense of presence may result in moments of grief because of the sudden memories. These should be moments of joy because they're filled with love and presence. Those moments of spontaneous grief we feel likely are from the sense of presence we don't realize. In those moments, instead of grieving, we must enjoy the presence, warmth, and love. It's the signal our loved one has come close by.

They send thoughts about what we need to do, watch out for, or take advantage of. That intuitive feeling we really should call Aunt Mary very possibly is coming from them. That is also a real, valid sense. They do what they can to help, but as we go on with our lives, they do not watch us every moment. They're busy with their own continuing lives, learning about life and eternity. They have their own occupations and preoccupations, often what they wished they could have done on the earth realm but couldn't. They haven't forgotten you, but just as many people must leave their families to go to work or other activities each day, those who are in the life after this life aren't preoccupied with being around you. They're busy, and they know you have your life to live.

They also communicate through bodily sensations, such as our feelings of being touched, cobwebby feelings, tingles, pains, and other such bodily sensations. One medium describes becoming anxious when she is receiving communication from people. Another has males giving her a sensation on the left side of her body and females on the right side. Sometimes, a guide or a loved one will use the same bodily sensation each time they are present to signal to you that the person or guide is present.

They Come When You Need Them or Talk with Them

They will return to be with you when you have thoughts that involve them. They don't observe birthdays and anniversaries because there is no time as we know it in the life after this life. However, when you are thinking about an anniversary or birthday when the family is coming together, they often stand with you, although you can't see them. Your thoughts come to them in the life after this life and they respond by going to be with you on special occasions.

Some people think their loved ones have abandoned them because they aren't receiving the strong physical signs they expect. No one is abandoned. If someone isn't receiving communication, it's because they're not responding to the communication when it comes.

Will I Hold them Back by Connecting?

I've been asked often whether connecting with our loved ones often will hold them back from going on to the next levels of life. Absolutely not! Here's why.

1. They have an eternity to grow. This idea that they have to get on with their progress is a peculiarly modern idea that comes out of our goal-driven, fast-paced lives. There's no hurry.

2. Many people in the life after this life spend the years their loved one is still on this side of life staying close by and taking care of them or giving them guidance. I'm not suggesting everyone's loved ones do that. However, staying close by is perfectly normal.

3. We have records through mediums of people saying that helping people on the earth realm is part of their spiritual growth. They grow by becoming increasingly compassionate and understanding our struggles. They also grow by ministering to us.

4. Our loved ones can go on to the next planes of life and still return to communicate at any time. They're only a thought away. They receive our thoughts and feelings wherever we are, and will come when we want to talk, when we're disturbed, or when something exciting is happening in our lives. They'll often look in on us even after they go on to

other levels of life. They'll go on with their lives, moving to other levels, but still are available to communicate.

So don't worry about continuing to connect with them. Many newly transitioned people tell us that the greatest burden they carry is that the people on this side of life <u>don't</u> communicate.

Your loved one is still very much a part of your life, just in a new relationship. Keep communicating.

If the Person on This Side Doesn't Communicate, They Just Go on to Their Activities on the Other Side

Speakers in the life after this life explain that they endeavor to help their loved ones still on the earth realm by inspiring them and giving them guidance. However, if the people don't believe the guidance is real or ignore it, those in spirit go on with their life activities without trying to communicate. This is what one experiencer wrote that her loved one said to her during her Self-Guided Afterlife Connection:

> Tom tells me every Soul wants to connect. Some have no one that validates how they tried to connect. Eventually those may stop trying. Then those like Tom who knew I would never not notice send a sign. The person on this side of life acknowledges the sign, so the person in spirit does something else. Tom says that the more those in spirit do, the more we on the earth realm see, and they do more because we validated the connection. And so on and so on.[268]

A man named Claude, killed in World War I, spoke to his mother through medium Gladys Osborne Leonard, about the problem.

> Everyone works here as he is best fitted. In helping others in some way or other, many help those they love and have left on earth, if they can get through to people there as I can to you; but for those whose relatives, either through ignorance, fear, disbelief, or religious bigotry, do not desire to get it to touch with them, there is work to be done by helping less developed spirits on the lower spheres.[269]

The communication becomes easier and more frequent as we establish the new relationship by communicating.

To learn more about Self-Guided Afterlife Connections you can learn so you can more easily receive the impressions and messages from people in spirit, go to www.earthschoolanswers.com/selfguided/.

What Is Communication with Loved Ones Like?

Nearly all of the communication from our loved ones living in the next life and from our guides, helpers, and Soul is in whole thoughts, transferred Mind to Mind without a syllable or word. The receiver simply knows what they're communicating. However, they also may communicate in words that come to your Mind. The sound vibrations that come into our ears when we hear someone speaking on the earth realm are just vibrations when they come to the ear, with no meaning. They don't take on meaning until they come to the Mind. Our Minds recognize the vibrations as symbols that represent words. We assemble the words and apprehend the meaning. When someone in the life after this life communicates with us, at times we may "hear" their words, but what we're doing is having the experience of the words without the vibrations coming into the ear. The words are just as real as if they had come from someone on the earth realm through our ears. The experience is the same, but it happens Mind to Mind.

However, nearly always, the communication is Mind to Mind, or telepathic.

Religious Beliefs against Communication with the Next Realm of Life

For anyone concerned about communicating with those who have left the earth, you must know that the Old Testament injunctions against mediums and speaking with the people who have transitioned referred to the religions that were popular at the time that were based on seeking advice about how to live using mediums. Yahweh, the God of the Old Testament, was a jealous god who would have no other gods before him. The writers were saying Yahweh didn't like people getting advice from anyone but him. That was the reason for the injunctions.

At the same time, the New Testament contains nothing about not connecting with loved ones. In fact, there is ample evidence of the connections the Early Christians were making. For more, go to www.earthschoolanswers.org/christians/.

Concerns about Earthbounds and Negative Entities When Communicating with Loved Ones

You can read more about earthbounds and negative entities on pages 59–71 of this book.

"Earthbounds" are people who have transitioned from the body but have not left the earth environment. They have no bodies, so they travel unseen. Because they are still attuned to the earth environment, they can sit on chairs, travel in buses, attend gatherings, and do the things people using bodies do. They almost never can actually disturb things by moving objects. Their primary mischief is in influencing people through thought.

For our connections with loved ones, there are minimal dangers from earthbounds or negative entities. We are performing out of love, so they can't influence us, and they find us incredibly boring. You may do a simple prayer of protection before making a connection with someone unseen, including our loved ones. That is just insurance. This is an example prayer.

> During this time of communication, surround and fill me, the room I am in, and all in this house with a white light of love and divine protection.

We also must be especially vigilant in any activities that open us up to influence from the unseen. We can participate in the activities but must maintain our higher spiritual stance. The Ouija board or "spirit board" has been instrumental in helping Spiritualists communicate with loved ones in the life after this life and with entities that are benevolent and helpful to humankind. Pearl Curran, a housewife from Saint Louis with only an eighth-grade education, first used a Ouija board to connect with spirit entity, Patience Worth, who had lived in the seventeenth century. Patience Worth inspired Curran to write in astonishingly accurate Middle English. Pearl Curran produced sixty novels, plays and poems, including a 60,000-word epic poem, all in perfect Middle English, a language Curran could not have known.[270]

Much of William Butler Yeats' later poetry was inspired by the Ouija board his wife used.[271] Poet James Merrill's work, *The Changing Light at Sandover*, which won the National Book Critics Circle Award in 1983, benefited from consulting a Ouija board.[272] Many Spiritualists used it to connect with people living in the life after this life.

Parents use the Ouija board to communicate with their children in spirit. A man named Leslie Stringfellow transitioned at age 26 in his hometown of Galveston, Texas, in 1886 after a brief illness. Leslie communicated to his parents through a Ouija board for 15 years. The result was a book written by Alice Stringfellow, Leslie's mother, describing the life after this life.[273]

Because the Ouija board opens the people involved to the desired communication, it also opens people not on a higher spiritual level to influence from earthbounds and negative entities. The Ouija board should be used only in spiritual efforts to contact specific loved ones, not as a game and certainly not in an effort to attract "ghosts."

In normal activity to communicate with loved ones, there are no problems with earthbounds or entities.

People Can Learn to Communicate with Loved Ones Living in the Life after This Life

Resources for connecting with loved ones living in the life after this life are at www.earthschoolanswers.com/connect/. Included is a free online training program AREI has developed to teach people how to enter the state of mind in which afterlife communication can take place.

The key to communication is love. Few of us have the ability to perform psychic medium readings for people we don't know. However, at least 98 percent of the general public can have psychic medium communication with their own loved ones.[274] The reason anyone can have afterlife connections is that the telepathic communication is strengthened by the bond of love.

After presenting many statements by people living in the next life about what impedes and fosters communication with people living on earth, Robert Crookall wrote ". . . the declaration that grief depresses the dead is the converse of the statement that love provides the best conditions in which they can communicate."[275]

If humankind is to have consistent, clear communication with the people living in the next life, our motives must be based in love. A woman named Julia, living in the life after this life, wrote through William T. Stead in automatic writing:

> It will make all the difference to your results ... if you pursue the investigation from a love motive and not for mere cold curiosity. ... The communion between the quick and the dead can only persist when the borderland is bridged by love. And unless there be self-sacrificing love and the desire for service on both sides, there will not, and cannot, be more than a brief, intermittent, and not altogether pleasant, intercourse between the two roads. [276]

Anyone who seeks to communicate with people living in the life after this life must do so from an attitude of love.

Grief Is a Major Impediment to Communication

Grief is a heavy, dense emotion. It creates a cocoon around the grieving person that loved ones in spirit trying to communicate cannot easily penetrate. The general rule for people having an Induced After Death Communication therapy session is that the person must wait one year after the death for emotions to stabilize. The sadness and periods of grief do not go away, but the person's emotions stabilize so grief, guilt, anger, and the other tapestry of emotions are not so great that they dominate the person's Mind.

Robert Crookall reports the statements by people living in the next realm about the effect of grief on their communication with loved ones still on earth.

> "I was still conscious of all that went on in my home. ... I saw my daughter weeping ... and it seemed to put a cloud between

us and give a numb sort of pain. ... Grief makes a barrier through which we cannot come, and it also hinders our progress upwards, for we are affected by *thoughts* and not by *physical conditions,* as we were on earth. ... Happiness in the hearts and faces of our dear ones on earth radiates waves of light that attract us ... grief radiates dark clouds and gives the appearance of a heavy black cloud enveloping our friends. Our new bodies are tuned to a higher key than were our earth-bodies. We are extremely sensitive to impressions."

A similar statement was made in England: "Do not grieve. Grief is so short-sighted. It blocks the outlets." (L. M. Bazzett, *After-Death Communications*, Kegan Paul, Trench, Trubner & Co. Ltd., p. 108). A discarnate soldier's communication, cited in *Light,* Vol. XLII, 1922, p. 706, included the following: "I could tell when mother was fretting about me. ... I was glad when you got a bit better: it made me miserable."

... [A woman] described how she received communications from her (dead) son, first by "automatic writing" and later by telepathy. She found that "It was only when *a cloud of depression* descended on me that he could *not* contact me, and *"the fog,"* as he called it, made him miserable."

... grief depresses the dead.

... On the one hand, he said, to his mother, "When you cry I can't get near you because clouds come up round you." On the other hand, he said: "I am so glad of father's thoughts of me, because I get such big help from them: they give me a lift up and make me strong. I am helping other boys and they make me able to do it."[277]

What It Is Like to Communicate with Someone Living in the Life after This Life

We must learn a new way of communicating when we communicate Mind to Mind with someone living in the next life. We're not accustomed to having someone communicate within our Minds.

We've been thinking, remembering, daydreaming, and talking to ourselves in the privacy of our Minds since we were children. Now, having someone else come in and start thinking and talking in that space in our Minds is a very different experience. To be able to connect and communicate, we must learn new ways of speaking and listening. That takes time and patience. It's like learning a new language. We can't learn a new language by flying into a country, stepping off a plane, and spending a half hour with native speakers. We'll just be bewildered by what we hear. In the same way, we mustn't expect that we'll learn this new language of Mind-to-Mind communication in one session. We must give it time. We're about to step off the plane into a new realm, and there we'll receive thinking, images, sentiments, memories, and messages that are coming from deep inside us where we are one with the person with whom we're communicating. We will be thinking, reminiscing, and viewing together. That's going to feel like our accustomed thinking, remembering, and talking to ourselves, but it's not coming from us.

To learn Mind-to-Mind communication, we must learn how to allow the new communication to come to us, we must learn to accept what comes, and we must be patient. We can learn how to communicate.

When we receive a message from someone on earth, that person makes word sounds by vibrating the air. The sound waves travel through the air, enter your ear, and eventually get to your Mind. The Mind interprets the vibrations as words and assembles a message from the words. The words drop off and the message remains as a whole, integrated memory.

When we get the vibrations from someone speaking on the earth realm, males generally have lower voices and females higher. Mom sounds different from Aunt Rose, even though she's Aunt Rose's sister. The vibrations are different because each person has different vocal cords, mouth shape, nasal cavities, and the rest of the vocal mechanism.

However, when we get the communications from our loved ones, guides, Higher Selves, and Souls, they come Mind to Mind, so there are no sounds and there are *usually* no words (although sometimes words come to mind). We just receive the messages. These messages have the qualities of memories or daydreaming, not the experiences of seeing, hearing, and feeling we're accustomed to when we communicate with someone in the physical world. The thoughts from them come to us as our thoughts do. We may then create words from the messages using our inner voice. That makes it difficult at first to realize the difference between our thinking or imagination and their messages—it's the same inner voice we've thought with since we were children. We must get past feeling like their messages should come in the voices they used on the earth realm. They usually don't. They usually come without words at all. They come in fully formed messages in the Mind.

We do have memories of their speaking when they were using a body. Our memories carry the exact voice, as though they were speaking through a microphone. When they speak to us Mind to Mind, they are not using that voice. They're using no voice. They are conveying messages, not speaking using the voice they had.

So it's a very normal part of learning how to communicate to go through having to get over the mistaken notion that what's coming into our minds is "just imagination." That will happen when we experience having images, thoughts, feelings, bodily sensations, and messages come to us that we just couldn't originate. The more we experience that, the more confident we become that the messages are coming from them, and the messages flow more smoothly. We must be patient. Learning Mind-to-Mind communication is like learning to speak a new language. But we will learn it if we just trust and allow the unfoldment to teach us.

Having said that, experiencers occasionally report that they hear clear words spoken in their minds, with the sound of the voice the person in the life after this life used on the earth realm. That may happen for you also, because the person is projecting to your Mind their voice. However, that isn't the usual way of communicating that those on the other side use.

All the Connections Are Positive Experiences

All of the experiences we have with loved ones are positive. They are always filled with love and a concern for the person living on the earth realm. If we ever have an experience or feeling that is negative, such as feeling the person on the other side shunned us or told us something disturbing or anything else negative, **that wasn't from them**. That unfoldment has come from fears and negative emotions we all have while on the earth realm that have risen in our Mind. Push them aside and say, "That's not from (your loved one). I put that in the trash." Think of putting that in a trash can. Then go back to your communication. Receiving negative feelings or messages is very unlikely to happen. Your communications will always be positive.

Although the approach to us is positive, our loved ones may feel negative emotions about what happened to them on earth, or about our separation. Our loved ones may be very sad at not being in the physical world with us or may be frustrated that something is happening in the family or may even be angry at some injustice. The person has the same personality, loves, fears, intolerances, sentiments, humor, and all the rest of what makes them an individual, just as had on earth. And so, we might see them come to us crying over something or frustrated and even angry, but the negative emotions will be from situations, not individuals. Their approach to us is full of love and concern. They have grown out of much of the pettiness they may have felt while in the body. The transition from the earth realm is a life-changing event! It results in changed sentiments.

The Experiences You May Have

In your communications with people living in the life after this life, you may have the following experiences.

A Sense of Presence

You may have a sense of presence. You will just know that person you want to connect with is there. It's as real as the senses of seeing and hearing. So when you're getting the Mind-to-Mind communication, you'll have a very real sense of their presence. You won't see anything and won't "hear" with your ears. But the knowledge or sense that they're with you is a very reliable validation you're connected.

Some people report having chills or tingling or other such physical sensation when a love one is near. You can get to know those sensations as the signal you loved one is present and anxious to communicate.

Conversations

You will have conversations with your loved one. The more you become accustomed to this Mind-to-Mind communication, the more easily the conversations will flow. They are very fast. You have no time to doubt or wonder or judge what is coming. There is no hesitation.

Colors

We have been told by those on the other side that when we see colors sweeping through our consciousness during the experience, the colors are them communicating with us. A psychotherapist had client in a Repair & Reattachment Grief Therapy session describe what his loved one on the other side told her about colors.

While I was connecting to her and seeing her, she told me something very interesting. She said the colors experiencers see when they are inside are actually the loved one in spirit. They are showing the person here what they can do, how they are now as spirit. They don't wait to show up as the human face or body we are expecting. When the colors come, it is the loved one already there.[278]

When they send an image or appear in a dream, they send an image that is their projection, rather like bringing an image into their Mind that we then have come to our Mind. We're thinking together. We aren't seeing them as they are now unless they decide to project that image to us. Some have had to project the image of what they looked like in a picture because they can't recall what they looked like when in Earth School. As a result, you may have the image appear as the young, vibrant person they are now, or you may see an image as they were when you last saw them when they were healthy. You may see one, then the other. They likely will be wearing what they wore in Earth School so they look familiar to you, not the robes most wear now in the life after this life. They are controlling the image by projecting it to our Minds.

Images and Scenes

Our loved ones project images and scenes to us. They may seem irrelevant at the time, as though they were just passing fantasies. When you allow free unfoldment, you may access a variety of images and scenes. They come Mind to Mind, bypassing the eyes, ears, skin, and brain. The result is the same sights in the Mind you might have with your eyes, but since the body limitations aren't there, what comes is fluid, easily changed, and not limited to mundane physical realities. They may seem to jump around or be in fragments. That's because in our Minds, loved ones, guides, Higher Selves, and Souls can take us from scene to scene easily and immediately to get messages to us, so they take advantage of that unrestricted ability.

They often give participants experiences instead of words. Instead of telling the participant something, they guide the person into experiencing it. This is an illustration from the journal someone wrote about her Self-Guided Afterlife Connection experience when she asked for a message from her husband.

> I asked Ben if he had any messages for me, and just because I asked, he said "come on." We jumped into a golf cart lol and meandered off. The golf course we started on became more like a safari. We got to a very tall and thin mountain, with people on either slope slogging away, getting to the top. Ben was laughing and said "I'll show you something." He went to a secret door in the bottom of the mountain, and it was an elevator! We both got in it, and were quickly at the top. "Sometimes people make it so hard for themselves" he said. The understanding I got from that, was that it was referring to our efforts to "get to" the other side and communicate. My medium friend is always telling me I'm trying too hard, thinking too much.[279]

This person could have received a Mind-to-Mind message: "Well, you're trying too hard and thinking too much." Instead, this person was given the experience that allowed her to discover the truth that she was trying too hard to make the communication happen; she should just take the elevator and let it take her to where she wants to go. The teaching often happens in experiences and senses of messages, not in words.

The person in spirit is in charge of the images, scenes, and messages. Our role is to allow them to unfold naturally, even if they seem irrelevant.

Sensations of Being Touched, Hugged, and Kissed

Our body experiences include sensations of being touched, but the sensations are entirely in the Mind, just as pain and pleasure are in the Mind, not in a body that is apart from the Mind. As a result, people describe being touched, caressed, hugged, and even kissed during afterlife communications, especially during dreams, Induced After-Death Communications, Repair & Reattachment Grief Therapy, and Self-Guided Afterlife Connections. The experiences are as real as physically being touched. They are conveyed Mind to Mind.

We Must Have No Expectations

Successful connections require patience and time. We must not go into our first experiences expecting a connection. If we anticipate a connection, that will block the flow of free unfoldment that eventually will result in the connection. We must be willing for the entire session to contain impressions, images, and experiences that seem to have no meaning. We must allow the communications to come in their own time, in their own way. When we're getting images or impressions that aren't meaningful, we should not think "But where is she? I want to connect and she's not here!" That will shut down the free unfolding and block the connection. The meaningless experiences are part of the process.

We also must not "project" or "imagine" things in an effort to stimulate them. Imagining them running to us or in some scene blocks them from being able to bring to us what they have in Mind. It is very important for us to realize that our loved one or guide has experiences or a message to give us. They are waiting for us to relax and give up control so they can give us what they have planned. If we keep control or intend to have something happen or expect to have a connection as we envision it, we block the image or message they have waiting for us. We can't *make* it come. We must *allow* it to come. We must give up control, no matter how much we want a connection.

We Must Learn to Acknowledge and Process the Natural Unfoldment

Some of what comes into the Mind comes without our intention. Unintended images, thoughts, feelings, bodily sensations, and messages come in deep-sleep dreams, hypnogogic dreaming when half awake, inspirations or flashes of insight, notions, and inspirations. They unfold without our intention to have them come. This entry into our Minds is called "free unfoldment." We don't control free unfoldment. Our language has a number of words or phrases to describe them coming to us because they're so common. We might describe them coming to us by saying "It just came to me," "I suddenly realized," "I had a flash of inspiration," or "a light bulb went on."

We have these freely unfolding images, thoughts, feelings, bodily sensations, and messages all the time, so we believe they're coming from inside our Minds, privately. We call them "my imagination." We have words for the belief we created these unusual insights: "I thought it up," "I imagined it," or "I dreamed it up." But neuroscience has no explanation for how something that wasn't in our memory or experience could suddenly come to us. The reason it can't be explained is that these unusual insights don't come from us. They come from some source outside of our Minds.

The sources of these unusual images, thoughts, or messages are our loved ones, guides, Souls, Higher Selves, Soul, and people interested in helping us. They all communicate with us regularly, throughout the day.

However, as a culture we have lost the ability to acknowledge and process the communication we're receiving. It registers at the subconscious level but doesn't rise into awareness, so we miss much of what is given to us. It's easier to have the communication enter awareness when we're being creative because we want these inspirations that we call "my imagination." However, in the rest or our lives we may reject the natural unfoldments from the subconscious, regarding them as irrational and unreliable. "It was *just* my imagination," we say.

We are taught by our society not to regard the messages as real or valid, so we don't listen to them. We thus miss many messages from our loved ones, guides, Souls, and Higher Selves. Jose Silva, the originator of the Silva method, wrote about our blindness and deafness to the intuition.

> Somewhere along the path of evolution, humankind made a wrong turn. We lost our way and became separated from our source. We became hypnotized by the physical world. Our senses now dominate our lives. For most of us, there is nothing else except the physical world. It is a world of bodily pain, bodily pleasure, bodily comfort. It is a world of physical skills, of physical sight, sounds, smells, and tastes. Our preoccupation with the physical world has led to education that is materially oriented. Each generation has become more and more of this physical world—and less and less respectful of what cannot be seen but only intuited, imagined, or visualized.[280]

You Must Be Open and Positive

Open yourself to whatever comes. That will help you become more attuned to the natural unfoldment that comes from your guides, helpers, Soul, and loved ones in the life after this life. Something may come to you: a sense of presence, a feeling of warmth and love, a memory, or a song. Allow whatever comes to come. Don't try to make something happen or change what comes to you. The experiences are like soap bubbles floating past you. If you reach out to draw one closer, as soon as you touch it, the bubble will pop. That is what will happen to your naturally unfolding experiences if you try to make them become something you want or expect.

Our loved ones, guides, helpers, and Souls are in charge of the experiences. They decide what to give us, and they develop what comes. They create the experiences from whatever is in our minds that's coming up naturally. If we judge, try to change, or otherwise do something with them, we're disturbing their effort to create messages and scenes for us. Then they have to start over. It's very important that we have the confidence that they're in charge and whatever comes to us is going to turn out to be what we need, even if to us it seems trivial, silly, or strange.

Don't reject anything that comes. If you're communicating and suddenly think of the seashore, don't reject that because you saw a picture of a seashore just before trying to make the connection. Stay with whatever comes. If you have the image of Mom or message from Mom and you really wanted to connect with Dad, don't stop the connection. Allow it to unfold. Often the person we want to communicate with intentionally steps aside to allow someone else to come through. The person you want may be next.

Connections may come in subtle feelings, senses, changes in your body, and a host of other things that are not pronounced or strong. Allow those feelings to unfold. Over time, with repeated sessions, your connection likely will become stronger. If you have no sense of anything, stay with the procedure. This is just one session, and you may have many sessions before you have a connection. If you don't have a connection, it doesn't mean there's something wrong with you or the person on the other side doesn't want to come to you. It just means that the conditions aren't right. You likely will need more sessions to let your connection mature.

Let the Doubt Flow Past

It's natural and normal to have occasional doubts about whether the unfoldment is from your loved one. Our culture is so spiritually backward that we were reared to doubt the reality of our eternal lives, even though the religions teach about eternal life. We all continue to second guess what we're getting from someone living in the life after this life. Just remember that unfoldment isn't coming from you. If you were trying to create the communication, you'd have to think about the content, then think about the words your loved one would use, then decide if they're the right ones, then change the wording; it would be like writing a novel. It would take you hours to get a few sentences together.

The unfoldments flow just like a conversation because they are a real conversation. You'll learn that the messages couldn't be coming from you. That will become more obvious to you over time. But don't feel you're not doing well because of the doubts. They're natural and normal.

How to Have an Afterlife Connection

Anyone can have an afterlife connection with a loved one. It takes relaxing into the state of mind to allow the connection to happen and being hyper attentive to what comes, accepting everything without judgment. Follow this procedure.

Set aside 15 to 30 minutes of time when you are in a quiet area without interruptions. Bring no cell phones to the area. Tell your family or others living with you that you are not to be disturbed. Wear comfortable clothing, preferably without belts or other restrictions. A jogging suit is ideal. Sit in a comfortable chair or recliner. Lying down is not good for most people because there's a good chance you will fall asleep.

Have in mind the person or pet who lives in the life after this life. The person or pet must be significant for you. It shouldn't be someone you know of but don't have a relationship with, such as an actor or historical figure. You may be grieving for this person or pet, or you may have someone in mind you aren't grieving for but have a close relationship with.

Follow this procedure.

1. Begin with a prayer of protection such as "During this time of communication, surround and fill me, the room I am in, and all in this house with a white light of love and divine protection."

2. Close your eyes and relax. Be aware of your breathing for a few minutes.

3. Then start from your head and think about relaxing your muscles in groups going down to your feet. Relax your head, jaw, neck, shoulders, arms, torso, thighs, calves, and feet, in that order, taking time with each. Stay aware of your breathing.

4. After you feel you are totally relaxed, invite your loved one to come to communicate with you. Be hyper-aware of everything that happens. Assume your loved one is there.

5. If you just see blackness, you're not being attentive enough. Within what seems to be blackness search for anything you might see. It will be there.

6. When you have a sense of presence, speak in your mind or audibly about your love for that person.

7. The first notion or thought that comes into your mind is the response. Don't judge it or analyze it. Your communication will be very fast. Keep the dialogue going without pauses and with only the content of the communication.

8. Carry on the communication as long as you want. We normally suggest you allow the person in spirit to decide when to stop. As you stay in the communication, you'll find it becoming more natural and you'll lose track of where you are.

The Afterlife Research and Education Institute has developed a training program that is free online to teach you how to come into the state of mind in which you can have an afterlife connection. You can learn about it at www.earthschoolanswers.org/selfguided/.

Coffee Time with Phil G.

Medium Phil G., author of *Recognise the Signs of Afterlife Contact*, developed a video in which he explains clearly and simply how to have an afterlife connection by meeting with the person in spirit over coffee. You can view the video at www.earthschoolanswers.com/phil/.

Phil G. suggests you get two coffee cups (or two glasses with a beverage) and sit at a table. Place one cup on the table before an empty chair and one before you. You're going to have a casual conversation with your loved one. Invite your loved one to come and sit. Then start a conversation. You might ask a question like "How are you?" The first notion that comes to you is a response. Don't judge it. Don't wonder if that's them. Keep the conversation going. It will happen very quickly because you'll get the responses or answers entirely, without a string of words. Their response will come to you whole, in an instant.

Don't be disappointed if you are clumsy at first. Try this eight or ten times on different days. You will find yourself easing into it more comfortably each time. You'll also find you accept the responses more easily and quickly.

If you get something that is negative or harsh or judgmental, that's your own Mind filling in, as Minds always do. Just know that's not them. Stay with the dialogue. After a while, your Mind won't be able to intrude because you're having such an easy, loving dialogue.

Automatic or Inspired Writing

One very good way of learning to keep the flow of the dialogue going is through automatic writing, also called inspired writing. Have a sheaf of a dozen blank pieces of paper and a pen on a table or clipboard. Relax your mind to shut out the physical world following the procedure explained in "How to Have Afterlife Connections" above. Then invite your loved one to communicate with you. Ask a question. As you ask the question, scribble it on the top sheet of paper.

Don't worry about legibility. Don't look at the writing. You might do this with your eyes closed. After you've scribbled the statement or question, keep scribbling the first words that come to mind immediately, without a break. You may receive a thought instead of words. Scribble the thought in words. Then scribble your response. Don't worry about penmanship. And don't stop scribbling. If you stop to wait for a response, you've already missed it. The response came either immediately after you scribbled your question or statement, while you were scribbling your question or statement, or even before you scribbled your question or statement. Your loved one is responding to the question in your Mind, not what you scribble, so they know and respond to the question before you write it.

Do this regularly and you will find you have less and less need to write all the words coming to you. You'll get the words in whole blocks of thought so quickly you can't write down words. Be patient and allow the weeks and months it may take for this fluency to happen.

14

We Graduate from Earth School

> Death is not extinguishing the light ~ it is only putting out the lamp because the dawn has come.
>
> ~ *Rabindranath Tagore*

At some point in our Earth School experience, it comes time to graduate. This chapter explains what happens at graduation.

Why Is There a Graduation Transition from Earth School?

Everything in Earth School has a reason for it. This is the world of causes and effects. We need light, so there is a sun. We need warmth, so the sun warms us. We need to maintain the body, so we eat and drink. We tire and need rest, so we have sleep. These seem necessary for life, but in the life after this life, there is no sun, only ambient light. There is no need for warmth; the temperature is always pleasant. Bodies don't require nourishment, so there is no need to eat or drink. People don't sleep unless they want to, although people go into a restful period when they want to.

Earth School is created to have what we need to love, learn, and enjoy experiences. A necessary part of the creation is to have causes and effects, even though they are relevant only to Earth School.

There are specific causes and effects that pertain to our bodies. We are born as an explanation for how our body enters Earth School. We mature by growing physically and psychologically. If we reach old age, our bodies deteriorate. We know these causes and effects well; they give us stability in life.

One of these cause-and-effect sequences is when the person exits Earth School. We must graduate by having the body cease to function to give a reason for our no longer engaging in Earth School experiences. We have finished our lessons and are ready to graduate, so we drop off the body as we would drop off an old, tattered coat that is no longer important to us. Unfortunately, the exit leaves people still in Earth School in grief because the familiar body and effortless communication are no longer present.

Transitioning is just part of the story. It's a natural, normal ending to our stay in Earth School and return home. We're on to the next exciting page in this engrossing drama of our lives.

The Race Is Run. The Reward Is Earned.

When someone exits Earth School, it is because the purpose of the Earth School experience has been achieved to the level it could be. The exception is suicides and victims of murder. For all others, several potential exit points were decided in the pre-birth planning. All the events were planned to learn life lessons, help others learn life lessons, and help humanity grow. The person's Higher Self, Soul, and guides planned the exit point for the time when the person most likely would achieve all of the objectives of the individual's period in Earth School.

The reward is in the life after this life. Riley Heagerty's home circle received this message from those living in the life after this life.

> It is so difficult to explain to you the conditions over here. I am where I would most wish to be, that is, with my loved ones, where I can keep in close touch with you all on the earth realm. … [We don't have food] in your sense, but much nicer. Such lovely essences and wonderful fruits and other things besides, which you don't have on earth. Much awaits you which will very much surprise you, all beautiful and high, and so sweet

and sunny. Life was a preparation for this sphere. Without that training I could not have been able to enter this glorious, wonderful world. The earth is where we learn our lessons, and this world is our great reward, our true and real home and life— the sunshine after the rain.[281]

The Transition Is Just a Change in Focus

It is just like opening a door and coming into the sunshine.[282]

~ Silver Birch

It may seem that something has ceased to exist at the transition, but the person simply is changing attunement to another reality in the Mind of the Universal Intelligence. It is much like our change of focus from computing our taxes to being interrupted by the phone ringing and talking with a close friend. When we're doing our taxes, we don't have our friend in mind at all. When we're talking to our friend, we don't have the taxes in mind at all. We have just changed focus.

During our lifetimes, we are focusing on having experiences with everyone else in our Earth School lives. It has only been a focus, however, not a location in space or time within a world that exists apart from the Universal Intelligence. At the transition, we simply change focus to another set of experiences with the people we love and others.

The collection of intelligences known as "Abraham," speaking through channel Esther Hicks, explains what happens at the transition: "You will withdraw your attention from this time/space reality and you'll reemerge in the nonphysical."[283]

Does the Person's Soul Plan the Exit Point?

There is a consensus based on contacts from people who have gone on to the next stage of life that the Soul plans more than one potential exit point before enrolling in Earth School. Loved ones left in Earth School need never feel there should have been something they could have done to stop the transition. When the appointed time comes, the transition will occur regardless of what measures are taken.

The exit point is chosen by the Soul and guides is at a time based on the person's progress in achieving their life goals. There is also evidence that the exit point can be changed if the Soul and guides feel something must be learned before the exit happens. There are verified accounts of people asking for additional time in Earth School because of a task or event coming up and being granted the stay. A boy transitioning from leukemia said that God spoke to him and he asked God to allow him to live another year so he could explain his death to his three-year-old brother. Amazingly, against medical odds, the boy lived one more year.[284]

There are also many verified accounts of people not wanting to transition with certain others in the room or anyone in the room. They pass quietly when someone leaves or in the middle of the night when no one is with them. Others hold onto life until they hear from loved ones that it's okay to pass.

Is Suicide in the Person's Plan?

We understand from the Masters of Light, the team working with AREI's physical mediumship circle, that people do not plan a suicide. It is a free will choice that truncates the person's plan.[285]

Suzanne Giesemann received the same message from Sanaya, a collective of minds from a higher dimension that she channels. When she discussed the message with Susanne Wilson, an extremely talented medium who often works with Suzanne, Susanne responded that she had the same messages about suicide: "It is not planned, but it exists in a higher potential for souls who take on tougher life lessons." Susanne then added, "Those who successfully take their life may have had an exit point right around there anyway, and if they didn't have an exit point, then their guardian angel would have stepped in."[286] If their guardian angel had stepped in, the result would have been that the attempt didn't succeed because medics arrived soon enough, or the attempt didn't work, or some other circumstance created by the guardian angel saved the person from making the transition.

People who end their life are met with great empathy, love, and concern by loved ones who are living in the next stage of life. There is no judgment or condemnation. However, sorrow that the person chose to leave Earth School early is felt by loved ones already in the life after this life as well as loved ones still in Earth School.

When someone ends their life, the life plans of the others involved with the person may be affected. In that case, their Souls and guides work to change the circumstances in the Earth School environment to bring the others back into alignment with their pre-birth plans.

How Do People Stop Fearing the Transition?

People needlessly fear the transition from Earth School out of ignorance. We do not fear moving from one country to continue our lives in another country. Before modern communication devices, people moving to another country would not hear from each other for years if at all. In the nineteenth century, sailors would leave their families on merchant ships and be gone for two or three years. There was sadness, homesickness, and missing loved ones, but not grief and despondence.

People lose their fear of transition from Earth School when they understand the truth that our loved ones are just moving to another country by changing focus. They are not "lost." They are very much alive, available to communicate, and looking forward to the reunion in a few short years when everyone is in the same realm.

Perhaps the greatest impact of a near-death experience is that the experiencer no longer fears the transition. Having glimpsed what life is like after this life, NDE experiencers are looking forward to their lives after the transition. The conviction that we live after leaving this life is the antidote to the fear of death.

What If We Can't Make It to a Loved One's Funeral?

The person memorialized in the funeral knows our every thought and feeling. We don't have to be physically at a funeral to let the person know we love them. Our thoughts and feelings are completely known to the person. Being at a funeral matters to people living in Earth School, but not to the person who graduates. Our love is all that person wants, and by wishing we could be at the funeral and feeling our feelings toward that person, we have given them the greatest expression of love we could give.

15

The Lead-Up to the Transition

Every person has unique experiences in the transition from Earth School that suit the individual. However, there are general occurrences leading up to the transition and during the transition that are similar. This chapter explains what we know about the lead-up to the transition. Much of the information in this chapter and the next comes from people living on this side of life because it is primarily from witnesses just before and during the transition. The next chapters then provide information about the periods after the transition provided exclusively by people now living in the life after this life.

Do People Have a Feeling They Are about to Transition?

The transition is in the plan for the person's life. If the transition is sudden, the person may have portents of the change. In one example, Suzanne Giesemann describes a young man named Wolf who, well before his sudden transition, drew pictures of where he would transition and the mode of transition by a lightning strike.[287] You can hear Suzanne describing a young man's premonitions of his transition and the remarkable story of Wolf's startling message at www.earthschoolanswers.com/wolf/.

The "Call" to Loved Ones

When the transition is expected, as at the end of protracted illness, there is a "call" to loved ones to come in the period leading up to the transition and at the time of the transition. Those in the life after this life answer the call and are with the person in the days before the transition and are there to help at the moment of transition.

In the case of a sudden transition, there is no time for the call, so loved ones are not immediately with the person. However, there are always "deliverers" who come to help the person make the adjustment.

Healers from the Other Side Revitalize the Spirit Energy to Help During the Lead-Up to the Transition

When the end of the Earth School experience is near, the Universal Intelligence facilitates movement into the next realm to aid us in the transition and revitalize our spirit energy while the body is failing. During this period, "counselors" from the next life and the spirits or Souls of people still on earth help the person make the adjustment. Timothy Gray, speaking from spirit through medium August Goforth, explains what happened during the period leading up to his transition.

> I spent a great deal of time in bed during my final days of illness on the earth, most of it sleeping from exhaustion and heavy medication. I was often very depressed, but eventually I found some peace in just letting any kind of consciousness take over. I wasn't fully aware that I sometimes left my body, or that special helpers would come and take me to places on an astral plane where I could rest even more deeply—was told about this later. There were many healers who would revitalize my spirit energy, while explaining what was happening and what to expect as my earth life neared its natural conclusion. …
>
> When out of my body I met with the spirits of my parents, who were still earth-embodied and caring for me in their home, as well as with the spirit of my earthly doctor. During these out-of-body periods we were counseled about various aspects and on

probable courses of action. I don't remember who the counselors were and haven't seen them since, but my impression is that they were just doing a job and then moved on to work with others in similar conditions. We all gathered together while our bodies were asleep—the counselors, my parents, the earthly doctor, and myself. We often met when daydreaming, which was frequent, as we were all exhausted from the ordeal. For me it felt like trying to get a stubborn zipper on a coat unstuck— meaning that my body was trying to die.[288]

Pre-death and Deathbed Visions in the Period before Death

For people who transition over time from old age or illness, guides, helpers, and loved ones who have preceded the person make preparations in the hours and days before the transition. The loved ones who have gone on before help the transitioning person make the transition by appearing to the person in dreams or visions.

One study found 63.3 percent of the 60 terminally ill patients in the study reported dreams and visions of loved ones. Of those, 79.9 percent recalled the visions vividly. The types of visions included deceased relatives or friends (78.9 percent), living friends and relatives (52.6 percent), and people the individual did not recognize (21 percent).[289]

Deathbed visions occur across cultures, tend to be of short duration, and in 62 percent of cases reported in a study by Otis and Haraldsson, the patient transitioned within 24 hours of reporting or showing signs of such visions.[290] Some people not predicted to transition have had the deathbed vision experiences followed shortly by the transition.[291]

The visions come at various times and under various conditions. A study found that 21 percent of the transitioning people saw visions when they were asleep, 13.1 percent while awake, and 65.7 percent during both sleep and wakefulness.[292]

You can watch a video of Dr. Christopher Kerr, medical director for Hospice Buffalo, describing the dreams transitioning people experience at www.earthschoolanswers.com/dreams/.

Family members and hospital personnel commonly report that a transitioning person stares at a corner of the room and points or calls the name of a deceased loved one, often when the person was previously weak or even comatose. Transitioning people have described seeing or hearing people not physically present, usually who already transitioned to the next stage of life, at their bedside. The visions are real enough that the person becomes calm and even delighted. The visions result in a change of attitude.

Dr. Karlis Osis and Dr. Earlendur Haraldsson, leading scholars in the study of pre-death and deathbed visions, describe a man on his deathbed who would

> ... look into the distance; these things would appear to him and seemed real to him. He would look up to a wall, eyes and face would brighten up as if he saw a person. He'd speak of the light, brightness, saw people who seemed real to him. He would say, "Hello," and "There's my mother." After it was over he closed his eyes and seemed very peaceful. He gestured with outstretched hands. Before the hallucination he was very ill and nauseous; afterwards he was serene and peaceful.[293]

Mothers living in the next stage of life most often appear, although other comforting figures may appear, including pets.[294] More than one person or a group may be present. The transitioning person becomes preoccupied with the visions and may begin speaking with the other-worldly visitors. A bright light is common in the deathbed experiences, often with figures coming out of the light.[295]

Patients typically report or show signs of being peaceful, loved, or joyful. They become more accepting of their impending deaths and describe a renewed connection with the loved one in the vision. The patients often report that the visitors convey the message that they have arrived to go with the patient on a journey or into another mode of existence.[296] In the same study, 21 percent of patients had visions of making preparations or going on a journey.[297]

Osis and Haraldsson describe an Indian woman on her deathbed who said her mother was coming to take her to the "land of God."

She kept uttering words. I listened because the relatives thought she wanted to tell me something. She told me her mother, who had died many years before, had come, calling her to accompany her to the land of God. When I told this to her relatives, they asked me to tell her not to go. They took this as a bad omen: that she was dying and nothing could be done. The patient said she was going and seemed happy about it. "I am going; Mother is calling me. I am going to the land of God." These were her last words. Before this experience, the patient had expected to recover.[298]

The other-worldly visitors in the visions do not threaten or scare the patients, but some have no understanding of the significance of their dreams, so they see them as distressing. However, when they discuss the visions with those present, 94.7 percent said they felt much better about the nature of the visions.[299]

Some transitioning people have deathbed visions of people they didn't know had passed away. Doctor Mynatt Savage, a Unitarian clergyman, wrote that two close friends, Jenny and Bessie, ages eight and nine, both had diphtheria. Jennie transitioned on Wednesday, but no one told Bessie about Jennie's death because her family felt it might stress her and impede her recovery. On Saturday, Bessie began telling her parents which of her brothers, sisters, and playmates should receive her belongings. She pointed out certain things she was very fond of that were to go to Jenny, so it was clear she had not found out from anyone that Jenny had transitioned at that point in time. However, a little later, as she approached death, she described seeing deceased grandparents and others gathered around her bed. Then she turned to her father with her face and voice both expressing great surprise. She said to him, "Why Papa, why didn't you tell me that Jennie had gone? Why didn't you tell me of it?" Jennie had come to Bessie to comfort her during her transition.[300]

Children are truth-tellers because of their youthful naiveté, so when they experience such visions, they describe them matter-of-factly. In *Closer to the Light*, Dr. Melvin Morse describes children's deathbed visions, explaining that they are astonishing scientific proof of the validity of the experiences at the point of death.[301]

Elisabeth Kübler-Ross wrote that children nearing death acquire the ability to leave the physical body and experience the presence of people they refer to as "playmates." She wrote, "The churches have called them Guardian Angels. Most researchers would call them guides." They have come to ease the child into the life after this life.[302]

Mike Tymn, in his book *The Afterlife Revealed*, describes what a senior coordinator of bereavement services at a hospice said to him about the visitors who come just prior to a person's transition:

> "They're so common I don't think much about them anymore," said Ginny Chapelear, senior coordinator of bereavement services at the Tidwell Hospice in Sarasota , Florida, when I asked her if deathbed visions and visitations (DBVs) are common among hospice patients. "We call them the 'gathering of spirits.'"[303]

Many people at the point of their transition see visions of the realm into which they are going. This is an account of Steve Jobs' last words:

> Before embarking, he'd looked at his sister Patty, then for a long time at his children, then at his life's partner, Laurene, and then over their shoulders past them.

> Steve's final words were: "Oh wow. Oh wow. Oh wow."[304]

In the biography of Thomas Edison, *Edison: Inventing the Century*, America's greatest inventor is reported to have emerged from a coma hours before his death and said, "It is very beautiful over there."[305]

The visions may be of religious figures, such as angels or other beings that are part of the person's religious tradition. In one of the most dramatic of such visions, Osis and Haraldsson describe a remarkable event a transitioning patient had with a vision of angels.

> He was unsedated, fully conscious and had a low temperature. He was a rather religious person and believed in life after death.

We expected him to die and he probably did too as he was asking us to pray for him. In the room where he was lying, there was a staircase leading to the second floor. Suddenly he exclaimed, "See the angels are coming down the stairs. The glass has fallen and broken." All of us in the room looked towards the staircase where a drinking glass had been placed on one of the steps. As we looked, we saw the glass break into a thousand pieces without any apparent cause. It did not fall; it simply exploded. The angels, of course, we did not see. A happy and peaceful expression came over the patient's face and the next moment he expired. Even after his death the serene, peaceful expression remained on his face.[306]

In one case a college educated woman in her 80s was transitioning from cardiac failure. She had the vision of a heavenly panorama.

She was an unusual patient, very alert and intellectual, keen sense of humor. She was a down-to-earth person. That morning she was listless, but her temperature and pulse were normal. She told me that the taxi driver had taken her to a beautiful garden where she saw beautiful, endless gardens, all kinds of flowers. She said that she had never seen anything like it, it was gorgeous. She did not want to return, but the taxi driver was impatient to get started. He took too long to get home, taking all the wrong streets. She would go back there any day— beautifully done garden. It sounded like a dream to me, but it seemed real to her. Four days later she died peacefully.[307]

In another experience, Osis and Haraldsson describe the visions of a woman in her fifties transitioning from cardiac disease.

She saw a beautiful garden with the gate. God was standing there and an angel was nearby. She insisted that God had appeared to her. She would get well if she stayed with me [the doctor]. She had just been transferred to my care. The vision gave her serenity and confidence in her recovery. She followed church doctrines, but wasn't a regular churchgoer.[308]

A registered nurse in her twenties was suffering from malignant hypertension that led to a stroke. She described what she saw that eliminated her fear of death.

She said she saw gates leading into a vast country, vast space. She felt utter peace, no fear, no worries. As the gates were opening she began to improve. Her speech, which had been affected, cleared up. The experience was very reassuring to her, completely eliminating her fear of death.[309]

Watch videos of hospice nurses describing incidents they witnessed with transitioning patients at www.earthschoolanswers.com/visions/.

View a video of Martha Atkins, death and dying educator and executive director at Contemplative Care for the Dying and founder of the Children's Bereavement Center of South Texas speaking about deathbed and near-death visions at www.earthschoolanswers.com/atkins/.

View a video of Dr. Christopher Kerr, CEO of the Center for Hospice & Palliative Care, speaking about deathbed and near-death visions at www.earthschoolanswers.com/kerr/.

Terminal Lucidity

Patients with severe psychiatric or neurological disorders who have not been lucid, perhaps for months, may suddenly regain their normal conscious self just before their transition and have lucid conversations with loved ones. The phenomenon is called "terminal lucidity." Their moods are elevated and they speak with vitality. In many cases, the brain has deteriorated so much that such an event is impossible.

In one study in the U.K., 70 percent of nurses had observed patients with dementia and confusion become completely lucid in the hours before death.[310]

Dr. Bruce Greyson, Professor of Psychiatric Medicine at the University of Virginia, describes 49 case studies of terminal lucidity, most of which occurred within a week of the person's transition, with 43 percent occurring on the final day of life. In an article in *The Journal of*

Nervous and Mental Disorders, Greyson and Michael Nahm describe 83 cases in which patients had brain abscesses, tumors, strokes, meningitis, Alzheimer's disease, dementia, schizophrenia, and mood disorders, all of which would preclude normal, lucid mental functioning. In spite of their conditions, the 83 patients experienced a brief, completely lucid recovery of consciousness just before their transition.[311]

Two remarkable, illustrative cases follow. Dr. Scott Haig, assistant clinical professor of orthopedic surgery at the Columbia University College of Physicians and Surgeons describes one of his patients named David whose lung cancer had spread to his brain. X-rays showed the metastasized tumors had destroyed virtually off of his brain tissue and replaced it with cancer cells. "David's head was literally stuffed with lung cancer," Dr. Haig wrote. In the days before his transition, he had lost all ability to speak or move. When Dr. Haig left the hospital one evening, David was close to transitioning. His family was with him. The next morning, the nurse in attendance told Dr. Haig what had happened the night before.

> He woke up, you know, doctor—just after you left—and said goodbye to them all. Like I'm talking to you right here. Like a miracle. He talked to them and patted them and smiled for about five minutes. Then he went out again, and he passed in the hour.[312]

In another case, a 42-year-old man had a tumor that had formed in his speech center. Over time, he became bedridden, blind in one eye, incontinent, increasingly incoherent in his speech, and bizarre in his behavior. He was unable to make sense of his surroundings. When his family touched him, he would slap at their hands as though slapping at an insect. He stopped sleeping and talked deliriously through the night. After continued deterioration for several weeks, he suddenly one night appeared calm and started speaking coherently. That night, he slept peacefully. The next morning, he remained coherent and talked with his wife about his imminent death for the first time. Later that day, he became immobile, lost his abilities to communicate, and two weeks later passed away.[313]

16

The Moment of the Transition

At the moment the earth body stops functioning, the person ceases to have body experiences. The person has not changed. The person's experiences are different. The transition is always painless. Those who have made the transition all remark how easy the transition is. For those who experience a catastrophic death, there may be a brief coma or period of unconsciousness during which the event takes place, or the person may suddenly be standing next to the lifeless body with no experience or recollection of the separation itself.[314] There is never any pain. There are accounts of people being taken away from an impending disaster and watching it happen from the safety of a lofty position. (See page 293). For those who have made the transition after a period of declining health, the individual is greeted by people in spirit as the transition occurs all fear or anxiety dissolves and a profound peace comes over the person.

Allan Kardec, the nom de plume of Hippolyte Léon Denizard Rivail, a French educator and author who originated the philosophy he called "Spiritism," wrote that he learned from mediums communicating with people in the next realm of life that the process of separation can be quick or can take some time. People who are materialistic and have no understanding of the survival of consciousness and have a fear of death inhibit their own separation so it takes longer.[315]

Monsignor Robert Hugh Benson, speaking from spirit through the medium Anthony Borgia, describes his own transition that gave him the impression that the transition is so seamless it seems this world and the next interpenetrate each other. He had no indication he had made the transition, except that, in a moment, the physical sensations of his illness left him and he experienced a feeling of peace.

> I have told you how, when I had reached a critical moment and I lay upon my final bed of earthly sickness, I at length felt an irresistible urge to rise up, and that I yielded to that urge easily and successfully. In this particular case the line of demarcation was very fine between the end of my earthly life and the beginning of my spirit life, because I was in full possession of my senses, fully conscious. The actual transition from one world to the other was in this respect imperceptible.

> But I can narrow things down still further by recalling that there came a moment when the physical sensations attendant upon my last illness left me abruptly, and in place of them a delightful feeling of bodily ease and peace of mind completely enveloped me. I felt that I wanted to breathe deeply, and I did so. The impulse to rise from my bed, and the passing of all physical sensations, mark the instant of my physical "death" and my birth into the world of spirit.

> But when this took place I was still in my own earthly bedroom, and therefore a part, at least, of the spirit world must interpenetrate the earth world.[316]

In another example of the ease with which the transition takes place, Private Thomas Dowding, a 37-year-old British soldier killed on the battlefield in World War I gave this description of his transition on the battlefield through the mediumship of Wellesley Tudor Pole.

> It was a fine evening. I had no special information of danger, until I heard the whiz of a shell. Then following an explosion, somewhere behind me, I crouched down involuntarily, but it

was too late. Something struck, hard, hard, hard, against my neck. Shall I ever lose the memory of that hardness? It is the only unpleasant incident that I can remember. I fell and as I did so, without passing through an apparent interval of unconsciousness, I found myself outside myself! You see I am telling my story simply; you will find it easier to understand. You will learn to know what a small incident this dying is.

Think of it! One moment I was alive, in the earthly sense, looking over a trench parapet, unalarmed, normal. Five seconds later I was standing outside my body, helping two of my pals to carry my body down the trench labyrinth toward the dressing station. They thought I was senseless but alive. I did not know whether I had jumped out of my body through shell shock, temporarily or forever. You see what a small thing is death, even the violent death of war! I seemed in a dream. I had dreamt that someone or something has knocked me down. Now I was dreaming that I was outside my body. Soon I should wake up and find myself in the traverse waiting to go on guard. ... It all happened so simply. Death for me was a simple experience— no horror, no long-drawn suffering, no conflict. It comes to many in the same way. ...

As in my case, thousands of soldiers pass over without knowing it. If there be a shock, it is not the shock of physical death. Shock comes later when comprehension dawns: "Where is my body? Surely I am not dead!" In my own case, I knew nothing more than I have already related, at the time. When I found that my two pals could carry my body without my help, I dropped behind. I just followed, in a curiously humble way. Humble? Yes, because I seemed so useless. We met a stretcher party. My body was hoisted onto the stretcher. I wondered when I should get back into it again. You see, I was so little "dead" that I imagined I was still physically alive. Think of it a moment before we pass on. I had been struck by a shell splinter. There was no pain. The life was knocked out of my body; again, I say, there was no pain. Then I found that the whole of myself—all, that is, that thinks and sees and feels and knows—was still alive and conscious! I had begun a new chapter of life. I will tell you what I felt like. It was as if I had been running hard until, hot and breathless, I had thrown my overcoat away. The coat was my body, and if I had not thrown it away I should have suffocated. I cannot describe the experience in a better way; there is nothing else to describe.[317]

There are many accounts of floating out of the body in the moments after the body is abandoned. Some of the descriptions note a snapping of what seem to be strings attaching the person's spirit to the body. This account is given by a physician in the life after this life communicated through a medium.

I could feel myself gradually raised from my body, and in a dreamy, half conscious state. It seemed as though I was not a united being—that I was separated into parts, and yet despite this there seemed to be an indissoluble connecting link. My spirit was free a short time after the organs of my physical body had entirely ceased to perform their functions. My spiritual form was then united into one, and I was raised a short distance above the body, standing over it by what power I was unable to tell. I could see those who were in the room around me and knew by what was going on that a considerable time must have elapsed since dissolution had taken place, and I presume I must have been for a time unconscious; and this I find is a common experience not however, universal."[318]

People in proximity of the body often describe phenomena in the room: a sudden light, at times blinding, a white, grey, or blue-white "soul mist," coming up from the body, a vaporous body shape with the features of the transitioning person, a silver or grey cord or many threads from the body connecting to the vaporous body shape that dissolve or snap, the vaporous body rising and disappearing into a corner of the room, and the vision of loved ones who have come to escort the person from the earth realm. Some report seeing a transfer of energy from the physical body to the new, separate body, called an etheric body, life-body, subtle body, vital body, astral body, or spirit body that is a duplicate of the physical body. The spirit seems to move toward the head and exit from the top of the head, although some have described witnessing some vaporous form exiting from the solar plexus.

These phenomena are described by Dr. R. B. Hout, a physician, who gave this account of his personal observations at the deathbed of his aunt.

> I suddenly became aware that there was much more in that room than the physical senses had been able previously to detect. For my attention was called, in some inexplicable way, to something immediately above the physical body, suspended in the atmosphere *about two feet above the bed.* At first I could distinguish nothing more than *a vague outline of a hazy, fog light substance.* There seemed to be only a mist held suspended, motionless. But as I looked, very gradually there grew into my sight a denser, more solid, condensation of this inexplicable vapor. Then I was astonished to see definite outlines present themselves, and soon I saw *this fog-like substance was assuming a human form.*

> Soon I knew that the body that I was seeing resembled that of the physical body of my aunt. … This astral body hung suspended horizontally a few feet above the physical counterpart: it was quiet, serene, and in repose. But the physical body was active in reflex movements and subconscious writhing of pain. I continually watched and … the spirit-body now seemed complete to my sight. I saw the features plainly. They were very similar to the physical face except that a glow of peace and vigor was expressed instead of age and pain. The eyes were closed as though in tranquil sleep, and a luminosity seemed to radiate from the spirit-body. …

> As I watched the suspended spirit-body, my attention was called, again intuitively, to a silver-like substance that was streaming from the head of the physical body to the head of the spirit double. Then I saw the connecting cord between the two bodies. As I watched, the thought, "the silver cord," kept

running through my mind. I knew, for the first time, the meaning of it. *This "silver cord" was the connecting link between the physical and spirit bodies, even as the umbilical cord unites the child to its mother. ...*

It was attached to each of the bodies at the occipital protuberance, immediately at the base of the skull. Just where it met the physical body had spread out, fanlike, and numerous little strands separated and attached separately to the skull-base. But other than at the attachments, the cord was round, being perhaps about an inch in diameter. The color was a translucent luminous silver radiance. The cord seemed alive with vibrant energy. I could see the pulsations of light stream along the course of it, from the direction of the physical body to the spirit double. ... With each pulsation the spirit-body became more alive and denser, whereas the physical body became quieter and more nearly lifeless. ...

My uncle, the deceased husband of my aunt, stood there beside the bed. Also her son. ... By this time the features were very distinct. The life was all in the astral body and the physical body had entirely stopped the restless moving, was entirely oblivious to all reflexes and death seemed imminent. The pulsations of the cord had stopped. ... I looked at the various strands of the cord as they spread out, fanlike, at the base of the skull. Each strand snapped and crawled back as would a taut wire if it was suddenly cut. ... The final severance was at hand. A twin process of death and birth was about to ensue. ... *The last connecting strand of the silver cord snapped and the spirit-body was free.*

The spirit-body, which had been supine before, now rose and stood erect behind the bed, where it paused momentarily before commencing its upward flight from the room. The closed eyes opened and a smile broke from the radiant features. *She gave a smile of farewell, then vanished from my sight.* The above phenomenon was witnessed by me as an entirely objective reality. These spirit-forms I saw with the aid of my physical eye.

… The whole of this event covered 12 hours. I watched, commented, and moved about during the occurrence.[319]

The Transitioning Person May See Long-Dead Loved Ones Coming to Take Them on a Trip

The deathbed visions described in the previous chapter continue during the transition itself. Transitioning people who have been bedridden often talk of going on a trip at the moment of their transition. Then, as they are in the transition experience, they say they see long-dead loved ones who have come to take them away. They have been called "deliverers."

The dying person is lying quietly, when suddenly, *in the very act of expiring,* he looks up—sometimes starts up in bed—and gazes on (what seems to be) vacancy, with an expression of astonishment, sometimes developing instantly into joy. … If the dying man were to see some utterly-unexpected but instantly-recognized vision … his face would not better reveal the fact. *The very instant this phenomenon occurs death is actually taking place.*[320]

A nurse named Joy Snell, with 20 years' experience caring for transitioning patients, described the same phenomenon.

I notice that often, just before the end, the dying would seem to recognize someone who was not of those at the bedside and was by the latter unseen. I have seen a woman who had been in a coma for hours suddenly open her eyes with a look of glad surprise, stretch forth her hands as though to grasp invisible hands outstretched towards her, and then with a sigh of relief, expire. … That at such moments as I have described the dying really see some spirit-form—I have never doubted. And the time came when it was revealed to me that they really do see.[321]

The Society for Psychical Research in London documented shared-death experiences in the late 1800s, calling them "death-bed visions" or "death-bed coincidences" based on observations by obstetrician Florence Elizabeth Barrett. This is an account of a woman's transition from William Barret's book, *Deathbed Visions*, published in 1926.

> Suddenly she looked eagerly towards one part of the room, a radiant smile illuminating her whole countenance. "Oh, lovely, lovely," she said. I asked, "What is lovely?" "What I see," she replied in low, intense tones. "What do you see?" "Lovely brightness—wonderful beings." Then—seeming to focus her attention more intently on one place for a moment—she exclaimed, almost with a kind of joyous cry, "Why it is father! Oh, he is so glad I am coming; he is so glad."[322]

Pain at the Transition

There is no pain during the transition. People who transition because of illness have no experience of the body's pain at the end, even though the people gathered around the deathbed see struggles or signs of pain. Frederic William Henry Myers, the well-known psychic researcher, spoke from the life after this life through medium Geraldine Cummins.

> The average man or woman when he or she is dying suffers no pain. They have become so dissevered already from the body that when the flesh seems to be in agony the actual soul merely feels very drowsy and has a sensation of drifting hither and thither, to and fro, like a bird resting on the wind.[323]

If the person becomes lucid, the individual's spirit has returned to the body for the lucid period. People may be experiencing going out of the body and back in through a series of experiences before the final transition.

People who transition because of a horrendous accident are spared the pain of the trauma that results in their transition, although they may experience the fear and trauma leading up to the accident, such as a plane crash. Laurel Parnell, an eye-movement desensitization and reprocessing (EMDR) psychotherapist, writes about the case of a client who received messages from the loved one for whom she was grieving during her EMDR therapy. The woman in spirit, who transitioned from a plane crash, described to Dr. Parnell's client that she experienced the plane's plummet toward the ground, but not the crash.[324]

People may describe being removed from the body before the traumatic incident that results in their transition and being taken to a vantage point at which they watch the event. Mike Tymn describes the account of a person now living in the life after this life communicating through South African trance medium Nina Merrington, explaining that he was spared the pain of a fatal auto accident and actually observed the event from outside of it.

> Mike Swain, who died in an auto accident, told his father Jasper Swain, a Pietermaritzburg, South Africa lawyer, that he left his body an instant before the cars actually impacted. Heather, his fiancée's young sister, was also killed in the accident. Mike told of being blinded by the glare of the sun reflecting off of the windscreen of the oncoming car. "All of a sudden, the radiance changes from silver to gold. I am being lifted up in the air, out through the top of the car. I grabbed little Heather's hand. She too is being lifted up out of the car." When they were about 30 feet above the car, they witnessed the collision below them and heard a noise like the snapping of steel banjo strings. They had suffered no pain.[325]

An Anglican nun named Frances Bakes, describing her death transition through medium Helen Greaves, explained that those who have made the transition do not recall any pain in the process.[326]

Mike Tymn describes the message from a man who had drowned: "I did not suffer. I was drowned and felt nothing.[327]

An airman who transitioned in World War II when his plane was hit communicated to his mother through a medium these insights about the lack of pain during the transitioning process.

> Even when death has been apparently less instantaneous, as in drowning, in hanging, in burning, etc., I have been told the same: they felt no struggle nor any pain. It would appear that when the summons has come, the "man" is not left in the body to wrestle for life but is emerging from it, leaving the struggle a

purely mechanical one. The struggle by the "man" takes place only when the period of death is to be warded off.[328]

Leslie Flint, the direct-voice medium in the twentieth century, had people living in the next life come through and speak using an ectoplasmic voice box that formed on his shoulder. We now have thousands of the recordings of these people speaking. A man living in the next life named Ted Butler came through describing his transition. He said that he was walking with his wife and saw a truck coming directly toward him. The next thing he remembered was seeing a group of people standing around looking at a body on the ground. He looked at the body and said, "The body looked just like me. Could have been my twin." It was him. However, he had no memory of the truck hitting him. He had been removed before the painful impact.[329]

You can listen to the recording of Ted Butler describing his transition at www.earthschoolanswers.com/butler/.

Suzanne Giesemann, the talented mental medium and channeler, received messages from a man in the process of transition, still in hospice. He said to her, "My physical body may appear to be suffering, but I'm fine." The person was not participating in the suffering the body, still alive, was experiencing.[330]

You can view Suzanne describing the fact that people do not suffer at the time of the transition at this link: www.earthschoolanswers.com/suzanne/.

We have no accounts from people living in the next life of suffering the pain of a sudden, accidental transition. The person goes on to the next life before the body dies.

People May Experience Glimpses of the Life after This Life as They Gradually Transition

Timothy Gray, quoted earlier speaking from spirit through medium August Goforth, explains what happened at the time of his transition. He describes glimpses of beautiful landscapes and the sound of music, as though a curtain were gradually opening.

It was soon realized and resolved by all of us, as informed and supported by our spirit counselors, that it was no longer necessary for me to remain embodied, and my body's sleep could begin to deepen enough so that I could be fully released. This decision was made from the greater reality of spirit, with support from experts there. It seemed as if my parents and doctors simply reached consensual understanding and acceptance in one instant while gathered round my bed the day before Christmas. I'm told that besides risen helpers, there were also a few people assisting who were still in their bodies on earth, but who did healing work with people like me while out of their bodies.

Sometimes I opened my eyes and found myself resting in an endless summer meadow, warmed by the sun and caressed by breezes which felt like hands gently touching me. Each time I awoke it was with a little more consciousness. It was as if curtains in the room were gradually opening up a little bit at a time, letting in more and more light. Often there was indescribable music that sounded from far away. Sometimes I seemed to be immersed within a pool of glowing lights. There were people whose chants took form in the air, manifesting as vines growing over a trellis or fountains tumbling over a path of iridescent stones. Several times I saw you sitting far off in the rain, and the rain was the sadness you felt, which surrounded you and made you feel lost and alone, and I felt your sorrow as my own. I began to feel strength returning and consciousness increasing. Nothing was in focus for what seemed a long time, and I just rested. I would have faint memories of sitting at the top of a hill, gazing over a field of blueish-white flowers that chimed softly as they moved with the breezes.[331]

Shared Deathbed Experiences

There are many accounts of people sharing the experience of transitioning with the person moving on to the life after this life. Raymond Moody, who coined the term "near-death experience" in his book *Life After Life*[332] in 1975, introduced the concept of shared-death experiences in his 2009 book *Glimpses of Eternity: An Investigation into Shared Death Experiences.*[333]

Dr. Moody described being at the bed of his transitioning mother with other family members waiting for his mother's transition. Dr. Moody said he saw their deceased father in the room, and all reported seeing an unusual light in the room, "like looking at light in a swimming pool at night," he wrote. "It was as though the fabric of the universe had torn and for just a moment we felt the energy of that place called heaven."[334]

View a video of Dr. Moody talking about shared-death experiences at www.earthschoolanswers.com/shared/.

Peter Fenwick, MD, and Elizabeth Fenwick, RN, who research end-of-life phenomena, have collected hundreds of shared-death experiences in the United Kingdom and Northern Europe.[335] They describe one account containing the lights common in these shared experiences. This is an account by a wife at her transitioning husband's bedside.

> Suddenly there was the most brilliant light shining from my husband's chest and as the light lifted upward there was the most beautiful music and singing voices, my own chest seemed filled with infinite joy and my heart felt as if it was lifting to join the light and music. Suddenly there was a hand on my shoulder and a nurse said, "I'm sorry love. He has just gone." I lost sight of the light and music. I felt so bereft at being left behind.[336]

The second from the Fenwicks' accounts is a description by a hospice chaplain.

> Sometimes I've seen a light, which is in a corner, like candle lights, it's a golden light. It's not electric lights and it's not one of the hospice lights. It just appears sometimes. It goes when they die. They take their last breath and everything settles down and the light goes out.[337]

A third account in the Fenwicks' research is from a pastoral caregiver in a hospice.

When her mother was dying this amazing light appeared in the room. The whole room was filled with this amazing light and her mother died.[338]

The Fenwicks describe a woman's experience as her brother was transitioning.

One woman described how, as her brother lay dying of cancer, those around him saw "odd tiny sparks of bright light" emanating from around the dying body. "Not many, just two or three very brief instances." She did not mention it to anyone but then her brother's wife mentioned seeing the same thing.[339]

Dr. Pim van Lommel, who has written extensively about near-death experiences, refers to the shared-death experience as an "empathetic NDE."[340] Dr. van Lommel describes a shared-death experience of a man whose loving partner, Anne, had been killed in a traffic accident. Her seven-year-old son was severely injured in the accident and was not expected to live. As the boy's transition neared, Anne's family gathered at the hospital to console each other. The man stood at the back of the room by a window. This is Dr. van Lommel's account of what happened.

The moment he died, when his EEG flatlined, I "saw" that his mother came to collect him. You must bear in mind that she'd died five days earlier. There was this incredibly beautiful reunion. And at one point they reached out for me and included me in their embrace. This was an indescribable, ecstatic reunion. Part of me left my body and accompanied them to the light. I know this must sound very strange indeed, but I was fully conscious with Anne and her son as they went to the light, just as I was fully conscious and in the room where all the relatives were incredibly sad because their nephew and grandson had just died. And I joined them. We were heading toward the light, but at a certain point it was clear that I had to return, so I fell back. I simply fell back into my body. It was such an overwhelming experience, I glowed with happiness, but then I suddenly realized that I had a big smile on my face amid all these people who'd just lost a child dear to them. I quickly covered my face with my hands because I didn't want to be disrespectful toward all these mourning and crying people in the room. And I never said a word about the experience. Talking about it seemed completely inappropriate at the time, and besides I didn't have the words to describe what had happened to me. I used to think that I knew what was what. But my worldview underwent a radical transformation.[341]

Melvin Morse, MD, describes a case in his book *Parting Visions* in which a soldier named Skala was cradling his friend on the battlefield as he lay transitioning. He found himself having a shared-death experience.

[Skala] felt himself being drawn up with his friend, above their bodies and then above the battlefield. Skala could look down and see himself holding his friend. Then he looked up and saw a bright light and felt himself going toward it with his friend. Then he stopped and returned to his body. He was uninjured except for a hearing loss that resulted from the artillery blast.[342]

In another shared-death experience, Jeff Olson was in a car accident in which his wife was killed instantly. He describes seeing her after she transitioned in a near-death experience. Jeff was transported to a hospital where a medical doctor named Dr. Jeff O'Driscoll had a shared-death experience in which he experienced communications from Jeff Olsen's deceased wife.[343] To view their descriptions, go to www.earthschoolanswers.com/jeff/.

Author David Sunfellow, founder of New Heaven New Earth, has a website with a marvelous, complete explanation of shared-death experiences. The website contains this summary of the phenomena people with the transitioning person experience during shared-death experiences:

- Mist at death
- Hearing beautiful music
- Change in the geometry of the room
- Strong upward pull on the body
- Shared out-of-body experience

- Seeing a mystical light
- Empathically co-living the life review
- Greeted by beings of light
- Encountering heavenly realms
- Boundary in the heavenly Realm[344]

Sunfellow's website explains that the shared-death experience offers the following benefits for the transitioning person and those who have the shared-death experience:

- Dramatic grief reduction, knowing that the one who has died is actually alive and well in the afterlife
- Greatly reduced fear and apprehension of death
- Increased belief in an afterlife
- A deeper understanding and refocusing on one's purpose in this life[345]

The Shared Crossing Project, founded by psychotherapist William Peters, helps families and the transitioning person understand what happens to consciousness as the body dies and teaches them how to facilitate a shared-death experience. The Internet address of the Shared Crossing Project website is at www.earthschoolanswers.com/shared/.

Visitations by the Transitioning Person to People Distant from the Body at the Moment of the Transition

Reports of people receiving a visit from a person at the moment of the transition are common. I was told by an acquaintance of mine named Mike Thomson about his encounter. Mike was driving down a highway alone and suddenly his ex-wife's Uncle Neely was sitting in the passenger seat. Mike was startled. He hadn't seen Uncle Neely since his divorce from Uncle Neely's niece years ago. Uncle Neely said, "Mike, the mass is over. Thanks be to God." That was an old joke between Mike and Uncle Neely. Mike converted to Catholicism at his marriage to Uncle Neely's niece, but he hated going to mass. When the family left the mass together, Uncle Neely would wryly remark to Mike, "Mike, the mass is over. Thanks be to God."

Mike glanced at the road and when he looked back at the passenger seat, Uncle Neely was gone. When Mike arrived at home, he was shaken and said nothing to anyone. He thought he must be losing his mind. A few minutes later, the phone rang and his son answered. His son shortly came into the room and said, "Dad, I have bad news. Uncle Neely just passed away."

Peter Fenwick gives the account of a similar appearance to someone far removed from the person who has just made the transition.

> I drifted back to sleep and had the most vivid dream. I saw my 22-year-old son walking toward me, his clothes dripping wet. He was talking to me, telling me that he was dead but that I was not to worry or be upset because he was alright. … When I woke I was very disturbed and tried to contact my son. I found out later that day that he had been drowned the previous night. I am convinced that he did contact me. … I have drawn great comfort from his visit to me over the years.[346]

Dr. Allan Botkin developed a psychotherapy method that puts grieving people into a state of mind in which they have their own afterlife communication with the person for whom they are grieving. The method is called an Induced After-Death Communication (IADC™). I co-authored the book describing the method and actual cases. In one case, a client described the odd encounter he had with his wife in a dream.

> Jerry had come to see me for psychotherapy about an unrelated matter, but after developing some trust in me, felt he could tell me his spontaneous ADC [after-death communication] story "without being labeled a nutcase." Jerry was living in the Midwest and his ex-wife was living on the East Coast with their three children. One night, he experienced the clear image of his ex-wife while he was asleep. "She looked beautiful, peaceful and happy," he said, "and she wanted to tell me about something of great concern to her." Jerry said she told him that he needed to start playing a more important role in rearing their children and even offered very specific suggestions about each child. Jerry said his experience was much clearer than a dream.

Jerry awoke right after his experience baffled by its remarkable clarity. He could remember the entire experience, and for him it felt like a real conversation with his ex-wife. After lying awake awhile trying to make sense of his experience, he managed to get back to sleep.

The next morning as he was making coffee, the phone rang. It was his ex-wife's sister. Tearfully, she told Jerry that his ex-wife had been killed in a car accident during the night.

Suddenly, the meaning of his experience became clear. Since then, Jerry's ex-wife has appeared to him five times in spontaneous ADCs, each time offering further advice about their children. "Every time," he said, "she did all the talking." And after each experience, Jerry followed her advice closely. In all instances, the advice turned out to be very helpful.[347]

Accounts of Transition Experiences after Periods of Illness

Crookall explains that many of those who transitioned after an illness describe notable sensations during the transition:

- Little if any physical pain
- A sensation of sinking
- A sensation of floating above the body, then standing beside it
- A dreamy state
- Watching the lifeless body and people standing around it
- Passing through a tunnel, passage, or door
- Going into a coma or blackout briefly and coming to awareness separate from the physical body
- Going into a period of sleep or semi-sleep and waking two to four days later in an environment away from the body or deathbed
- Feeling an expansion
- Not realizing they had permanently vacated the body

- Being saddened because of the grief experienced by loved ones and friends

- Not being able to make people in bodies see or respond to them

- A feeling they might be dreaming[348]

Many Describe Finding Themselves Out of the Body, Floating Above It or Standing Beside It

At the moment of the transition, people commonly realize their physical body is lying motionless while they are floating above it or standing beside it. One example is from the direct-voice medium Leslie Flint archives. During one of Leslie Flint's direct-voice sessions, a man in spirit known as Mr. Biggs described what happened at his transition. He was sitting in his easy chair, felt odd, and found himself standing over his body, which was still slumped in the chair.[349] You can hear Mr. Biggs describing his transition at this link: www.earthschoolanswers.com/biggs/.

Monsignor Robert Hugh Benson, who had passed into the life after this life in 1914, spoke clairaudiently through medium Anthony Borgia, describing seeing his body as he made the transition from it.

> I suddenly felt a great urge to rise up. I had no physical feeling whatever, very much in the same way that physical feeling is absent during a dream, but I was mentally alert, however much my body seemed to contradict such a condition. Immediately I had this distinct prompting to rise, I found that I was actually doing so. I then discovered that those around my bed did not seem to perceive what I was doing, since they made no effort to come to my assistance, nor did they try in any way to hinder me. Turning, I then beheld what had taken place. I saw my physical body lying lifeless upon its bed, but here was I, the real I, alive and well. For a minute or two I remained gazing, and the thought of what to do next entered my head, but help was close at hand. I could still see the room quite clearly around me, but there was a certain mistiness about it as though it were filled

with smoke very evenly distributed. I looked down at myself wondering what I was wearing in the way of clothes, for I had obviously risen from a bed of sickness and was therefore in no condition to move very far from my surroundings. I was extremely surprised to find that I had on my usual attire, such as I wore when moving freely and in good health about my own house. My surprise was only momentary since then, I thought to myself, what other clothes should I expect to be wearing? Surely not some sort of diaphanous robe? Such costume is usually associated with the conventional idea of an angel, and I had no need to assure myself that I was not that!

Such knowledge of the spirit world as I had been able to glean from my own experiences instantly came to my aid. I knew at once of the alteration that had taken place in my condition; I knew, in other words, that I had "died." I knew, too, that I was alive, that I had shaken off my last illness sufficiently to be able to stand upright and look about me. At no time was I in any mental distress, but I was full of wonder at what was to happen next, for here I was, in full possession of all my faculties, and, indeed feeling "physically" as I had never felt before.[350]

Another man described through a medium what happened in the moments of his transition.

I felt a peculiar sensation all through my body. Then I seemed to rise up out of my body and come down quietly on the floor. I was in the same room, but there seemed to be two of me, one on the bed and one beside the bed. All about me were my family in deep grief, why I could not tell, for my great pain was gone and I felt much better. Some of those whom I recognized as persons who had died, asked me to go, and with that thought I was outside and apparently could walk on the air.[351]

The Silver Cord and Threads

There are many accounts of a silver cord connecting the physical body to an etheric or astral body that is the consciousness of the person.

It is also known as the *Sutratman,* or life thread. The silver cord is described as a white or silver elastic umbilical-like cord that must be attached for the body to have vitality. Some describe two silver cords, one coming from the solar plexus (conveying vitality to the body) and one coming from the head (transmitting consciousness).[352] The silver cord makes a notable snap when the body loses its vitality and the person is freed.

The communicators sometimes describe glue-like threads that connect the physical body to the etheric or astral body. These threads similarly snap in a chorus as the physical body gives up the spirit.

The silver cord is not reported in cases of sudden death.[353] Apparently the cord is severed immediately upon the body's demise.

Does Anyone Make the Transition Alone?

No one makes the transition alone. In gradual transitions, the transition is anticipated, people appear to the person during the period before the transition, and there are people to help the newly transitioned person. When the transition is sudden, as in an explosion, the family already in the life after this life will not be there at the moment of the transition, but there will be someone called a "deliverer" to help the person adjust until loved ones arrive. Many people take on the role of helper or counselor as part of their spiritual growth that continues in the life after this life.

17

The Time Immediately
After the Transition

We receive our understanding of what happens in the moments and days after a full transition from Earth School from descriptions conveyed through mediums by people who have made the transition. Today we have a great many descriptions. We know what happens.

When each person comes to the appropriate pre-planned exit point in their life, the body ceases to function in some way. The individual is not affected by this change, except to be released from the conditions, imperfections, and rules of life in Earth School. The person is the same person an hour after the transition as an hour before. The Mind doesn't change.

What happens in the moments after the body stops functioning without resuscitation is different from what happens in a near-death experience (NDE). In an NDE, the person is still learning lessons and progressing in this life. As a result, the experience prepares the person for a more loving, compassionate life after the experience. At times, the NDE contains elements not at all in the experience after transition, such as the negative NDEs. Everything that happens as long as the person remains in Earth School, including the events in an NDE, happen for reasons relevant to the person's progress.

This chapter explains what happens in the time immediately after the transition.

People Speaking from the Next Life Remark How Easy the Transition Is

The transition is quite smooth and without incident. The person may not realize they have transitioned, however, and need help understanding the change. Some are bewildered for a period of time until they make the adjustment. A number of those living in the next life who have spoken about their transitions have described how, in the moments after their bodies died, they felt that they must be dreaming and would wake up.

People who are materialists, with no belief in the survival of consciousness and no understanding of the life they will enter after the transition, may have difficulty accepting the reality of their transition. Their adjustment may be difficult because of the fears they create within themselves about where they are and what will happen to them. It is important for us in Earth School to help people understand who they are in eternity and what happens after the transition to make their transition smoother.

After the transition, people describe a feeling of expansiveness, or having vast knowledge, of having a highly developed memory, and having acute sensory experiences. They have a feeling of being unified with the universe. They remark that the reality of where they are has all the feeling of being the true reality; earth is an imperfect facsimile.

All People Have a Joyous Realization They Are Alive

All people who have made the transition have the same joyous reaction to finding that they continue to live after the body dies. One example is from a woman known only as "Mrs. M." speaking through the talented medium Gladys Osborne Leonard.

> I cannot tell you much about my first days here because I seemed to be living in a dream of joy, yet dream is not the correct word since it was more real than any hour or moment I have had on earth. I was rather an alive person on earth, as you

will remember, but I feel so much more alive here. Why I said "dream" was it seemed almost too good to be true, but I had no fear of it ending like a dream, I knew it was going to be everlasting. It was the kind of experience which on earth might be termed a dream of joy. I simply walked on air for several days, to use the old phrase, I lived in happy reunion with my dear husband, a little later meeting with many old friends. You may remember that I did all I could to spread the knowledge of communion with the beyond and help people by sharing with them my own happy experiences. Many told me I had helped them. Well, here those people gathered around me by and by and gave me quite an impressive reception. They told me how right I had been to speak straight from my heart to them, that what I had said, even when not evidential, had carried weight because of my intense conviction. All that was most pleasant.[354]

People who have made the transition describe a feeling of being light and free. Any maladies they might have had in Earth School are gone. They experience no pain, even if their bodies were wracked with pain in the last moments of Earth School.

Crookall describes the sentiments of people after the transition. When they become aware of their transition, the reaction is very positive.

Many do not describe a "partial awakening": their awareness of a stable environment emerged simultaneously with their assurance of personal identity, and of having survived the death of the body. In such accounts the first feeling described is one of "peace," "security,", "well-being," "expansion," "release," "intense reality," etc. Many declare that they were "astonished" that death had not been what had been expected ... on the contrary, it had been "natural" and the new environment was "real," "familiar," "pleasant," "beautiful" and "earth-like."[355]

When They Realize They Have Transitioned, They Must Adjust to the New Reality

The first perspective of the newly transitioned is that it's very strange to suddenly leave Earth School and be in this new world that is so much more wonderful. Cyrus Kirkpatrick, an afterlife researcher, out-of-body traveler, and author, writes about encountering his mother in the life after this life during one of his out-of-body experiences. He describes her reaction to being in the next life:

> It's actually very difficult adjusting to what happened. That's been the hardest thing for me, is comprehending where I am and how it all works. Like, that I used to be THERE, and now I'm HERE. It's hard to understand and it's hard to think about.
>
> ... this new reality is fine. There's nothing altogether that different about it, there's nothing I can't do here. It's a normal and fine place to be. It's just realizing where you are, in an "afterlife." It's very strange sometimes![356]

People Do Not Suddenly Change after the Transition

The person's Mind does not change after the transition. The transition is like getting on a plane and landing in another country. The traveler is the same person, just in a different location. Some people believe they are going on with their lives as they were before their transition, although they are mystified by the odd occurrences resulting from not being in the familiar environment. Others believe they are dreaming and will awaken. And still others move smoothly into the new next life.

The person has the same feelings as before the transition. If the person was angry and hostile in this life, the anger and hostility remains. If the person was humble and loving, the humility and loving nature are still part of the person's nature. All the person's skills, memories, attitudes, preferences, and desires remain the same. The person does not become all-knowing. The person is still the same Mind, just in a different environment.

The Swedish visionary philosopher Emanuel Swedenborg corroborates the fact that the person remains the same after dropping off the body.

The first state of man after death is like his state in the world, because he is still in like manner in externals. He has therefore a similar face, similar speech, and a similar disposition, thus a similar moral and civil life; so that he knows no other than that he is still in the world, unless he pays attention to the things that he meets with, and to what was said to him by the angels when he was raised up—that he is now a spirit. Thus one life is continued into the other, and death is only the passage.[357]

Mike Tymn has a marvelous description of the fact that even additions and cravings carry on after the transition.

Communicating through a medium, Dr. Frederick H. Wood asked his discarnate mother how victims of drink fare in the afterlife. "The craving goes over with the etheric body," his mother replied, "and it goes over with the mind, too. Disease of that kind affects the whole personality. It is true of other vices, too and also the mental ones of greed, malice, vanity, or selfishness. These become part of yourself unless you conquer them."[358] She added that such addictions are sometimes more difficult to eradicate on her side than on earth.[359]

In the days and weeks after the transition, the person's perspective changes. After all, this person now knows the reality that life continues after the body stops functioning, and the importance of everything on earth diminishes.

People who have transitioned to the next stage of life do have a change in perceptive abilities. They communicate telepathically with each other, animals, and even plants in what the ITC pioneer Friedrich Jürgenson described as "direct perception."[360]

The Person Does Not Go into "Soul Sleep"

The belief among some Christians that people who have left Earth School are sleeping is based on Paul's statements that Christians who had transitioned have just fallen asleep and are "sleeping in Jesus" (1 Thessalonians 4:13-18). This belief that people who have left Earth School sleep until the resurrection is commonly referred to as "soul sleep." The term for this belief given by John Calvin is "psychopannychia."[361]

There are reports of Christians living in the next stage of life who have not given up on this belief. They are banded together feeling they are sleeping until the resurrection. The collective of minds in the higher levels of being who spoke through the medium Maurice Barbanell as Silver Birch remarked about these Christians.

> There is no eternal sleep, because we disturb the dead. There are some who go to sleep because they are taught that that is what will happen. ... You are taught some funny things in your world. They cannot sleep forever, though.[362]

People Are Given Help after the Transition

In the period after the transition, some people are bewildered and must become accustomed to the new reality. Loved ones provide perspectives for the newly arrived person and help that person understand the realities of the life after this life. Mrs. M., referred to earlier, explained from spirit through Gladys Osborne Leonard that people who have no loved ones to guide them are given help by caring counselors.

> [We went to] one of the centers where guidance is given to newcomers who have no relatives to welcome and instruct them. Kind people take them in hand, answering questions and talking things over with them and guiding them to find any relatives whom they speak of as having predeceased them, but who did not come to welcome them on arrival. In some such work as that I shall soon be taking part.[363]

The Most Prominent Occurrences after the Transition

After the transition, people experience a wide range of occurrences.

Being Aware of the Body and Leaving It Behind

The first of these prominent occurrences happens after the person has risen out of the body fully conscious. The person then may continue away from the room and may encounter someone who acts as a guide. The whole time, the person is as awake as during a normal wakefulness.

Robert Crookall explains that the transition out of the body is so natural the person usually doesn't realize what has happened.

> Many insisted the act of dying involved no pain, and said that they saw the physical body lying on the bed, reminding them of the discarded garment. Everything was so natural that the fact of transition was often unrealized at first. They found that they could not be seen or heard by friends still in the flesh.[364]

Edward C. Randall, speaking through medium Emily French, describes what happened after he had risen from his body.

> Some of those whom I recognized as persons who had died, asked me to go, and with that thought I was outside and apparently could walk on the air. My next thought was that it was a dream and that I would awake and feel again the terrible pain. I was gently told what had happened, and I felt that God had been unjust to take me when I had so much to do, and when I was so needed by my family. I was not satisfied with the place I was in. About me there was a fog, and I started to walk out of it, but the farther I walked, the more dense it got, and I became discouraged and sat down by the wayside in deep grief. I had ever tried to provide the very best for those dependent on me. Where was my reward? Then someone approached, came as it were out of the fog, and I told him of my life work and complained of the condition I was in, and questioned the justice of it. He replied, "Yours was a selfish love; you worked for self. You should have made others happy as well as your own." He promised to help me in my great trouble, if I would help myself.[365]

A farmer named George Hopkins in the life after this life came through in a Leslie Flint session on April 11, 1959. He explained that he dozed off and when he awakened saw his body and tried to awaken himself. He "shook" his body and entreated it to "wake myself up." You can listen to him speaking the following and more at www.earthschoolanswers.com/hopkins/.

Well, I just had a stroke or seizure or heart attack or something of the sort. As a matter of fact I was in the harvesting. I felt a bit peculiar, I thought it was the sun and well, I sat down in the 'edge. As far as I was concerned I felt a bit drowsy and peculiar and must have dozed off.

But dear, oh dear, I had such a shock. I woke up, as I thought, and the sun had gone down and there was me, or at least what appeared to be me. I couldn't make it out at all, I was so puzzled. I just didn't know what to do. I tried to shake myself— if you can do such a thing—I …wake myself up, sort of thing. I thought, well this is funny, I must be dreaming. I tried to sort of get, you know, some sense out of meself. I tried to talk to meself, try and understand what had been going on. I thought this must be some sort of crazy sort of dream or something. I couldn't make head nor tail of it.

It never struck me at all that I was dead. Anyway I wondered what I am I going to do now. I don't know. Anyway I found myself walking, as I thought I was, I went along the road to the doctor's. I thought well, perhaps he can help me. Perhaps he can sort of, sort it all out, like, you know.

Anyway I got to the doctor's and I knocked on the door, but no one answered. I thought well, I shouldn't have thought he would have been out, because he had surgery hours. Then I saw people coming and going in the surgery door and I thought, I dunno, nobody seems to take any notice and I saw one or two of my old cronies. They all sort of seemed to walk through me almost, you might say. No one seemed to make any comment about me. Course, I don't know I thought "Well this is a funny how-de-do."

Anyway I stood there for a bit trying to work it out. Then I saw someone hurrying down the road like mad to the doctor's. He got to the doctor's rushed in and pushed past me and everybody and next moment, I heard them talking about me. Which puzzled me. I thought what the hell's wrong with them? I'm here. I heard them say I was dead!

The doctor went in his car up the road, and I thought "Well I don't know about dead. I can't be dead. I'm here. I can see what's going on, I can hear what they're talking about. How the hell can I be dead?"

Then I thought to myself, that's funny, I saw myself lying down. I don't know, how can I be? I mean you're dead and you're done for and you're in heaven or hell. I'm certainly not in heaven and not in hell. I mean I'm 'ere, listenin' to what they're talkin' about. And of course, gradually I suppose it dawned on me that I must be dead.[366]

Entering a Period of Sleep without Realizing What Happened

The second prominent occurrence is a period of sleep without the person being conscious of what has happened. People who experience the transition after an extended illness often go through a period of sleep for two to four earth days that helps them make the transition into the next life.[367] The length of time may depend on the person's spiritual development that prepares them for the transition. Someone who understands the transition and anticipates it may experience a shorter sleep.[368] They may awaken in a recovery area appearing much like a hospital to them, with attendants who greet them upon their awakening and help them adjust to their new condition. This period of sleep is different from the brief unconsciousness some people describe, especially people who have transitioned from the body suddenly.

Robert Crookall cites a writer named Constance Wiley describing the sleep period.

> The only sleep there is after "passing" is that given to those who have passed through severe illness with much weakness and pain, who cannot free their minds from thoughts of sickness and weakness . ... Many think that there is a long interval between "passing" an active life on this side . ... If we are suffering from some complaint that gave us weakness and great pain, then we are taken to a home and tenderly nursed ... because, although we can't with our spiritual bodies feel pain or weakness, yet our minds continue to think we are suffering, unless we are brought back to health . ... Then, when we have recovered, we are taken where our lives, ill or well spent, entitle us to be.[369]

The period of sleep may be protracted if the person needs the time to adjust to the new reality. The medium Anthony Borgia, author of *Life in the World Unseen*, writes the explanation of the period of sleep he heard from a person in the life after this life:

> Long illness has a tiring effect upon the spirit body and when, at last, the physical body is cast off, the spirit body usually goes to one of the numerous halls of rest. ... There the new resident sleeps, ultimately to wake fully refreshed. ... With some, a short time serves; with others it takes months of earth-time. In my own case, I was ill for only a brief period on earth; I passed without losing consciousness. I was able to gaze upon my physical body. ... A friend who had passed on before me came to me, at the instant of departure, and took me to my new home. After a brief survey of it he recommended a rest period. I awoke in perfect health. [370]

The Body Has Died but the Person Continues Acting Normally

The third common occurrence is when the person's body has died but the etheric or spirit body continues acting as though nothing has happened. This happens after a sudden transition on a battlefield, an accident, a massive stroke, a heart attack, a homicide, or other such unexpected event that thrusts the person from the body without pain or recollection of what happened. The person is conscious and functioning as though still using the body on earth.

They continue with their activities in the moments after transitioning, often watching events unfold around their lifeless bodies. Finally someone comes to them to help them understand that they have transitioned out of the body. It could be a loved one, an acquaintance whom they knew had passed, or a helper who has accepted the role of helping people confused when they have crossed into the next stage of life.

One World War I soldier named Alf Pritchett described himself running toward the enemy on the battlefield, but noticing that the enemy was running past him as though they couldn't see him. It wasn't until some time later that he realized he had been killed suddenly, most likely in an explosion, but was still running on the battlefield as the spirit person. His physical body was lying on the battlefield somewhere but all the rest—his Mind, personality, and memories—were exactly the same.[371]

Listen to the recording of Alf Pritchett describing his experience in a Leslie Flint session in 1960, 43 years after his transition in World War I: www.earthschoolanswers.com/alf/.

A man named Ted Butler said that before his death he was walking down the street with his wife and remembered seeing something coming at him. He then saw a crowd of people standing around staring at something. He "had a look" and saw someone lying on the street who looked just like him. "Could've been my twin brother," he said. His wife was crying hysterically, but for some reason, she couldn't see him. The reason was that he had been hit by a runaway truck and transitioned instantly. He got into the ambulance with the body and sat next to his grief-stricken wife, who still couldn't see him. Then he went to his own funeral. He remarked, "It was all very nice, but it was so damned silly because there I was!"[372]

Listen to the recording of Ted Butler describing what happened to him at www.earthschoolanswers.com/butler/.

People Who Transition Suddenly Have Unique Experiences

People who transition suddenly and unexpectedly in the prime of life typically describe transitions that are markedly different from those who transition after a period of illness. Crookall summarizes the events in these transitions that differ from occurrences experienced by people who transition over time. He calls the sudden transition an "enforced death."

> (1) The natural death of average man is typically followed by a "sleep" but in enforced death the person concerned tended to be awake and alert at once or almost at once; (2) in natural death consciousness was characterized by such words as "peace," "security," "happiness," "freedom," etc; in enforced death it was at first "confused," "bewildered," etc; (3) whereas in natural transition the environment was described as "beautiful," "clear," "light," and "brilliant," in enforced death it was often (at first) "misty," "foggy," even "watery"; (4) whereas many who died naturally are conscious of having seen (or felt the presence of) the "silver cord," that feature is very seldom mentioned by those whose death was enforced; (5) whereas men who died naturally were often aware that they were met by discarnate friends (and death-bed visions are common in natural transitions), there was some delay on the part of men whose death was enforced in seeing those who met them (friends and undescribed pre-death visions of discarnate friends).[373]

When the transition is expected, as at the end of protracted illness, there is a "call" to loved ones to come. They are with the person in the days before the transition and are present to greet the person at the moment of transition. In a sudden transition, there is no time for the call, so loved ones are not immediately with the person. However, there are always "deliverers" who come to help the person make the adjustment.

The clearest description of the work by these deliverers is in Robert Crookall's *Life in the World Unseen*.

Again, although the man whose death is enforced may not have time to "call" friends who have "gone before," he is not without aid; as already said, there are experts who undertake such special duties. Although it may be some little time before he is aware of their presence, these "deliverers" soon take him in charge and in this work they may have the "cooperation" of mortals who are psychic. The newly-dead man thus comes to realize what has happened—that a transition of an abnormal nature has caused a temporary abnormal state. Discarnate friends whom he himself was unable to "call" are then brought by the "deliverers": as in the case of those who passed on naturally, he recognizes them and knows that they are "dead." He realizes what has happened to himself. He then enjoys a period of rest under special conditions. This prepares the soul body to operate at a rate higher than that of the physical body. The effect of any shock, due to his sudden transition, is illuminated and the newly dead man enters upon the normal sequence of after-death experiences, shedding the vehicle of vitality, awakening in "paradise," conditions, passing through his "judgment," and thereafter going to his "his own place." [374]

The newly dead person is aware of the thoughts and feelings of physically embodied friends through telepathic and clairvoyant senses. [375]

Awareness after the Transition

After the transition, people describe a feeling of expansiveness, or having vast knowledge, of having a highly developed memory, and a feeling of being unified with the universe. Many remark that their senses were more acute than ever before. Robert Crookall describes the accounts from people living in the next realm of life:

> During earth-life, consciousness, though "normal" to us, is actually limited, "blinkers"- like, by the physical body. At death, this valuable, though restricting, instrument is shed, "normal" consciousness gives place to the "super-normal " type: there is an "expansion," and a "deepening" of awareness, and not only

do remarkable faculties (of which we may have had occasional effort evanescent activities during earth-life) become normal to us, but we find that we are "nearer" than before to loved ones who are still in the flesh. The true causes and the necessary consequences of our words and deeds, our underlying motives and true characters (which were more or less hidden from the lesser self) become clear to us in the un-enshrouded Soul Body.[376]

The accounts given by many people who have made the transition include their astonishment at how wonderful they feel and how glorious their surroundings are.

Many Do Not Realize They Have Transitioned

After they have transitioned, people are the same as they were before the transition, with all the senses they had and body experiences. When we transition, we will have experiences as we are having now, with no announcements to alert us to the change of status. Monsignor Hugh Benson, speaking from the life after this life through medium Anthony Borgia, explains.

> There is a surprising number of people who do not realize they have passed from the earth in the death of the physical body. Resolutely they will not believe that they are what the earth calls "dead." They are dimly aware that some sort of change has taken place, but what that change is they're not prepared to say.[377]

Many people believe themselves to be in a dream from which they will soon awaken. A priest named Edwin, now in the life after this life, speaking through Anthony Borgia, describes his impressions of being in a dream when he transitioned to the next realm of life.

> His first impressions upon his awakening in the spirit were—to use his own words—absolutely breathtaking. He had visualized subconsciously perhaps, some sort of misty state as condition of a future life, where there would be a great deal of 'prayer and praise.' To find himself in a realm of inexpressible beauty, with

all the glories of earthly nature purged of its earthliness, refined and eternalized, with the enormous wealth of colour all around and about him; to behold the crystal purity of rivers and brooks, with the charm of the country dwellings and the grandeur of the city's temples and halls of learning; to find himself in the centre of all such glories without an inkling of what had thus been in store for him, was to cast doubts upon the veracity of his own eyes. He could not believe that he was not in the midst of some beautiful, but fantastic, dream, from which he would shortly awaken to find himself once again in his old familiar surroundings. He thought how he would relate this dream when he returned to consciousness. Then he considered how it would be received — as very beautiful, no doubt, but just a dream.[378]

A woman named MaryAnn Ross living in the life after this life described her feeling she was in a dream after her transition. She spoke in a Leslie Flint session on January 20, 1969. You can listen to this portion of her session and the rest of her description of her experiences in the life after this life at www.earthschoolanswers.com/ross/.

And there was my mother, but she did not look the same as when I saw her in ma [sic] dream, as I thought. She looked young, as I'd seen her in the picture that used to hang in my bedroom, when she was married, many years before. And she'd got a white dress and she had a black bow ribbon in her hair, so like I'd seen her in early pictures, when I was very young. We used to have everything, collection of old photos, that mother'd keep in the tin. Yes, it was just as if I was seeing her as she was then.

She said to me that I was alright and that I'd nothing to worry about and I was not going back, and I thought this is just a dream. And then she said no, it's not a dream, it's real, you're alive now, you're not to worry about anything. And she said, soon, when you're really recovered over this, she said, we'll go out we'll meet all sorts of people that you used to know when you were a wee bairn [baby], you know, when you were young.

I could not quite see and understand, I could not realize at that stage that I was dead. It was like a beautiful dream.[379]

Guides and Helpers Meet with Some Deceased

In most cases, the person is greeted by a loved one or acquaintance. Such is the case with the priest named Edwin in spirit.

As soon as I had had this brief space in which to look about me and to appreciate my new estate, I found myself joined by a former colleague—a priest—who had passed to this life some years before. We greeted each other warmly, and I noticed that he was attired like myself. Again this in no way seems strange to me, because had he been dressed in any other way I should have felt that something was wrong somewhere, as I had only known him in clerical attire. He expressed his great pleasure at seeing me again, and for my part I foresaw the gathering up of the many threads that had been broken at his death. ... He, himself, was in the best of spirits as he stood there giving me such a welcome, as on the earth-plane, two old friends accord each other after a long separation. That, in itself, was sufficient to show that all thoughts of being marched off to my judgment are entirely preposterous. We both were too jolly, too happy, too carefree, and too natural, and I, myself, was waiting with excitement for all manner of pleasant revelations of this new world, and I knew that there could be none better than my old friend to give them to me. He told me to prepare myself for an immeasurable number of the pleasantest of surprises, and that he had been sent to meet me on my arrival. As he already knew the limits of my knowledge, so his task was that much easier.[380]

A Variety of Events Follow the Period of Sleep

For those who enter a period of sleep after the transition, a range of events may occur. No single event occurs for everyone. Examples of the variety of events follow.

Awakening in a Reception Area or Hospital Setting

Some awaken in a hospital-like setting called a "reception area" or "rest house" where people help them make the adjustment to being dead and their loved ones come to visit. It is most often described as having many beds and no walls. Three example descriptions follow.

It was a home of rest for those who had come into spirit after long illness, or who had had a violent passing, and who were inconsequence, suffering from shock. ... It was built in the classical style, two or three stories high, and it was entirely open upon all sides. That is to say, it contained no windows as we know them on earth.[381]

A curious characteristic of places where newly arrived souls are brought to recover from the shock of passing—a lack of walls.[382]

I "woke up" here in this hospital of the rest home. My room had no walls and the sunlight seemed to flow over one all the time.[383]

A woman who gave her name as "Mary Ivan" spoke in a Leslie Flint session describing her awakening in a rest house that seemed like a hospital to her. You can listen to Mary speaking these words about what happened when she awoke in the rest-house setting at www.earthschoolanswers.com/ivan/.

Ah, I woke up and found myself in a kind of place like a hospital. I thought, "Well what's this?" Because I was in my own house and, you know, I was sick-a-bed and everything. And I had a sister who was looking after me. And I remember waking up here and I was in a kind of ward place in the hospital.

But very nice and very clean, and everything seemed so fresh and airy, and everyone seemed to be so efficient and quiet and peace, and the sun or whatever it was—at least I thought it was the sun then—was shining through the windows, and everywhere around was pretty and clean. There were pictures hanging on the walls and somehow it seemed like a very special kind of hospital.

And I thought, well, this is strange. And then a very sweet woman came to me and said, "You know," she says, "you just have to rest a little while and then you'll soon be all right, once you sort of, sort yourself out and get to know things. And your people will be coming in to see you in a wee while." And I thought, "This is strange." I felt sure I was at home in my own bed, and here I am in a hospital, so I must have been unconscious and they must have brought me into hospital. I did not think at first that I was dead.[384]

Monsignor Robert Hugh Benson speaking through Anthony Borgia explains why people like Mary awaken in a hospital-like setting. He describes an entire floor of a building, with people he calls "recumbent forms" sleeping on couches. He explains that the people had lingering illnesses or sudden and violent transitions and needed this period because of the debilitating effects of their illnesses or violent event on their minds.

Occupying the whole of the floor space were extremely comfortable-looking couches, each of which bore a recumbent form, quite still, and obviously sleeping profoundly. Moving quietly about were a number of men and women intent upon watching the different couches and their burdens.

I noticed as soon as we entered this hall that we came under the influence of the blue ray, and its effect was one of pronounced energizing as well as tranquility. Another noticeable quality was the entire absence of any idea of an institution with its inevitable officialdom. There was no question of patronage, nor did I feel the least shade of being among strangers. Those in attendance upon the sleepers did so, not in the attitude of a certain task to be done willy-nilly, but as though they were performing a labour of love in the sheer joy of doing it. Such, indeed, was precisely the case. The glad awakening of these sleeping souls was an ever recurrent joy to them, no less than to the people who had come to witness it.

I learned that all the "patients" in this particular hall had gone through lingering illnesses before passing over. Immediately after their dissolution they are sent gently into a deep sleep. In some cases the sleep follows instantly—or practically without break—upon the physical death. Long illness prior to passing into the spirit world has a debilitating effect upon the mind, which in turn has its influence upon the spirit body.

The latter is not serious, but the mind requires absolute rest of varying duration. Each case is treated individually, and eventually responds perfectly to its treatment. During this sleep-state the mind is completely resting. There are no unpleasant dreams, or fevers of delirium. …

Constant watch is kept upon them, and at the first flutterings of returning consciousness, others are summoned, and all is ready for the full awakening. …

We were shown another large hall similarly appointed, where those whose passing had been sudden and violent were also in their temporary sleep. These cases were usually more difficult to manage than those we had just seen. The suddenness of their departure added far greater confusion to the mind.[385]

A man named Dr. Franke had been killed at Dachau death camp during World War II because he would not perform the heinous acts the Nazis required him to perform. He came through in a Leslie Flint session describing what happens in the recovery areas. You can listen to Dr. Franke describing in detail what he does in the facilities where he counsels people still suffering from problems they had while alive on earth at www.earthschoolanswers.com/franke1/.

There were doctors too, I meet. They take me to place where we look after people who are … come here from the earth whose mind is in terrible condition. For they have not been able to rid themselves of the old thoughts old ideas. So they are housed …

housed in large place, like a hospital or infirmary and there they are looked after, but it is an education of the mind. It is the transforming of the individual from the old material unhappy self, into a new being full of light, full of joy, full of happiness.

In this I base my work. So, my real work is now in these large places to which sometimes certain people are brought whose minds are in the state of unhappiness and turmoil. And I help, and like many other souls here, to reinstate or to rehabilitate them into this new way of thinking, that they can rid themselves of all the old ideas and horrible things which still cling to them.[386]

Rupert Brooke, the celebrated British poet, transitioned in military action in Greece in 1915. He came through in a Leslie Flint session on September 15, 1957, explaining that he didn't awaken in a reception area, but when it was clear he was wandering around perplexed, he was taken to what he called a "cleansing station." The many who were watching over him decided he was confused enough that he needed a period of rest in a relaxed setting.[387] You can hear him describe the place at www.earthschoolanswers.com/rupert/.

Awakening in a Comfortable Home Setting

Some who have transitioned describe awakening in a comfortable room, with beautiful furniture and light streaming through windows. Edward C. Randall, speaking through medium Emily French, described the room he found himself in when he awakened in the life after this life.

The last physical sensation that I recall was one of falling, but I had no fear—it seemed so natural. At the same time I heard voices speaking words of encouragement, voices that I recognized as those of loved ones that I thought dead. For a time I had no recollection. Then I awoke in this spirit sphere, and never will I forget the joy that was mine. I found myself, saw my body, which appeared as usual, except lighter and more ethereal. I was resting on the couch in a beautiful room filled with flowers. I looked through a window and saw the landscape, bathed in rose-colored light. There was a quiet that was impressive, then music, the harmonious vibration of which seemed to rise and fall softly.[388]

Others describe awakening in familiar surroundings, such as a room in which they grew up as children. Their family now in the life after this life is there when they awaken. In a Leslie Flint session, Princess Alexandra of Denmark, Queen Consort of Edward VII of England, described from spirit what happened to her when she awoke in the next life. She found herself in familiar surroundings from her youth. Her family and friends she had known were there. You can hear her speaking this description and more at www.earthschoolanswers.com/alexandra/.

I remember very vividly awakening in a room which was very reminiscent of a room that I've been very fond of, many years previously in my earthly existence. In every way it seemed to be an exact replica: the colourings, the materials, the furnishings. In fact everything about it was a perfect reproduction; in fact, so much so, that I did not realise at first that I passed on at all. And I remember only too well the very beautiful view from the window, with the beautiful green grass, lawn and terrace and at the bottom, far in the distance, the river.

It was a spot which I had been most fond. And in this room on my awakening were many of my relations and friends that I had known. It was almost like a kind of reception, which of course it was. And I must admit it was a great joy to me, to meet all these friends and all these souls that had meant so much to me in my Earthly life, and to have the feeling of peace and the realization that it was an environment in the very room in which I was most happy. It was a room that had given me great joy and pleasure many, many years previously.[389]

Awakening in a Natural Setting

In other accounts given by people who have made the transition, the person awakens in a natural setting and is greeted by a loved one. In one example from Leslie Flint's session recordings, a man named George Wilmot, who had been a "rag and bone" merchant on the earth realm, described waking after his transition in a field under a tree. You can listen to this account at www.earthschoolanswers.com/jenny/.

> And the first thing I remember when I woke up over here was being in a—well, I suppose you'd call it a field. I seemed to be sitting, lying under a tree. And I remember, sort of, waking up. And I could see this horse coming towards me. And it was my old Jenny. Cor! She looked younger, of course, and she was … oh, she was so thrilled and so happy you could sense and feel it, I can't say how, I mean this is something I can't explain. But it's almost as if she was talking to me. It was extraordinary. I couldn't hear any voice and you don't expect to hear a horse speak. But it was somehow mentally, I suppose, now I realize. It must have been as though she was speaking to me and welcoming me and she came and stood beside me and was licking my face. Goodness me, I'll never forget this as long as I live. I was so thrilled and so excited. …[390]

The Reunions

There are always reunions with the people and pets the person loved while in Earth School, although the reunion may be delayed when the transition is sudden or when the person goes through a period of rest or sleep. Family, friends, and even acquaintances have a joyous coming-home experience with the new arrival.

A man named Sam Woods came through in a Leslie Flint session describing the environment he found himself in after awakening and his reunion with his wife. You can hear the recording of this account at www.earthschoolanswers.com/sam/.

The actual idea of leaving your lot, your world, and coming over here, oh it's nothing, it's just like going to sleep and waking up into a new environment. You might say that it's so much nicer and pleasanter than anything you might know on earth. And all your old pals and your relations that you're fond of standing around and about you, all giving you a welcome. It's a very nice how d'ya do, I'll tell you.

I remember waking up in what appeared to be a nice little place, in a nice room, nice flowers, oh, beautiful little house it was, the sort of place I'd hoped one day I might have, but I knew jolly well from my own experience on earth that I'd never have it on your side, because I never had the wherewithal to buy it or even rent such a place. Here, I found myself in a very nice, oh, a lovely little place, it was. It was not too big, it was just my cup of tea. Just very pleasant.

And there, there was my old lady looking as I remember her, oh, many years ago, oh, looking thirty years younger. She was standing there looking down at me. I was lying on this here sort of couch arrangement. And I remember sort of waking as it were from sleep. And first thing I saw was this lovely room and then my dear lady standing there at the bottom of the bed, as it were, or couch rather, and one or two other people that I had known. There was my wife's brother who died, oh 1914-18 war, he came over, he was torpedoed or something in the first World War aboard ship.

And there was me mother; at first I didn't even know it was me mother, I didn't cotton on to that at all. Then I recognized her and realized how much younger she looked. It was my mother, but you know, I didn't recognize her. She looked like a young woman about twenty. I'd seen a photo taken of her many years ago, but I never cotton on onto the fact that it was me mother. It soon dawned on me who she was. At first, she looked like a beautiful lady that I had some vague idea of but never knew. It's a funny thing, you know, but a bit. Oh, various people were there, people I'd known.

What amazed me more than anything there, squatted down on the side there was my old dog Timothy. Oh, a lovely old creature Tim was. We had him for about fifteen years and oh, he was a nice old dog. And there was a cat that my wife had always been fond of, ginger cat, it was. We used to call her "Old Marmie," it was a marmalade cat, "Marmie."[391]

Most are joyful reunions with family members. However, Michael Newton writes about the description he received of a reunion event of one of his hypnotherapy subjects organized by his soul group.

After my last life, my group organized one hell of a party with music, wine, dancing and singing. They arranged everything to look like a classical Roman festival with marble halls, togas and all the exotic furnishings prevalent in our many lives together in the ancient world. Melissa (a primary soulmate) was waiting for me right up front, re-creating the age that I remember her best and looking as radiant as ever.[392]

People without Family Have People Assigned to Help Them

A sailor named Terry Smith came through in a Leslie Flint session describing a woman who had been assigned to take care of him. Terry found himself first in the life after this life walking down an avenue. He came to a house and a woman greeted him. She told him she was expecting him, and she would be taking care of him. She explained that he drowned when his ship was sunk, along with a great number of other men. A portion of Terry Smith's account follows. The entire description in Terry's voice of his meeting his caregiver is at www.earthschoolanswers.com/terry-2/.

So she says, "Yes and everyone of those lads has got someone, somewhere to look after them. Some have got their own people; relations or friends. Some have got other souls and I'm one [who's] in charge of you." She says, "You didn't realize," she says, "but you were directed. You thought you were walking on your own up the road," she says. "But you wasn't." She says,

"You were being helped by inspiration from a soul whose job it is to help people when they come over suddenly, like you did."

So I says, "Oh yeah?" You know, sort of listening, like, not quite taking it all in, you know. So I says, "Well I don't understand this at all."

So she says, "Well don't you worry," she says. "You stay with me. I'll look after you. I'll be like your Mum."[393]

Meeting People We Do Not Want to Meet

There is no requirement that we meet people we do not want to meet and we will not meet them even though they want to connect.[394] As with all of our activities forever in our lives, we choose the people we want to meet and those we want to live with.

Visiting Loved Ones Still on Earth

The first thoughts of many who make the transition is of their loved ones still on earth. They wonder how they are or wish to see them and are either guided to them or immediately are in their presence in Earth School. However, most are very disappointed when their loved ones cannot see or her them. Their loved ones make no response to their presence.

Edward C. Randall, speaking through medium Emily French, explains that when he visited his loved ones after this transition, he was deeply saddened that they could not see or feel him.

My greatest disappointment after my awakening was when I returned to my old home, before I discovered that none could see or feel me and all grieved for me as one dead, and their sorrow held me. I wept with them, and could not get away, until time healed their sorrow.[395]

A man named Alfred Higgins came through in a Leslie Flint session describing how he explained to the guide helping him that he was concerned about his family. With his guide's help, he visited his wife. A short excerpt follows. You can listen to Higgins describing the entire lead-up to the visit at www.earthschoolanswers.com/higgins2/.

I'm beginning to realize what you say is so, I must admit I'm a bit concerned about my people. It must be a terrible shock for them, you know. I have no recollection of dying. I don't remember anything bar falling. At least I had a feeling I was falling and then I don't remember no more." ...

So he says, "Would you like to go back for just a little while to see your people? Do you think that would help you? ...They won't take any notice of you, you know... they won't realize that you're there because they can't see you and they won't hear you if you speak to them." ...

So I just held his hand and ... I don't know, it seems so strange, but as soon as I touched his hand it's just as if everything went sort of peculiar. It was as if everything gradually seemed to disappear. It was as if I was sort of—I don't know—going to sleep I suppose in a kind of way and yet it wasn't like sleep. It was just a sort of lacking of understanding and realization of things around and about me. I became sort of unconscious, I suppose.

The next thing I knew I was standing in our kitchen and I was watching my wife.[396]

People Often Go to Their Own Funeral

People generally are no longer interested in their bodies after the transition, but those speaking from the life after this life often describe going to their own funerals.

A man named Ted Butler earlier described as being hit by a truck, described his staying with his body for a period of time after his transition, including going to the morgue and his own funeral.[397] You can listen to the recording of Ted Butler speaking about going to his funeral at www.earthschoolanswers.com/funeral/. Below is his reaction to going to his funeral.

Then there was the funeral and all that. Of course, I went to that and I thought to meself at the time, 'well I don't know. There's all this fuss and how-d'ya-do and expense for nothing'.

'Cause there I was. I was in the carriage, an horse-drawn carriage the wife had, 'cause she knew my love of horses. They did have motors, but she wanted this horse-drawn I suppose. And I thought, "it's all very touching," but at the same time it all seemed so damn silly to me, because there I was.

Loved Ones' Grief Holds the Newly Transitioned on Earth

People, especially children, who have left the earth quite often comment that their greatest disturbance after transition is experiencing the grief of loved ones still on earth. Those in the next life receive our thoughts and emotions. Crookall provides statements by several children speaking from the next life about the effect of their parents' grieving on them.

Phillip urged his mother: "Shake off your dumps; ... It hinders me in visualizing you clearly." He also told her the converse — namely, that her wish to help him (when newly-dead) had had "a great effect" on his post-death experiences. One of Randall's girl communicators pleaded, "Oh, mummy, don't cry so. It makes me so unhappy. If only you would smile and be glad I'd be quite happy because I see ever so many lovely people who seem to be waiting to take me to someplace ... but I just can't leave *you*." Later this girl complained, "Why do you grieve so? I am well and could be happy, only your sad face keeps me wanting to be near you and comfort you." A boy-communicator of Randall's made identical statements: "When earth conditions do not bind me, I can attend lectures, etc. But I am bound to earth by the sorrow of my parents. ... That holds me like bands of steel so I can only at times do what other boys do. They don't understand that I am more alive than ever before, but until they give me happier thoughts ... I am as unhappy as they are. I could be so happy, and accomplish so much, if they would let me go!" Catherine, a child commentator (whose identity was also well established) said, "Do not cry for me — it makes me sad." Freddie Grisewood [a famous British broadcaster] ... an honors graduate of Oxford, having described "seeing," at various times, friends and relatives who had "passed on," noted that they looked "well and happy." But he observed: "All made the same requests—that those whom they had left behind should not grieve for them unduly." He continued: "In Mark's case this request was reiterated time after time. He would say, "Freddie, do tell mother (Lady Mackenzie) not to grieve so much—she's holding me back."[398]

Edward C. Randall, speaking through medium Emily French, described the effect of grief on him after his transition to the next life.

> The grief of my people kept me so sad at first that I was not able to see or think of anything but earthly sorrow. That is why grief for departed friends and relatives is so wrong, and is so harmful, both to those on earth and to those who come over. The longer that grief continues and the more hopeless it is, the more those mourned for are kept to earth.[399]

Dr. Alice Gilbert's son, speaking to her from spirit, said "Great grief, persistent and self-centered, keeps the departed 'tied up,' yet frustrated and helpless."[400]

On the other hand, Frances Banks, communicating from the life after this life through medium Helen Greaves, reported that loving thoughts and prayers "could be likened to a draft of healing water for the newly transmitted soul."[401]

Where Does the Person Go After Leaving the Body?

Everyone goes to "Heaven." But the commonly understood meaning of "Heaven" is incorrect.

The other realms, including the next stage of life, are in different focuses for the Mind. They are not in a location. Everything is one, but we change focus when we attune from one realm to another. It is much like our Minds when we are sitting thinking. We remember a concert we attended last week, and for that time, the concert is our focus. We hear the instruments and remember the grandiose hall. When we think of what to have for dinner, our focus is on food. When we are focused on the concert, the images and thoughts of food are still part of us, but we are focused on the concert with no thought of food. And when we are focused on dinner, the memories of the concert are still part of us, but our focus is on dinner. They coexist in us, but we focus on one at a time.

In the same way, while in Earth School, we are focused on the Earth School accessible to us through the Universal Intelligence. Matter and energy are the Universal Intelligence giving substance to the focus called "Earth School" so we can love, learn, and be happy. Our Minds are focused on Earth School in the twenty-first century. However, we could be focusing on Earth School during Elizabeth I's reign or focusing on another realm entirely different from Earth School. They are not in locations. They are different focuses our individual Minds take on in the Universal Intelligence.

When we have the experience of the body transitioning, the Mind just changes focus from Earth School to the life after this life. The Earth School body experiences are no longer available or desirable. Instead, we have a vital, healthy, young body in the life that is the new focus of our lives. The life after this life is just like Earth School, with its own matter and energy as we know them created by the Universal Intelligence. Earth School is a spiritual plane. The next plane is another spiritual plane, but much better and without the negatives.

We are experiencing Earth School together because we have the same focus. The Universal Intelligence gives us each the same experiences so we can participate in Earth School together.

The answer to "Where does the person go after the transition?" is "nowhere"; there is only here, and there is only now. The person has a new focus with new experiences in realms with experiences, matter, and energy created by the Universal Intelligence that has people, animals, rivers, roads, flowers, and all the rest of the solid substance we have on the Earth School spiritual plane.

The Second Death

Most people find themselves in the next stage of life naturally after the body dies. They wake from a sleep in a recovery location many describe as being like a hospital, or they wake in a familiar setting with loved ones around, or they awake in some other circumstances. A few, however transition from the body and are as much a part of the earth environment as they were before the body ceased to function. They may wander around in the earth environment, riding in cars, walking, going to favorite places, and otherwise acting as though still in a body. If they don't realize fully that they have transitioned from the body, it may be a frustrating time of unsuccessfully trying to communicate with people.

At some time, the person who has been wandering the earth environment realizes they have transitioned away from the body and move on to the next realm of life away from Earth School. Counselors and loved ones who have previously made the transition work at trying to help the person move on. The first transition stopped the body experiences. The second transition for some is when they finally leave the Earth School environment. It has been called the "second death." It is a change of state of mind resulting in a change in a focus on the new life in what has been called "Summerland" or "Level 3." The activities such as the life review and living in a new home with loved ones do not begin until this second transition has occurred.

Crookall describes the transition as shedding the vital body that was used after the person left the physical body. When the vital body is shed, the person goes on to Level 3 or Summerland with a causal body, which is the body with all the characteristics we associate with a normal body in Earth School, except that it has no defects and the person usually assumes a body the same as the body the person had in his or her prime.[402]

What Happens to the Body

The body is just a body experience, not a physical object in a material universe. Consciousness does not "enter" the body. Consciousness gives rise to the body experience; consciousness creates the body. For the sake of causes and effects in the Earth School realm, the cessation of the body and transition away from the body experience has physical phenomena: snapping of the silver cord, snapping of the threads holding the physical body to the spirit body or etheric body. At times, "spirit doctors" called "deliverers," who have come to help the person make the transition, may sever the silver cord.[403]

The testimony of those living in the life after this life is that when the person no longer uses the body, it can be buried, cremated, or left to the elements; the person has no need for it or interest in it. Never once in all that I have read from people who have lived through the transition did someone remain attached to their body in any way after the transition, although someone may attend their funeral unaffected by and uninterested in the body lying in the casket.

As to whether the individual who used the body is affected by embalming, effects of the elements, or cremation, this is what Carl Wickland, MD, learned through the communications received by his medium wife:

> During the three days of sleep which usually follow transition, the spirit is unaware that his physical body has been cremated or removed to the cemetery and when he wakens he fails to comprehend the new situation, since he still occupies a [spirit or etheric] body, although one of finer substance, and still retains old habits, desires and ideals. Being as alive as ever, it does not enter his mind that anything unusual has happened [in a transition] and he may remain oblivious to his condition for years.[404]

The Life Review

Evidence from near-death experiences and mediums who have reported what people living in the life after this life have described to them, corroborate the understanding that people experience a life review after making the transition. In the life review, the individual reviews all the significant actions and events during the person's life, feeling them from the points of view of people involved as well as the person's point of view. There is no judgment or punishment involved. In the life review, people judge themselves, thereby experiencing profound learning from reviewing the actions and feeling the sentiments of the others involved.

For excellent descriptions of the life review provided by people who have made the transition to the life after this life, read Mike Tymn's *The Afterlife Revealed: What Happens after We Die*, Chapter 5, "The Life Review" and Robert Crookall's *The Supreme Adventure: Analyses of Psychic Communication*, pages 86 to 95.

Those living in the life after this life who have gone through the experience describe the life review as an "unreeling" of their entire life experienced as though it were happening now.

> One of the first things noticed is that, without mental effort, everything we have done ... comes before us as a present memory.[405]

> I saw clearer and clearer the events of my past life pass, in a long procession, before me.[406]

A life review during a near-death experience happens during the short period of the experience, but in detail because time is suspended. The person will return to consciousness and use the experience to change their life. This account one woman gave of her life review during her NDE is so vivid and uplifting that I am providing it here.

> I actually could feel the joy each person felt when I touched their life in a loving way. I was getting "caught" doing something right for once in my life. During the good he was telling me "I am so proud of you!" I felt such joy for making him so proud because I never realized what that felt like because I always felt like I couldn't do anything right. Reviewing my random acts of kindness gave me the most joy because I was able to feel the difference I made in someone's life that I hadn't realized at the time ... and I didn't even know them. Little acts of kindness mean so much to God.
>
> Also, I had to see and feel all the hurtful things I had done (even the hurtful things I didn't know I did). I had to feel the person's hurt I caused. But God was not judging me. I was looking at my actions with God by my side loving me while I was judging

myself. And believe me, no one can judge me any harsher than I already judge myself. He was asking me, "What different choices could you have made? What are you learning from this? This was clearly not the punishing God I had been taught to believe in. The hardest part of this was realizing he had already forgiven me. I was having a hard time forgiving myself. He showed me that I couldn't let His love in without first forgiving myself. Punishing myself didn't make me better in His eyes. Accepting his love is what he wanted from me. Once I was able to accept that God only loved, it was easier for me to openly and honestly look at my life.[407]

The life review may take place at any time after the full transition from the earth. A man named Bill Wooton in the life after this life speaking through direct-voice medium Lilian Bailey explained that some people put off the life review for many years of earth time, not wanting to face what happened and the reactions of people involved.[408] One source reports that people may put off the life review for hundreds or thousands of years.[409]

Rob Schwartz's research reveals that, as the life review proceeds, our spirit guides sit with us, conversing about the events and occasionally pointing out incidents we could have handled better, such as by showing love and compassion when the other person involved needed it. However, these comments are made in a loving tone, with no hint of judgment or negativity.[410]

There are some descriptions of two life reviews. The first is a review of life events without examining them emotionally. The second is termed "the judgment," in which the person goes through a life review feeling all the feelings and realizing all the thoughts of all people involved in the most salient life events. The first, non-emotional review happens quickly, and is experienced by earthbounds as well as people who have gone on to Level 3 or Summerland. The emotional life review occurs after the person has left the earth environment and has gone on to Level 3.[411]

The purpose of the life review is for the person to learn from the Earth School experience. Michael Newton, founder of the Newton

Institute for Life Between Lives Hypnotherapy, explains that during the life review there is a gentle probing by perceptive, caring teacher-guides to facilitate the learning experience.[412]

> Generally, the composition of a group of souls is made up of beings at about the same level of advancement, although they have their individual strengths and shortcomings. These attributes give the group balance. Souls assist one another with the cognitive aspects of absorbing information from life experiences as well as reviewing the way they handled the feelings and emotions of their host bodies directly related to those experiences. Every aspect of a life is dissected, even to the extent of reverse role playing in a group, to bring greater awareness. By the time souls reach the intermediate levels they begin to specialize in those major areas of interest where certain skills have been demonstrated.[413]

W. H. Myers, the founder of the Society for Psychical Research, speaking from spirit said that through the experience he became "purified through his identification with the sufferings of his victims."[414]

It may seem that reviewing an entire life would take a long time, but outside of Earth School, time does not have the same meaning. The life review happens in great detail. All events are reviewed as they happened, in normal time. The whole process takes little of what we refer to as time in Earth School.

Professor Camille Flammarion told of a man who fell into a ravine and said he had reviewed his entire life during his near-death experience. The review occupied only a second or two, even though the events reviewed covered many years.[415]

Mike Tymn explains the life review in P. M. H. Atwater's near-death experience.

> P. M. H. Atwater, whose NDE took place during 1977, reported that she saw every thought she had ever had, every word she had ever spoken, and every deed she had ever done during her life review. Moreover she saw the effects of every thought,

word, and deed on everyone who might have been affected by them. As she interpreted it, she was judging herself.[416]

James Sherwood, a British automatic-writing medium, received messages from a spirit referred to as "E. K.," who described his life review after his transition.

His thoughts turned inward and moved at a surprising rate. "It raced over the record of a long lifetime which is lit up with a searchlight that spared no blunders, sins or weaknesses, but impartially illumined it all, as one holds up an old, finished garment to the light and notes with dismay its rents and stains. This clear breeze recollection showed me the honest shape and cut of the thing too. I reviewed it as though I had no longer a special responsibility for it but had to understand clearly in what it had failed and in what succeeded."[417]

Francis Banks, an Anglican nun, spoke from spirit through the mediumship of Helen Greaves, comparing the life she had planned before her entry into Earth School with the life she actually lived, event by event.

Somewhere in the deeps of my mind two "blueprints" are brought forward into my consciousness. These are so clear that I can (literally) take them out, materialise them and study them. One is the Perfect Idea with which my spirit went bravely into incarnation. The other is the resultant of only a partially-understood plan ... in fact my life as it was actually lived. ... First of all the mind looks at the whole comparison, and sets the blueprints side by side. This is the first shock; a true humbling of yourself to find that you did so little when you would have done so much; that you went wrong so often when you were sure that you were right. During this experience the whole cycle of your life-term unfolds before you in a kaleidoscope series of pictures. During the crisis one seems to be entirely *alone*. Yours is the judgment. You stand at your own bar of judgment. ... You make your own decisions. You take your own blame. ... You are the accused, the judge and the jury.[418]

Michael Newton also explains that there is a review in minute detail within the person's soul cluster group, the group of souls who entered Earth School together.[419]

Are We Judged?

There is no judgment. There is no condemnation. We evaluate our lives in the life review and come to our own sentiments about the life we led. The life review helps the person learn from the results of their actions and perhaps the person feels regretful, sad, and dismayed, but those emotions are not inflicted upon the person. They are signs we understand the impact our actions had on people so we learn about loving through reviewing our actions.

Is There a Hell?

No one speaking through mediums from the next life describes a hell or place of torment. The concept of Hell is a myth invented by the church in the second century CE. It is simply inconceivable that the Universal Intelligence, embodying pure love, would put people into torture for a moment, let alone an eternity.

There is so much evidence that Hell is a myth that I have devoted an entire webpage to it at www.earthschoolanswers.com/hell/.

There is no being called a "devil," "Satan," "Lucifer," or "Beelzebub." That creature is mythology borrowed from Zoroastrianism.

18

Our Life after the Transition

Just as the seventeenth through the nineteenth centuries saw the rise to prominence of the Newtonian universe and the twentieth century saw the revelation of the quantum universe, the twenty-first century is seeing the ascendence of the spiritual universe.

We are continually expanding our knowledge of this life and the life after this life as humankind could never do during its 200,000-year history. Mental mediums, physical mediums, trance mediums, channelers, and others are receiving clear communication from people very much alive whose bodies have died. They are excitedly describing their lives in the realm we have called the "afterlife" and humankind's place in eternity. Ordinary people are learning to have their own inspiring contacts with loved ones living in the life after this life. What they are learning is being disseminated to masses of people over the Internet and in publications. Amazon lists over 10,000 books fitting the key term "afterlife." Our accumulated knowledge is revealing to humankind the true nature of this life and the life after this life. Humankind is undergoing a spiritual revolution.

This chapter presents a small sampling of what we now know about life in the next life. We know much more that would fill hundreds of books. For the clearest, most enlightening description of life in the afterlife, read Anthony Borgia's books, especially the trilogy of books in *Life in the World Unseen*.[420] In his books, medium Anthony

Borgia conveys descriptions of life in the next life from Monsignor Robert Hugh Benson, a priest now living in the life after this life.

The Physical World in the Life after This Life Is Very Much Like the Physical World We Are Living in Now

The world we are living in now is a spiritual realm, with matter, energy, and forces woven by the Universal Intellect. The next spiritual realm of life is the same, but with a different set of matter, energy, and forces we will experience together. On arriving in the next life, people are astonished at how similar life there is to life on earth. A young man killed over Flanders in World War I in 1914 communicated to his mother from the life after this life through medium Gladys Osborne Leonard. He described his astonishment at the solid, earthlike nature of the world he had entered.

> I asked one of my guides if it was a "thought-world" we were in, though the ground felt quite substantial to my feet; and he said, "It is more real and permanent than the one you have left." I bent down and poked my finger in the soil and found it left a hole, and the soil stuck under my nail. … We went for a walk through beautiful woods and fields; the turf was springy, the air soft and clear, and soft sunshine over everything. We then returned to the house and explored the grounds. There was a beautiful fountain with sparkling water in it. I made a cup of my hands and drank a little, but did not need it, and asked my companion what would happen if I drink too much. "You will not drink too much, that would be foolish; and if you were foolish you would not be here, as each man earns his environment by his conduct. By the working of the natural law, you gravitate to the place for which you are suited; what is within you draws you automatically." I bathed in a glorious lake the water of which was slightly scented. It ran off my body as I stepped out, almost as if it were running off marble or alabaster.[421]

We Have a Change in Understanding and Perspectives

We transition to the life after this life by changing our focus, rather like our watching a sunset for a few minutes and then turning full circle to see a waterfall. When we enter the next stage of life we are the same person we were before we left Earth School. We've just changed the focus of our attention. It is as though we had boarded a plane to a distant country and landed as the same person we were when we boarded the plane.

However, the change in focus results in changes in some of our perspectives. We realize we are eternal beings who just graduated from a temporary Earth School experience. We also have some changes in mental faculties. We are able to communicate telepathically with people and animals. We can travel to a location by intending to be there.

Some people who have had deformities on earth may not easily lose their sense that they still have the deformity. Medium John Sebastian Marlow Ward received the following response to a question from his brother in spirit.

> *What sorts of diseases do you get there?* … Here it is almost entirely a matter of healing the mind and spirit. … [One condition is] hysteria of different kinds, especially a kind which makes the victim believe that he is crippled. Of course, though normally such physical defects which belonged to the earth life do not remain with the astral body, yet in these cases the mind makes the astral body behave as if it were crippled.[422]

Upon entering the next realm, people identify themselves as male and female because of their identities in Earth School. As a result, people believe they are males or females. But they don't regard each other in quite the same way as on earth: "… they seem to have the same feeling to each other, with a different expression of it."[423] However, they assume the identities as one gender or the other. There is no biology that assigns them to one or the other.

The Senses Are Much More Alert and Keen

People's senses in the life after this life are much more alert. The residents of the next life refer to this life as a dream, with impeded sensory experiences. They refer to their new stage of life as the real life. They realize they just allowed their real senses and capabilities to be diminished for the Earth School experience. When they shed their Earth School bodies, their sensory experiences are richer and fuller than when they were in Earth School.

Speaking from the life after this life through a medium, John Thomas told his son, Charles Drayton Thomas, that his spirit body was much more powerful than his physical body.

> I wish to emphasize that not only am I surrounded by greater beauty and happiness, but that my powers of appreciation are greatly expanded. You know how one used to walk past beautiful flowers, and grand sites, without seeing all that was in them; we are able to see the complete beauty. In short, our powers are 1,000 times greater than yours."[424]

Residents of the life after this life also say they remember many more details of their time in Earth School.

> Our minds are like a complete biography of our earthly life, wherein is set down every little detail concerning ourselves, arranged in an orderly fashion, and omitting nothing. The book is closed, normally, but it is ever there, ready to hand, for us to turn to, and we merely recall the incidents as we wish.[425]

When they apply themselves to learning in the next stage of life, they have what amounts to a photographic memory. They recall everything they set about learning.

People with Mental Conditions on Earth Are Helped to Grow from Where They Are Mentally to a Normal State

People with mental conditions are given treatment so they advance to normal functioning. Doctor David Hossack, a noted

American physician, spoke from spirit about the progress of people with mental conditions.

> The insane passed from the earth-life insane still, and countless numbers of our people are required to care for them and give them proper treatment so that their mentality may be restored to the normal. Murderers at war with humanity, hanged or electrocuted on the earth-plane, are liberated in this community, and we are obliged to do what the world of men failed to do— control and educate them. Then, again, we have the ignorant and vicious. The atom of good that has found expression in them must be developed and directed.[426]

When a person who has been mentally disabled from a condition such as Down syndrome, fetal alcohol syndrome, brain injury, hydrocephalus, or other issue that results in little mental development beyond an infant's or young child's Mind, the person loses the physical limitations upon transition to the life after this life and is able to begin developing as a child does. The physical disabilities no longer affect the individual, so development from the level of mental growth into adulthood happens unimpeded. However, it is a growth at the same pace with the same procedures as growing from a child to an adult in Earth School.

For example, a person with an autism spectrum disorder, who has the mental age of an eight- or nine-year-old and communication difficulties, will begin life in the next realm with their mind at the mental age of eight or nine and the same limited communication level. Since their mental capacities are freed from the limitations their physical bodies imposed on them, they advance to become mature and capable over time, just as a child advances to become an adult in Earth School.

Timothy Gray, speaking from spirit through medium August Goforth, explains.

> We may not have been able to carry a tune in Earth School, but all the limitations of the body are gone in the next stage of life, so we can learn to sing melodically or play an instrument adeptly.

Those who were developmentally disabled in Earth School lose the physical limitations, but enter the next stage of life with the knowledge and maturity they had in Earth School. As a result, a person who was a Down's syndrome adult in Earth School will begin as more or less a child in the next stage of life, but without the limitations will mature into a fully functioning adult.[427]

Aviator Amy Johnson, speaking from spirit in a Leslie Flint session, describes what happens to people with mental disabilities when they transition to the next life. You can listen to Amy Johnson speaking at www.earthschoolanswers.com/amy2/.

We do get people come over here who were very retarded on earth, and mentally sort of—well not *compos mentis*. You know, I mean who really are like children. ... we have vast places here like lecture halls and places where people can go and be helped. And I suppose you call them kind of clinics, cum hotel, cum schools, cum colleges, you know. I mean ... vast places, so vast and there's so much that one can do and learn oneself, even when one's helping others. ...

The physical side is purely physical anyway, and ... that no longer applies so therefore they are not under the same condition with the same handicap. But of course there has been a retarded condition ... a mental condition and it is this mental aspect that they have to work on.

But usually of course they are quite bright in themselves even when on Earth, it's just that they cannot express themselves or their brain doesn't function properly. But it doesn't alter the fact that there is the ability there, there is the possibility and of course here it is all ability and possibility to achieve ... and of course under the different conditions they are different and they're much more able to assimilate knowledge and experience, they're much more teachable you know.[428]

The Attitudes and Beliefs People Transition with May Affect Them for Many Years

People transition with all the attitudes and beliefs they held while in the earth environment. Some gather with like-minded people and carry on with the customs of their belief systems, especially religious belief systems. Matthew Ward, speaking through the mediumship of his mother, explains about Christians who believe they are "sleeping" until the resurrection.

> People of stubborn nature whose rigid religious or scientific indoctrination opposes almost everything they encounter here ... may sleep and wake intermittently for hundreds of years before recognizing that they simply had been incorrectly taught.[429]

People who were atheists on earth have an especially difficult time reconciling their experiences after the transition with their belief systems. Psychic Arthur Ford, speaking from spirit to Ruth Montgomery through automatic writing, explains.

> When [an atheist] finds himself on this side of the open door, he will not accept the fact, for he knows that there is no such place. ... For a long time this soul may lie in stupor, waiting for the so-called hallucination to pass away. He is vaguely conscious of activity around him, but to him it has no reality. Sometimes a soul wastes eons in this state.[430]

Some materialist scientists are still materialists in the afterlife. They congregate in the life after this life sure there's some physical explanation for what has happened to them and endeavoring to understand it. They work in teams as they did in Earth School to study what has happened. They still won't allow themselves to believe in the life after this life and spiritual existence.

People Have a Set of Living Circumstances That Fit the Dispositions They Enter With

We find ourselves in circumstances that fit our moral character developed in Earth School. Dr. Robert Hare conveyed from spirit that one's immediate place in the afterlife is determined by a sort of "moral specific gravity." The moral specific gravity is evident in the person's good works or lack of good works. The afterlife is made up of many planes, spheres, or realms. Someone with a low moral specific gravity will gravitate to a lower plane, but can still gradually evolve to a higher plane with the help of more enlightened spirits.[431]

Most people find themselves in the realm for people with a higher specific gravity that the Theosophists called "Summerland." People who are loving and compassionate live in pleasant circumstances with others who are loving and compassionate. Their world is full of love and devoid of discord and loneliness. On the other hand, people who on earth were violent, cruel, and despicable find themselves with others who are violent, cruel, and despicable. Their surroundings match their mental and spiritual condition: they are darker, with unpleasant odors and regular unpleasant sounds coming from their bickering and fights. Living in darker, unpleasant circumstances is not the result of a judgment and certainly isn't any form of a hell. The unfortunate people in these regions and those with them are creating the environment through their thoughts and dispositions.

Dr. Robert Hare, a renowned inventor and an emeritus professor of chemistry at the University of Pennsylvania medical school while on earth, conveyed from spirit that one's immediate place in the life after this life is determined by a sort of "moral specific gravity." The moral specific gravity is evident in the person's good works or lack of good works. The afterlife is made up of many planes, spheres, or realms. Someone with a low moral specific gravity will gravitate to a lower plane, but can still gradually evolve to a higher plane with the help of more enlightened spirits.[432]

Jasper Swain, receiving messages from his son after his death, explains his son's description of the life conditions each person experiences in the life after this life.

> While you are still on earth, your thought, your intentions, everything you do, gives your soul a certain rate of vibration. … When you die and manifest here, you would go straight to the part of our world that vibrates at [that rate].[433]

Elizabeth Fry, who led the eighteenth-century reformation of UK prisons, explains that people coming into the life after this life find themselves in circumstances that fit their mental and spiritual status. You can hear Elizabeth Fry explain this more fully at www.earthschoolanswers.com/fry2/.

> The average person certainly finds, coming here, a happy state of being and great opportunity for knowledge, experience and rest, if it's necessary. There is no depression. The only depression, of course, that one would find is if a person coming here has a great deal that they have cause to regret in their make up and in their life. And in consequence, people do go through a state of readjustment, where they themselves assess themselves, for the first time probably, and they begin to feel they could have done so differently when on Earth and they could have helped so much more than they did.

> The very self-centered people find things very difficult at first. But, of course, we must remember and realize that everyone finds, eventually, that state of existence which one could call happiness. It's something which is never denied, but everyone must earn it. And so everyone goes through changes and stages of evolution, until such time as they have reached a certain goal, if you like, and probably for a very long time … uh, they will stay in that environment until they feel the need or the urge to go further.[434]

Monsignor Robert Hugh Benson in the life after this life, speaking through medium Anthony Borgia, explains that his spiritual development affected the living circumstances in his new life.

Both the house and the garden, he told me, were the harvest I had reaped for myself during my earth life. Having earned the right to possess them, I had built them with the aid of generous souls who spend their life in the spirit world performing such deeds of kindness and service to others. ... Frequently this work is undertaken and carried out by those who, on earth, were expert in such things, and who also had a love for it.[435]

Dr. Franke, who was killed at Dachau death camp, spoke in a Leslie Flint session on April 6, 1964. He explains that the world in the life after this life is created for the individual by their thoughts. As a result, people create the world they expect to have without realizing it. You can listen to him speaking these words at www.earthschoolanswers.com/franke/.

But, it is so strange because it is as if the very thoughts of man can create for himself that which for him is the most best or most necessary. That is why when your friend here, he say to me, "describe your world" I know of course that it is expect for me to describe my world. I describe my world as I know it or try to describe it. But every man who come to you from this side would describe to you exactly what he has experienced. But what his experience may be, may be perhaps very different to another. And if you can realize that this world is a world where thoughts are so powerful, that a man can create for himself, even at first perhaps unknowingly, the kind of conditions which are best for him.

It is as if it is a law, a natural law here, for man to enter into a condition or condition or state of being which is best suited for him. Of course I have explained a little of how some people's minds are so confused and whose conditions of thought are so bad, that they need to be tended. And their thoughts needed to be changed, by the good thoughts and the real thoughts of people who have knowledge, and they are taken to certain places for this. But most people entering into this world for the first time, are usually of course met by their loved ones. They're taken to the homes of their loved ones and they are treated like a lost soul that has been found. They are shown everything, but you must remember that even though you may show a soul from your world certain things, if it is not for them ready to see, they do not see in the same way. It is difficult to explain this, but a person cannot always understand something immediately.[436]

The Lower Realms

Residents of the life after this life speak often about "thought regions" where people who were degenerate on earth are together because of their common attitudes. They indicate that these people are still bent upon impeding humankind's growth to spiritual maturity. As such, they sometimes use the word "hell" to describe the thought region, but never suggest that it is a place of torture. That hell with fire and brimstone is a myth. This is an account Mike Tymn had on his always-fascinating and informative blog of a deceased soldier's description of the thought region where some degenerate people remain of their own choosing:

> … Private Thomas Dowding, a 37-year-old British soldier, was killed on the battlefield in WWI. On March 12, 1917, he began communicating through the mediumship of Wellesley Tudor Pole. After floundering in the ethers, not even realizing he was dead for a time, as time goes on that side, he was met by his brother, William, who had died three years earlier, and began his orientation.

> "Hell is a thought region," Thomas Dowding communicated on March 17, 1917. "Evil dwells there and works out its purposes. The forces used to hold mankind down in the darkness of ignorance are generated in hell! It is not a place; it is a condition. The human race has created the condition."[437]

This thought region, he explains, "depends for its existence on human thoughts and feelings." People are there because they choose to be there, but "Release will come from within some day." When any person chooses to mature out of the condition, they rise from it immediately. [438]

When people leave Earth School, they enter an environment that suits their mental condition, attitudes, and spiritual level of growth. Those who have been selfish and cruel in Earth School will be on a sphere or plane with others who are also selfish and cruel. It happens automatically, without deliberation. That isn't a punishment and it certainly isn't a hell. It's a condition they create by their own expectations for the way life is and ought to be. These realms are created by the negative thoughts and attitudes of the inhabitants. They expect life to be dog-eat-dog, full of greed and selfishness, so that is the way it is for them. And they are with others who have the same inclinations.

These lower areas are described as being dark, dank, and unpleasant. There are unpleasant sounds, such as mad, raucous laughter and shrieks. The beauties of the higher realm are not present there. James M. Peebles, considered the father of the Spiritualist movement, received this communication through a medium from a resident of the life after this life.

I have seen in the lower spheres of darkness clusters, societies, and cities of moral degradation, in the streets of which undeveloped spirits were engaged in disputations, quarrels, enmities, and pitiful ravings. They delighted to annoy and torture each other—delighted to live, in a measure, their earthly lives over again, and to influence gamblers in their dens, inebriates in their wretched retreats, and debauchees in their haunts of crime.[439]

Monsignor Robert Hugh Benson describes through Anthony Borgia descending into the lower realms.

As we proceed slowly from our own realm towards these dark lands, we shall find a gradual deterioration taking place in the countryside. The flowers become scanty and ill-nourished, giving the appearance of a struggle for existence. The grass is parched and yellow, until, with the last remnants of sickly flowers, it final disappears altogether, to be superseded by barren rocks. The light steadily diminishes until we are in a grey land, and then comes the darkness—deep, black, impenetrable darkness; impenetrable, that is, to those who are spiritually blind. Visitors from a higher realm can see in this darkness without themselves being seen by the inhabitants, unless it becomes vitally necessary so to indicate their presence. ...

The inhabitants were variously occupied: some were seated upon small boulders, and gave every appearance of conspiring together, but upon what devilish schemes it was impossible to say. Others were in small groups perpetrating unspeakable tortures upon the weaker of their kind who must, in some fashion, have fallen afoul of their tormentors. Their shrieks were unbearable to listen to, and so we closed our ears to them, firmly and effectively. Their limbs were indescribably distorted and malformed, and in some cases their faces and heads had retrograded to the merest mockery of a human countenance. Others again we observed to be lying prone upon the ground as though exhausted from undergoing torture, or because of expending their last remaining energy upon inflicting it, before they could gather renewed strength to recommence their barbarities.[440]

The residents remain on that lower plane of life until they grow out of it. No one put them there; no one demands they change; no one punishes them. They remain there until they choose to grow into a higher spiritual level. Then they simply evolve into a higher level naturally.

Residents of the lower realms are continually urged to rise out of the unpleasant region by loved ones and guides. Alice Stringfellow received messages from her cousin Bettie in spirit about these darker regions.

They are what you would call the scum of the earth and have passed their lives in vice and crime. There is but one such place for this class, but its extent is incredible and its population immense. They live in discord and misery and everything is dark and forbidding, a dull, leaden fog pervades the air at all times. ... Every good spirit who has friends there goes often to see them and makes every effort to awaken in them sorrow for their past lives and the desire for the pure and higher life. But such efforts are usually a thankless task, for many of them are so wedded to their terrible life that they actually take pleasure in it, and resist every effort that is made in their behalf. But some see their error and are brought to feel the wrong of such a life, and embrace the first opportunity to escape. They have no settled occupation, but live in idleness and it is sad to think how many, by their lives on earth, are preparing a residence for themselves in this dreadful place [441]

Reverend Charles Drayton Thomas, speaking through direct-voice medium Leslie Flint, describes going to those living in ignorance in the lower levels to help them rise out of their circumstances. You can listen to this and more of Rev. Thomas speaking about going to the lower levels to counsel people at this link: www.earthschoolanswers.com/thomas1/.

A lot of these people, they stay on this, sort of, odd, strange level of consciousness—which isn't terribly far removed from earth—but they are living in a kind of dream-state in which they need jerking out of. And that's what we try to do.

Many of us, we go and we enter into their homes and into their lives and we even try to make them appreciate the power that they have within them, that they can manifest that power in that particular environment. Even if they cannot yet aspire or at that moment, as it were, aspire to something higher.

In other words, we try to give them a rejuvenating force which, in itself, will make them start to think more deeply and with more concern about themselves and the possibility of change.

You see, there's this great, this is a great sort of atmosphere and attitude of mind with a lot of these people. They are quite, in their own fashion and way, content to stay on that level of consciousness. And some of them haven't, of course, met souls that, they were drawn to or attached to when on Earth.[442]

People Have Familiar, Substantial Bodies Just As They Did on Earth

All who cross to the next realm describe having a tangible body just as they had when in a physical body. They have no aches and pains, however, and they feel healthy and light. When they see themselves in a reflection, they look as they did in their twenties or thirties if they transitioned at an older age. If they transitioned as children, they grow up on the other side of life. There are no diseases, deformities, or mental difficulties. People have bodies that are whole, healthy, vibrant, and young. There are no "old people," and no old-people ailments.

People May Wear Any Type of Clothing

People may wear the type of clothing they wore in Earth School when they first enter the next realm of life, but most eventually abandon the Earth School garb for comfortable, colorful, exquisitely designed robes and prefer a light sandal for footwear. However, some prefer to go barefoot.

A man named Claude, killed in World War I, described his garments through medium Gladys Osborne Leonard.

> I dress as I did with you, but some people wear white robes because they think when out of the mortal body it is the correct thing to do. If I chose to wear a tunic and sandals, or Beefeater's get up, no one would laugh and jeer; they would realize it made me happy, and that is reason enough.[443]

Who Do We Live With?

We live with people who love us and whom we love. They live with us because they chose to live with us and we chose to live with them. We are not required to live with someone we don't want to be with. We never have to even see them. Hopefully, as the person matures, old animosities fall away, but we always have the free will to be with people we want to be with. Henry Thibault explains in *Letters from the Other Side*:

All who are in the sphere of love and light dwell in families, communities, groups … a world of mutual loves and affections and pursuits. Parents and children are reunited only if that love tie persists, and friends and relatives have no other reason for being together but that they love to have it so.[444]

The collective of brilliant minds named Silver Birch, speaking through Maurice Barbanell, described the loving relationships in the life after this life.

Wherever there has been love between a man and a woman and that love has brought them together and made them as one, and they have lived on the same spiritual plane in your world, then "death" will not part them. "Death" will be a door which will give them a greater freedom for their souls to be more closely united than they were in your world of matter. But if their coming together, their marriage as you call it, was not a marriage of souls but only of bodies, and their souls did not dwell on the same plane, then "death" will drive them further apart, for it will relegate them to their own spiritual spheres.[445]

Another commentator explains about living arrangements in the life after this life when people have more than one spouse.

If someone has more than one spouse or more than one close relationship on earth, the person may live with any one or none of them. Relationships continue to be based on mutual interest and love. We live with whomever we want to live with, and no one can compel someone to live with another.[446]

Jane Sherwood, communicating with her husband in spirit, writes, "There is no sense of possession in even the most intimate relationships."[447]

Where Do We Live?

We live in houses just as we do in Earth School, with yards, flowers, trees, streets, and towns. Houses are described as being elegant and clean. The houses have gardens around them, with natural soil just as on earth. People who enjoyed gardening on earth or wished they had been able to garden tend the gardens. Beautiful flowers grow continually and profusely. No one picks the flowers, however. They are left to grow naturally.

The environment and homes are what the person was accustomed to on earth. A man in spirit speaking through medium William W. Aber explains that people live in circumstances that are similar to those they experienced on earth.

> I have traveled a great deal in spirit life, and I find spirits live as they did on earth. The Hollander does not change his dress or his quaint ways for something that would appear more modern to the Anglo-Saxon visitor. I have often seen the picturesque Swiss homes in spirit life. The Indian villages are here just as on earth, and Red Feather has even treated me to a ride on his pony, and I, in return, took him to a Chinese home. So I find that different nations have different ideas of what constitutes the beautiful in their spirit homes, the same as they had in earth life. [448]

Alice Stringfellow, who received messages from her son Leslie in the life after this life, received this description of a region with Chinese people:

> The Chinese people resemble very much their earthly bodies and their faces have the same almond eyes and flat noses, and they dress for all the world like they did on earth. In fact, I believe every nation, when its people first pass over, keeps the same characteristics that marked them on earth. [449]

The homes reflect who we have become through our Earth School experiences and the activities we engaged in. Edward C. Randall, speaking through medium Emily French, described the living conditions he found himself in upon awakening in the next life. When he awoke he saw a woman who communicated to him telepathically.

> Then one appeared, and, though she spoke no words, I seemed to understand and answered.

In this thought language she told me that she had been my guardian while in the old body, and now that I had been released she would take me over to the home that I had in my life been building. She said: "This room so beautiful is the result of your self-denial and the happiness you brought to others, but there are others not so pleasing; and we passed into another that was dark and filled with rubbish; the air was heavy. This my guide said was built through my selfishness. Then to another, a little better lighted. I was told that every effort to do better created something brighter. Then into the garden where, among beautiful flowers, grew obnoxious weeds, the result of spiritual idleness. "The house must all be made beautiful," she said, "the weeds of idleness uprooted; and this can only be done by yourself, through work in the lower planes, by helping others."[450]

Each person lives in a home, possibly with loved ones, and otherwise with people who have been given the task to take care of the person. If one person has advanced to a higher level than a friend or relative, the two will see each other only occasionally.[451]

The homes are very often duplicates of the homes the people loved in Earth School. Sometimes people who were wealthy in Earth School are in smaller houses to help them learn that wealth isn't important. The construction can be changed at any time by an act of the will.[452]

People wander in and out of people's houses without being announced or invited. Everyone is welcomed and loved.

Monsignor Robert Hugh Benson in the life after this life describes his home as he toured it for the first time:

I have already mentioned that when I was first introduced to my spirit home I observed that it was the same as my earth home, but with a difference. As I entered the doorway I saw at once the several changes that had been brought about. These changes were mostly of a structural nature and were exactly of the description of those that I had always wished I could have carried out to my earthly house, but which for architectural and other reasons I had never been able to have done. Here, earthly needs had no place, so that I found my spirit home, in general disposition, exactly as I had ever wished it to be. The essential requisites indispensably associated with an earthly homestead were, of course, completely superfluous here; for example, the severely mundane matter of providing the body with food. That is one instance of the difference. And so with others it is easy enough to call to mind. As we traversed the various rooms together, I could see many instances of the thoughtfulness and kindness of those who had labored so energetically to help me reconstruct my old home in its new surroundings. While standing within its walls I was fully aware of its permanence as compared with what I had left behind me. But it was a permanence that I knew I could end; permanent only so long as I wished it to be so. It was more than a mere house; it was a spiritual haven, an abode of peace, where the usual domestic cares and responsibilities were wholly absent. The furniture that it contained consisted largely of that which I had provided for its earthly original, not because it was particularly beautiful, but because I had found it useful and comfortable, and adequately suited my few requirements. Most of the small articles of adornment were to be seen displayed in their customary places, and altogether the whole house presented the unmistakable appearance of occupancy. I had truly "come home."[453]

There are no fences or hedges because boundaries are not needed. The homes have no heating or air conditioning because the temperature is always pleasant. The air is comfortably warm, with "gentle perfume-laden breezes."[454]

The homes don't need to be cleaned; nothing becomes dirty. There is no dust or dirt.

Social Activities Are the Same As on Earth

The activities in the life after this life are much the same as activities in Earth School. In our lives today, we often gather to socialize. Gatherings of people in the life after this life are identical. We attend a concert here, sitting in rows of seats with other music lovers listening to performances that excite us. The same scene with equally keen music lovers is played out regularly in the next realm. Here we have family gatherings where we meet with great joy and affection. We have the same gatherings in the next life.

Dr. Robert Hare in spirit explains.

> In addition to our studies we have many other sources of intellectual, moral, and heartfelt enjoyment, from which we derive the most ineffable pleasure: one of which is social reunions and convivial meetings; a coming together of dear friends, brothers , sisters, children and parents; where the liveliest emotion and tenderest affections of our nature are excited, and the fondest and most endearing reminiscences are awakened; where spirit meets in unison with spirit, and heartbeats responsive to heart.[455]

Doctor David Hossack, a noted American physician, spoke from spirit about gatherings and reunions in the next life.

> In addition to our research, we have our diversion from which we obtain great pleasure. We come together in social intercourse, just as you do. Families meet and have reunions, just as you do. Not one particle of love is lost, but rather it is intensified. Everything is intensified to a degree that you cannot imagine. Your pleasure and amusements can in no way compare to those which we are privileged to enjoy.[456]

The Life After This Life Is a World of Thought

The life after this life is a world of thought, explained a man in the life after this life through medium Grace Rosher:

> It is a world in many ways similar to the one we have left, but far more beautiful, as there is nothing to damage or destroy. All our activity is controlled by thought. We realize that the power of thought is the greatest force. Right thinking is the most potent force there is to combat all the so-called horror of evil.[457]

Just as Earth School is created by the Universal Intelligence based on our individual thoughts and expectations, the next realm of life is co-created by the inhabitants. Monsignor Hugh Benson, in spirit, explains through medium Anthony Borgia.

> The united thoughts of the inhabitants of the whole realm will sustain all that grows within it, the flowers, and the trees and the grass, and the water, too, whether of lake, river, or sea.[458]

Summerland Has Exquisitely Beautiful Environments

In Summerland, there are a great many environments, but all are pleasant, with surroundings reminiscent of the environment of Earth School, only more beautiful than the residents are able to describe.

The environment depends on the person's state of being and expectations. If someone is still tied to the earth and its environment, they will experience a very earthlike existence for as long as they remain at that level of thought. The descriptions we receive of the Summerland environment are filled with ecstatic descriptions of a realm just like the earth realm, but much more glorious. Everything that is lovely on earth is exceedingly lovely in the life after this life, and the environment contains additional features undreamt of on earth.

Leland Stanford, speaking to his father from spirit through medium Fred Evans, explained the environment in the life after this life.

> Try and understand, if you can, that not only are the landscapes spiritual, but so is the beauty of all that there is on the other side of life. The physical is only a gross imitation of the spiritual. There is no tongue which can describe the beauty of the spiritual realms, wherein are the souls of those who have just entered on their progressive existence — souls who have striven to do their best according to their light. I say that there is no tongue that can describe the beauties of that land. Take the best that you have, and it is poor in comparison.[459]

Dame Alice Ellen Terry, the Shakespearean actress living in the nineteenth and early twentieth centuries, described the realm of the life

after this life in a Leslie Flint session. You can listen to Ellen Terry
speaking these words at www.earthschoolanswers.com/terry3/.

But I can say that that which constitutes my life is full of beauty,
full of color, full indeed of every aspect of loveliness that words
could depict or experience could experience. There is so much.
There are great buildings, beautiful to behold. There are great
cities in which all can be found that is good for the life of the
individual. There are great theatres, of course, in which great
plays are performed. Great operas, even, are sung. Great
musicians compose great works, so the great orchestras can play
and many can be blessed by music and the color which suffuses
the whole auditorium during its performance.

If only I could even just depict the colorings of this world, this
place in which I find myself now, so far removed from your
realization. Colors beyond description; ever changing in their
subtlety and ever giving forth, as it were, a luminosity and a
beauty so far removed from material ideas, that one cannot hope
to recapture. Thinking, as one must, in comparison to the
rainbow of the earth, one can see here, as it were, the colorings
of innumerable rainbows with innumerable colorings, far more
vast and comprehensive in their spectrum.

There is a diffused subtlety of light at times. There is never
darkness. There is a kind of, what you might call perhaps, a
twilight, and yet this is something which in itself is so unlike
yours. There is a time for quietude with us and rest and yet
there is never any need for rest or sleep; but a peacefulness that
comes upon us when we feel the need. And then our energies,
which never seem to flag, are ever present, ever calling upon us
to do more, to experience more, to endeavor more.

There is all the beauty and magnificence of the countryside and
the colorings of nature, but even more glorified and beautified
than anything you know. There are all the conditions that one
would expect of your life, but much more rarefied and more

beautiful, much more vast in its comprehension and its experience.[460]

The Flowers Are in Glorious Profusion

This description of flowers from Anthony Borgia's *Life in the World Unseen* gives a flavor of how much more remarkable the life after this life is than the earth environment. He was noting that the gardens are very orderly.

By this I do not mean the regular orderliness that one is accustomed to see in public gardens on the earth-plane, but that they were beautifully kept and tended. There were no wild growths or masses of tangled foliage and weeds, but the most glorious profusion of beautiful flowers so arranged as to show themselves to absolute perfection. Of the flowers themselves, when I was able to examine them more closely, I must say that I never saw either their like or their counterpart, upon the earth, of many that were there in full bloom.

Numbers were to be found, of course, of the old familiar blossoms, but by far the greater number seemed to be something entirely new to my rather small knowledge of flowers. It was not merely the flowers themselves and their unbelievable range of superb colorings that caught my attention, but the vital atmosphere of eternal life that they threw out, as it were, in every direction. And as one approached any particular group of flowers, or even a single bloom, there seemed to pour out great streams of energizing power which uplifted the soul spiritually and gave it strength, while the heavenly perfumes they exhaled were such as no soul clothed in its mantle of flesh has ever experienced. All these flowers were living and breathing, and they were, so my friend informed me, incorruptible.

There was another astonishing feature I noticed when I drew near to them, and that was the sound of music that enveloped them, making such soft harmonies as corresponded exactly and perfectly with the gorgeous colors of the flowers themselves. I am not, I am afraid, sufficiently learned, musically, to be able to give you a sound technical explanation of this beautiful phenomenon, but I shall hope to bring to you one with knowledge of the subject, who will be able to go into this more fully. Suffice it for the moment, then, to say that these musical sounds were in precise consonance with all that I had so far seen—which was very little—and that everywhere there was perfect harmony.[461]

The Light Is Higher Quality Than Sunlight, But There Is No Sun

The sky is blue, with no sun, moon, or stars. There is an ambient light of higher quality than the light from the sun. One resident of Earth School describes the light in this way.

The light we have is obtained from the action of our minds on the atmosphere. We think light, and there is light. That is why people who come over in evil condition are in the dark; their minds are not competent to produce light enough for them to see. There is greater intensity of light as we go up through the spheres, which comes from the blending of the more spiritual minds. … When you speak of the sun in the spirit world, you mistake, for there is no such thing. There is light here, radiated from the atoms. Our light is very different from your sun. Your light is grosser than ours; it is unnatural to us, and, therefore, painful to the spirit. Our light is soft, radiant and very brilliant. Your physical eye can never behold it; it is so ethereal, so beautiful, that it blends with sensation.[462]

There is no night, although some describe a "twilight" period each day in which the ambient light is not so bright. People do "rest," but don't sleep unless they want to sleep.

The Temperature Is Always Pleasant

The temperature is always pleasant, with no inclement weather, although there is one description of a "mist" that happens every two earth weeks[463] and another of rain that "is good for our bodies."[464]

There Are Grand Buildings and Halls

Buildings such as halls of learning, schools, art galleries, concert halls, and museums are described as being made of a solid material that has a pearl-like luminescence. The buildings are assembled in vast, beautiful, clean cities. In these halls of learning, all people studiously read out of self-motivated interest.

There Is a Natural Environment Much Like That on Earth

Any of the Summerland environments have all the attributes of Earth School. There are mountains, rivers, lakes, forests, meadows, and vast fields of flowers. There are seas and beaches. Monsignor Hugh Benson, speaking through medium Anthony Borgia, describes a sea.

> Never had I expected to behold such a sea. It's covering was the most perfect reflection of the blue of the sky above, but in addition it reflected myriad rainbow tints in every little wavelet. … From where we were, I could see islands of some considerable size in the distance. … Beneath us was a fine stretch of beach upon which we could see people seated at the water's edge.[465]

The environment is consistently described as being exceptionally beautiful. Stafford Betty, in *The Afterlife Unveiled: What the Dead Are Telling Us About Their World*, includes a description of the environment and homes conveyed through William Stainton Moses, in trance, taking a tour with Mentor, a spirit communicator.

> I have no recollection of losing consciousness, but the darkness seemed to give place to a beautiful scene which gradually unfolded itself. I seemed to stand on the margin of a lake, behind which rose a chain of hills, verdant to their tops, and shrouded in a soft haze. The atmosphere was like that of Italy, translucent and soft. The water beside which I stood was unruffled, and the sky overhead was of cloudless blue. I strolled along the margin of the lake, meditating on the beauty of the scene. I met a person coming towards me [and] knew it was Mentor [one of a group of 49 spirit communicators]. … His voice

as he addressed me was sharp and decisive in tone: "You are in spirit-land, and we are going to show you a scene in the spheres." He turned and walked with me along the margin of the lake till we came to a road which branched along the foot of the mountain. A little brook flowed by its side, and beyond was a lovely stretch of verdant meadow, not cut up into fields as with us, but undulating as far as the eye could reach. We approached a house very like an Italian villa, situated in a nook, amidst a grove of trees like nothing I ever saw before; more like gigantic ferns of the most graceful and varied description. Before the door were plots of flowers of the most lovely hues and varieties. My guide motioned me to enter, and we passed into a large central hall, in the middle of which a fountain played among a bank of flowers and ferns. A delicious scent filled the air, and the sound of sweet music, soft and soothing, greeted the ear.[466]

Music and Art Are Integral Parts of Life in the Next Life

Music and art are integral, vital components of Summerland life. The air seems to be full of music. Not everybody has to hear it, though. The people living there can hear the music only if they want to hear it. Anyone can shut it out and be in silence.[467]

There are vast concert halls and orchestras made up of thousands of people playing instruments, some of which are like those in Earth School while others are unique. Music is both heard and seen. As an orchestra plays, beautiful colors appear around the orchestra in keeping with the music, with no devices responsible for the lights. As Monsignor Benson said through Anthony Borgia, "In music, it can be said that the spirit world starts where the earth world leaves off."[468]

The master composers from earth continue writing works that are performed by the vast orchestras. Great painters, sculptors, poets, novelists, dramatists, and others who were talented on earth continue their work in the life after this life.

This is the world where the artist finds all his dreams come true, where the painter and the poet realize their ambition, where genius has full power of expression, where the repressions of earth are swept away and all gifts and talents are used in the service of one another. [469]

People who wanted to pursue an art while on the earth realm but were unable to do so may learn the art form and develop into accomplished performers. There are many "amateur" displays of the early artwork.

> Amateur … concerts take place continually and every locality has its own. But sometimes there are grand concerts by the great artists.[470]

People Travel by Walking or by Simply Intending to Be Somewhere

People may walk to destinations, although they do have the ability to simply focus on where they would like to be and they are transported there instantly.[471] However, people may not will themselves into another's presence unless the person wants the visitor there. People still have privacy and free will to choose those they want to associate with. Arthur Ford, speaking from spirit through medium Ruth Montgomery, explains.

> It is true that we are able to think ourselves into any locale to see almost anyone, but … if no one wants to see you, you are not able to intrude on his solitude or other activities. It must be a two-way street.[472]

However, in the early periods after the transition, people prefer to walk unless the destination is far or in another realm.

There are automobiles, but they do not burn petroleum products and emit noxious gasses. In some communities, hobby groups of people interested in automobiles have created replicas of particular models of automobiles. They ride in them for sport and pleasure.[473]

People May Speak or Communicate Telepathically

People may communicate by making vocal sounds or through telepathy. The longer someone is a resident of the life after this life, the more interested the person is in foregoing the ponderous action of stringing words together to convey thoughts. Minds are more open to each other so thoughts are accessible by anyone through telepathy.[474]

Henry Thibault conveys the messages of a speaker coming through a medium known as A. B. using automatic writing. The speaker describes a remarkable blending of minds between people.

> On this side, when I met my beloved wife, I became herself—she was transformed into me. All that she knew and felt became the content of my consciousness. All that I had attempted and achieved, all that I had failed to accomplish, yet battled and struggled to complete, was known to her as no words, no thoughts even, as earth uses the terms, could have conveyed. We were one, yet individually our own very separate selves, knowing as we were known, to the full extent of each other's capacity. [475]

However, it is possible to use our free will to deliberately keep our thoughts to ourselves. That requires more effort, so if someone is freely, spontaneously speaking, the thoughts will simply pour out into the discourse.

There is a "universal spirit language," so that people who came from various language backgrounds are all able to understand conversations and discourses.[476] They explain that people in groups with similar customs from earth keep their languages as long as they want to, but in communicating with people who speak other languages, the communication is through telepathy of messages so language is not a barrier.[477]

Children in the Life after This Life

D. E. Bailey, meeting with medium Mrs. Swain in 1886, received the following message about children in the life after this life from Bailey's daughter, Eva, and wife, Dora.

> [Children] are placed in a kind of intermediate condition between the upper and lower spheres. They are given in charge of pure and holy spirits. They are always brought back to their

parents, not because of their wisdom, but of their purity and, too, because they can more readily take up and act upon the forces surrounding the parents. They are continually hovering around their earth homes, and if they find pure and harmonious conditions, these children progress very fast, but they do not increase in size any faster than they would have done had they remained in earth life. They are often sent on errands of great importance by higher spirits. They are strongly attached to parents and to those to whom they have to go to gather earth knowledge and, oftentimes, when the parents are wrapped in slumber, these little ones are allowed to come, fondle and caress them, until that part of their nature, which never found expression in earth life, has been gratified.

Those who die in infancy and childhood, after they have been in spirit long enough to attain the stature of manhood and womanhood, have the power to reduce themselves to their former size, and so appear the same as when on earth and, by this means, parents and friends, when they entered the spirit world, recognized them at once.[478]

Monsignor Benson, speaking from spirit through medium Anthony Borgia, describes a children's realm that has been called "the nursery of heaven." Children who have transitioned from Earth School live in a special area, called the "children's sphere," where they learn with other children.[479]

Leslie Stringfellow, speaking from spirit through his mother, Alice Stringfellow, describes the place where children grow up, including children who had not been born on earth:

There are many homes for children here, and today we visited one situated in an immense grove of trees and the buildings covered a space of ground as large as a small town.

This was for small children under seven and eight years. Older ones have other homes, where they go after leaving these infant ones.

The children are watched over and cared for by the most beautiful and motherly spirits who in their earth-life were especially fond of children. These are entirely orphans, as we call them, or children whose parents are still on earth, but who will take them home when they themselves come over.

These children are educated in every branch of knowledge and those who have special tastes for music, painting and other accomplishments are given every opportunity to cultivate these talents.

In talking to these little ones, it was easy to tell those who had had no earth life or experience [aborted, miscarried, or stillborn]. They seemed more spiritual, but not so sympathetic and affectionate, as the others who had known a mother's love on earth.

Not in this whole spirit world is there a child who would for a moment think of wishing to leave this bright and happy home, in exchange for the pains and sorrows of your world.[480]

You can listen to a resident of the next stage of life describing his reunion with his sister who had transitioned in infancy and grew up in the life after this life at www.earthschoolanswers.com/alf2/. You can listen to Annie Nanji in spirit speaking about meeting her miscarried children whom she didn't realize were alive in the next life: www.earthschoolanswers.com/children/.

Monsignor Benson explains that "there were to be found children of all ages, from the infant, whose separate existence upon the earth-plane had amounted to only a few minutes, or who even had had no separate existence at all, but had been born 'dead,' to the youth of sixteen or seventeen years of earth time."[481]

Dr. David Hossack, a noted American physician, spoke from spirit about the caregivers who take care of children unborn on the earth who have been born in the life after this life.

There are countless millions of children unborn physically who are plunged into this world of ours, and there are millions of women here who have never known motherhood in earth life, who take and care for them, watch and aid their growth, mentally and physically, and in that manner satisfy the craving of motherhood.[482]

The child's physical and intellectual advancement is much faster and richer than in Earth School. The children are "given knowledge of a particular subject rather than taught it."[483] They are taught to read, but most of the other teaching found in Earth School classrooms is not taught to the children. When they reach a suitable age, the children choose their vocation and focus their studies on becoming proficient in its practices.

Historian and author N. Riley Heagerty explains what he has learned about schools from people living in the life after this life.

There are great schools to teach the spirit children. Besides learning all about the universe and other worlds, about other kingdoms under God's rule, they are taught lessons of unselfishness and truth and honor. Those who have learned first as spirit-children, if they should come into your world, make the finer characters.[484]

The Ability to Relive Life Experiences

All experiences that ever were or ever will be are accessible from the Universal Intelligence. In the next realm we are able to access events from our own lives from this vast archive. John Thomas, speaking from spirit to his son, Charles Drayton Thomas, explains.

… it will be possible someday to reenact all the brightest and best scenes of one's earthly life … and also those which one has missed on earth; all that which once was possible, but which did not come to fruition. You will realize the good of what you have done, and the happiness which you had, and beyond that, also, the happiness which you might have had, and which, just because you might have had it, it is still yours.[485]

John Thomas, speaking from spirit to his son, Charles Drayton Thomas, explains that it is possible for someone to review specific lifetime events at any time.

We can [live over again the happiest scenes of our earth life] and do. It is especially wonderful and beautiful when two recall such things together.[486]

Desires and Expectations

A person's desires and expectations are the same immediately after the transition as before. The mind does not change.

As a result, people may want to eat, sleep, drink, smoke, and all the other things they did when on the earth realm. Since they expect food, sleep, drinks, and smoking to be available, it is there. They don't will it into being. What the person expects to be in their environment is there because of the expectation. However, drinking a beverage with all the properties of wine or stronger drinks does not intoxicate.[487] It isn't necessary to sleep, but if someone wants the experience, they lie down, and sleep comes naturally.

As the person matures away from the earth habits, expectations and desires, the need to eat, drink, sleep, smoke, and other activities carried over from earth, extinguish.[488]

George Harris, a builder in the life after this life, came through in a Leslie Flint session describing the fact that people can choose to eat or not, but if they eat, he was amazed to realize they never have to make a trip to a toilet. You can listen to George Harris speaking at www.earthschoolanswers.com/harris/.

> I get the impression that we . . . I don't know. When I first came here it seemed, I suppose, it was necessary to me to have certain things, meals and that. And now I don't feel the urge so much. It's funny that. And in consequence I don't seem to need to eat. You don't have to go to the toilet even. Isn't it funny? I mean, you have a darn good meal and you'd think, well, later on, you'd have to go the joey [toilet], you know, but you don't!

> That's a thing that shook me at first. Couldn't make head or tail of this. And then they said, "Oh well it's different. It ain't the same old physical body," as they call it, and "it hasn't got the same, sort of, construction," or whatever that is. And, uh, they said, "Really, this business that you want to eat and, others like

you, feel the need for a cup of tea and all that, it's only a state of mind."

Course, I suppose, in some sort of way, what they say is true enough but, um, I suppose it is. But I'm so happy as I am in my own natural surroundings and carrying on the kind of things that appeal to me. And I meet many people now that I've made pals with.[489]

A woman named Rose Hawkins living in the life after this life came through in a Leslie Flint session explaining that if she wants tea, it is simply available. If she loses her taste for tea, it will no longer be available. You can listen to her speaking these words at www.earthschoolanswers.com/rose/.

Of course, I don't feel the urge to eat. I did when I first came here, but it was mostly fruit and that sort of thing that one had. But, um, I suppose it is that as you lose the desire for something, you realize it ain't so important, then it ceases to exist for you. But, um, I was a one for my cup of tea, and I still like it and have it.

Now, I suppose, people will say where do you get your tea from? Do you get it from... from some place on your side? Well, of course, it must come from some place on this side, so it must be grown and it must be, sort of, made, mustn't it? . . .

Well, it's a funny thing though. You know, I'm not conscious, for instance, I don't go into a kitchen and put a kettle on ... and make myself a cup of tea, in that sense. But if I feel the need for a cup of tea ... well, all I can say is, that it's there. . . .

Of course, some people say, and even people over here, have said that it's, uh... not a reality. It's only because I think it's necessary I have it, and it's made possible. But when I lose the desire for a cup of tea, which, um, I've been used to having all my life, uh, when I lose the desire for it, it will no longer exist for me. Because that's a—and I'll tell you the honest truth—that's one of the reasons why I'm afraid of going too far.[490]

One person who came through in a Leslie Flint session loved to smoke a pipe, so he had a pipe. Of course, the smoke was not deleterious to his health and didn't affect the atmosphere. All the pleasurable sensations of smoking a pipe were there, however. Since there is nothing but Mind and experiences, the same experiences will occur. There never was a physical pipe in a world outside of the person on the earth realm—just the experience of smoking. As a result, the same is true in the life after this life.

Raymond Lodge, speaking in the life after this life, said that some of the newly transitioned soldiers smoked cigars. [491]

Frederick Myers in the next life, speaking through medium Geraldine Cummins, described that, in this realm, what a person wants is simply available:

> Myers pointed out that the average unthinking man in the street may desire or glorify a brick villa and will likely find it. If he were to long for a superior brand of cigar, he can have the experience of smoking this brand. If he wanted to play golf, he may continue to play golf. "But he is merely dreaming all the time or, rather, living within the fantasy created by his strongest desires on earth. After a while, this life of pleasure ceases to amuse and content him. Then he begins to think and long for the unknown, long for a new life. He is at last prepared to make the leap in evolution and this cloudy dream vanishes." [492]

People new to the next stage of life may prefer to wear the clothes they wore in Earth School, so those clothes are provided without their request. What they are given suits their desires and expectations. After a while, people lose their interest in retaining the habits of Earth School and don a spirit robe. The spirit robes are a variety of colors. The residents of the life after this life don't change clothing one sleeve at a time. When the person wants the spirit robe, it is simply on their body, without effort. If the person wants to put on clothes from Earth School for an occasion, the clothes appear on the person's body.

Creating with the Power of Thought

People can also create consciously. They can will things into being. There is only Mind and experiences, so thoughts have power. A. D. Mattson, speaking from spirit through medium Margaret Flavell Tweddell, explains.

> Here you think up your clothes, they materialize, and you put them on. When you want to change what you are wearing, you can thought-power off the clothes you have on and create something else. We all tend to wear the kind of things that we enjoy … Whatever we create remains as objective reality as long as we wish it to.[493]

However, the process of creating by thought is something that must be learned, as Dr. Alice Gilbert's son in spirit told her.

> It is not easy to explain how thought creation works. … Some timid unadvanced folk take centuries [to learn how to create]. It is very funny to watch them practicing.[494]

The architects and builders who create large buildings must work together in a concerted effort. Matthew Ward, speaking through his mother, explained.

> Manifesting huge, elaborate buildings with exalted purposes requires immense amounts of increasingly controlled power.… The arrangements that enable that process to happen involve extensive cooperation and intricate planning by our large force of expert architects and engineers.[495]

George Harris, who was a builder on earth, continues his trade in the life after this life. He explains that he lays bricks just as he did on earth, but he has been told that he's laying bricks because he expects and wants to lay bricks rather than build walls using more of his Mind. George mentions going to meetings, presumably with the building contractor, where he was told to have a different outlook, which he mistakenly refers to as a "look out." We can glean from the content of the talks between the contractor and George that he is having trouble understanding. He laid bricks on earth and is determined to lay bricks in the life after this life, so the Universal Intelligence makes bricks, mortar, and a trowel available to him without his asking, because he wants to feel the bricks in his hands and lay the mortar to place one brick at a time.

George's description of wanting to lay bricks follows. You can listen to him speaking at www.earthschoolanswers.com/harris2/.

> But then they do try and tell me, for instance, and others that have been to these meetings and that, where they say as how it's a state of mind; that everywhere where you live's a state of mind and if you think you want to do certain things, then you do certain things. But until you learn to, sort of, "look out" in a different way, then you carry on in the same old way.
>
> Well, I mean, that's all very well, as far as it goes, but why should I want to change? I'm quite happy. I was a builder on your side. I got pleasure out of my work. I always enjoyed it. Do the same here. … To me, the bricks I use are as solid as any I ever used on Earth. Mind you, I don't know where they come from. That's a … you asked me that and I don't know. I suppose there must be places where they… brick kilns?... I don't know. But everything looks real to me. Everything seems real. And everything seems much as it was on Earth.
>
> But that's what these others tell me; that, uh, you know, that it's a state of mind. I don't know whether they're trying to tell me that because of my state of mind—and I think I can't build unless I have bricks and I have all the things that are necessary, like.
>
> And therefore, they seem to try and say to me (of course I don't believe a word of it) they try and say to me that I do all of this out of my own state of mind—and the same applies to all the other people where I am; that we're working on a certain, what do you call it, state of mind, vibration or material vibration or something they try to tell me, you know. … I mean, the bricks are as real as real, and the houses that we build are as real as

real. And we go through the same old process as we did on Earth. I mean we … we really build.[496]

Negative Emotions

The people living in the life after this life are human beings living in a different country. They still feel the emotions we all feel on earth. They feel joyful, excited, frustrated, sad, and the range of other emotions. Stafford Betty describes Leslie Stringfellow's statements from spirit about negative emotions he and others feel.

> But all is not fun and games in Summerland. Even though Leslie describes it as a thousand times better in every way than our world, he later admitted that his mother's depression following his death—a depression that stretched out for 11 years—"has many times been bitterness to me." Other spirits suffer from neglect. They want to be remembered, to be in their loved ones' thoughts, to have even a single flower left on their gravestone. A loneliness can figure prominently in Summerland. At one point Leslie makes a plea to all of us on earth to make more use of the medium's gift. If we did, if we kept up a running conversation with "the dead," fewer of them would be so soon forgotten.[497]

Occupations and Preoccupations

People are industrious because being active, accomplishing goals, and serving others brings them bliss. Their work is recreation.[498] People act out of love for one another, without expecting compensation for the work. They give of themselves in ways that make both them and the receiver joyful. Builders build houses for people who desire to have a house without expectation of being paid. They use their thoughts to create, but there is still labor involved in the building. Everyone works out of enjoyment and a desire to serve others.

> … It is a busy world where everyone is doing his or her part. We do not have any strife for money or need for money; so you see the occupation of the great majority of your people is gone. It is only by helping others in this life—and this is equally true of the

earth-life—that one betters his conditions and enriches himself. This is the law. The only happiness that the inhabitants of earth really get is through being charitable, doing good, and making the world happier. The only wealth that any man carries beyond the grave is what he gives away before he reaches the grave.[499]

Medium Eliza Duffey reports this narrative she received from someone living in the life after this life describing employment available to the speaker:

Unlike the manners of earth, where circumstances or misjudgment of others force many into employments entirely uncongenial to them … in the new life with which I was trying to familiarize myself, the work of each was that best suited to his or her tastes and abilities, and for that reason was an enjoyment and not a task. Labor was no longer a bondage enthralling body and soul, and dwarfing the intellect, but added light which aided the faculties to expand and develop themselves in healthful ways. All professions, all occupations, seemed represented.[500]

All occupations known to people on earth are represented in the life after this life, except police, prison guards, undertakers, and other such occupations that fit only the earth environment solely.[501] No one is compelled to perform any task.

Thoughts have power. Through thoughts, people build solid things, such as buildings. Architects design the buildings and draw up plans. Builders take their hand at the various activities required to make an exquisite building. All the usual materials associated with earth builders are present. However, the building process occurs through intention, one portion and one level at a time. There is still great effort in creating the building but thought results in the design and assemblage. However, each person must come to the point of wanting to use thoughts as part of the building process. Until the person does, they can continue to use the methods they used on earth.

There are gardeners, musicians, architects, counselors of newly transitioned people, teachers of children, craftsmen in all crafts, and all manner of occupations. A Lutheran minister, theologian, and professor,

Alvin D. Mattson, spoke through medium Margaret Flavell about the plethora of occupations he had to choose from when he arrived in the life after this life.

> I find the latitude in our choices here to be quite incredible. I don't know what field I will enter at the present time. I will have to pray over this and inquire into various fields, because once we are committed, we are committed for a considerable time. Here we don't work so much as individuals. We work more in bands and groups.[502]

A person may continue an occupation from Earth School. Artists still paint; builders still build houses; scientists still perform their research; and teachers still teach. Shakespeare and Oscar Wilde are still writing plays. However, people are not required to be anything they don't wish to be. If a person always desired to play the piano while in Earth School but never had the chance, they may learn to play the piano in the life after this life and give recitals or be part of the vast orchestras. Someone who loved to grow flowers on earth but ended up being an auto mechanic can become a gardener in the life after this life.

Medical doctors in the next life are helping doctors in Earth School to practice medicine and surgery. "Many a spirit doctor has guided the hand of an earthly surgeon when he is performing an operation," Monsignor Benson explains from spirit.[503] There are great "halls of rest" for people who have transitioned suddenly and violently where nurses and doctors tend to them.

Counselors or support people work with individuals who had a difficult time while on earth and are still recovering from the experiences. The counselors help the person go through growth as on earth. Dr. Franke, who came through in a Leslie Flint session, explains that he is a counselor and explains how he helps people.

> In this hospital ... I call it that, though it is more than that, and you would not even first realize it was hospital, but even so, it is a form of hospital. And it is a hospital for curing of the sickness of the mind or the thoughts, which must be changed to help people to forget many things which it is better they should not remember, which hold them back, which still make them

materially minded and, in consequence, retard their progress. So, we have to work very much perhaps like some of your psychologists or perhaps those whose task it is on earth to try to trace back the causes which create the unpleasant effect. We have to know individuals, we have to understand them, we have to talk with them. We have to learn exactly what it is that is holding them back in their progress. And there are many different reasons and different things why a person does not adapt immediately or even after some time, into the fuller life here.[504]

You can listen to a fuller explanation of Dr. Franke's activities counseling people in recovery areas at www.earthschoolanswers.com/franke2/.

Since there are no manufacturing plants, people who engaged in manufacturing occupations on earth find other occupations and preoccupations. Many teach children who have left Earth School and grow up in the afterlife. Some people do "rescue" work, helping people who have made the transition to understand where they are and guiding them along as they adjust to their new lives. People engage in the occupations that give them bliss.

A man in the life after this life named Lester Coltman gave messages through automatic writing to his aunt, Lillian Walbrook. He describes his choice of a profession.

My work is continued here as it began on earth, in scientific channels, and, in order to pursue my studies, I visit frequently a laboratory possessing extraordinarily complete facilities for the carrying on of experiments. I have a house of my own, delightful in the extreme, complete with library filled with books of reference—historical, scientific, medical—and, in fact, with every type of literature. To us these books are as substantial as those used on earth are to you.[505]

Colton also describes occupations in the life after this life in detail.

If he has a great talent, that he brings to perfection here; for if you have beautiful music, or any other talents, we have them here much more. … Work is a wonderful life, and those who become teachers of souls learn so much themselves. Literary souls become great orators, and speak and teach in eloquent language. There are books, but of quite a different kind from yours. One who has studied your earth-laws would go into the spirit-school as a teacher of justice. A soldier, when he himself has learned the lessons of truth and honor, will guide and help souls, in any sphere or world…[506]

People are not required to work, but if someone chooses not to work, that person eventually rises out of the indolence.

There are among spirits, as among men, some who live only for themselves; but their idleness weighs upon them, and, sooner or later, the desire to advance causes them to feel the need of activity, and they are glad to make themselves useful.[507]

Scientists and Engineers Continue Their Work in the Next Life

People who were scientists on earth do not become all-knowing when they transition to the life after this life. They continue to learn from the point at which they were before the transition, using more advanced technology and equipment they develop using their newly found knowledge. New principles and discoveries are conveyed to them from higher-level minds. They in turn impart them to scientists in the earth realm working in the same field, although virtually all the scientists on earth are not aware of it. As a result, the scientists working in the next life and scientists on earth are advancing together, with the scientists in the next life slightly ahead of the scientists on earth.[508]

The same is true of engineers in the life after this life. John Thomas, speaking from spirit to his son, Charles Drayton Thomas, explains.

When engineers come here whose minds are bent upon engineering, and who may not be ready to take up another line of study or work, they continue experimenting in a limited way, especially with electrical engineering. They are sometimes able to discover certain things which they then endeavor to impress upon the minds of suitable people on earth.[509]

The inspirations that provide humankind with discoveries that make life more enjoyable are provided when the time is right, as Monsignor Benson explains from spirit.

> The people of the earth have it in their power to see that modern inventions are employed solely for their spiritual and material good. When the time comes that real spiritual progress is made, then the earth-plane can expect a flood of new inventions and discoveries to come through from the scientists and engineers of the spirit world. But the earth-plane has a long and sorrowful way to go before that time comes. And in the meantime the work of the spirit scientist continues.[510]

Lutheran minister Alvin D. Mattson spoke through medium Margaret Flavell about his father in the life after this life, who accepted the role of helping specialists on the earth work to alleviate world hunger. He influenced their minds to help them make discoveries.

> Eventually he decides to work with a group analyzing hunger problems and tries to transfer, telepathically, their solutions to specialists on earth working on the same problem from their end. The silent transfer to earth of helpful ideas is a common activity of spirits ...[511]

The scientists on earth have no idea how many of their discoveries are inspired by scientists in the life after this life. Marie Curie describes from spirit how much she found out she had been inspired by scientists in the life after this life. You can listen to her speak at www.earthschoolanswers.com/curie/.

> I don't know, I think to myself as I look back on my life, I realize now that what I had to do I did. It was not just by myself, you know. A lot of things you know, we call inspiration, you know, which in a way is so. I did not know then that I was to some extent induced by people from this side of life. A lot of the

things that we sometimes think come from ourselves do not necessarily come that way. But we are inspired, inspiration, you know, guidance from people on this side of life who help us, you know. I was I suppose in a way a medium. I never thought it was like that. I did not understand this Spiritualism. I had some experience of it, yes, but not much.

But now I know that many of the things that have been done and the things that I did, you know, were things that were given to me from people on this side, people that I have now met, you know. I have met many souls here who are deeply involved, you know, in the work, to heal the sick and the suffering, to find ways of curing diseases. And I now know that some of the things that happened with me which I thought at the time I was aware were truths of my own invention, I was inspired, you know, impress what to do and how to go about it. You know, we are all children. We don't understand perhaps sometimes. In a way, we are being impressed, we are given guidance, we are helped. We are children and we need guidance and help, but we don't always understand or accept, you know.[512]

Masters of the Arts Inspire Performers and Artists on Earth

Those on the next planes of existence are greatly interested in inspiring people in Earth School and helping them to create beautiful art works, symphonies, performances, and other artwork. Some explain that they are looking for promising people to inspire. They also continue their own development of their craft far beyond the capabilities they had while in Earth School.

Chopin explained from spirit in a Leslie Flint session that musicians gather together and compose and play compositions, make comments to each other, and receive helpful advice. Together, they go to other realms to listen to the music composed there, which is unique to that realm and condition.[513]

He was having one of several conversations he had with a musician named Rose Creet, who was sitting with Leslie Flint. He had explained that he was helping Rose perfect her performance. In this conversation, Chopin remarked to her, "I'm going to make of you an excellent pianist."[514]

Recreation

Monsignor Robert Hugh Benson, speaking from the life after this life,[515] explains that people do not suffer fatigue of body or mind. However, if someone becomes restless with one form of work, the person may engage in another form of work for a while or an endless variety of recreation activities. Whatever people enjoy doing in Earth School, they may continue it in the next stage of life. There are concerts, halls of art, gardening, beautiful scenic paths, and the whole abundance of pleasurable activities we have in Earth School, plus more.

> In our theaters, just as in our concert halls, we have those exceptionally talented people who once performed so brilliantly for you. ... We have marvelous theatrical comedy productions and also performances by masterful comedians.[516]

Performances are given of historical events in which the actual people involved in the activities perform as they did in the events.[517]

When someone wants to engage in a pleasurable activity, the circumstances are available. The desire for the activity among people interested in it makes the equipment or circumstances available, without request. Mary Ann Ross, speaking in a Leslie Flint session, says that she always wanted to play the piano when she was on the earth. After her transition, when she entered the house in which she was to live, she was amazed to see a piano there. The man accompanying her was a piano teacher. When she sat to play the piano, she received mental guidance from her teacher so she played well very quickly.[518] You can listen to the recording of Mary Ann Ross describing from spirit when she first saw the piano and played it at www.earthschoolanswers.com/ross4/.

There is no hunting or other activity that would terrorize or injure animals. There is no slaughter allowed, under whatever cloak it masquerades, such as sport. In this realm, animals cannot die, but they can be subject to terror. Therefore that constitutes injury and is not allowed. [519]

There are races and other contests, but those engaged in them have only a friendly rivalry. There is no reward involved. The participants enjoy becoming more capable and accomplished, not being better than someone else. People play sports such as baseball and football in areas designed for the sports.[520]

Monsignor Benson explains that there are beautiful theaters for concerts and plays, and vast libraries that contain every work produced by humankind both in this stage of life and the next. There are halls devoted to painting, sculpture, literature, fabrics, tapestries, and many other subjects, filled with people practicing their skills and enjoying the camaraderie of people with the same interests. Every art object and discovery is represented there. None is lost.[521]

Lester Kolterman in spirit, giving messages through Miss Lillian Walbrook, his aunt, describes his recreation activities.

I have a music-room containing every mode of sound-expression. I have pictures of rare beauty and furnishings of exquisite design. I am living here alone at present. Many friends frequently visit me as I do them in their homes and, if a faint sadness at times takes possession of me, I visit those I loved most on earth.[522]

There are recreational devices such as boats and motorcycles. They are not powered by machinery. The boats sail effortlessly and the motorcycles travel with ease because of the intention of the person controlling the effort to have the boat or motorcycle propel itself forward.[523]

Animals Are Abundant and Communicate with People

The fields and woodlands are populated with all the animal species, but they don't prey on one another, and they are not afraid of each other. The animals are described as living in separate areas, but people can walk up to them and hold them. The animals are at a higher state of being than in Earth School, able to communicate through a telepathy that doesn't require speech. They understand themselves as being one with humankind and are completely comprehended by those with whom they come into contact. No animals are killed. No animal products are used in making things.

There are beautiful birds with gorgeous plumage singing and twittering in a symphony of sound. As with the other animals, the birds can communicate. Monsignor Hugh Benson, speaking from spirit through Anthony Borgia, explains.

> But it was their trusting friendliness that was so delightful by comparison with the earthly birds, whose life there takes them into another world almost. Here we were part of the same free world, and the understanding between the birds and ourselves was reciprocal. When we spoke to them we felt that they knew just what we were saying, and in some subtle way we seemed to know just what their thoughts were. To call to any particular bird meant that that bird understood, and it came to us.[524]

Dame Alice Ellen Terry, speaking from spirit through the direct-voice mediumship of Leslie Flint, explains that the life after this life contains animals of all kinds, and people communicate telepathically with them. You can listen to Ellen Terry speaking these words at www.earthschoolanswers.com/terry2/.

> We have, of course, all the animals that constitute nature, but there again in a more highly developed state of being. There are all the domestic animals that one has loved, but even with them there is the realization of that oneness with man's world and man's kingdom. There is the ability for the animal world to make itself understood and we to understand them. They do not have to convey in words, because it is not necessary or possible, possibly.

> But the point is, that we know what they think, we know what they feel and they know what we say unto them. They read our thoughts and they are able to understand all that we feel. That, I think, is one of the greatest things of this life: is that being completely and absolutely comprehended, not only by the human race similar to oneself, but to the lesser (so called)

kingdom of the animal and the birds and the freedom and the beauty.[525]

A man named Terry Smith came through in a Leslie Flint session describing his experience of communicating telepathically with a cat. His companion in his new environment explained that animals are more capable than people on earth give them credit for. You can listen to Terry Smith speaking these words at www.earthschoolanswers.com/smith/.

> Then all of a sudden, during the middle of the conversation this cat did the most funny thing, I thought. It may sound silly, but it jumped off this chair and it came up to me and it sat on its hind legs and it looked up at me. And it sort of cocked its ears up and it didn't meow, it didn't make that noise like a cat—but it was just as if the thing spoke! Do you know I nearly dropped ... I was so shaken.
>
> She says, "Oh, hmm," she says, "don't worry," she says, "You'll get used to that." She says, "The animals," she says, "over here have developed, to a great extent, their ability to make themselves understood. Of course, on Earth in a way they can do that, but we don't hear them speak because they haven't language as we understand it. But over here their thoughts are such that they can, sort of, vibrate ..." she says, "... the atmosphere and you can hear the sounds. And it's merely their thoughts being transmitted to you so that you can hear them."
>
> Then she says ... hmm, this cat says, "How are you?" You know, and I thought, "by cripes, this is quite mad," you know. Cats don't say "how are you?" and, hah, I didn't know what to do, what to say.
>
> She says, "Don't worry," she says, "You'll get used to that." She says, "Animals," she says, "are much more sensitive than people realize and they have their own knowledge of things. They can transmit thoughts and they pick up thoughts and you'll get used to the fact that animals can convey a great deal more from this side than they can on Earth."

Anyway I got, sort of, adjusted to the idea and I said, "Very well thanks." And then the cat … it seemed as if the cat said—I don't say the cat said this, but it seemed as if it said, "Well, I hope you'll be happy here."

And I thought, "well this is most peculiar." Then the cat went back and sat on the chair and curled up and as far as I was concerned it went to sleep.

Of course I still couldn't get this at all. She says, "Don't worry," she says, "you'll understand, that animals have a great, uh, capacity of understanding and over here they can transmit their thoughts, the same as I can transmit mine to yours, without even the effort of speaking if I want to." She says, "You can read my thoughts and I can read yours. Thought is a real thing to us and it's very tangible and that's why animals can communicate by thought-force," she said.[526]

Mary Ann Ross, coming through in a Leslie Flint session, describes a dog the family had in her childhood that, in the next life, jumped up into her bed and startled her. She then describes seeing other animals. You can listen to Mary Ann Ross speaking these words and more at www.earthschoolanswers.com/ross3/.

Then there was a dog jumped on ma bed and this really gave me a fright, in a way. Not that I was afraid of dogs, I was fond of animals, but this was a dog that we'd had many years ago, that ma father adored and that was killed by a cart, many years ago, when I was, oh—in my twenties, I suppose. And this dog we called it Nipper. And do you know, to see Nipper jump on this bed startled me and I just couldn't realize. My mother said, of course we've animals here too. Ah, I thought well this is—you know, I just couldn't understand it, if they were dead. As my mother said, that there'd be animals too. And she said, oh that's nothing. She said, out in the yard, she said, you'll see a lot of other animals too.[527]

A man named Wagstaff came through in a Leslie Flint session on November 2, 1970, explaining that he and a friend of his regularly talk to the animals telepathically.

> My friend and I, we love the countryside. We talk to the animals, and it's a funny thing that. You say talk to the animals, you can talk to animals here and they understand you too, and they have their own little way of life.[528]

The Vastness of the Afterlife

The people communicating to us from the life after this life explain that it is vaster than we can imagine. There are millions of realms of existence, occupied by vast numbers of people at various levels of spiritual maturity and interest. It is incorrect to view the next life as a few discrete planes. Instead, there is level after level of continuously different planes where people are together based on their interests and attitudes.

People remain individuals who continue to grow spiritually until they have developed into celestial beings inhabiting the highest realms. These higher-order beings do come to work with people on the lower levels. They also teach in a chain of being, providing guidance and instruction to people on lower levels who then administer it to the general public in the life after this life or to people living in Earth School.

People are able to visit lower levels, but may not visit higher levels unless accompanied by a guide, and even then can only venture to the outer fringes of the higher level. John Thomas, speaking from spirit to his son, Charles Drayton Thomas, explains.

> If it is someone on a higher sphere whom I wish to see, that person must share my wish or nothing will come of it. On the other hand, when I wish to see one who is living on a sphere lower than my own the desire need not be mutual.[529]

Schools and Learning

There are schools, but they are not places where students memorize facts. The memory works perfectly, so there is no need to memorize. Students are able to learn quickly, with sharpened understanding. Each student follows their own course of study, independent of others. John Thomas, cited previously, explains.

> We have schools here for the development of the soul of man, and to teach him his relation to humankind; to instruct him in the wonders of creation, impart to him knowledge of the inhabitants of the numerous worlds in space, to aid man also, and experimenting in chemistry and all other branches of science, for in this life we can explore the uttermost extent of the universe. We also instruct in political economy and laws governing humanity. We also point out conditions and means whereby to help the unprogressive and helpless portion of mankind.[530]

There are expansive halls of learning where people are being taught or are practicing their skills. Raymond Lodge, communicating from spirit to his father through the medium Gladys Osborne Leonard, explained that they attend lectures at the halls of learning, where they prepare themselves for the higher spheres while living in lower ones.[531]

Books and Libraries

There are libraries with vast numbers of books. However, much more knowledge is available from sources other than libraries containing books. Jane Sherwood's husband in spirit, communicating through her, explains.

> We can study in libraries, which are very much like the libraries you have on earth. … The time comes when you no longer want to go around in a regular library. … We can then go to memory bank reference libraries, which contain records of everything that has ever happened.[532]

Every book ever written is in the libraries. However, people don't need to check them out. They can simply have the book read itself to them. People can even get the original meaning of the author, as though the author were with them explaining it. At the following link you can listen to a woman in the life after this life, who came through in a Leslie Flint session, describing the fact that books read themselves to people: www.earthschoolanswers.com/alice/.

> Oh, as far as you can take the books out, I should say, you know, but, oh yes, you can take things home, but it's really not necessary. That's the funny part about it, when you come to think about it. There's everything, everything there that you expect, that you would want, but you soon begin to realize that many of the things are not really necessary in quite the same sort of way. If you mentally sort of tune in to a particular something or somebody that you want a communication, or telepathy. It isn't as if you have to borrow a book and read it as such. It's as if you want to know about the book, perhaps a very famous book, you can either read it, but when you begin to realize that this book can express itself to you. But honestly how it's done I don't know. It's as if you can sit there and you can close your eyes and you can hold the book in your hands and all the happenings in the book can just sort of tell you. You know, yes it's funny, but I don't know. So instead of getting, you know, your own idea, which may not be quite what was intended, you can get the identical thought impressions of the author and publisher, you know.[533]

People can converse with the authors rather than read the books. Charles Drayton Thomas received this description of the government in the life after this life through medium Gladys Osborne Leonard.

> We have books, and people who delight in making them very much as do authors on earth. Perhaps we do not read quite as much as you do; because we are now able to converse personally with the authors. … Still, we have the books and

there are libraries. In those libraries are many books which have never been published on earth.[534]

Edward C. Randall, speaking through medium Emily French, describes the temples of learning, libraries, and books.

Earth people, as a rule, think that when they have passed through high school and universities, they are through with study. When they arrive here and appreciate that knowledge is the stepping-stone of their progression, they attend our temples of learning in great things, where more advanced teachers instruct them. In the spirit world, as in your world, are numerous libraries. These men and women grow intellectually. Many books are composed and written in spirit spheres, and the authors endeavor sometimes to impress their words and wisdom upon the brains of some sensitive ones upon the earth sphere. Again, a book written by one in your plane is by mental activity first created in spirit substance. It had to be before it could be closed in the physical substance by you, and we have all those books, as well as those holy written by spirits, but none are permitted in our libraries that are not founded upon truth. It is interesting to see the vast number of spirit people thronging our libraries, studying the works of the more advanced spirits, similar to what is done in the libraries of earth.[535]

People Who Have Graduated from Earth School Continue to Grow in Wisdom, Love, and Compassion

We continue to grow in wisdom, love, and compassion after leaving Earth School. Earth School provided experiences we could not have while in the comfortable environment we enter in the next stage of life. Earth School contains people of different spiritual levels, some hostile and violent, others kind, loving, and other-centered. As we live with this great variety of people, we face challenges, hostility, conflict, success, joy, and tragedy. We grow in spiritual maturity by facing obstacles and overcoming them.

The conditions in Summerland that most people enter are so pleasant that many choose not to evolve into higher levels of being for a long time. They remark that they are content to stay where they are, although they know there are higher levels. Some people prefer to stay where they are for long periods of time. Higher-level teachers and guides try to help them learn so they can advance, but there is no pressure, and no one requires anyone to leave a level and progress to another level.

However, most people want to advance spiritually. They want to grow in their sensitivities, love, and compassion. There are courses of study they may choose to go through, and they may be tasked to help people still on earth, including family, so they deepen their empathy and sensitivity.

In the life after this life, we know we are one with all people, both those in the next life and those on the earth realm, and one with the Universal Intelligence. As a result, our spiritual growth is accelerated. People continue learning and growing, but without the struggles of Earth School. There are schools, workshops, teaching by ascended masters, gatherings where people talk about their experiences and learning, and all the other experiences that help people to grow. As a result, people change over time. They become more wise, educated, loving, compassionate, and other-centered.

Alvin D. Mattson, speaking from the life after this life through medium Margaret Flavell, describes a group of 20,000 people who had been Lutheran on earth gathering to hear Martin Luther speak.[536]

Time

Because the afterlife has no sun, there are no days or years to count. Changes occur, and people have the same types of experiences as they had on earth that occur over time, so there is a time of sorts. However, they don't count time, and since they realize their eternal nature, there is no hurry to accomplish things. Their sense of time, in other words, is quite different. There are no clocks or references to time using "o'clock," meaning "of the clock."

This is the clear description given by Robert Hugh Benson in the life after this life through Anthony Borgia in response to Borgia's question about how those in the life after this life schedule meetings, such as spiritual events, if there is no measure of time.

To gather the people to the church was perfectly simple, he said. Whoever is in charge has only to send out his thoughts to his congregation, and those that wish to come forthwith assemble! There was no need for bell-ringing. The emission of thought is far more thorough and exact! That is simple so far as the congregation is concerned.

They have merely to wait until the thought reaches them, either in a direct call to attend, or by the urge to attend. But where does the ministering clergyman obtain his indication of the approach of service time? That question, I was told, raised a much greater problem.

With the absence of earth-time in the spirit world, our lives are ordered by events; events, that is, that are part of our life. I do not refer now to incidental occurrences, but to what, on earth, would be regarded as recurrent happenings. We have many such events here, as I hope to show you as we proceed, and in doing so you will see how we know that the performance of certain acts, individually or collectively, are clearly brought to our minds. The establishment of this church we were now inspecting saw also the gradual building up of a regular order of services, such as those who belong to its particular denomination on earth are familiar with. The clergyman who is acting as pastor to this strange flock would feel, by his duties on earth, the approach of the usual "day" and "time" when the services were held. It would be, in this respect, instinctive. It would, moreover, grow stronger with practice, until this mental perception would assume absolute regularity, as it is considered on the earth-plane. With this firmly established, the congregation have but to await the call from their minister.[537]

When Monsignor Benson refers to a "congregation," and "church," he doesn't mean a religious gathering as we know it. He explained, "We have our communal worship here, but it is purged of every trace of meaningless creeds, of doctrines and dogmas. We worship the Great and Eternal Father in truth, absolute truth. We are of one mind, and one mind only."[538]

They do have celebrations. Some who would have celebrated Christmas and Easter on earth celebrate them. Visitors from higher realms who are perfect beings come into the celebrations.

There are people in higher levels who know the events to come at any period in Earth School. Not all who are now living in the next life know the future. Those with this talent sometimes convey information when someone on the earth realm wants to have a glimpse into the future.

Government

As with all collections of people, there is a need for a form of government to help with decisions that will affect all people. Charles Drayton Thomas received this description of the government in the life after this life through medium Gladys Osborne Leonard.

> There is a government, but not one which limits and restricts; it is more in the nature of an inquiry bureau to which one can apply for advice and guidance when needing it. There will be an area which corresponds in general to a county. In this is one of these bureaus. It is managed by a band of experienced people who have been here for some considerable time, and who do not belong wholly to our sphere, but return periodically for work. They know exactly where the newly arrived are most likely to make mistakes.[539]

On higher levels, there is a governing by general consent of the individuals. Medium Lenora Huett provided a report from a resident of the life after this life about government. She said that people are not truly self-governing on an individual basis at the higher levels, "for as they reach the higher levels there is more of a communal governing or a governing by general consent, so that it is not an individual thing or an I am my own law."[540]

Religious Beliefs and the Life After This Life

Those in the life after this life all say there are no established churches or religions for all people. People gather for spiritual discussions, but there are no holy scriptures, rituals, or dogma among those who have released themselves from Earth School's belief systems.

However, some people still cling to the old beliefs, staying in pockets with others who have the same worldviews. Everyone enters the life after this life with all the same assumptions and perspectives they had on earth. As a result, there are some Christian groups living together who are sure they're in a holding pattern waiting for the rapture and their return to a physical existence in Earth School. Some who believed that the spirit sleeps until the resurrection are "sleeping," although they're given guidance and inspiration to begin understanding that they're already in the next stage of their eternal life.

A man named Dr. Franke explained in a Leslie Flint session how difficult it is to help people with strong religious convictions to grow out of them.

> They must first learn to undo. They must first learn to free themselves of all these preconceived ideas or phobias, and even religious things which are perhaps very strong in them. Indeed, sometimes the religious type of individual is more difficult to deal with because, as you know, often they think they are right and they're so sure. They are so adamant that they cannot be wrong, that only they are right. They are often the most difficult people to deal with.[541]

Some people continue to hold to their theological teachings for extended periods so they don't progress. Julia Ames, living in the life after this life, explained this in automatic writing through William T. Stead.

> In this world where I now find myself, one of the strangest of my discoveries was this. There were spirits here utterly un-progressed, although they had been "dead," as you count, 50, in one case nearly 100 years. They were holding views, theological teachings, abandoned when I was a lad. And another wildly perplexing fact was that some atheists, who had been here only a few years, have become the leaders and teachers even of such as myself.[542]

All of these people with narrow, restricting views eventually grow out of them into freedom and spiritual maturity. No one stays in these conditions forever.

Attitudes toward Jesus and God among People in the Next life

Concerning Jesus (Yeshua bar Yosef), those living in the life after this life agree that Jesus came to earth to teach humankind, but was not a god and could not "save" someone. A man named Claude, killed in World War I, spoke of Jesus to his mother through medium Gladys Osborne Leonard.

> I believe that Christ is a great and wonderful personality, a great spirit in the form of a man, as near as possible to God, because the God-force plays so strongly in and through him … but he did not come to save men from the results of their sins. It is a comfortable theory, but not true. Here we learn that every man has to earn his own salvation.[543]

Episcopal Bishop James A. Pike learned about the figure of Jesus from his son in spirit speaking through a medium. Pike asked his son who those living in the life after this life believe Jesus was. His son was concerned that the truth would be harmful to his father because of his position in the church, but he conveyed this message.

> I told you before. I am telling you again. … Oh, it is difficult. I'm afraid I might hurt you. I might hurt you. This is what I was telling you: people must have an example you know. They talk about him [Jesus]—a mystic, a seer, yes, a seer. Oh, but, Dad, they don't talk about him as a savior. As an example, you see? … I would like to tell you, Jesus is triumphant, you know … not a savior, that's the important thing—an example.[544]

The messages from residents of the life after this life also describe God as the foundation of all being, not a male figure separated from humankind. A speaker through medium J. H. Conant explains.

> We do not believe in a God outside and apart from Nature. We believe in a God that is in humanity. We believe in a God that makes all things divine. We believe in a God that hallows the

flowers as he hallows our souls; and we most fervently pray that we may never so far forget ourselves as to believe in a God who would bestow special favors upon any one of his children more than upon the whole. [545]

Sex in the Life After This Life

We have been assured that if we want to enjoy the pleasures of sex in Summerland, we are able to do so. The psychical researcher Frederick Myers, speaking after his death through medium Geraldine Cummins, described sexual activity in the life after this life. Myers describes a man who lived for sex in his earthly life. After his transition, he found he was able to indulge in his desires.

> When he enters the Kingdom of the Mind, that as his mental perceptions are sharpened so his predominant earth-desire is intensified, his mental power being far more considerable. He can, at will, summon to himself those who will gratify this over-developed side of his nature. Others of his kind gravitate to him. And for a time these beings live in a sex paradise. ... They yearn still for gross sensation, not for that finer life, which is the spirit of sexual love, that perfect comradeship without the gratification of the grosser feelings. They obtain it in abundance, and there follows a horrible satiety. They come to loathe what they can obtain in excess and with ease; and then they find it extraordinarily difficult to escape from those who share these pleasures with them.[546]

J. M. Peebles, considered a father of the Spiritualist movement, describes the same sexual activity and full pleasures in the life after this life.

> Men and women, continuing as they do their individuality, sex necessarily exists in the world of spirits, but in heaven there are no perversions of these functions. [547]

Does Gender Identity or Sexual Orientation on Earth Have Any Effect on the Person in the Next Life?

There is no discrimination according to a person's sentiments about their gender identity or sexual orientation. The person carries on with the attitudes and interests they had on earth. These are not assigned to a gender or sexual orientation.

Matthew Ward, speaking from spirit to his mother through her mediumship, explains.

> Homosexuality is an evolutionary stage of the spirit … and it is not to be condemned or honored any more than any other physical or spiritual stage. … If [an] earth lifetime was homosexual in orientation, it will enter here the same way. … Whether heterosexual or homosexual in nature, the soul-level energy and bonding commitment of all couples is totally respected.[548]

What If Someone Had Two Partners?

Consistently, those in the life after this life tell spouses still in Earth School to have a full life, including feeling free to have another partner. There is no possessiveness, jealousy, or covetousness in spirit.

When two or more partners with one spouse come into the life after this life, they will choose to live with each other or not, without concerns about who is whose mate. The feeling of possessiveness is created on the earth realm only. Concerns about whether I can spend eternity with my soul mate are only held by people still on the earth realm. Those issues resolve themselves in the next realm of life.

No one is forced to live with anyone. We still have free will in the life after this life.

19

Our Life after the Next Life

We are able to stay in the next life for as long as we want to. One man named Omar in Monsignor Robert Hugh Benson's messages from spirit through Anthony Borgia said he had been in the Summerland stage of life for 2,000 earth years.[549] In another place, Monsignor Benson says that the rulers of realms have spent many thousands of earthly years in the spirit world before they are placed in charge of people.[550] Leslie Flint had people come through in his séances from the Roman Empire.[551]

Alice Stringfellow received this description of the time we may spend in the Summerland environment from Leslie, her son in the life after this life:

> Progression to the higher spheres depends greatly upon the desire of each person, and also upon the effort to acquire knowledge. We will stay here perhaps thousands of years. We feel that this is good enough and that is what keeps us here. The higher one goes the more elevated he is in knowledge and goodness. We must stay here as long as we are satisfied.[552]

However, staying forever in one place would be a miserably dull eternal existence. People advance beyond the Summerland level eventually. Judge David Hatch, speaking from spirit through medium Elsa Barker, explains.

You should get away from the mental habit of regarding your present life as the only one. Get rid of the idea that the life you expect to lead on this side, after your death, is to be an endless existence in one state. You could no more endure such an endless existence in the subtle manner [of Hatch's world] than you could endure to live forever in the gross matter in which you are now incased. You would weary of it. You could not support it.[553]

As we advance in our wisdom and spiritual stature, we are able to ascend to higher levels of consciousness. People advance to higher levels gradually, not by graduating from one sphere to another.

Elizabeth Fry, who led the eighteenth-century reformation of UK prisons, explains that we progress from horizon to horizon in eternity.

… in your world you can see so far and you can see no further. And yet, as you travel forward, you are approaching that which was before out of sight. So it is with us. We have perspective, we can see so far and as we are travelling forward other aspects of perspective come into view, other parts of existence and life that we did not know existed gradually become within our conscious range.

You must look upon eternity and eternal life like that; a gradual process of going and marching forward and as one is going forward, new vistas strike the horizon. And as you approach them, they become more clear and you see a different picture and a different scene. That is why different souls from different spheres must surely depict life rather differently, one to another. It all depends on the individual, how far they have progressed and what their experiences are.[554]

There are a number of descriptions of realms referred to as "planes," "spheres," "vibrations," or "levels." They are not spatial locations; they are states of mind. Some refer to seven levels.[555] The spheres or levels are only gross descriptions of millions of conditions and environments. For example, there might be millions of environments with untold numbers of people living in circumstances that fit the criteria for being on Level 3. Allan Kardec describes these levels as "heavens."

> You ask them which heaven they inhabit, because you have the idea of several heavens, placed one above the other, like the stories of the house, and they therefore answer you according to your own ideas; but, for them, the words "third," "fourth," or "fifth" heaven expressed different degrees of purification, and consequently of happiness.[556]

There are no boundaries, as in geographical divisions. However, each sphere is completely invisible to the inhabitants of the spheres below it, so there is a boundary of awareness.[557] People on lower levels cannot visit higher levels unless brought close to a higher level by one of the higher-level people. A man named Mike Swain, communicating from spirit to his father, Jasper Swain, described attempting to enter a higher-level sphere:

> Many communicating from the next life have reported that they have been able to visit higher planes for a short period, but the light there is too great for them, and they are forced to return to their proper abode. Mike Swain, speaking from the life after this life through his father, said, "These worlds above us are even richer in light and happiness. If I go there, and I can, I find it too bright; the light hurts my eyes. And the vibrations are so refined that I can't respond to them! So I reverse gear and return to this world—which suits me just fine."[558]

Sanaya, the collective of wise beings channeled by Suzanne Giesemann, gave Suzanne this description of those higher levels:

> As your learning increases and your growth increases along with it, you are "rewarded" by your own actions and you move up the ladder as it were. Now you no longer need a robe. Now you are pure light. Now you circulate more freely amongst those at the other levels. You may visit those in the human consciousness realms on particular missions, or at the other levels. You may be seen as an orb or as an angel. Those with

eyes to see will see your glow. Your fellow lights know you by the particular glow or vibration of your light, and so, you see, you have no need for names or clothes. What do you do all day? You are. You love. By your very presence you raise the consciousness of the whole. You teach. You glow. You need not DO anything. Your environment is not an environment. You no longer have need for houses, or schools, or music, or things. Your music is the vibration of love. It is all around you and you know it as you. Yet still, you know there is more. There is the entirety of all that is you.[559]

We needn't fear advancing to this state of being. We remain individuals; we do not merge into some higher being called the Source. The collective of celestial beings communicating through Maurice Barbanell as Silver Birch explains that we keep our individuality.

The ultimate is not the attainment of Nirvana. All spiritual progress is toward increasing individuality. You do not become less of an individual. You become more of an individual. You develop latent gifts, you acquire greater knowledge, your character becomes stronger, more of the divine is exhibited through you. You do not lose yourself. What you succeed in doing is finding yourself.[560]

Descriptions of the Levels

Most people transition from Earth School to Level 3 or Summerland. Those with degenerate personalities gather together naturally in the second sphere. The fourth, fifth, and sixth levels are described as filled with light, love, and happiness. Among the residents of the seventh level are Jesus of Nazareth, John the Beloved, Confucius, Seneca, Plato, Socrates, and Solon.[561] These celestial beings remain individuals, capable of communicating with people on the earth realm. Confucius, described as being in the seventh level, has come through in a Leslie Flint session[562] and in a session Dr. Neville Whymant had with medium George Valiantine.[563]

The movement from Level 3, or Summerland, to the fourth is a change in mentality or spirit. Robert Crookall, author of *The Supreme*

Adventure, refers to the transitions as "deaths," but they are simply welcomed transitions.

We have been concerned with the first and second "deaths"(actually births) and the immediate after-life. But there is a third "death" — that transition in which the soul body itself is discarded. After this event, consciousness operates at spiritual "levels" in the spiritual or celestial body, with the indescribable true "heavens" as the environment. The third "death," more properly described as the third unveiling of the greater self, there is no "corpse," "husk" or "shell" (as do the first and second): in this process the body undergoes a progressive refinement and purification and consequently an increase in responsiveness.[564]

Elsa Barker, through automatic writing, recorded the words of Judge David Hatch in the life after this life describing the fourth level.

Within the subtle world of which I speak you will perceive a variety of forms which are not known on earth and therefore may not be expressed in words. Yet there is a certain similarity, a correspondence between the appearances on this luminiferous plane. Flowers are there; but these are in shapes unknown to you, exquisite in color, radiant with light. Such colors, such lights are not contained within any earthly octave, are expressed by us in thoughts and not in words. For, as I previously remarked, words are for us obsolete. However, the soul, in this plane of consciousness, must struggle and labor, know sorrow but not earth sorrow, know ecstasy but not earth ecstasy. The sorrow is of a spiritual character, the ecstasy is of a spiritual kind. [565]

We receive hints and glimpses into the fifth through the seventh levels. Stafford Betty quotes Frederick Myers in spirit, speaking through trance medium Geraldine Cummins, describing the levels.[566] The fifth level is called the Plane of Flame.

Myers tells us that an inhabitant here remains himself, yet is all those other selves [in his group] as well. He no longer dwells in form—as it is conceived by man—but he dwells still in what might be described as an "outline" ... an outline of emotional thought: a great fire which stirs and moves this mighty being. Such a being is continuously conscious. ... He tastes of heaven and yet the revelation of the last mystery tarries, still awaits the completion of the design of which he is part.[567]

On the sixth plane, the individuals are formless white lights. The Minds of the inhabitants are dominated by reason. Myers describes the sixth plane.

Emotion and passion, as known to men, are absent. White light represents the perfect equanimity of pure thought. Such equanimity becomes the possession of the souls who entered this last rich kingdom of experience. ... They are capable of living now ... as the pure thought of their Creator. They have joined the immortals.[568]

Myers continues to describe the seventh plane.

Without a body of any kind, you merge with the Great Source and reign in the great calm of eternity. Yet you still exist as an individual [and] are wholly aware of the imagination of God. So you are aware of the whole history of the earth from Alpha to Omega. Equally all planetary existence is yours. Everything created is contained within that imagination, and you . . . know it and hold it. An eon of spiritual evolution is usually required before taking this final step: only a very few pass out Yonder during the life of the earth. A certain number of souls attain to the sixth state, but remain in it or, in exceptional cases for a lofty purpose, descend again into matter. They are not strong enough to make the great leap into timelessness, they are not yet perfect.[569]

Throughout these ascensions into increasingly higher levels, there is no loss of individuality by merging with a universal consciousness. We remain individuals, even when we have left behind any interest in earth-like environments and bodies. Crookall explains,

"Only the Absolute, Transcendent, Unmanifested, Infinite 'Father' is 'pure spirit,' 'purely subjective.'"[570]

Our attachment now to our bodies, our lives, and our relationships causes us to recoil from the thought of leaving behind all we are familiar with by graduating to higher and higher levels. However, we will never be forced to advance. And when we decide to advance, we will have matured far beyond where we are now, just as an adult has matured far beyond being an infant. We will not want to stay an infant forever. We will yearn to become more than we have been.

Bibliography

Abbot, N. C. "Healing as a therapy for human disease: a systematic review." *Journal of Alternative and Complementary Medicine* 6, no. 2 (2000): 159-169.

Aber, William W., and Jabez Hunt Nixon. *Beyond the Veil: Being a Compilation, with Notes and Explanations.* Whitefish, MT: Kessinger Publishing, 2003; originally published in 1906.

"Abraham Hicks – Must we return to this earth?" Produced by Esther Hicks. October 5, 2010. YouTube video, 13:15, https://www.youtube.com/watch?v=IW7uF3kUAME.

Achterberg, J., and K. Cooke. "Evidence for correlations between distant intentionality and brain function in recipients: A functional magnetic resonance imaging analysis." *Journal of Alternative and Complementary Medicine* 11, no. 6 (2005): 965-971.

Admin, M. "Hundreds in India Ritually Starve Themselves to Death Each Year." Knowledge Nuts. Accessed April 1, 2014. https://knowledgenuts.com/2014/04/01/hundreds-in-india-ritually-starve-themselves-to-death-each-year/.

Afterlife Research and Education Institute, Inc. "Afterlife Communication: David Thompson's Séances Today." https://adcguides.com/davidthompson1.htm.

Akiane's Gallery. http://www.artakiane.com/.

Allen, Miles. *The Realities of Heaven: Fifty Spirits Describe Your Future Home.* CreateSpace Independent Publishing Platform, 2015.

Alton, Larry. "Why Low Self-Esteem May Be Hurting You at Work." NBC News. November 15, 2017. https://www.nbcnews.com/better/business/why-low-self-esteem-may-be-hurting-your-career-ncna814156.

"Amazing blind teen uses echolocation to 'SEE.'" Familes.com. October 26, 2006. https://www.families.com/amazing-blind-boy-uses-echolocation-to-see-watch-the-video-clip .

"Americans are the unhappiest they've been in 50 years, poll finds."
NBC News. June 16, 2020.
https://www.nbcnews.com/politics/politics-news/americans-are-
unhappiest-they-ve-been-50-years-poll-finds-n1231153.

Anonymous. *The Bridge Over the River*. Translated by Joseph Wetzl.
Hudson, NY: Steiner Books, 1974.Astin, J. A., E. Harkness, and
E. Ernst. "The efficacy of 'distant healing': a systematic review of
randomized trials." *Annals of Internal Medicine* 132 (2000): 903-
910.

Austin, A. W., ed. *Teachings of Silver Birch*. London: Psychic Book Club,
1938.

Baird, A. T. *A Casebook for Survival*. London: Psychic Press Ltd., 1942.

Baird, J. L. *Sermons, Soap and Television—Autobiographical Notes*. London:
Royal Television Society, 1988.

Baldwin, Neil. *Edison: Inventing the Century*. New York: Hyperion, 1995.

Bander, P. *Voices from the Tapes*. New York: Drake Publishers, 1973.

Barbash, Fred. "Near-death experiences are a kind of high, even if
you're not really near death." *The Washington Post*, July 7, 2014.
https://www.washingtonpost.com/news/morning-
mix/wp/2014/07/07/study-the-near-death-experience-is-
generally-positive-even-when-death-isnt-really-near/.

Barker, Elsa. *Letters from a Living Dead Man*. Dallas, TX: Hill-Pehle
Publishing, 2012, originally published in 1914.

Barrett, William. *Death-Bed Visions*. Guildford, UK: White Crow Books,
2011.

Barry, J. "General and comparative study of the psychokinetic effect on
a fungus culture." *Journal of Parapsychology* 32 (1968): 237-43.

Basar, E. "Memory as the 'whole brain work': A large-scale model based
on 'oscillations in super-synergy.'" *International Journal of
Psychophysiology* 58, no. 2-3 (2005): 199-226.

Bates, B. C., and A. Stanley. "The epidemiology and differential
diagnosis of near death experience." *American Journal of
Orthopsychiatry* 55 (1985): 542-9.

Baumeister, Roy F., Arlene M. Stillwell, and Todd F. Heatherton.
"Personal Narratives About Guilt: Role in Action Control and

Interpersonal Relationships." *Basic and Applied Social Psychology* 17, no. 1-2 (1985): 173-198.

Becker, Carl B. *Paranormal Experience and Survival of Death.* SUNY Series in Western Esoteric Traditions. New York: State University of New York Press, 1993.

Begley, S. "In our messy, reptilian brains." *Newsweek.* Accessed April 9, 2007. http://www.msnbc.msn.com/id/ 17888475/site/newsweek/.

Beischel, J., and G. E. Schwartz. "Anomalous information reception by research mediums demonstrated using a novel triple-blind protocol." *Explore* 3, no. 1 (January/February 2007).

Bengston, W. F., and D. Krinsley. "The effect of the 'laying on of hands' on transplanted breast cancer in mice." *Journal of Scientific Exploration* 14, no. 3 (2000): 353-364.

Bennett, E. *Apparitions and Haunted Houses: A Survey of Evidence.* London: Faber, 1939.

Bennett, Olivia. Art with Olivia. http://www.oliviabennett.com/.

Bering, Jesse. "One Last Goodbye: The Strange Case of Terminal Lucidity." *Scientific American.* November 25, 2014. https://blogs.scientificamerican.com/bering-in-mind/one-last-goodbye-the-strange-case-of-terminal-lucidity/.

Berkovich, S. "A scientific model why memory aka consciousness cannot reside solely in the brain." Near-Death Experience Research Foundation. Accessed October 25, 2007. https://www.nderf.org/NDERF/Research/Berkovich.

Berman, M. *Reenchantment of the World.* Ithaca, NY: Cornell University Press, 1981.

Besant, Annie, and Charles Webster Leadbeater. *Thought Forms: A Record of Clairvoyant Investigation.* Brooklyn: Sacred Bones Books, 2020; originally published in 1901.

Betty, Stafford. *The Afterlife Unveiled: What the Dead Are Telling Us About Their World.* Blue Ridge Summit, PA: 6th Books, 2011.

Bierman, D. J., and D. Radin. "Anomalous anticipatory response on randomized future conditions." *Perceptual and Motor Skills* 84 (1997): 689-690.

Billikopf, Gregorio. "Cultural differences? Or, are we really that different?" University of California, Berkeley. 1999.

http://www.cnr.berkeley.edu/ucce50/ag-labor/7article/article01.htm.

Blackburn, Elizabeth, and Elissa Epel. *The Telomere Effect: A Revolutionary Approach to Living Younger, Healthier, Longer.* New York: Grand Central Publishing, 2017.

Blackmore, S. "Out of body experiences in schizophrenia." *Journal of Nervous and Mental Disease* 174 (1986): 615-9.

Blum, D. *Ghost Hunters: William James and the Search for Scientific Proof of Life After Death.* London: Penguin Press, 2006.

Borgia, Anthony. *ABC of Life.* London: Feature Books, Ltd., 1945.

Borgia, Anthony. *Life in the World Unseen.* London: Corgi Books, 1970.

Borum, Randy. *Psychology of Terrorism.* Tampa, FL: University of South Florida, 2004.

Borysenko, J. *Fire in the Soul: A New Psychology of Spiritual Optimism.* London: Warner Books, Inc., 1993.

Botkin, A., with R. C. Hogan. *Induced After-Death Communication: A Miraculous Therapy for Grief and Loss.* Charlottesville, VA: Hampton Roads Publishing, 2014.

Botkin, A., with R. C. Hogan. *Induced After-Death Communication: A New Therapy for Grief and Trauma.* Charlottesville, VA: Hampton Roads Publishing, 2005.

Braud, W. "Empirical explorations of prayer, distant healing, and remote mental influence." *Journal of Religion and Psychical Research* 17, no. 2: 62-73. Accessed July 15, 2007. http://www.integral-inquiry.com/docs/649/empirical.pdf.

Braud, W., and M. Schlitz. "A methodology for the objective study of transpersonal imagery." *Journal of Scientific Exploration* 3 (1983): 43-63.

Braud, W., and M. Schlitz. "Possible role of intuitive data sorting in electrodermal biological psychokinesis (bio-PK)." *The Journal of the American Society for Psychical Research* 83, no. 4 (October 1989): 289-302.

Braud, W., and M. Schlitz. "Remote mental influence of animate and inanimate target systems: A method of comparison and preliminary findings." *Proceedings of Presented Papers,* 32nd

Annual Parapsychological Association Convention. San Diego, California, 1989, 12-25.

Braud, W., D. Shafer, and S. Andrews. "Electrodermal correlates of remote attention: Autonomic reactions to an unseen gaze." *Proceedings of Presented Papers*, 33rd Annual Parapsychology Association Convention, 1990, 14-28.

Braud, W., D. Shafer, and S. Andrews. "Reactions to an unseen gaze (remote attention): A review, with new data on autonomic staring detection." *Journal of Parapsychology* 57 (1993): 373-390.

Braun, Bennett. *Treatment of Multiple Personality Disorder*. Washington, D.C.: American Psychiatric Publishing, 1986.

Bray, S. *A Guide for the Spiritual Traveler*. Queensland, Australia: Scroll Publishers, 1990.

Browning, C. R. *Ordinary Men: Reserve Police Battalion 101 and the final solution in Poland*. New York: Harper Collins, 1992.

Brune, P. F. "The rediscovered beyond." World ITC. December 2006. www.worlditc.org/d_07_brune_rediscovered_beyond.htm.

Bryner, J. "Huge stores of oxygen found deep inside earth." MSNBC. October 1, 2007. http://www.msnbc.msn.com/id/21082196/.

Buengner, P. "Morphic Fields can now be measured scientifically!" The Global Oneness Commitment. Accessed October 13, 2007. http://www.experiencefestival.com/a/Morphic_fields/id/10320.

Buffet, Howard. *Fragile: The Human Condition*. Washington, D.C.: National Geographic Society, 2009.

Burbidge, Augustus Henry. *The Shadows Lifted from Death*. Stuart, FL: Roundtable Publishing, 2011.

Burrowes, Robert J. "Love Denied: The Psychology of Materialism, Violence and War." Feelings First Blog. May 2013. https://feelingsfirstblog.wordpress.com/key-articles/love-denied/.

Burt, C. *The Gifted Child*. New York: Wiley, 1975.

Butler, T., and L. Butler. *There Is No Death and There Are No Dead*. AA-EVP Publishing, 1947.

Byrd, R. C. "Positive therapeutic effects of intercessory prayer in a coronary care unit population." *Southern Medical Journal* 81, no. 7 (1988): 826-829.

Byrne, Brian Patrick, Leon Markovitz, Jody Sieradzki, and Tal Reznik. "All the People God Kills in the Bible." *Vocativ*, April 20, 2016. https://www.vocativ.com/news/309748/all-the-people-god-kills-in-the-bible/index.html.

Calvin, John. *Psychopannychia*. Warrendale, PA: Ichthus Publications, 2018; originally published in 1542.

Campbell, Joseph, with Bill Moyers. *The Power of Myth*. New York: Doubleday, 1988.

Carnegie Mellon University. "Happy People Are Healthier, Psychologist Says." ScienceDaily. November 8, 2006. https://www.sciencedaily.com/releases/2006/11/061108103655.htm.

Carrington, H. *The World of Psychic Research*. New Jersey: A.S Barns & Co., Inc., 1973.

Carroll, Lee, and Jan Tober. *The Indigo Children: The New Kids Have Arrived*. Carlsbad, CA: Hay House, 1999.

Carter, C. Rebuttal to Keith Augustine's Attack of "Does Consciousness Depend on the Brain?" Accessed May 30, 2007. https://www.survivalafterdeath.info/articles/carter/augustine.htm.

Cassirer, M. *Medium on Trial—The Story of Helen Duncan and the Witchcraft Act*. Stansted, Essex: PN Publishing, 1996.

Chalmers, D. J. "The Puzzle of Conscious Experience"; "Mysteries of the Mind." *Scientific American* (special issue, 1997): 30-37.

Chesterman, John. *An Index of Possibilities: Energy and Power*. New York: Pantheon Books, 1974.

Choi, C. "Strange but True: When Half a Brain Is Better than a Whole One." *Scientific American*. May 24, 2007. http://www.sciam.com/article.cfm?articleId=BE96F947-E7F2-99DF-3EA94A4C4EE87581&chanId=sa013&modsrc=most_popular.

Chopra, Deepak, Menas Kafatos, Bernardo Kastrup, and Rudolph Tanzi. "Why a Mental Universe Is the 'Real' Reality." Chopra Foundation. November 30, 2015. https://choprafoundation.org/consciousness/why-a-mental-universe-is-the-real-reality/.

"The Church of England and Spiritualism—the full text of the Majority Report of the Church of England committee appointed by Archbishop Lang and Archbishop Temple to investigate Spiritualism." London: Psychic Press Ltd., 1960s (completed 1939). https://www.cfpf.org.uk/articles/religion/cofe_report/cofe_repor t.html.

Cobbe, Francis Power. *The Peak in Darien: An Octave of Essays.* Charleston, NC: Nabu Press, 2010.

Colella, Francesca. "How Many People Are Starving Around the World?" The Borgen Project. January 20, 2018. https://borgenproject.org/how-many-people-are-starving-around-the-world/.

Conradt, Stacy. "The Quick 10: 10 Famous Uses of the Ouija Board." Mental Floss. https://www.mentalfloss.com/article/26158/quick-10-10-famous-uses-ouija-board.

Conte, H. R., M. B. Weiner, and R. Plutchik. "Measuring death anxiety: Conceptual, psychometric, and factor-analytic aspects." *Journal of Personality and Social Psychology* 43 (1982): 775-785.

"A conversation with John Giorno." *Artful Dodge Magazine.* College of Wooster. Accessed October 14, 2007. https://artfuldodge.spaces.wooster.edu/interviews/john-giorno/.

Cook, E. W., B. Greyson, and I. Stevenson. "Do any near-death experiences provide evidence for the survival of human personality after death? Relevant features and illustrative case reports." *Journal of Scientific Exploration,* 12 (1998): 377-406. http://www.near-death.com/evidence.html#a2.

Cooke, Ivan. *The Return of Arthur Conan Doyle.* Liss, UK: White Eagle Publishing, 1980.

Corey, M. *The God Hypothesis: Discovering Design in Our "Just Right" Goldilocks Universe.* Rowman & Littlefield Publishers, Inc., 2007.

Counts, D. A. "Near-death and out of body experiences in a Melanesian society." *Anabiosis* 3. No. 2 (1983): 115-135.

Crookall, Robert. *The Supreme Adventure, Analyses of Psychic Communications.* Cambridge, UK: James Clarke & Co., Ltd., 1961.

Cummins, Geraldine. *Beyond Human Personality*. London: Ivor Nicholson and Watson, Ltd., 1935.

Cummins, Geraldine. *The Road to Immortality*. London: The Aquarian Press, 1955.

Currie, I. *You Cannot Die*. London: Book Club Associates, 1995.

Dalai Lama XIV. *A Policy of Kindness: An Anthology of Writings by and about the Dalai Lama*. Boulder, CO: Snow Lion Publications, 2012.

Dam, Abhijit Kanti. "Significance of end-of-life dreams and visions experienced by the terminally ill in rural and urban India." *Indian Journal of Palliative Care* 22, no. 2 (April-June 2016): 130-134.

"Daniel Dunglas Home 1833-1886." SurvivalAfterDeath.info. Accessed July 16, 2007. https://www.survivalafterdeath.info/mediums/home.htm.

Davis, Andrew Jackson. *Death and the After Life*. Boston: Kobe and Rich, 1865.

De Morgan, Sophia Elizabeth. *From Matter to Spirit*. London: Longman, Green, Longman, Roberts & Green, 1863.

DePanfilis, Diane. *Child Neglect: A Guide for Prevention, Assessment, and Intervention*. U.S. Dept. of Health and Human Services, Children's Bureau, Office on Child Abuse and Neglect, 2006.

Desmedt, J. E., and D. Robertson. "Differential enhancement of early and late components of the cerebral somatosensory evoked potentials during forced-paced cognitive tasks in man." *Journal of Physiology* 271 (1977): 761-782.

Dillbeck, M. C., G. S. Landrith, and D. W. Orme-Johnson. "The Transcendental Meditation program and crime rate change in a sample of forty-eight cities." *Journal of Crime and Justice* 4 (1981): 25-45.

"Documenting Numbers of Victims of the Holocaust and Nazi Persecution." *Holocaust Encyclopedia*. U.S. Holocaust Memorial Museum. https://encyclopedia.ushmm.org/content/en/article/documenting -numbers-of-victims-of-the-holocaust-and-nazi-persecution.

Dodds, E. R. "Presidential Address." *Proceedings of the Society for Psychical Research*. London: 1962.

Doğan, Recep. "Can Honor Killings Be Explained with the Concept of Social Death? Reinterpreting Social Psychological Evidence." *Homicide Studies* 24, no. 2 (February 14, 2019): 127–150.

Dolgoff, S. "Life is good. So why can't you stop worrying?" MSNBC. November 28, 2007. https://www.nbcnews.com/health/health-news/life-good-so-why-cant-you-stop-worrying-flna1c9463693.

Dossey, L. *Healing Words*. New York: HarperOne, 1997.

Dossey, L. *Recovering the Soul: A Scientific and Spiritual Search*. New York: Bantam Books, 1989.

Dossey, L., and S. Schwartz. *Therapeutic Intent/Healing Bibliography of Research*. Accessed December 15, 2007. http://www.stephanaschwartz.com/wp-content/uploads/2010/03/Healing-Therapeutic-Intent-Biblio.pdf.

Doyle, A. C. *The History of Spiritualism, Vols. I and II*. New York: Arno Press, 1926.

"Dr. Bruce Lipton—A New Hope: Epigenetics and the Subconscious Mind." Dr. Ron Ehrlich. https://drronehrlich.com/dr-bruce-lipton-a-new-hope-epigenetics-and-the-subconscious-mind-2/.

Duffey, Eliza B. *Heaven Revised: A Narrative of Personal Experiences After the Change Called Death*. London: Forgotten Books, 2019; originally published in 1921.

Dunne, Brenda J. "Co-operator experiments with an REG device. PEAR Technical Note 91005." *Cultivating consciousness for enhancing human potential, wellness and healing*, edited by K. R. Rao (Westport, CT: Praeger, 1993), 149-163.

Dunne, Brenda J., and R. G. Jahn. "Experiments in remote human/machine interaction." *Journal of Scientific Exploration* 6, no. 4 (1992): 311-332.

Easton, J. C. "Survey on physician's religious beliefs shows majority faithful." *The University of Chicago Chronicle* 24, no. 19 (July 14, 2005). http://chronicle.uchicago.edu/050714/doctorsfaith.shtml.

Eccles, J. C. "The effect of silent thinking on the cerebral cortex." *Truth Journal* 2 (1988). http://www.leaderu.com/truth/2truth06.html,.

Edmonds, John Worth, and George T. Dexter. *Spiritualism*. New York: Partridge & Brittan, 1855.

"Edward VIII Abdicates the Throne." The History Place.
    https://www.historyplace.com/speeches/edward.htm.
Einstein, Albert. Letter to Robert S. Marcus, Princeton, NJ, February 12,
    1950.
Eisen, William. *The Agashan Discourses: The Agashan Teachers Speak on the*
    Who, What, Where, When, and Why of Life on the Earth Plane.
    Camarillo, CA: Devorss & Co., 1978.
Emerson, Ralph Waldo. *The Complete Works— Volume II, Essays: First*
    Series. Boston: Houghton, Mifflin and Company/The Riverside
    Press, 1883.
Emoto, Masaru. *The Secret Life of Water.* New York: Atria Books, 2005.
"Failure in meditation: A detailed analysis." *Meditation Is Easy.* Accessed
    October 14, 2007.
    http://www.meditationiseasy.com/mCorner/failure_in_meditati
    on.htm.
Fenwick, Peter. "Approaching-Death Experiences and the NDE: A
    model for the dying process." International Association for
    Near-Death Studies. Accessed June 21, 2007.
    https://iands.org/research/nde-research/important-research-
    articles/42-dr-peter-fenwick-md-science-and-
    spirituality.html?showall=1.
Fenwick, Peter. "Dying: a spiritual experience as shown by near death
    experiences and deathbed visions." Royal College of
    Psychiatrists. 2004. https://www.rcpsych.ac.uk/docs/default-
    source/members/sigs/spirituality-spsig/spirituality-special-
    interest-group-publications-
    pfenwickneardeath.pdf?sfvrsn=686898bc_2.
Fenwick, Peter, and Elizabeth Fenwick. "All the questions are
    essentially simple but the answers remain elusive." *The Daily*
    Mail, March 2, 1995.
Fenwick, Peter, and Elizabeth Fenwick. *The Art of Dying: A Journey to*
    Elsewhere. London: Continuum International Publishing, 2008.
Fenwick, Peter, and Elizabeth Fenwick. *The Truth in the Light—An*
    Investigation of Over 300 Near-Death Experiences. Terra Alta, WV:
    Headline Book Publishing, 1996.

Fenwick, Peter, Hilary Lovelace, and Sue Brayne. "Comfort for the dying: Five year retrospective and one year prospective studies of end of life experiences." *Archives of Gerontology and Geriatrics* 51, no. 2 (2009): 173-179.

Fisher, Joe. *The Case for Reincarnation.* London: Grafton Books, 1986.

Flint, Leslie. "The Leslie Flint Séance Recordings Archive." Leslie Flint Trust. https://www.leslieflint.com/recordings-archive.

Flint, Leslie. *Voices in the Dark.* New York: Macmillan Publishing, 1971.

Fodor, Nandor. *These Mysterious People.* London: Rider & Co. Ltd., 1934.

Fontana, David. *Is There an Afterlife?: A Comprehensive Overview of the Evidence.* Washington, D.C.: O Books, 2005.

Gabbard, G. O., and S. W. Twemlow. *With the Eyes of the Mind: An Empirical Analysis of Out-of-Body States.* New York: Praeger, 1984.

Geley, Gustave. *Clairvoyance and Materialization: A Record of Experiments.* London: T. Fisher Unwin Limited, 1927.

Giesemann, Suzanne. *Awakening: Lessons from Beyond the Veil.* E-book, 2016. https://www.suzannegiesemann.com/books/.

Giesemann, Suzanne. *Wolf's Message.* Cardiff, CA: Waterside Productions, Inc., 2014.

Gilbert, Alice. *Philip in the Spheres.* Detroit: The Aquarian Press, 1952.

Giovetti, P. "Near-death and deathbed-experiences: An Italian survey." *Theta* 10, no. 1 (1982): 10-13.

"Global Consciousness Project: Meaningful Correlations in Random Data." Global Consciousness Project. Princeton University. Accessed October 22, 2007. http://noosphere.princeton.edu/.

Goldsmith, S. K., T. C. Pellmar, A. M. Kleinman, and W. E. Bunney, eds. "Reducing Suicide: A National Imperative." Washington, D.C.: Institute of Medicine, The National Academies Press, 2002.

Gonzalez, Guillermo, and Jay W. Richards. *The Privileged Planet: How Our Place in the Cosmos Is Designed for Discovery.* Washington, D.C.: Regnery Publishing, 2004.

Goodrich, Joyce. "Psychic healing: A pilot study." Unpublished doctoral dissertation. Union Graduate School, Yellow Springs, OH, 1974.

Goodrich, Joyce. "Studies of paranormal healing." *New Horizons* 2, no. 2 (1976): 21-24.

Gorius, Léa. "How Much Does It Cost to End Poverty?" The Borgen Project. December 16, 2017. https://borgenproject.org/how-much-does-it-cost-to-end-poverty/.

Goswami, Amit. *The Self-Aware Universe: How Consciousness Creates the Material World.* New York: TarcherPerigee, 1995.

Grad, B. R. "Some biological effects of laying-on of hands: a review of experiments with animals and plants." *Journal of the American Society for Psychical Research* 59 (1965): 95-127.

Grad, B., R. Cadoret, and G. I. Paul. "The influence of an unorthodox, method of treatment on wound healing in mice." *International Journal of Parapsychology* 3 (1961): 5-24.

"Graham Wallas' model." Accessed September 11, 2007. members.optusnet.com.au/charles57/Creative/Brain/wallis_intro.htm.

Greaves, Helen. *The Challenging Light.* Suffolk, UK: Neville Spearman, 1984.

Greaves, Helen. *Testimony of Light: An Extraordinary Message of Life After Death.* New York: TarcherPerigee, 2009.

Grey, Margot. *Return from Death: An Exploration of the Near-Death Experience.* London: Arkana, 1985.

Greyson, B. "The near death experience scale: construction, reliability and validity." *Journal of Nervous and Mental Disease* 171 (1983): 369-75.

Greyson, B. "Near death experiences as evidence for survival of bodily death." Survival of Bodily Death: An Esalen Invitational Conference, February 11-16, 2000.

Grinberg-Zylverbaum, J., M. Delaflor, M. E. Sanchez-Arellano, M. A. Guevara, and M. Perez. "Human communication and the electrophysiological activity of the brain." *Subtle Energies* 3, (1993): 3.

Grossman, Dave. "Trained to Kill: Are We Conditioning Our Children to Commit Murder?" *Christianity Today.* August 10, 1998.

Groth, A. N. *Men Who Rape.* New York: Plenum Press, 1979.

Guggenheim, Bill, and Judy Guggenheim. *Hello from Heaven.* New York: Bantam Books, 1995.

Gurney, Edmund, F. W. H. Myers, and Frank Podmore. *Phantasms of the Living*. London: Trubner, 1886.

Gustafson, Craig. "Bruce Lipton, PhD: The Jump from Cell Culture to Consciousness." *Integrative Medicine: A Clinician's Journal* 16, no. 6 (December 2017): 44–50.

Hadamard, J. *The Psychology of Invention in the Mathematical Field.* Princeton, NJ: Princeton University Press, 1949.

Hagelin, John S., Maxwell V. Rainforth, David W. Orme-Johnson, Kenneth L. Cavanaugh, Charles N. Alexander, Susan F. Shatkin, John L. Davies, Anne O. Hughes, and Emanuel Ross. "Effects of Group Practice of the *Transcendental Meditation* Program on Preventing Violent Crime in Washington, D.C.: Results of the National Demonstration Project, June-July 1993." *Social Indicators Research* 47, no. 2 (1999): 153-201.

Haig, Scott. "The brain: the power of hope." *Time Magazine* 169 (2007): 118-119.

Hallenbeck, James L. *Palliative Care Perspectives.* Chapter 7, "Psychosocial and Spiritual Aspects of Care: Altered States of Consciousness at the End of Life." Oxford, UK: Oxford University Press, 2003.

Hameroff, Stuart. "Overview: Could life and consciousness be related to the fundamental quantum nature of the universe?" Quantum Consciousness. Accessed December 15, 2007. https://philpapers.org/rec/HAMOCL.

Hamilton, Craig. "Is God all in your head?" *What is Enlightenment?* (June-August 2005).

Hamilton-Parker, Craig. *What to Do When You Are Dead: Exploring Life After Death.* New York: Sterling Publishing Co., 2001.

Hamilton, T. G. *Intention and Survival.* London: Regency Press, 1942.

Hapgood, Charles H. *Voices of Spirit.* New York: Delacorte Press / Seymour Lawrence, 1975.

Haraldsson, E. "Survey of claimed encounters with the dead." *Omega* 19 (1989): 103-13.

Haraldsson, E., and T. Thorsteinsson. "Psychokinetic effects on yeast: An exploratory experiment." *Research in Parapsychology* (pages 20-21). Metuchen, NJ: Scarecrow Press, 1973.

Hare, Robert. *Experimental Investigation of the Spirit Manifestations: Demonstrating the Existence of Spirits and Their Communion with Mortals. Doctrine of the spirit world respecting heaven, hell, morality, and God. Also, the influence of Scripture on the morals of Christians.* New York: Partridge & Brittan, 1855.

Harris, W. S., M. Gowda, J. W. Kolb, C. P. Strychacz, J. L. Vacek, P. G. Jones, A. Forker, J. H. O'Keefe, and B. D. McCallister. "A randomized, controlled trial of the effects of remote, intercessory prayer on outcomes in patients admitted to the coronary care unit." *Archives of Internal Medicine* 159, no. 19 (October 25, 1999): 2273-2278.

Hawking, Stephen. *A Brief History of Time.* New York: Bantam, 1998.

Hay, David. "The Spirituality of the Unchurched." British and Irish Association for Mission Studies Conference, 2002.

Heagerty, N. Riley. *The Hereafter: Firsthand Reports from the Frontiers of the Afterlife.* New York: Circle of Light Research, 2020.

Heffern, Rich. "Spirituality and the fine-tuned cosmos." *National Catholic Reporter.* December 12, 2003. https://natcath.org/NCR_Online/archives2/2003d/121203/121203 a.htm.

"Helen Duncan: The Official Pardon Site." Accessed July 29, 2007. http://www.users.zetnet.co.uk/helenduncan/.

Hertzog, D. B., and J. T. Herrin. "Near death experiences in the very young." *Critical Care Medicine* 13 (1985): 1074-5.

Hogan, R. Craig, ed., *Afterlife Communication: 16 Proven Methods, 85 True Accounts.* Chicago: Greater Reality Publications, 2014.

Hogan, R. Craig. *Your Eternal Self: Science Discovers the Afterlife.* Chicago: Greater Reality Publications, 2020.

Holladay, April. "Expanding space." WonderQuest. Accessed December 10, 2007. http://www.wonderquest.com/ExpandingUniverse.htm.

"Holmes and Rahe Stress scale says divorced men seeking contact are at most risk." BBC Action Network. Accessed October 25, 2007. http://www.bbc.co.uk/dna/actionnetwork/A3539522\.

Holzer, H. *Ghost Hunter.* New York: Bobbs Merrill Company, 1963.

Homans, George C. "A Conceptual Scheme for Describing Work Group Behaviour." *The Human Group.* New York: Harcourt, Brace and Company, 1950.

Honorton, C., and D. C. Ferrari. "Future telling: A meta-analysis of forced-choice precognition experiments, 1935-1987." *Journal of Parapsychology* 53 (1989): 281-308.

"Hornell Hart 1888-1967." SurvivalAfterDeath.info. Accessed April 16, 2007. https://www.survivalafterdeath.info/researchers/hart.htm.

Howe, Neil. "Millennials and the Loneliness Epidemic." *Forbes.* May 3, 2019. https://www.forbes.com/sites/neilhowe/2019/05/03/millennials-and-the-loneliness-epidemic/#59174e247676.

"Humans with amazing senses." ABC Primetime. August 9, 2006. http://abcnews.go.com/Primetime/story?id=2283048&page=1.

Hymowitz, Kay S. "Alone: The decline of the family has unleashed an epidemic of loneliness." *City Journal.* Spring 2019. https://www.city-journal.org/decline-of-family-loneliness-epidemic.

"Hypnosis for Pain Relief." Arthritis Foundation. https://www.arthritis.org/health-wellness/treatment/complementary-therapies/natural-therapies/hypnosis-for-pain-relief.

"Hypnosis, No Anesthetic, for Man's Surgery." CBS News. April 22, 2008. https://www.cbsnews.com/news/hypnosis-no-anesthetic-for-mans-surgery/.

Hyslop, J. H. *Life After Death: Problems of the Future Life and Its Nature.* Whitefish, MT: Kessinger Publishing, 1918.

"IADC Therapy for Grief." https://iadctherapy.com/about.

"Indicators of School Crime and Safety: 2006." Institute of Education Sciences, U.S. Department of Education. December 2006. http://nces.ed.gov/programs/crimeindicators/.

Inglis, B. *Science and Parascience—A History of the Paranormal 1914-1939.* London: Hodder and Stoughton, 1984.

Ingraham, Christopher. "Americans are getting more miserable, and there's data to prove it." *Washington Post.* March 22, 2019.

https://www.washingtonpost.com/business/2019/03/22/american
s-are-getting-more-miserable-theres-data-prove-it/.

"An introductory analysis of the NDE (Near-Death Experience)."
Originally published in *Two Worlds* (1996).
https://cryskernan.tripod.com/intro_analysis_of_the%20NDE%2
0_.htm.

Jacobi, Jolande. *The Way of Individuation.* New York: New American
Library, 1983.

"James Hyslop 1854-1920." Accessed December 22, 2007.
https://www.survivalafterdeath.info/researchers/hyslop.htm

Jankowski, M. S. *Islands in the street: Gangs and American urban
society.* Berkeley: University of California Press, 1991.

Johnson, Ian. "Who Killed More: Hitler, Stalin, or Mao?" *The New York
Review.* February 5, 2018.
https://www.nybooks.com/daily/2018/02/05/who-killed-more-
hitler-stalin-or-mao/

Johnson, R. C. *The Imprisoned Splendour.* Wheaton, IL: Quest Books,
1982.

Jonas, W. B., and C. C. Crawford. "Science and spiritual healing: a
critical review of spiritual healing, 'energy' medicine, and
intentionality." *Alternative Therapies* 9, no. 3 (2003): A56-71.

Jung, C. G. *Collected Works of C. G. Jung, Volume 11; Psychology and
Religion.* Princeton, NJ: Princeton University Press, 1975.

Jung, C. G. *Collected Works of C. G. Jung, Volume 17: The Development of
Personality.* Princeton, NJ: Princeton University Press, 1954.

Jung, C. G. *Letters, Volume 1.* Princeton, NJ: Princeton University Press,
1973.

Jung, C. G., *Memories, Dreams, Reflections.* New York: Vintage Books,
1989.

Jürgenson, Friedrich. *Sprechfunk mit Verstorbenen.* Freiburg im Br.:
Hermann Bauer Verlag, 1967.

Kalish, R. A., and D. K. Reynolds. "Phenomenological reality and post
death contact." *Journal for the Scientific Study of Religion* 12, vol. 2
(1973): 209-21.

Kardec, Allan. *The Spirits' Book.* Westlake Village, CA: Spiritist
Educational Society, 2019; originally published in 1857.

Kean, Leslie. *Surviving Death: A Journalist Investigates Evidence for an Afterlife.* New York: Crown Archetype, 2017.

Kearney, Patrick. "Still crazy after all these years: Why meditation isn't psychotherapy." Accessed October 15, 2007. http://www.buddhanet.net/crazy.htm.

Keen, M. "Physical phenomena at the David Thompson séance of October 25th 2003." https://www.survivalafterdeath.info/articles/keen/thompson.htm.

Keen, M., and A. Ellison. "Scole: A response to the critics? The Scole Report." *Proceedings of the Society for Psychical Research* 58, part 220 (1999).

Kelly, Edward F. "Inadequacies of contemporary Mind/brain theories." Paper presented at the Esalen Invitational Conference on Survival of Bodily Death, February 11-16, 2000.

Kelly, Edward F., Emily Williams Kelly, Adam Crabtree, Alan Gauld, and Michael Grosso. *Irreducible Mind: Toward a Psychology for the 21st Century.* Lanham, MD: Rowman & Littlefield, 2006.

Kelway-Bamber, L., ed., *Claude's Book.* New York: Henry Holt and Company, 1919.

Kendall, J. *Michael Faraday.* London: Faber, 1955.

Kenny, Robert. "The science of collective consciousness." *What Is Enlightenment?* 25 (May-July 2004): 78.

Kenny, Robert. "What Can Science Tell Us about Collective Consciousness?" Institute for Global Transformation. http://www.ifgt.net/wp-content/uploads/2016/09/What-Can-Science-Tell-Us-About-Collective-Consciousness-1.pdf.

Klopfer, Bruno. "Psychological Variables in Human Cancer." *Journal of Prospective Techniques* 31 (1957): 331-40.

Knoblauch, H., Ina Schmied, and Bernt Schnettler. "Different Kinds of Near-Death Experience: A Report on a Survey of Near-Death Experiences in Germany." *Journal of Near-Death Studies* 20, no. 1 (2001): 15-29.

Knoll, Max. "Transformations of science in our age." *Papers from the Eranos Yearbooks, Eranos 3: Man and Time,* edited by Joseph Campbell. Princeton, NJ: Princeton University Press, 1957.

Komp, Diane M. *A Window to Heaven: When Children See Life in Death*. Grand Rapids, Michigan: Zondervan Publishing, 1992.

Konrath, Sara H. "The empathy paradox: Increasing disconnection in the age of increasing connection." *Handbook of Research on Technoself: Identity in a Technological Society*, edited by Rocci Luppicini. Hershey, PA: IGI Global. 2013.

Kornfield, J. *A path with heart: A guide through the perils and promises of spiritual life*. New York: Bantam, 1993.

Kounang, Nadia. "What is the science behind fear?" CNN. October 29, 2015. https://www.cnn.com/2015/10/29/health/science-of-fear/index.html.

Krieger, D. "Therapeutic touch: the imprimatur of nursing." *American Journal of Nursing* 7 (1975): 784-787.

Kübler-Ross, Elisabeth. *Is There Life After Death?* Sounds True audio, 2006.

Kübler-Ross, Elisabeth. *On Children and Death*. New York: MacMillan Publishing, 1983.

Kübler-Ross, Elisabeth. *On Life After Death*. Berkeley, CA: Celestial Arts, 1991.

Laberge, S., and M. Schlitz. "Covert observation increases skin conductance in subjects unaware of when they are being observed: A replication." *The Journal of Parapsychology* 61 (1997).

Landsman, Klaas. "The Fine-Tuning Argument: Exploring the Improbability of Our Existence." *The Challenge of Chance: A Multidisciplinary Approach from Science and the Humanities*. Switzerland: Springer Nature, 2016.

Larson, E. J., and L. Witham. "Leading scientists still reject God." *Nature* 394 (1998): 313.

Latz, N. M., D. P. Agle, R. G. DePalma, and J. J. DeCosse. "Delirium in surgical patients under intensive care." *Archives of Surgery* 104, no. 3 (March 1972): 310-313.

Lawrence, Madelaine, and Elizabeth Repede. "The Incidence of Deathbed Communications and Their Impact on the Dying Process." *American Journal of Hospice and Palliative Care* 30, no. 7 (2013): 632-639.

Lazarus, Richard. *The Case Against Death*. London: Warner Books, 1993.

LeShan, L. *The Medium, the Mystic, and the Physicist*. New York: Viking Press, 1974.

Libet, B. "Subjective antedating of a sensory experience and Mind-brain theories: Reply to Honderich." *Journal of Theoretical Biology* 114, no. 4 (May 31, 1985): 563-570.

Libet, B., E. W. Wright, B. Feinstein, and D. K. Pearl. "Subjective referral of the timing for a conscious sensory experience." *Brain* 102, no. 1 (1979): 193-224.

"Life After Death: Episode 8, The testimony of science." Hosted by Tom Harpur, based on his book (1998; Phoenix, AZ: Wellspring Media). TV documentary.

Linzmeier, B. M. "Attitudes toward near-death experiences." Accessed December 6, 2006. https://www.nderf.org/NDERF/Articles/nde_attitudes.htm.

Lipka, M., and C. Gecewicz. "More Americans now say they're spiritual but not religious." Pew Research Center. September 6, 2017. https://www.pewresearch.org/fact-tank/2017/09/06/more-americans-now-say-theyre-spiritual-but-not-religious/.

Lipton, Bruce. *The Biology of Belief*. Carlsbad, CA: Hay House, 2016.

Lipton, Bruce. "Dr Bruce Lipton—At Last, Scientific Proof of How Our Thoughts Can Make Us Healthy or Sick." 180 Nutrition. https://180nutrition.com.au/psychology/bruce-lipton-interview/.

Lipton, Bruce. "THINK Beyond Your Genes—March 2018," Bruce H. Lipton, PhD, https://www.brucelipton.com/think-beyond-your-genes-march-2018/.

Lisansky, Jonathan, Rick J. Strassman, David Janowsky, and S. Craig Risch. "Drug induced psychoses." *Transient Psychosis: Diagnosis, Management and Evaluation*, edited by Joe P. Tupin, Uriel Halbreich, and Jesus J. Pena, 80-111. New York: Bruner/Mazel, 1984.

Lives in Hazard. Directed by Susan Todd and Andrew Young (1994; Pleasantville, NY: Archipelago Films). NBC-TV movie.

Lodge, Oliver. *Raymond or Life and Death*. New York: George H. Doran, 1916.

Lombroso, Cesare. *Criminal Man*. Durham, NC: Duke University Press, 2006.

"Loneliness Is at Epidemic Levels in America." Cigna.
    https://www.cigna.com/about-us/newsroom/studies-and-
    reports/combatting-loneliness/.
Long, Dr. Jeffrey. "How Many NDEs Occur in the United States Every
    Day?" Near-Death Experience Research Foundation.
    https://www.nderf.org/NDERF/Research/number_nde_usa.htm.
Loughran, Gerry. "Can There Be Life after Life? Ask the Atheist!" 2001.
    Reprinted as "An Analysis of the Near-Death Experiences of
    Atheists." http://www.near-
    death.com/experiences/atheists01.html.
Maalouf, Amin. *In the Name of Identity: Violence and the Need to Belong.*
    New York: Arcade Publishing, 2012.
Machado, C., and D. A. Shewmon, eds. *Brain Death and Disorders of
    Consciousness.* Springer e-book. 2004.
Mack, Eric. "Forget Dying and Public Speaking: Here's the 47 Things
    Americans Fear More in 2017." Inc. https://www.inc.com/eric-
    mack/forget-dying-public-speaking-heres-47-things-americans-
    fear-more-in-2017.html.
"Many Americans are lonely, and Gen Z most of all, study finds." CBS
    News. May 3, 2018. https://www.cbsnews.com/news/many-
    americans-are-lonely-and-gen-z-most-of-all-study-finds/.
Maraldo, Pamela. *Medicine: In Search of a Soul: The Healing Prescription.*
    Carlsbad, CA: Balboa Press, 2017.
Mars, Brigitte. "Improve your brain power—with a healthy diet." BNET
    Research Center. *Natural Journal* (October 2000).
Marshall, R. S., R. M. Lazar, J. Pile-Spellman, W. L. Young, D. H.
    Duong, S. Joshi, and N. Ostapkovich. "Recovery of brain
    function during induced cerebral hypoperfusion." *Brain* 124,
    no. 6 (June 2001): 1208-1217.
Matchett, W. F. "Repeated hallucinatory experiences as part of the
    mourning process among Hopi Indian women." *Psychiatry* 35
    (1972): 185-194.
Mayell, Hillary. "Thousands of women killed for family 'honor.'"
    National Geographic. February 12, 2002.
    https://www.nationalgeographic.com/culture/article/thousands-
    of-women-killed-for-family-honor.

Mayer, E. L. *Science, Skepticism, and the Inexplicable Powers of the Human Mind.* New York: Bantam Books, 2007.

McCraty, R. *The energetic heart: Bioelectromagnetic interactions within and between people.* Boulder Creek, CA: Institute of HeartMath, 2003.

McKenna, P., and G. O'Bryen. *The Paranormal World of Paul McKenna.* London: Faber, 1997.

McKenzie, A. *Apparitions and Ghosts: A Modern Study.* London: Arthur Baker Ltd., 1971.

McRobbie, Linda Rodriguez. "The Strange and Mysterious History of the Ouija Board." *Smithsonian Magazine.* October 27, 2013. https://www.smithsonianmag.com/history/the-strange-and-mysterious-history-of-the-ouija-board-5860627/.

McTaggart, L. *The Field: The Quest for the Secret Force of the Universe.* New York: Harper Paperbacks, 1998.

Meek, G. *After We Die, What Then?* Columbus, OH: Ariel Press, 1987.

"Michelangelo's Prisoners or Slaves." Accademia.org. http://www.accademia.org/explore-museum/artworks/michelangelos-prisoners-slaves/.

Miller, L. H., A. D. Smith, and L. Rothstein. "The stress solution: An action plan to manage the stress in your life." New York: Pocket Books, 1993.

Miller, R. N. "Study of the effectiveness of remote mental healing." *Medical Hypotheses* 8 (1982): 481-490.

Milton, Richard. "Skeptics who declared discoveries and inventions impossible." Alternative Science

Moeller, Rachael. "Study Suggests Common Knee Surgery's Effect Is Purely Placebo." *Scientific American.* July 12, 2002. https://www.scientificamerican.com/article/study-suggests-common-kne/.

Montgomery, Guy, Katherine DuHamel, and William Redd. "A meta-analysis of hypnotically induced analgesia: How effective is hypnosis?" *International Journal of Clinical and Experimental Hypnosis* 48 (2000): 138-153.

Moody, Raymond. *Glimpses of Eternity: An Investigation into Shared Death Experiences.* London: Rider, 2011.

Moody, Raymond. *Life After Life.* New York: HarperOne, 1975.

Moody, Raymond. *Reunions: Visionary Encounters with Departed Loved Ones*. New Delhi, India: Ivy Press, 1993.

Moore, C. A. The unseen realm: Science is making room for near-death experiences beyond this world. *Desert Morning News*. February 18, 2006.

Moorjani, Anita. *Dying to Be Me: My Journey from Cancer, to Near Death, to True Healing*. Carlsbad, CA: Hay House, 2014.

Morin, R. "Do Americans Believe in God?" *Washington Post*. April 24, 2000. www.washingtonpost.com/wp-srv/politics/polls/wat/archive/wat042400.htm.

Morse, M. L. "Near death experiences and death-related visions in children: implications for the clinician." *Current Problems in Pediatrics* 24 (1994): 55-83.

Morse, M. L. with P. Perry. *Parting Visions*. New York: Villard Books, 1994.

Morse, Melvin, and Paul Perry. *Closer to the Light*. London: Souvenir Press, 1991.

Murphet, H. *Beyond death — The Undiscovered Country*. Wheaton, IL: Quest Books, 1990.

Murphy, M., and R. A. White. *The psychic side of sports*. Reading, MA: Addison-Wesley, 1978.

Muthumana, Sandhya P., M. Kumari, A. Kellehear, S. Kumar, and F. Moosa. "Deathbed visions from India: A study of family observations in northern Kerala." *Omega* 62, no. 2 (2010-2011), 97-109.

Myers, F. W. H. *Human Personality and Its Survival of Bodily Death*. Whitefish, MT: Kessinger Publishing, 1903.

Nahm, Michael, and Bruce Greyson. "Terminal Lucidity in Patients with Chronic Schizophrenia and Dementia: A Survey of the Literature." *The Journal of Nervous and Mental Disease* 197, no.12 (2009): 942-944.

Nash, C. B. "Test of psychokinetic control of bacterial mutation." *Journal of the American Society for Psychical Research* 78, no. 2 (1984): 145-52.

Naylor, William, ed. *Silver Birch Anthology: Wisdom from the World Beyond*. London: Spiritualist Press, 1974.

Neehall-Davidson, Joan. *Perfecting Private Practice.* Bloomington, IN: Trafford Publishing, 2004.

Neff, Kristin. "Why self-compassion is healthier than self-esteem." Self-Compassion.org. https://self-compassion.org/why-self-compassion-is-healthier-than-self-esteem/.

Nelaraw, Mohnish. "90% people have low self-esteem: Experts." TOI. September 12, 2017. https://timesofindia.indiatimes.com/city/nagpur/90-people-have-low-self-esteem-experts/articleshow/60469457.cms

Newton, Michael. *Destiny of Souls: New Case Studies of Life Between Lives.* Woodbury MN: Llewellyn Publications, 2000.

Nietzsche, Friedrich. *Thus Spake Zarathustra: A Book for All and None.* "Zarathustra's Discourses, I. The Three Metamorphoses." The Project Gutenberg. https://www.gutenberg.org/files/1998/1998-h/1998-h.htm#link2H_4_0006.

Nisargadatta, Maharaj. *I Am That: Talks with Sri Nisargadatta Maharaj.* Charlottetown, Canada: The Acorn Press, 1990.

Novak, M. *The joy of sports.* New York: Basic Books, 1976.

Olson, Jeff, and Jeff O'Driscoll. "Shared Near-Death Experiences Between Doctor and Patient." Produced by International Association for Near-Death Studies. January 6, 2021. YouTube video, 19:47, https://youtu.be/lwkOnahGlsc.

Onetto, B., and G. H. Elguin. "Psychokinesis in experimental tumorgenesis. (Abstract of dissertation in psychology, University of Chile 1964)." *Journal of Parapsychology* 30 (1966): 220.

Oppenheim, J. *The Other World.* Cambridge, UK: Cambridge University Press, 1985.

Orme-Johnson, David W., K. L. Cavanaugh, C. N. Alexander, P. Gelderloos, M. C. Dillbeck, A. G. Lanford, and T. M. Abou Nader. "The influence of the Maharishi Technology of the Unified Field on world events and global social indicators: The effects of the Taste of Utopia Assembly." 1989. In *Scientific research on Maharishi's Transcendental Meditation and TM-Sidhi program: Collected papers, Vol. 4 Vlodrop,* edited by R. A.

Chalmers, G. Clements, H. Schenkluhn, and M. Weinless. The Netherlands: Maharishi Vedic University Press.

Osborne, Samuel. "Four genocides we should also remember on Holocaust Memorial Day." *Independent*. January 27, 2016. https://www.independent.co.uk/news/uk/home-news/four-genocides-we-should-also-remember-holocaust-memorial-day-a6837246.html.

Osis, Karlis. "Core visions of psychical research: Is there life after death? A cross-Cultural Search for the Evidence." *Journal of the American Society for Psychical Research* 92 (July1998): 252.

Osis, Karlis, and Erlendur Haraldsson. *At the Hour of Death*. Norwalk, CT: Hastings House, 1997.

"Other Types of Experiences We Study." University of Virginia School of Medicine, Division of Perceptual Studies. https://med.virginia.edu/perceptual-studies/our-research/types-of-cases/.

Owen, G. Vale. *The Life beyond the Veil: A Compilation (Life on Other Worlds* series). Schenectady, NY: Square Circles Publishing, 2014; originally published in 1921.

"Paradise Polled: Americans and the Afterlife." Roper Center. https://ropercenter.cornell.edu/paradise-polled-americans-and-afterlife.

"Paranormal Voices Assert: Death No End." Man and the Unknown. Accessed October 3, 2007. https://wichm.home.xs4all.nl/deathnoe.html.

Parish, C. "The ultimate adventure." What Is Enlightenment? WIE Unbound audiotape, 2007.

Parnell, Laurel. *Transforming Trauma: EMDR*. New York: W. W. Norton & Company, 1998.

Pasricha, S. "Near-Death experiences in South India: A systematic survey." *Journal of Scientific Exploration* 9, no. 1 (1986): 4.

Patt, Stephan. "Brain localization of consciousness? Neurological considerations." Seventh International Interdisciplinary Seminar, "Exploring the human mind: the perspective of natural sciences," Ponte di Legno, Italy. December 28, 2003.

http://web.quipo.it/glopresti/pdl/ppt/Patt%20-
%20Brain%20localization%20of%20consciousness.pdf.

Patterson, Jill. "How Evil Is a Socially Constructed Concept: Evil Across Societies." *The Manitoban*. February 9, 2021. http://www.themanitoban.com/2012/10/how-evil-is-a-socially-constructed-concept-evil-across-societies/12309/.

Pearson, Ronald. "Alternative to relativity including quantum gravitation." Second International Conference on Problems in Space and Time, St. Petersburg, Russia. Academy of Sciences & Arts. September 1991, 278-292.

Pearson, Ronald. "Consciousness as a Sub-quantum Phenomenon." *Frontier Perspectives* 6, no. 2 (Spring/Summer 1997): 70-78.

Pearson, Ronald. *Intelligence Behind the Universe!* Headquarters Publishing Company, 1990.

Pearson, Ronald. "Quantum Gravitation and the Structured Ether." Sir Isaac Newton Conference, St. Petersburg. March 1993, 39-55.

Peebles, James M. *Immortality and Our Employments Hereafter: With What a Hundred Spirits, Good and Evil, Say of Their Dwelling Places.* London: Forgotten Books, 2015; originally published in 1907.

Penman, D. "Many scientists are convinced that man can see the future." May 5, 2007. https://www.redorbit.com/news/science/925987/many_scientists_are_convinced_that_man_can_see_the_future/.

Persinger, M. A., and S. Krippner. "Dream ESP experiments and geomagnetic activity." *The Journal of the American Society for Psychical Research* 83 (1989).

Peters, Adele. "It would cost just $330 billion to end global hunger by 2030." Fast Company. October 15, 2020. https://www.fastcompany.com/90564107/it-would-cost-just-330-billion-to-end-global-hunger-by-2030.

"Physicists Challenge Notion of Electric Nerve Impulses; Say Sound More Likely." Science Blog. University of Copenhagen. March 7, 2007. https://scienceblog.com/12738/physicists-challenge-notion-of-electric-nerve-impulses-say-sound-more-likely/.

Pike, James A., and Diane Kennedy Pike. *The Other Side: An Account of My Experiences with Psychic Phenomena*. Eugene, OR: Wipf and Stock, 1968.

Playfair, Guy L. *Twin Telepathy: The Psychic Connection*. London: Vega Publish, 2003.

"Poll: Stress Squeezes 4 in 10 Americans." CBS News. 2007. www.cbsnews.com/news/poll-stress-squeezes-4-in-10-americans-30-01-2007/.

Post, Jerrold M. "It's us against them." *Terrorism* 10 (1987): 23-35.

Prescott, James W. "The Origins of Human Love and Violence." Institute of Humanistic Science. *Pre- and Perinatal Psychology Journal* 10, no. 3 (Spring 1996): 143-188.

Presti, David E. Review of Edward F. Kelly et al., *Irreducible Mind: Toward a Psychology for the 21st Century*. Rowman & Littlefield. Accessed October 5, 2007. https://rowman.com/ISBN/9781442202061/Irreducible-Mind-Toward-a-Psychology-for-the-21st-Century.

"Prodigy, 12, compared to Mozart." CBS News. November 24, 2004. https://www.cbsnews.com/news/prodigy-12-compared-to-mozart/.

"Psychic Detectives." Transcript. CNN. "Nancy Grace." December 30, 2005. http://transcripts.cnn.com/TRANSCRIPTS/0512/30/ng.01.html.

Puryear, Anne. *Stephen Lives!* New York: Pocket Books, 1992.

Puthoff, H. E. "CIA-initiated remote viewing at Stanford Research Institute." Journal of Scientific Exploration 10 (1996): 63-76.

Puthoff, H. E., and R. Targ. "A perceptual channel for information transfer over kilometer distances: historical perspective and recent research." *Proceedings of the IEEE* 64, no. 3 (March 1976).

Putnam, Allen. *Flashes of Light from the Spirit-Land: Through the Mediumship of Mrs. J. H. Conant*. London: Forgotten Books, 2015; originally published in 1872.

Radin, D. *The Conscious Universe: The Scientific Truth of Psychic Phenomena*. New York: HarperCollins Publishers, 1997.

Radin, D., G. Hayssen, M. Emoto, and T. Kizu. "Double-blind test of the effects of distant intention on water crystal formation." *Explore* 2, no. 5 (September/October 2006): 408-411.

Radin, D., C. Rae, and R. Hyman. "Is there a sixth sense?" *Psychology Today* 39, no. 4 (July/August 2006).

Radin, D., R. Taft, and G. Yount. "Effects of Healing Intention on Cultured Cells and Truly Random Events." *The Journal of Alternative and Complementary Medicine* 10, no. 1 (2004): 103-112.

Randall, E. C. *The Dead Have Never Died.* New York: A. A. Knopf, 1917.

Rees, W. D. "The hallucinations of widowhood." *British Medical Journal* 4 (1971): 37-41.

Rein, G. "A psychokinetic effect on neurotransmitter metabolism: Alterations in the degradative enzyme monoamine oxidase." In *Research in Parapsychology 1985,* edited by D. H. Weiner and D. Radin, 77-80. Metuchen, NJ: Scarecrow Press, 1986.

Rhine, J. B., C. E. Stuart, and J. G, Pratt. *Extra-Sensory Perception after Sixty years: A Critical Appraisal of the Research in Extra-Sensory Perception.* Boston: Bruce Humphries, 1966.

Richards, Jay, and Guillermo Gonzalez. "Are we alone?" *The American Spectator* (May 1, 2004).

Ring, K., and S. Cooper. *Mindsight: Near-Death and Out-of-body experiences in the Blind. The Journal of Nervous and Mental Disease* 188, no. 11 (November 2000): 789-790.

Ring, K., and M. Lawrence. "Further evidence for veridical perception during near-death experiences." *Journal of Near-Death Studies* 11, no. 4 (1993): 223-229.

Ring, P. "Dr. Larry Dossey champions the healing power of prayer." *Mysteries Magazine 16.*

Rogge, M. "Direct Voice: Conversation between mother and her deceased son." Man and the Unknown. Accessed October 5, 2007. http://www.xs4all.nl/~wichm/fearon.html.

Rogo, D. S. *Leaving the Body: A Complete Guide to Astral Projection.* New York: Fireside/Simon & Schuster, 1993.

Rogo, D. S. "Researching the out-of-body experiences." In *Best Evidence,* Michael Schmicker, 203. Bloomington, IN: iUniverse, 2002.

Roland, P. E., and L. Friberg. "Localization in cortical areas activated by thinking." *Journal of Neurophysiology* 53 (1985): 1219-1243.

Rommer, B. *Blessings in Disguise: Another Side of the Near Death Experience.* Woodbury, MN: Llewellyn Publications, 2000.

Rowse, A.L. "Justice for Robert Bridges." *Contemporary Review* 263, no. 1531 (August 1993): 86.

Roy, Archie. "Letter to Michael Roll (May 19, 1983): Psychic Phenomena."

Russell, P. *From Science to God: A Physicist's Journey into the Mystery of Consciousness.* Novato, CA: New World Library, 2004.

Sabom, M. *Light and Death.* Grand Rapids, MI: Zondervan Publishing, 1998.

Sabom, M. *Recollections of Death: A Medical Investigation.* New York: Harper & Row, 1998.

Sampson, R. J., and J. H. Laub. *Crime in the Making: Pathways and Turning Points Through Life.* Cambridge, MA: Harvard University Press, 1993.

Sathyanarayana Rao, T. S., M. R. Asha, K. S. Jagannatha Rao, and P. Vasudevaraju. "The Biochemistry of Belief." *Indian Journal of Psychiatry* 51, no. 4 (Oct-Dec 2009): 239–241.

Savage, Mynot J. *Life Beyond Death.* New York: G. P. Putnam's Sons, 1900.

Schlitz, M. "Embracing the mystery." *What Is Enlightenment?* WIE Unbound audiotape, December 13, 2003.

Schlitz M., and W. G. Braud. "Reiki-Plus natural healing: An ethnographic/experimental study." *Psi Research* 4 (1985): 100-123.

Schlitz, M., and S. LaBerge. "Covert observation increases skin conductance in subjects unaware of when they are being observed: a replication." *The Journal of Parapsychology 61* (1997): 185-196.

Schlitz, S., and C. Honorton. "Ganzfeld psi performance within an artistically gifted population." *Journal of the American Society for Psychical Research* 86 (1992): 83-98.

Schmicker, M. *Best Evidence.* Lincoln, NE: Writers Club Press, 2002.

Schnabel, J. *Remote Viewers — The Secret History of America's Psychic Spies.* New York: Dell, 1997.

Schroeder, G. L. *The Hidden Face of God*. New York: Simon & Schuster, 2001.

Schroeter-Kunhardt, M. "A review of near death experiences." *Journal of Scientific Exploration* 7, no. 3 (Fall 1993): 219-39, 1.

Schroter-Kunhardt, M. "Erfahrungen sterbender während des klinischen Todes." *Z Allg Med* 66 (1990): 1014-21.

Schwartz, G., and L. Russek. *The living-energy universe: A fundamental discovery that transforms science and medicine.* Charlottesville, VA: Hampton Roads Publishing, 1999.

Schwartz, G., and W. L. Simon. *The Afterlife Experiments, Breakthrough Scientific Evidence of Life After Death.* New York: Atria Books, 2003.

Schwartz, G., Lind G. S. Russek, Lonnie A. Nelson, and Christopher Barentsen. "Accuracy and Replicability of Anomalous After-Death Communication Across Highly Skilled Mediums." *Journal of the Society for Psychical Research* 65, no. 1 (2001): 1-25.

Schwartz, Robert. *Your Soul's Gift: The Healing Power of the Life You Planned Before You Were Born.* Chesterland, OH: Whispering Winds Press, 2012.

Schwartz, Robert. *Your Soul's Plan: Discovering the Real Meaning of the Life You Planned Before You Were Born.* Berkeley: North Atlantic Books, 2009.

Schweitzer, Tamara. "U.S. workers hate their jobs more than ever." Inc.com. Accessed October 15, 2007. https://www.inc.com/news/articles/200703/work.html.

Scull, Maggie. "Timeline of 1981 hunger strike." *The Irish Times*. March 1, 2016. https://www.irishtimes.com/culture/books/timeline-of-1981-hunger-strike-1.2555682.

Sharp, K. C. *After the Light*. Lincoln, NE: Author's Choice Press, 2003.

Sheldrake, Rupert. "The 'sense of being stared at' experiments in schools." *Journal of the Society for Psychical Research* 62, (1998): 311-323.

Sheldrake, Rupert. "Videotaped Experiments on Telephone Telepathy." *Journal of Parapsychology* 67 (2003): 147-166.

Sherwood, Jane. *The Country Beyond*. London: Neville Spearman, 1969.

Sherwood, Jane. *The Psychic Bridge*. London: Rider & Co., Ltd., 1942.

Shkurko, Tatyana A. "Socio-psychological Analysis of Controlling Personality." *Procedia - Social and Behavioral Sciences* 86 (2013): 629–634.

Sicher, F., E. Targ, D. Moore, and H. S. Smith. "A randomized, double-blind study of the effects of distant healing in a population with advanced AIDS." *Western Journal of Medicine* 169, no. 6 (1998): 356-363.

Silva, Jose. *The Silva Mind Control Method.* New York: Pocket Books, 1991.

Simpson, A. Rae. "MIT Young Adult Development Project." MIT. 2018. http://hrweb.mit.edu/worklife/youngadult/index.html.

Simpson, Mona. "A Sister's Eulogy for Steve Jobs." *The New York Times.* October 30, 2011. https://www.nytimes.com/2011/10/30/opinion/mona-simpsons-eulogy-for-steve-jobs.html.

Smith, G. *The Unbelievable Truth.* Carlsbad, CA: Hay House, 2004.

Smith-Moncrieffe, Donna. "Evidence of the Afterlife." Science of Mediumship Event, Toronto. November 9, 2013. https://www.slideshare.net/dmoncri/evidence-of-the-afterlife-science-of-mediumship-event.

Snyder, J. J. "Science confirms survival." The Campaign for Philosophical Freedom. Accessed September 20, 2007. http://www.cfpf.org.uk/articles/background/snyder.html.

Solfvin, G. F. "Psi expectancy effects in psychic healing studies with malarial mice." *European Journal of Parapsychology* 4, no. 2 (1982): 160-197.

Sonterblum, Laina. "Gang Involvement as a Means to Satisfy Basic Needs." New York University. https://wp.nyu.edu/steinhardt-appsych_opus/gang-involvement-as-a-means-to-satisfy-basic-needs/.

"Soul Planning." Produced by Suzanne Giesemann. June 25, 2018. YouTube video, 51:30, https://www.youtube.com/watch?v=-k35ozLYyW8&t=11s.

Spraggett, A. *The Case for Immortality.* Scarborough, Canada: New American Library of Canada, 1974.

Spraggett, A. *Probing the Unexplained*. New York: New American Library, 1973.

Stammar, G. "Drill preps personnel for violence at school." *The Daily Pantagraph*. September 20, 2007.

"The State of Depression in America." Depression and Bipolar Support Alliance. February 2006. https://www.yumpu.com/en/document/read/36079800/the-state-of-depression-in-america-depression-and-bipolar-support-.

Stead, William T. *After Death: Letters from Julia*. Guildford, UK: White Crow Books, 2011.

Stevenson, I. "Do we need a new word to supplement 'hallucination?'" *American Journal of Psychiatry* 140, no. 12 (1983): 1609-11.

Stevenson, I. *Xenoglossy*. Charlottesville, VA: University of Virginia Press, 1974.

Stevenson, I., J. E. Owens, and E. W. Cook. "Features of 'near-death experience' in relation to whether or not patients were near death." *The Lancet* 336, no. 8724 (1990): 1175-1177.

Stevenson, M. "Ancient child sacrifices found in Mexico." NBC News. April 17, 2007. https://www.nbcnews.com/id/wbna18164233.

Stringfellow, Alice Johnston. *Leslie's letters to his mother: Being a collection of messages received by Henry Martyn Stringfellow and Alice Johnston Stringfellow*. Fayetteville, AR: Democrat Pub. and Printing Co., January 1, 1926.

"Study suggests brain may have 'blindsight.'" NBC News. October 31, 2005. https://www.nbcnews.com/health/health-news/study-suggests-brain-may-have-blindsight-flna1c9437216.

"Suicide in Children and Teens." American Academy of Child & Adolescent Psychiatry 10 (June 2018).

"Supergirl Dilemma: Girls Grapple with the Mounting Pressures of Expectations: Summary Findings," Girls Incorporated, 2006.

Swain, Jasper. *Heaven's Gift: Conversations Beyond the Veil*. South Africa: Kima Global Publishers, 1996.

Swain, Jasper. *On the Death of My Son*. London: Turnstone Press, 1974.

Swedenborg, Emanuel. *Heaven and Hell*. West Chester, PA: Swedenbourg Foundation, New Century Edition, 2000.

Talbot, Michael. *The Holographic Universe*. New York: Harper Perennial, 2011.

Targ, R., and K. Harary. *The Mind Race*. New York: Villard Books, 1984.

Targ, R., and J. Katra. *Miracles of Mind*. Charlottesville, VA: Hampton Roads Publishing, 1998.

Targ, R., and H. Puthoff. "Information transmission under conditions of sensory shielding." *Nature* 251 (1974).

Tart, C. "Psychedelic experiences associated with a novel hypnotic procedure, mutual hypnosis." In *Altered States of Consciousness*, 291-308. New York: John Wiley & Sons, 1969.

Tart, C. "Psychophysiological study of out-of-the-body experiences in a selected subject." *Journal of the American Society for Psychical Research* 62, no. 1 (1968): 3-27.

Taylor, Ruth Mattson. *Witness from Beyond*. New York: Hawthorn Books, 1975.

Tedder, W. H., and M. L. Monty. "Exploration of long-distance PK: A conceptual replication of the influence on a biological system." In *Research in Parapsychology*, edited by W. G. Roll, R. L. Morris, and J. D. Morris, 90-93. Metuchen, NJ: Scarecrow Press, 1981.

Thaheld, F. "Biological non-locality and the mind-brain interaction problem: comments on a new empirical approach." *Biosystems* 2209 (2003): 1-7.

"Theodicy, God and Suffering – A debate between Dinesh D'Souza and Bart Ehrman." Produced by Gordon College Center for Christian Studies. November 11, 2010. YouTube video, 1:42:27. https://www.youtube.com/watch?v=Isg6Kx-3xdI.

"There's more than meets the eye in judging the size of an object." The All I Need. Accessed August 25, 2007. http://www.theallineed.com/medicine/06032012.htm.

Thomas, Charles Drayton. *Life Beyond Death with Evidence*. Hong Kong: Hesperides Press, 2008; originally published in 1923.

Thomas, Charles Drayton. "Report re Lodge via Leonard," *Journal of the Society for Psychical Research* 33 (1945): 136, 138-160.

Thibault, Henry. *Letters from the Other Side*. London: John M. Watkins, 1919.

Thorpe, Matthew, and Rachael Link. "12 Science-Based Benefits of Meditation." Healthline. October 27, 2020.

Tiller, W. A. "Subtle energies." *Science and Medicine* 6, no. 3 (May/June 1999).

Tiller, W. A., W. Dibble, and M. Kohane. *Conscious Acts of Creation: The Emergence of a New Physics.* Walnut Creek, CA: Pavior Publishing, 2001.

"Tiny-brained man's lifestyle wows doctors." NBC News. July 19, 2007. https://www.nbcnews.com/id/wbna19859089.

Touber, Tijn. "Life goes on." *Ode* 3, no. 10 (December 2005).

Treffert, D. "Kim Peek—The Real Rain Man." Wisconsin Medical Society. Archived September 9, 2008, at the Wayback Machine.

Twemlow, S. W., G. O. Gabbard, F. C. Jones. "The out-of-body experience: a phenomenological typology based on questionnaire responses." *American Journal of Psychiatry* 139, no. 4 (April 1982): 450-5.

Twenge, Jean M. "The Sad State of Happiness in the United States and the Role of Digital Media." World Happiness Report. March 20, 2019. https://worldhappiness.report/ed/2019/the-sad-state-of-happiness-in-the-united-states-and-the-role-of-digital-media/.

Twenge, Jean M., G. N. Martin, and W. K. Campbell. "Decreases in psychological well-being among American adolescents after 2012 and links to screen time during the rise of smartphone technology." *Emotion* 18, no. 6 (2018): 765-780.

Tymn, M. *The Afterlife Revealed: What Happens After We Die?* Guildford, UK: White Crow Books, 2011.

Tymn, M. "Automatic writing Explained." White Crow Books, http://whitecrowbooks.com/michaeltymn/entry/automatic_writing_explained.

Tymn, M. "Ghost Stories: Ghost loses chess match." All About Paranormal. September 1, 2008. https://www.allaboutparanormal.co/2008/09/ghost-stories-ghost-loses-chess-match.html#axzz6rppHBgXf.

Tymn, M. "Try Shock Therapy to Protect Against Vagabond Spirits?" White Crow Books. Blog. June 28, 2011. http://whitecrowbooks.com/michaeltymn/month/2011/06/.

Tymn, M. "A veridical death-bed vision." Paranormal and Life After
   Death. March 14, 2008.
   https://paranormalandlifeafterdeath.blogspot.com/2008/03/.
Ullman, Montague. "Herpes Simplex and Second Degree Burn Induced
   Under Hypnosis." *The American Journal of Psychiatry* 103, no. 6
   (May 1947).
Ullman, Montague, and S. Krippner. *Dream Studies and Telepathy: An
   Experimental Approach*. New York: Parapsychology Foundation,
   1970.
"United States: How afraid are you of death?" Statista. January 2019.
   https://www.statista.com/statistics/959347/fear-of-death-in-the-
   us/.
Utts, Jessica. "An Assessment of the Evidence for Psychic Functioning."
   Journal of Scientific Exploration 10, no. 1 (1996): 3-30.
Van den Berg, David P. G., and Mark van der Gaag. "Treating trauma
   in psychosis with EMDR: A pilot study." *Journal of Behavior
   Therapy and Experimental Psychiatry* 43, no.1 (March 2012).
Van Lommel, Pim. *Consciousness Beyond Life: The Science of the Near-
   Death Experience*. New York: HarperCollins, 2010.
Van Lommel, Pim. "Near-death experience in survivors of cardiac
   arrest; a prospective study in the Netherlands." *Lancet* 358
   (December 15, 2001): 39-45.
Van Lommel, Pim. "6. Neurophysiology in a normal functioning brain."
   International Association for Near-Death Studies. Accessed
   November 15, 2007. https://iands.org/research/nde-
   research/important-research-articles/43-dr-pim-van-lommel-md-
   continuity-of-consciousness.html?start=5.
Vargas, L., F. Loya, and J. Hodde-Vargas. "Exploring the
   multidimensional aspects of grief reactions." *American Journal of
   Psychiatry* 146, no. 11 (1989): 1484-9.
Varvoglis, M. "Telepathy: What is PSI? What isn't?" Parapsychological
   Association.
   http://archived.parapsych.org/psiexplorer/telepth2.htm.
Vinney, Cynthia. "Understanding Maslow's Theory of Self-
   Actualization." ThoughtCo. 2018.

https://www.thoughtco.com/maslow-theory-self-actualization-4169662.

Von Buengner, P. "Morphic fields can now be measured scientifically!" M.H. C - Angelfire. January 16, 2005. https://www.angelfire.com/indie/mhc/dyce/index.blog/333950/morphic-fieldz/.

Von Schrenk-Notzing, Baron. *Phenomena of Materialization, a contribution to the investigation of mediumistic teleplastics.* New York: E. P. Dutton, 1920.

Wade, W. C. *The Fiery Cross: The Ku Klux Klan in America.* New York: Touchstone/Simon & Schuster, 1987.

Wagner, S. "Deathbed visions." Liveabout.com. Updated January 2, 2019. http://paranormal.about.com/library/weekly/aa021901a.htm.

Ward, John Sebastian Marlowe. *A Subaltern in Spirit Land.* London: W. Rider, 1920.

Ward, Suzanne. *Matthew, Tell Me about Heaven.* Camas, WA: Matthew Books, 2012.

Watkins, G. K., and A. M. Watkins. "Possible PK influence on the resuscitation of anesthetized mice." *Journal of Parapsychology* 35, no. 4 (1971): 257-72.

Watkins, G. K., A. M. Watkins, and R. A. Wells. "Further studies on the resuscitation of anesthetized mice." In *Research in Parapsychology,* edited by W. G. Roll, R. L. Morris, and J. D. Morris, 157-59. Metuchen, NJ: Scarecrow Press, 1972.

Weiskrantz, L. "Blindsight revisited." *Journal of Cognitive Neuroscience* 6 (1996): 215-220.

Weiss, P. A. "The living system: Determinism stratified." In *Beyond reductionism: New perspectives in the life sciences,* edited by A. Koestler and J. R. Smythies. London: Hutchinson, 1969.

Wells, R., and J. A. Klein, "Replication of a 'psychic healing' paradigm." *Journal of Parapsychology* 36 (1972): 144-47.

Wells, R., and G. K. Watkins. "Linger effects in several PK experiments." In *Research in Parapsychology,* edited by W. G. Roll, R. L. Morris, and J. D. Morris, 143-47. Metuchen, NJ: Scarecrow Press, 1974.

Wenberg, Cy. *Gadflies.* Bloomington, IN: Trafford Publishing, 2006.

"What's the point of all of this?" Suzanne Giesemann. May 26, 2020. https://www.suzannegiesemann.com/what/.

White, Stewart Edward, *The Betty Book*. Westwood, MA: Ariel Pr, 1988; originally published in 1937.

Wickland, Carl. *The Gateway of Understanding*. Santa Ana, CA: National Psychological Institute, Inc., 1934.

Wickland, Carl. *Thirty Years Among the Dead*. Guildford, UK: White Crow Books, 2011.

Wilkinson, D., P. Knox, J. Chatman, T. Johnson, N. Barbour, Y. Myles, and A. Reel. "The Clinical Effectiveness of Healing Touch." *Journal of Alternative and Complementary Medicine* 8, no. 1 (2002): 33-47.

Williams, G. *A Life Beyond Death*. London: Robert Hale, 1989.

Williams, Kevin. "People Have Near-Death Experiences While Brain Dead." Near-Death Experiences and the Afterlife. Accessed April 1, 2007. http://www.near-death.com/experiences/evidence01.html.

Wills-Brandon, C. *One Last Hug Before I Go: The Mystery And Meaning Of Deathbed Visions*. Norwalk, CT: Hastings House, 2007.

Wills-Brandon, C. "Understanding departing visions or deathbed visitations." Empowering Caregivers. Accessed June 21, 2007. http://www.care-givers.com/DBArticles/pages/viewarticle.php?id=137.

Windbridge Research Center. "Major Findings to Date." 2019. http://www.windbridge.org/education/major-findings.

Winston, S. "Research in psychic healing: A multivariate experiment." Unpublished doctoral dissertation. Union Graduate School, Yellow Springs, OH, 1975.

"Within." *The Daily Way*. Suzanne Giesemann. January 10, 2021. https://www.suzannegiesemann.com/within-4/.

Woods, D.L., and M. Dimond. "The effect of therapeutic touch on agitated behavior and cortisol in persons with Alzheimer's disease." *Biological Research for Nursing* 4, no. 2 (2002): 104-114.

"Youth mental health report: Youth Survey 2012-16." Mission Australia, in association with the Black Dog Institute. April 18, 2017.

"Youth suicide fact sheet." National Youth Violence Prevention Resource Center. 2002.

Zaleski, C. *Otherworld Journeys*. New York: Oxford University Press, 1987.

Zammit, V. "Australian psychics beat 'orthodox' science." Victor Zammit. Accessed May 13, 2007. http://victorzammit.com/articles/sensingmurder.html.

Zammit, V. "Conversation with Victor Zammit." Victor Zammit. Accessed September 21, 2007. http://victorzammit.com.

Zammit, V. "15. Direct-voice mediums: Leslie Flint." https://www.victorzammit.com/book/4thedition/chapter15.html.

Zammit, V. *A Lawyer Presents the Case for the Afterlife*. Sydney, Australia: Ganmell Pty Ltd., 2006.

Zammit, V. "10. Materialization mediumship." Victor Zammit. Accessed December 12, 2007. http://www.victorzammit.com/book/chapter10.html.

Endnotes

[1] Lorraine Berry, "'They': the singular pronoun that could solve sexism in English," *The Guardian*, May 5, 2016, https://www.theguardian.com/books/booksblog/2016/may/05/they-the-singular-pronoun-that-could-solve-sexism-in-english.

[2] AfterlifeData.com, 2019. http://afterlifedata.com/.

[3] Dr. Jeffrey Long, "How Many NDEs Occur in the United States Every Day?" Near-Death Experience Research Foundation, https://www.nderf.org/NDERF/Research/number_nde_usa.htm

[4] Professor Dr. Hubert Knoblauch et al., "Different Kinds of Near-Death Experience: A Report on a Survey of Near-Death Experiences in Germany," *Journal of Near-Death Studies* 20, no. 1 (2001): 15-29.

[5] "About IADC," IADC Therapy for Grief, https://iadctherapy.com/about.

[6] Allan L. Botkin with R. Craig Hogan, *Induced After-Death Communication: A New Therapy for Healing Grief and Trauma* (Charlottesville, VA: Hampton Roads Publishing, 2005).

[7] Gary E. Schwartz, *The Afterlife Experiments: Breakthrough Scientific Evidence of Life after Death* (New York: Atria Books, 2003).

[8] "Major Findings to Date," Windbridge Research Center, 2019, http://www.windbridge.org/education/major-findings/.

[9] Donna Smith-Moncrieffe, "Evidence of the Afterlife," presentation, Science of Mediumship, Toronto, November 9, 2013. https://www.slideshare.net/dmoncri/evidence-of-the-afterlife-science-of-mediumship-event.

[10] "Afterlife Communication: David Thompson's Séances Today," Afterlife Research and Education Institute, Inc., https://adcguides.com/davidthompson1.htm.

[11] Leslie Flint Educational Trust, https://leslieflint.com.

[12] Miles Allen, *The Realities of Heaven: Fifty Spirits Describe Your Future Home* (CreateSpace Independent Publishing Platform, 2015).

[13] Stafford Betty, *The Afterlife Unveiled: What the Dead are Telling Us About Their World* (Blue Ridge Summit, PA: 6th Books, 2011).

[14] Anthony Borgia, *Life in the World Unseen* (London: Corgi Books, 1970).

[15] N. Riley Heagerty, *The Hereafter: Firsthand Reports from the Frontiers of the Afterlife* (New York: Circle of Light Research, 2020).

[16] Robert Crookall, *The Supreme Adventure: Analyses of Psychic Communications* (Cambridge, UK: James Clarke & Co. Ltd., 1961).

[17] Robert Schwartz, *Your Soul's Plan: Discovering the Real Meaning of the Life You Planned Before You Were Born* (Berkeley: North Atlantic Books, 2009).

[18] Robert Schwartz, *Your Soul's Gift: The Healing Power of the Life You Planned Before You Were Born* (Chesterland, OH: Whispering Winds Press, 2012).

[19] M. Tymn, *The Afterlife Revealed: What Happens After We Die?* (Guildford, UK: White Crow Books, 2011), 61-77.

[20] R. Craig Hogan, *There Is Nothing but Mind and Experiences* (Normal, IL: Greater Reality Publications, 2020).

[21] Klaas Landsman, "The Fine-Tuning Argument: Exploring the Improbability of Our Existence," *The Challenge of Chance: A Multidisciplinary Approach from Science and the Humanities* (Switzerland: Springer Nature, 2016).

[22] Stephen Hawking, *A Brief History of Time* (New York: Bantam, 1998), 125.

[23] Rich Heffern, "Spirituality and the fine-tuned cosmos," *National Catholic Reporter*, December 12, 2003. https://natcath.org/NCR_Online/archives2/2003d/121203/121203a.htm.

[24] "Interviews with Great Scientists, VI. Max Planck," *The Observer*, London, January 25, 1931.

[25] Heagerty, *The Hereafter*, 15.

[26] R. C. Henry, "The Mental Universe," *Nature* 436, no. 7 (2005): 29.

[27] Anton Zeilinger, "Essential quantum entanglement," in *The New Physics*, edited by Gordon Fraser (Cambridge, UK: Cambridge University Press, 2012), 257-267.

[28] Heagerty, *Hereafter*, 62 (citing August Goforth and Timothy Gary, *The Risen: Dialogues of Love, Grief & Survival Beyond Death*, 2016, Chapter 2, "Tim Speaks").

[29] "Amy Johnson séance," Leslie Flint Educational Trust, January 1970, https://www.leslieflint.com/amy-johnson.

[30] Hogan, *There Is Nothing but Mind and Experiences*, 187-192.

[31] Thomas Campbell, *My Big Toe: A Trilogy Unifying Philosophy, Physics, and Metaphysics: Awakening, Discovery, Inner Workings* (Huntsville, AL: Lightning Strike Books, 2007).

[32] "Soul Planning," produced by Suzanne Giesemann, June 25, 2018, YouTube video, 51:30, https://www.youtube.com/watch?v=-k35ozLYyW8&t=11s.

[33] "Soul Planning."

[34] Schwartz, *Your Soul's Gift*.

[35] Anabela Cardoso, *Electronic Voices: Contact with Another Dimension?* (Washington, D.C.: O Books, 2010).

[36] Raj Raghunathan, "The Need to Love," *Psychology Today*, January 8, 2014, https://www.psychologytoday.com/us/blog/sapient-nature/201401/the-need-love.

[37] Raghunathan, "The Need to Love."

[38] Steve Taylor, "Addiction and a Lack of Purpose," *Psychology Today*, November 30, 2018, https://www.psychologytoday.com/us/blog/out-the-darkness/201811/addiction-and-lack-purpose.

[39] M. A. Carrano, *Asleep in the Helix: Survival and the Science of Self-Realization* (North Haven, CT: Avatar Paradigms, 2009), 270.

[40] Taylor, "Addiction and a Lack of Purpose."

[41] Schwartz, *Your Soul's Plan*, 123.

[42] Norman Herr, "Television & Health: III Violence," Internet Resources to Accompany the Sourcebook for Teaching Science, http://www.csun.edu/science/health/docs/tv&health.html.

[43] "Suicide in Children and Teens," American Academy of Child & Adolescent Psychiatry, no. 10, June 2018, https://www.aacap.org/AACAP/Families_and_Youth/Facts_for_Familie s/FFF-Guide/Teen-Suicide-010.aspx.

[44] S. K. Goldsmith et al., eds. "Reducing Suicide: A National Imperative." (Washington, D.C.: Institute of Medicine, The National Academies Press, 2002).

[45] Jean M. Twenge et al., "Decreases in psychological well-being among American adolescents after 2012 and links to screen time during the rise of smartphone technology," *Emotion* 18, no. 6 (2018): 765-780.

[46] Jean M. Twenge, "The Sad State of Happiness in the United States and the Role of Digital Media," World Happiness Report, March 20, 2019, https://worldhappiness.report/ed/2019/the-sad-state-of-happiness-in-the-united-states-and-the-role-of-digital-media/.

[47] "Youth mental health report: Youth Survey 2012-16," Mission Australia, in association with the Black Dog Institute, April 18, 2017.

[48] "The Mahatma Gandhi séance," Leslie Flint Educational Trust, June 21, 1961, https://www.leslieflint.com/gandhi.

[49] Walter Sullivan, "The Einstein Papers. A Man of Many Parts." The *New York Times*, March 29, 1972. https://www.nytimes.com/1972/03/29/archives/the-einstein-papers-a-man-of-many-parts-the-einstein-papers-man-of.html.

[50] John Leland, "Are They Here to Save the World?" *The New York Times*, January 12, 2006, https://www.nytimes.com/2006/01/12/fashion/thursdaystyles/are-they-here-to-save-the-world.html.

[51] Lee Carroll and Jan Tober, *The Indigo Children: The New Kids Have Arrived* (Carlsbad, CA: Hay House, 1999).

[52] M. Lipka and C. Gecewicz. "More Americans now say they're spiritual but not religious." Pew Research Center. September 6, 2017. https://www.pewresearch.org/fact-tank/2017/09/06/more-americans-now-say-theyre-spiritual-but-not-religious/.

[53] Schwartz, *Your Soul's Plan*, 286.

[54] "The Mahatma Gandhi séance."

[55] "Michael Fearon séance," Leslie Flint Educational Trust, 1954, https://www.leslieflint.com/michael-fearon-1954.

[56] "Michael Fearon séance."

[57] William Stainton Moses, *Spirit Teachings: Through the Mediumship of William Stainton Moses* (CreateSpace Independent Publishing Platform, 2008; originally published in 1883), 35.

[58] "Sir Thomas Beechum [sic]," produced by Leslie Flint Educational Trust, YouTube video, 34:07, https://www.youtube.com/watch?v=Q_eHJWWwjTg.

[59] M. Tymn, "A Glimpse of Hell," White Crow Books, blog, http://whitecrowbooks.com/michaeltymn/feature/a_glimpse_of_hell_by_michael_e._tymn.

[60] M. Tymn, "A Glimpse of Hell."

[61] Betty, *The Afterlife Unveiled*, 21.

[62] Betty, *The Afterlife Unveiled*, 21.

[63] Heagerty , *The Hereafter*, 74-75 (citing M. T. Shelhamer, *Life and Labor in the Spirit World*, Christian Literature House, NY, 1985).

[64] "The Harry Price séance," Leslie Flint Educational Trust, 1963, https://www.leslieflint.com/harry-price.

[65] Kerry Pobanz, "Depossession Healing: A Comparison of William Baldwin's 'Spirit Releasement Therapy' and Dae Mo Nim's Ancestor Liberation," *Journal of Unification Studies* 9 (2008): 143-162, http://www.tparents.org/Library/Unification/Publications/JournalUnificationStudies9/JUS9-07.html

[66] Crookall, *The Supreme Adventure*, 105.

[67] A. W. Austin, ed., *Teachings of Silver Birch* (London: Psychic Book Club, 1938), 109.

[68] "Maurice Chevalier" recording by Leslie Flint Educational Trust, Afterlife Research and Education Institute, 1975, http://adcguides.com/LF_MauriceChevalierquicktime.htm.

[69] Edward C. Randall, *Frontiers of the After Life*, 2010.

[70] "Harry Price Speaks About Poltergeists," Afterlife Research and Education Institute, Leslie Flint Educational Trust recording, 1963.

[71] "The Dorcas séance," Leslie Flint Educational Trust, 1964, leslieflint.com/dorcas.

[72] E. C. Randall, *The Dead Have Never Died* (New York: A. A. Knopf, 1917), 165-166.

[73] "The Harry Price séance."

[74] Betty, *The Afterlife Unveiled*, 20.

[75] Betty, *The Afterlife Unveiled*, 42 (citing Elsa Barker, *Letters from a Living Dead Man*, Rider & Co. Ltd., London, 1914).

[76] Betty, *The Afterlife Unveiled*, 92 (citing Ruth Mattson Taylor, *Witness from Beyond*, New York: Hawthorn Books, 1975).

[77] Charles Drayton Thomas, *Life Beyond Death with Evidence* (Hong Kong: Hesperides Press, 2008; originally published in 1923), 43.

[78] Pobanz, "Depossession Healing," 143-162.

[79] William J. Baldwin, *Healing Lost Souls: Releasing Unwanted Spirits from Your Energy Body* (Hampton Roads Publishing, 2003): 27-38.

[80] "The Elizabeth Fry séance," Leslie Flint Educational Trust, 1963, https://www.leslieflint.com/elizabeth-fry-april-1963.

[81] M. Tymn. "Try Shock Therapy to Protect Against Vagabond Spirits?" White Crow Books, 2011, http://whitecrowbooks.com/michaeltymn/month/2011/06/.

[82] Bruce Lipton, "THINK Beyond Your Genes—March 2018," Bruce H. Lipton, PhD, https://www.brucelipton.com/think-beyond-your-genes-march-2018/.

[83] George Wehner, *A Curious Life* (New York: Liveright Company, 1929), 272.

[84] Wehner, *A Curious Life*, 295.

[85] Annie Besant and Charles Webster Leadbeater, *Thought Forms: A Record of Clairvoyant Investigation* (Brooklyn: Sacred Bones Books, 2020; originally published in 1901).

[86] Hillary Mayell, "Thousands of Women Killed for Family 'Honor,'" *National Geographic*, February 12, 2002, https://www.nationalgeographic.com/culture/2002/02/thousands-of-women-killed-for-family-honor/.

[87] Jill Patterson, "How Evil Is a Socially Constructed Concept: Evil Across Societies," *The Manitoban*, February 9, 2021, http://www.themanitoban.com/2012/10/how-evil-is-a-socially-constructed-concept-evil-across-societies/12309/.

[88] Brian Patrick Byrne et al., "All the People God Kills in the Bible," *Vocativ*, April 20, 2016, https://www.vocativ.com/news/309748/all-the-people-god-kills-in-the-bible/index.html.

[89] Thomas H. Holmes and Richard H. Rahe, "The Social Readjustment Rating Scale," *Journal of Psychosomatic Research* 11, no. 2 (August 1967): 213-218.

[90] "Documenting Numbers of Victims of the Holocaust and Nazi Persecution," United States Holocaust Memorial Museum, Holocaust Encyclopedia, https://encyclopedia.ushmm.org/content/en/article/documenting-numbers-of-victims-of-the-holocaust-and-nazi-persecution.

[91] Ian Johnson, "Who Killed More: Hitler, Stalin, or Mao?" *The New York Review*, February 5, 2018, https://www.nybooks.com/daily/2018/02/05/who-killed-more-hitler-stalin-or-mao/.

[92] Samuel Osborne, "Four genocides we should also remember on Holocaust Memorial Day," *Independent*, January 27, 2016, https://www.independent.co.uk/news/uk/home-news/four-genocides-we-should-also-remember-holocaust-memorial-day-a6837246.html.

[93] "Theodicy, God and Suffering – A debate between Dinesh D'Souza and Bart Ehrman," produced by Gordon College Center for Christian Studies, November 11, 2010, YouTube video, 1:42:27, https://www.youtube.com/watch?v=Isg6Kx-3xdI.

[94] Schwartz, *Your Soul's Plan*, 226-227.

[95] "Theodicy, God and Suffering."

[96] Francesca Colella, "How Many People Are Starving Around the World?" The Borgen Project, January 20, 2018, https://borgenproject.org/how-many-people-are-starving-around-the-world/.

[97] Howard Buffet, *Fragile: The Human Condition* (Washington, D.C.: National Geographic Society, 2009).

[98] Léa Gorius, "How Much Does It Cost to End Poverty?" The Borgen Project, December 16, 2017, https://borgenproject.org/how-much-does-it-cost-to-end-poverty/.

[99] Adele Peters, "It would cost just $330 billion to end global hunger by 2030," Fast Company, October 15, 2020, https://www.fastcompany.com/90564107/it-would-cost-just-330-billion-to-end-global-hunger-by-2030.

[100] M. Admin, "Hundreds in India Ritually Starve Themselves to Death Each Year," Knowledge Nuts, accessed April 1, 2014, https://knowledgenuts.com/2014/04/01/hundreds-in-india-ritually-starve-themselves-to-death-each-year/.

[101] Maggie Scull, "Timeline of 1981 hunger strike," *The Irish Times*, March 1, 2016, https://www.irishtimes.com/culture/books/timeline-of-1981-hunger-strike-1.2555682.

[102] Lipton, "THINK Beyond Your Genes— August 2019."

[103] Bruce Lipton, "Dr Bruce Lipton—At Last, Scientific Proof of How Our Thoughts Can Make Us Healthy or Sick," 180 Nutrition, https://180nutrition.com.au/psychology/bruce-lipton-interview/.

[104] "Dr. Bruce Lipton—A New Hope: Epigenetics and the Subconscious Mind," Dr. Ron Ehrlich, https://drronehrlich.com/dr-bruce-lipton-a-new-hope-epigenetics-and-the-subconscious-mind-2/.

[105] Elizabeth Blackburn and Elissa Epel, *The Telomere Effect: A Revolutionary Approach to Living Younger, Healthier, Longer* (New York: Grand Central Publishing, 2017).

[106] Carnegie Mellon University, "Happy People Are Healthier, Psychologist Says," ScienceDaily, November 8, 2006, https://www.sciencedaily.com/releases/2006/11/061108103655.htm.

[107] Anita Moorjani, *Dying to Be Me: My Journey from Cancer, to Near Death, to True Healing* (Carlsbad, CA: Hay House, 2014).

[108] Montague Ullman, "Herpes Simplex and Second Degree Burn Induced Under Hypnosis," *The American Journal of Psychiatry* 103, no. 6 (May 1947).

[109] Rachael Moeller, "Study Suggests Common Knee Surgery's Effect Is Purely Placebo," *Scientific American* (July 12, 2002), https://www.scientificamerican.com/article/study-suggests-common-kne/.

[110] Bruno Klopfer, "Psychological Variables in Human Cancer," *Journal of Prospective Techniques* 31 (1957): 331-40.

[111] Pamela Maraldo, *Medicine: In Search of a Soul: The Healing Prescription* (Carlsbad, CA: Balboa Press, 2017).

[112] Maraldo, *Medicine: In Search of a Soul.*

[113] Michael Talbot, *The Holographic Universe* (New York: Harper Perennial, 2011), 98-100.

[114] Bennett Braun, *Treatment of Multiple Personality Disorder* (Washington, D.C.: American Psychiatric Publishing, 1986).

[115] Schwartz, *Your Soul's Plan*, 46.

[116] "Arthur Conan Doyle séance," Leslie Flint Educational Trust, January 17, 1966, https://www.leslieflint.com/arthur-conan-doyle.

[117] "Mickey séance," Leslie Flint Educational Trust, October 14, 1987, https://www.leslieflint.com/mickey-october-14th-1987.

[118] "The Charles Drayton Thomas séance," Leslie Flint Educational Trust, June 29, 1970, https://www.leslieflint.com/charles-drayton-thomas.

[119] Carl Wickland, *Thirty Years Among the Dead* (Guildford, UK: White Crow Books, 2011).

[120] Tymn, *The Afterlife Revealed*, 137-138.

[121] Schwartz, *Your Soul's Plan*, 270.

[122] Guy Montgomery et al., "A meta-analysis of hypnotically induced analgesia: How effective is hypnosis?" *International Journal of Clinical and Experimental Hypnosis* 48 (2000): 138-153.

[123] "Hypnosis for Pain Relief," Arthritis Foundation, https://www.arthritis.org/health-wellness/treatment/complementary-therapies/natural-therapies/hypnosis-for-pain-relief.

[124] "Hypnosis, No Anesthetic, for Man's Surgery," CBS News, April 22, 2008, https://www.cbsnews.com/news/hypnosis-no-anesthetic-for-mans-surgery/.

[125] David P. G. van den Berg and Mark van der Gaag. "Treating trauma in psychosis with EMDR: A pilot study," *Journal of Behavior Therapy and Experimental Psychiatry* 43, no. 1 (March 2012): 664-671.

[126] Schwartz, *Your Soul's Plan*, 76.

[127] Schwartz, *Your Soul's Plan*, 103.

[128] Schwartz, *Your Soul's Plan*, 119.

[129] Michael Newton, *Destiny of Souls: New Case Studies of Life Between Lives* (Woodbury MN: Llewellyn Publications, 2000), 4.

[130] Ruth Montgomery, *A World Beyond: A Startling Message from the Eminent Psychic Arthur Ford from Beyond the Grave* (Robbinsdale, MN: Fawcett Publications, 1971), 160.

[131] Edward C. Randall, *Frontiers of the Afterlife* (Guildford, UK: White Crow Books, 2010; originally published in 1922), 54.

[132] "Mickey séance," Leslie Flint Educational Trust, December 8, 1973, https://www.leslieflint.com/mickey-december-8th-1973.

[133] Peter Boulton and Jane Boulton, *Psychic Beam to Beyond: Through the Psychic Sensitive Lenora Huett* (Camarillo, CA: DeVorss & Co., 1983), 59.

[134] Mary Blount White, *Letters from the Other Side: With Love, Harry and Helen* (Hinesburg, VT: Upper Access, 1995; originally published in 1917), 145.

[135] Jane Sherwood, *The Country Beyond* (London: Neville Spearman, 1969), 217.

[136] "John Grant séance," Leslie Flint Educational Trust, June 9, 1969, https://www.leslieflint.com/john-grant-june-1969.

[137] Schwartz, *Your Soul's Plan*, 74.

[138] Schwartz, *Your Soul's Plan*.

[139] Schwartz, *Your Soul's Gift*.

[140] Schwartz, *Your Soul's Plan*, 317.

[141] Suzanne Giesemann, "Soul Planning."

[142] Schwartz, *Your Soul's Plan*, 15.

[143] "Edward VIII Abdicates the Throne," The History Place, https://www.historyplace.com/speeches/edward.htm.

[144] Schwartz, *Your Soul's Plan*, 28.

[145] Schwartz, *Your Soul's Plan*, 228.

[146] Schwartz, *Your Soul's Plan*, 81.

[147] Richard Martini, "According to Michael Newton …," Quora, January 4, 2019, https://www.quora.com/According-to-Michael-Newton-the-majority-of-souls-whom-did-go-see-him-were-young-souls-and-a-small-were-old-souls-If-that-s-the-case-then-why-do-so-many-people-struggle-with-poverty-and-depression-when-only-the.

[148] Schwartz, *Your Soul's Plan*, 98-99

[149] Schwartz, *Your Soul's Plan*, 229.

[150] Giesemann, "Soul Planning."

[151] Tymn, *The Afterlife Revealed*, Appendix C.

[152] "Frédéric Chopin séance," Leslie Flint Educational Trust, December 17, 1962, https://www.leslieflint.com/chopin-dec-17th-1962.

[153] Amit Goswami, *The Self-Aware Universe: How Consciousness Creates the Material World* (New York: TarcherPerigee, 1995).

[154] Deepak Chopra et al., "Why a Mental Universe Is the 'Real' Reality," Chopra Foundation, November 30, 2015, https://choprafoundation.org/consciousness/why-a-mental-universe-is-the-real-reality/.

[155] A. Rae Simpson, "MIT Young Adult Development Project," MIT, 2018, http://hrweb.mit.edu/worklife/youngadult/index.html.

[156] A. Botkin with C. Hogan, *Induced After-Death Communication: A Miraculous Therapy for Grief and Loss* (Charlottesville, VA: Hampton Roads Publishing, 2014).

[157] Chopra, "Why a Mental Universe."

[158] Schwartz, *Your Soul's Plan*, 222-223.

[159] Tymn, *The Afterlife Revealed*, Appendix B.

[160] Tymn, *The Afterlife Revealed*, 166 (citing Geraldine Cummins, *The Road to Immortality*, The Aquarian Press, London, 1955, 62- 63).

[161] Schwartz, *Your Soul's Plan*, 71.

[162] Schwartz, *Your Soul's Plan*, 73.

[163] Schwartz, *Your Soul's Plan*, 73.

[164] Craig Hamilton-Parker, *What to Do When You Are Dead: Exploring Life After Death* (New York: Sterling Publishing Co., 2001), 114.

[165] Lipton, "THINK Beyond Your Genes—March 2018."

[166] Bruce Lipton, *The Biology of Belief* (Carlsbad, CA: Hay House, 2016).

[167] Eric Mack, "Forget Dying and Public Speaking: Here's the 47 Things Americans Fear More in 2017," Inc., https://www.inc.com/eric-mack/forget-dying-public-speaking-heres-47-things-americans-fear-more-in-2017.html.

[168] Nadia Kounang, "What is the science behind fear?" CNN, October 29, 2015, https://www.cnn.com/2015/10/29/health/science-of-fear/index.html.

[169] Sara H. Konrath, "The Empathy Paradox: Increasing Disconnection in the Age of Increasing Connection," *Handbook of Research on Technoself: Identity in a Technological Society*, ed. Rocci Luppicini (IGI Global, 2013), 967–991.

[170] "Americans are the unhappiest they've been in 50 years, poll finds," NBC News, June 16, 2020.

[171] Twenge, "Decreases in psychological well-being," 765-780.

[172] Twenge, "The Sad State of Happiness in the United States."

[173] "Many Americans are lonely, and Gen Z most of all, study finds," CBS News, May 3, 2018, https://www.cbsnews.com/news/many-americans-are-lonely-and-gen-z-most-of-all-study-finds/.

[174] Neil Howe, "Millenials and The Loneliness Epidemic," *Forbes*, May 3, 2019, https://www.forbes.com/sites/neilhowe/2019/05/03/millennials-and-the-loneliness-epidemic/#59174e247676.

[175] Kay S. Hymowitz, "Alone: The decline of the family has unleashed an epidemic of loneliness," *City Journal*, Spring 2019, https://www.city-journal.org/decline-of-family-loneliness-epidemic.

[176] "Loneliness Is at Epidemic Levels in America," Cigna, https://www.cigna.com/about-us/newsroom/studies-and-reports/combatting-loneliness/.

[177] Christopher Ingraham, "Americans are getting more miserable, and there's data to prove it," *Washington Post*, March 22, 2019, https://www.washingtonpost.com/business/2019/03/22/americans-are-getting-more-miserable-theres-data-prove-it/.

[178] Ingraham, "Americans are getting more miserable."

[179] "United States: How afraid are you of death?" Statista, January 2019, https://www.statista.com/statistics/959347/fear-of-death-in-the-us/.

[180] "Paradise Polled: Americans and the Afterlife," Roper Center, https://ropercenter.cornell.edu/paradise-polled-americans-and-afterlife.

[181] "Paradise Polled."

[182] Stan A. Ballard and Roger Green, *The Silver Birch Book of Questions & Answers* (London: Spiritual Truth Press, 1998), 147.

[183] Heagerty, *Hereafter*, 66 (citing Goforth, *The Risen*).

[184] C. G. Jung, *Collected Works of C. G. Jung, Volume 17: The Development of Personality* (Princeton: Princeton University Press, 1954).

[185] C. G. Jung. *Collected Works of C. G. Jung, Volume 11; Psychology and Religion.* (Princeton: Princeton University Press, 1975), 81.

[186] Joseph Campbell with Bill Moyers, *The Power of Myth* (New York: Doubleday, 1988).

[187] Dalai Lama XIV, *A Policy of Kindness: An Anthology of Writings by and about the Dalai Lama* (Boulder, CO: Snow Lion Publications, 2012).

[188] Jung, *"The Development of Personality."*

[189] Nisargadatta, *I Am That.*

[190] Albert Einstein letter to Robert S. Marcus, Princeton, NJ, February 12, 1950.

[191] John 3:1-21.

[192] Friedrich Nietzsche, *Thus Spake Zarathustra: A Book for All and None,* "Zarathustra's Discourses, I. The Three Metamorphoses," The Project Gutenberg, https://www.gutenberg.org/files/1998/1998-h/1998-h.htm#link2H_4_0006.

[193] William Naylor, ed., *Silver Birch Anthology: Wisdom from the World Beyond* (London: Spiritualist Press, 1974), 94.

[194] George C. Homans, "A Conceptual Scheme for Describing Work Group Behaviour," *The Human Group* (New York: Harcourt, Brace and Company, 1950).

[195] Eric Berne, *Games People Play: The Basic Handbook of Transactional Analysis* (New York: Ballantine Books, 1996).

[196] Mack, "Forget Dying and Public Speaking."

[197] Craig Gustafson, "Bruce Lipton, PhD: The Jump From Cell Culture to Consciousness," *Integrative Medicine: A Clinician's Journal* 16, no. 6 (December 2017): 44–50.

[198] T. S. Sathyanarayana Rao et al., "The Biochemistry of Belief," *Indian Journal of Psychiatry* 51, no. 4 (Oct-Dec 2009): 239–241.

[199] Fred Barbash, "Near-death experiences are a kind of high, even if you're not really near death," *The Washington Post*, July 7, 2014, https://www.washingtonpost.com/news/morning-mix/wp/2014/07/07/study-the-near-death-experience-is-generally-positive-even-when-death-isnt-really-near/.

[200] James W. Prescott, "The Origins of Human Love and Violence," Institute of Humanistic Science, *Pre- and Perinatal Psychology Journal* 10, no. 3 (Spring 1996): 143-188.

[201] Robert J. Burrowes, "Love Denied: The Psychology of Materialism, Violence and War," Feelings First Blog, May 2013, https://feelingsfirstblog.wordpress.com/key-articles/love-denied/.

[202] Randy Borum, *Psychology of Terrorism* (Tampa, FL: University of South Florida, 2004), 3.

[203] Jerrold M. Post, "It's us against them," *Terrorism* 10 (1987): 23-35.

[204] Amin Maalouf, *In the Name of Identity: Violence and the Need to Belong* (New York: Arcade Publishing, 2012).

[205] Roy F. Baumeister et al. "Personal Narratives About Guilt: Role in Action Control and Interpersonal Relationships." *Basic and Applied Social Psychology* 17, no. 1-2 (1985): 173-198.

[206] H. R. Conte et al., "Measuring death anxiety: Conceptual, psychometric, and factor-analytic aspects," *Journal of Personality and Social Psychology* 43 (1982): 775-785.

207 *Lives in Hazard*, directed by Susan Todd and Andrew Young (1994; Pleasantville, NY: Archipelago Films), NBC-TV movie.

208 M. S. Jankowski, *Islands in the street: Gangs and American urban society* (Berkeley: University of California Press, 1991).

209 Laina Sonterblum, "Gang Involvement as a Means to Satisfy Basic Needs," Applied Psychology Opus, New York University, https://wp.nyu.edu/steinhardt-appsych_opus/gang-involvement-as-a-means-to-satisfy-basic-needs/.

210 R. J. Sampson and J. H. Laub, Crime in the making: Pathways and turning points through life (Cambridge, MA: Harvard University Press, 1993).

211 W. C. Wade, *The Fiery Cross: The Ku Klux Klan in America* (New York: Touchstone/Simon & Schuster, 1987).

212 C. R. Browning, *Ordinary Men: Reserve Police Battalion 101 and the final solution in Poland* (New York: Harper Collins, 1992).

213 A. N. Groth, *Men Who Rape* (New York: Plenum Press, 1979).

214 Tatyana A. Shkurko, "Socio-psychological Analysis of Controlling Personality," *Procedia—Social and Behavioral Sciences* 86 (2013): 629–634.

215 Recep Doğan. "Can Honor Killings Be Explained With the Concept of Social Death? Reinterpreting Social Psychological Evidence." *Homicide Studies* 24, no. 2 (February 14, 2019): 127–150.

216 "The Ellen Terry séance," Leslie Flint Educational Trust, January 24, 1964, https://www.leslieflint.com/ellen-terry.

217 Jolande Jacobi, *The Way of Individuation* (New York: New American Library, 1983).

218 C. G. Jung, *Memories, Dreams, Reflections* (New York: Vintage Books, 1989).

219 Jacobi, *The Way of Individuation*.

220 Cynthia Vinney, "Understanding Maslow's Theory of Self-Actualization," ThoughtCo, 2018, https://www.thoughtco.com/maslow-theory-self-actualization-4169662.

221 Joan Neehall-Davidson, *Perfecting Private Practice* (Bloomington, IN: Trafford Publishing, 2004), 95.

[222] Nisargadatta, *I Am That.*

[223] "Michelangelo's Prisoners or Slaves," Accademia.org, http://www.accademia.org/explore-museum/artworks/michelangelos-prisoners-slaves/.

[224] Giesemann, "What's the point of all of this?"

[225] Giesemann, "What's the point of all of this?"

[226] Betty, *The Afterlife Unveiled,* 92 (citing Taylor, *Witness from Beyond*).

[227] Susanne Wilson, *Guidance Quest: Connect with Your Spirit Guide* (Portland, OR: CD Baby, 2015).

[228] "Supergirl Dilemma: Girls Grapple with the Mounting Pressures of Expectations: Summary Findings." Girls Incorporated, 2006.

[229] Larry Alton, "Why Low Self-Esteem May Be Hurting You at Work," NBC News, November 15, 2017, https://www.nbcnews.com/better/business/why-low-self-esteem-may-be-hurting-your-career-ncna814156.

[230] Mohnish Nelaraw, "90% people have low self-esteem: Experts," TOI, September 12, 2017, https://timesofindia.indiatimes.com/city/nagpur/90-people-have-low-self-esteem-experts/articleshow/60469457.cms.

[231] Kristin Neff, "Why self-compassion is healthier than self-esteem," Self-Compassion.org, https://self-compassion.org/why-self-compassion-is-healthier-than-self-esteem/.

[232] Matthew Thorpe and Rachael Link, "12 Science-Based Benefits of Meditation," *Healthline,* October 27, 2020, https://www.healthline.com/nutrition/12-benefits-of-meditation.

[233] "Within," *The Daily Way,* Suzanne Giesemann, January 10, 2021, https://www.suzannegiesemann.com/within-4/.

[234] "The 'Loneliness' Epidemic," Health Resources & Services Administration, n.d., https://www.hrsa.gov/enews/past-issues/2019/january-17/loneliness-epidemic.

[235] William T. Stead, *After Death: Letters from Julia* (Guildford, UK: White Crow Books, 2011), 118.

[236] Anonymous, *The Bridge Over the River*, translated by Joseph Wetzl (Hudson, NY: Steiner Books, 1974), 14.

[237] Jasper Swain, *Heaven's Gift: Conversations Beyond the Veil* (South Africa: Kima Global Publishers, 1996), 85.

[238] Crookall, *The Supreme Adventure*, 82-83.

[239] Heagerty, *The Hereafter*, 93 (citing L. Kelway-Bamber, ed., *Claude's Book*, New York: Henry Holt and Company, 1919).

[240] Rochelle Wright and R. Craig Hogan, *Repair & Reattachment Grief Therapy* (Normal, IL: Greater Reality Publications, 2015).

[241] William W. Aber and Jabez Hunt Nixon, *Beyond the Veil: Being a Compilation, with Notes and Explanations* (Whitefish, MT: Kessinger Publishing, 2003; originally published in 1906), 380.

[242] Tymn, *The Afterlife Revealed*, 89.

[243] Heagerty, *Hereafter*, 60 (citing Goforth, *The Risen*).

[244] Tymn, *The Afterlife Revealed*, 126.

[245] Rupert Sheldrake, "The 'sense of being stared at' experiments in schools," *Journal of the Society for Psychical Research* 62 (1998): 311-323.

[246] Tymn, *The Afterlife Revealed*, 126.

[247] "The Alfred Higgins séance," Leslie Flint Educational Trust, October 14, 1963, https://www.leslieflint.com/alfred-higgins.

[248] "The Alfred Higgins séance"

[249] Crookall, *The Supreme Adventure*, 158.

[250] L. Kelway-Bamber, ed., *Claude's Book* (New York: Henry Holt and Company, 1919), 58.

[251] Stewart Edward White, *The Betty Book* (Westwood, MA: Ariel Pr, 1988; originally published in 1937), 25.

[252] "The Alfred Higgins séance."

[253] M. Tymn, "Automatic Writing," White Crow Books, http://whitecrowbooks.com/michaeltymn/feature/automatic_writing_by _michael_e._tymn.

[254] Ivan Cooke, *The Return of Arthur Conan Doyle* (Liss, UK: White Eagle Publishing, 1980), 76.

[255] G. Vale Owen, *The Life beyond the Veil: A Compilation (Life on Other Worlds* series) (Schenectady, NY: Square Circles Publishing, 2014; originally published in 1921), 11.

[256] Baron von Schrenk-Notzing, *Phenomena of Materialization, a contribution to the investigation of mediumistic teleplastics* (New York: E. P. Dutton, 1920).

[257] Elizabeth Kübler-Ross, *On Life After Death* (Berkeley, CA: Celestial Arts, 1991), 51.

[258] Tymn, "Automatic Writing."

[259] "Types of Mediumship," Psychic Student, https://www.psychicstudent.com/types-of-mediumship/.

[260] William Stainton Moses, *Spirit Identity* (Palala Press, 2015; originally published in 1902).

[261] Wright, *Repair & Reattachment Grief Therapy.*

[262] Sir William Barrett, *Personality Survives Death* (Longman Green & Co. Ltd., 1937), 146.

[263] R. Craig Hogan, ed., *Afterlife Communication: 16 Proven Methods, 85 True Accounts* (Normal, IL: Greater Reality Publications, 2014).

[264] Anne Puryear, *Stephen Lives!* (New York: Pocket Books, 1992), 212.

[265] Helen Greaves, *Testimony of Light: An Extraordinary Message of Life After Death* (New York: TarcherPerigee, 2009), 75.

[266] Ruth Mattson Taylor, *Witness from Beyond* (New York: Hawthorn Books, 1975), 64.

[267] Elsa Barker, *Letters from a Living Dead Man* (Dallas, TX: Hill-Pehle Publishing, 2012, originally published in 1914), 15.

[268] Journal account by a woman who experienced a Self-Directed Afterlife Connection, June 4, 2017.

[269] Kelway-Bamber, *Claude's Book*, 15.

[270] Richard Lazarus, *The Case Against Death* (London: Warner Books, 1993), 19.

[271] Stacy Conradt, "The Quick 10: 10 Famous Uses of the Ouija Board," Mental Floss, https://www.mentalfloss.com/article/26158/quick-10-10-famous-uses-ouija-board.

[272] Linda Rodriguez McRobbie, "The Strange and Mysterious History of the Ouija Board," *Smithsonian Magazine*, October 27, 2013, https://www.smithsonianmag.com/history/the-strange-and-mysterious-history-of-the-ouija-board-5860627/.

[273] Alice Johnston Stringfellow, *Leslie's letters to his mother: Being a collection of messages received by Henry Martyn Stringfellow and Alice Johnston Stringfellow* (Fayetteville, AR: Democrat Pub. and Printing Co., January 1, 1926).

[274] R. Craig Hogan, *Your Eternal Self: Science Discovers the Afterlife* (Normal, IL: Greater Reality Publications, 2020), 188.

[275] Crookall, *The Supreme Adventure*, 156-157.

[276] Stead, *After Death*, 87.

[277] Crookall, *The Supreme Adventure*, 156-157.

[278] Repair & Reattachment psychotherapy session with Rochelle Wright, August 24, 2017.

[279] Self-Guided Afterlife Connections session, January 12, 2016.

[280] Jose Silva, *The Silva Mind Control Method* (New York: Pocket Books, January 15, 1991).

[281] Heagerty, *The Hereafter*, 57.

[282] Austin, *Teachings of Silver Birch*, 120.

[283] "Abraham Hicks – Must we return to this earth?" Produced by Esther Hicks, October 5, 2010, YouTube video, 13:15, https://www.youtube.com/watch?v=IW7uF3kUAME.

[284] Diane M. Komp, *A Window to Heaven: When Children See Life in Death* (Grand Rapids, Michigan: Zondervan Publishing, 1992).

[285] Masters of Light. AREI physical mediumship circle. Séance, December 23, 2018.

[286] Giesemann, "Soul Planning."

[287] Suzanne Giesemann, *Wolf's Message* (Cardiff, CA: Waterside Productions, Inc., 2014).

[288] Heagerty, *Hereafter*, 63-64 (citing Goforth, *The Risen*).

[289] Abhijit Kanti Dam, "Significance of end-of-life dreams and visions experienced by the terminally ill in rural and urban India," *Indian Journal of Palliative Care* 22, no. 2 (April-June 2016): 130-134.

[290] Karlis Osis and Erlendur Haraldsson, *At the Hour of Death* (Norwalk, CT: Hastings House, 1997).

[291] Osis, *At the Hour of Death*, 38.

[292] Dam, "Significance of end-of-life dreams," 130-134.

[293] Osis, *At the Hour of Death*, 37.

[294] Marilyn Mendoza, "Deathbed Visions," *Psychology Today*, October 5, 2016, https://www.psychologytoday.com/us/blog/understanding-grief/201610/deathbed-visions-part-i.

[295] Osis, *At the Hour of Death*, 38.

[296] Madelaine Lawrence and Elizabeth Repede, "The Incidence of Deathbed Communications and Their Impact on the Dying Process," *American Journal of Hospice and Palliative Care* 30, no. 7 (2013), 632-639; Peter Fenwick et al., "Comfort for the dying: Five year retrospective and one year prospective studies of end of life experiences," *Archives of Gerontology and Geriatrics* 51, no. 2 (2009), 173-179; Sandhya P. Muthumana et al. "Deathbed visions from India: A study of family observations in northern Kerala," *Omega* 62, no. 2 (2010-2011), 97-109; Osis, *At the Hour of Death*.

[297] Osis, *At the Hour of Death*.

[298] Osis, *At the Hour of Death*, 37.

[299] Osis, *At the Hour of Death*.

[300] Mynot J. Savage, *Life Beyond Death* (New York: G.P. Putnam's Sons, 1900), 310 – 311.

[301] Melvin Morse and Paul Perry. *Closer to the Light* (London: Souvenir Press, 1991).

[302] Kübler-Ross, *On Life After Death*, 51.

[303] Tymn, *The Afterlife Revealed*, 46.

[304] Mona Simpson, "A Sister's Eulogy for Steve Jobs," *The New York Times*, October 30, 2011,

https://www.nytimes.com/2011/10/30/opinion/mona-simpsons-eulogy-for-steve-jobs.html.

[305] Neil Baldwin, *Edison: Inventing the Century* (New York: Hyperion, 1995).

[306] Osis, *At the Hour of Death*, 44.

[307] Osis, *At the Hour of Death*, 165.

[308] Osis, *At the Hour of Death*, 165.

[309] Osis, *At the Hour of Death*, 165-166.

[310] Jesse Bering, "One Last Goodbye: The Strange Case of Terminal Lucidity," *Scientific American*, November 25, 2014, https://blogs.scientificamerican.com/bering-in-mind/one-last-goodbye-the-strange-case-of-terminal-lucidity/.

[311] Michael Nahm and Bruce Greyson, "Terminal Lucidity in Patients with Chronic Schizophrenia and Dementia: A Survey of the Literature," *The Journal of Nervous and Mental Disease* 197, no. 12 (2009), 942-944.

[312] Scott Haig, The brain: the power of hope, *Time Magazine* 169 (2007), 118-119.

[313] Nahm, "Terminal Lucidity," 942-944.

[314] Crookall, *The Supreme Adventure*, 174.

[315] Allan Kardec, *The Spirits' Book* (Westlake Village, CA: Spiritist Educational Society, 2019; originally published in 1857), 116.

[316] Borgia, *Life in the World Unseen*, 116.

[317] Heagerty, *Hereafter*, 82-83 (citing Wellesley Tudor Pole, *Private Dowding*, Watkins Publishing, London, 1917).

[318] Sophia Elizabeth De Morgan , *From Matter to Spirit* (London: Longman, Green, Longman, Roberts & Green, 1863), 148-149.

[319] Crookall, *The Supreme Adventure*, 119-120 (citing R . B. Hout, *Light* 55, 1935: 209).

[320] Francis Power Cobbe, *The Peak in Darien: An Octave of Essays* (Charleston, NC: Nabu Press, 2010).

[321] A. T. Baird, *A Casebook for Survival* (London: Psychic Press Ltd., 1942), 140.

[322] William Barrett, *Deathbed Visions* (Guildford, UK: White Crow Books, 2011).

[323] Geraldine Cummins, *The Road to Immortality* (London: The Aquarian Press, 1955), 61.

[324] Laurel Parnell, *Transforming Trauma: EMDR* (New York: W. W. Norton & Company, 1998).

[325] Tymn, *The Afterlife Revealed*, 68.

[326] Helen Greaves, *The Challenging Light* (Suffolk, UK: Neville Spearman, 1984), 14-15.

[327] Tymn, *The Afterlife Revealed*, 142.

[328] Crookall, *The Supreme Adventure*, 29.

[329] "The Ted Butler séance," Leslie Flint Educational Trust, February 10, 1964, https://www.leslieflint.com/ted-butler.

[330] Suzanne Giesemann video recorded January 3, 2018.

[331] Heagerty, *Hereafter*, 63-64 (citing Goforth, *The Risen*).

[332] Raymond Moody, *Life After Life* (New York: HarperOne, 1975).

[333] Raymond Moody, *Glimpses of Eternity: An Investigation into Shared Death Experiences* (London: Rider, 2011).

[334] Moody, *Glimpses of Eternity*, 49- 50.

[335] Peter Fenwick and Elizabeth Fenwick, *The Art of Dying: A Journey to Elsewhere* (London: Continuum International Publishing, 2008).

[336] Leslie Kean, *Surviving Death: A Journalist Investigates Evidence for an Afterlife* (New York: Crown Archetype, 2017), 140-141 (citing Peter Fenwick, "End-of-Life Experiences").

[337] Kean, *Surviving Death*, 141 (citing Fenwick, "End-of-Life Experiences").

[338] Kean, *Surviving Death*, 141 (citing Fenwick, "End-of-Life Experiences").

[339] Leslie Kean, *Surviving Death*, 141 (citing Fenwick, "End-of-Life Experiences").

[340] Pim van Lommel, *Consciousness Beyond Life: The Science of the Near-Death Experience* (New York: HarperCollins, 2010), 41.

341 Van Lommel, *Consciousness Beyond Life*, 41-42.

342 Melvin Morse with P. Perry, *Parting Visions* (New York: Villard Books, 1994).

343 Jeff Olson and Jeff O'Driscoll, "Shared Near-Death Experiences Between Doctor and Patient," produced by International Association for Near-Death Studies, January 6, 2021, YouTube video, 19:47, https://youtu.be/lwkOnahGlsc.

344 Shared Crossing Project, https://www.sharedcrossing.com/.

345 Shared Crossing Project, https://www.sharedcrossing.com/.

346 Kean, *Surviving Death*, 144 (citing Fenwick, "End-of-Life Experiences").

347 Botkin, *Induced After-Death Communication: A New Therapy*.

348 Crookall, *The Supreme Adventure*, 14-22.

349 "Mr. Biggs communicates," Leslie Flint Educational Trust, 1966, https://www.leslieflint.com/mr-biggs-1966.

350 Borgia, *Life in the World Unseen*, 11.

351 Heagerty, *Hereafter*, 77-78 (citing Randall, *Frontiers of the Afterlife*, 2010).

352 Crookall, *The Supreme Adventure*, 130-131.

353 Crookall, *The Supreme Adventure*, 129.

354 Heagerty, *The Hereafter*, 27.

355 Crookall, *The Supreme Adventure*, 64.

356 Cyrus Kirkpatrick Facebook page post, https://www.facebook.com/cyrus.kirkpatrick.

357 Emanuel Swedenborg, *Heaven and Hell* (West Chester, PA: Swedenborg Foundation, New Century Edition, 2000).

358 Frederick H. Wood, *Through the Psychic Door* (London: Psychic Book Club, 1954), 67.

359 Tymn , *The Afterlife Revealed*, 137-138.

360 Friedrich Jürgenson, *Sprechfunk mit Verstorbenen* (Freiburg im Br.: Hermann Bauer Verlag, 1967).

361 John Calvin. *Psychopannychia* (Warrendale, PA: Ichthus Publications, 2018; originally published in 1542).

362 Austen, *The Teachings of Silver Birch*, 193.

[363] Heagerty, *The Hereafter*, 27.

[364] Crookall, *The Supreme Adventure*, 17.

[365] Heagerty, *Hereafter*, 77-78 (citing Randall, *Frontiers of the Afterlife*, 2010).

[366] "The George Hopkins séance," Leslie Flint Educational Trust, April 11, 1959, https://www.leslieflint.com/george-hopkins.

[367] Crookall, *The Supreme Adventure*,132.

[368] Crookall, *The Supreme Adventure*,136.

[369] Crookall, *The Supreme Adventure*, 35 (citing Constance Wiley, *A Star of Hope to Those Who Seek Spiritual Truths*, C. W. Daniel Co. Ltd., London [1938], 7, 22).

[370] Anthony Borgia , *ABC of Life* (London: Feature Books, Ltd., 1945), 35.

[371] "The Alfred Pritchett séance," Leslie Flint Educational Trust, November 4, 1960, https://www.leslieflint.com/alfred-pritchett.

[372] "The Ted Butler séance."

[373] Crookall, *The Supreme Adventure*, 21-22.

[374] Crookall, *The Supreme Adventure*, 68.

[375] Crookall, *The Supreme Adventure*, 100.

[376] Crookall, *The Supreme Adventure*, 163.

[377] Borgia, *Life in the World Unseen*, 52.

[378] Borgia, *Life in the World Unseen*, 125.

[379] "The Mary Ann Ross séance," Leslie Flint Educational Trust, January 20, 1969, https://www.leslieflint.com/mary-ann-ross.

[380] Borgia, *Life in the World Unseen*, 125.

[381] Borgia, *Life in the World Unseen*, 23.

[382] Allen, *The Realities of Heaven*, 135.

[383] Greaves , *Testimony of Light*, 12.

[384] "The Mary Ivan séance," Leslie Flint Educational Trust, August 15, 1966, https://www.leslieflint.com/mary-ivan-1966.

[385] Borgia, *Life in the World Unseen*, 27.

[386] 'The Doctor Franke séance," Leslie Flint Educational Trust, April 6, 1964, https://www.leslieflint.com/doctor-franke.

387 "The Rupert Brooke séance," Leslie Flint Educational Trust, September 15, 1957, https://www.leslieflint.com/rupert-brooke.

388 Heagerty, *Hereafter*, 75-76 (citing Randall, *Frontiers of the Afterlife*, 2010).

389 "The Queen Alexandra séance," Leslie Flint Educational Trust, 1960, https://www.leslieflint.com/queen-alexandra.

390 "The George Wilmot séance."

391 "Sam Woods," produced by Leslie Flint Educational Trust, YouTube video, 1964, 23:13, https://www.youtube.com/watch?v=YkB3J6JPe8M.

392 Newton, *Destiny of Souls*, 4.

393 "The Terry Smith séance," Leslie Flint Educational Trust, July 16, 1966, https://www.leslieflint.com/terry-smith.

394 Austen, *The Teachings of Silver Birch*, 124.

395 Heagerty, *Hereafter*, 77-78 (citing Randall, *Frontiers of the Afterlife*, 2010).

396 "The Alfred Higgins séance."

397 "The Ted Butler séance."

398 Crookall, *The Supreme Adventure,* 155.

399 Randall, *Frontiers of the Afterlife,* 44.

400 Alice Gilbert, *Philip in the Spheres* (Detroit: The Aquarian Press, 1952).

401 Greaves, *Testimony of Light,* 58.

402 Crookall, *The Supreme Adventure,* 165.

403 Crookall, *The Supreme Adventure,* 137.

404 Carl Wickland, *The Gateway of Understanding* (Santa Ana, CA: National Psychological Institute, Inc., 1934), 65.

405 Jane Sherwood, *The Psychic Bridge* (London: Rider & Co., Ltd., 1942), 48.

406 Sherwood, *The Country Beyond*, 24.

407 Anonymous post, "The Purpose of a Life Review," produced by Off the Left Eye, YouTube video, July 15, 2002, 6:05, https://www.youtube.com/watch?v=j8L1tmJhizc.

[408] Tymn, *The Afterlife Revealed,* 98-99 (citing Marjorie Errands, *The Tapestry of Life,* Psychic Press Ltd., London, 1979, 56).

[409] Austen, *The Teachings of Silver Birch,* 202.

[410] Schwartz, *Your Soul's Plan,* 121-122.

[411] Crookall, *The Supreme Adventure,* 164-165.

[412] Newton, *Destiny of Souls,* 2-3.

[413] Newton, *Destiny of Souls,* 5.

[414] Geraldine Cummins, *Beyond Human Personality* (London: Ivor Nicholson and Watson, Ltd., 1935), 29, 44.

[415] Crookall, *The Supreme Adventure,* 90.

[416] Tymn, *The Afterlife Revealed,* 94-95.

[417] Sherwood, *The Country Beyond,* 63.

[418] Greaves, *Testimony of Light,* 77.

[419] Newton, *Destiny of Souls,* 3.

[420] Borgia, *Life in the World Unseen.*

[421] Heagerty, *The Hereafter,* 94 (citing Kelway-Bamber, *Claude's Book).*

[422] John Sebastian Marlowe Ward, *A Subaltern in Spirit Land* (London: W. Rider, 1920), 103.

[423] Oliver Lodge, *Raymond or Life and Death* (New York: George H. Doran, 1916), 197.

[424] Thomas, *Life Beyond Death with Evidence,* 178-184.

[425] Borgia, *Life in the World Unseen,* 132-133.

[426] Heagerty, *Hereafter,* 95 (citing Randall, *Frontiers of the Afterlife,* 2010).

[427] Heagerty, *Hereafter* (citing Goforth, *The Risen).*

[428] "Amy Johnson séance."

[429] Suzanne Ward, *Matthew, Tell Me about Heaven* (Camas, WA: Matthew Books, 2012), 164.

[430] Montgomery, *A World Beyond,* 118.

[431] Tymn, *The Afterlife Revealed,* 101.

[432] Tymn, *The Afterlife Revealed,* 101.

[433] Swain, *Heaven's Gift,* 38.

[434] "The Elizabeth Fry séance."

[435] Borgia, *Life in the World Unseen*, 13.

[436] 'The Doctor Franke séance."

[437] Tymn, "A Glimpse of Hell."

[438] Tymn, "A Glimpse of Hell."

[439] James M. Peebles, *Immortality and Our Employments Hereafter: With What a Hundred Spirits, Good and Evil, Say of Their Dwelling Places* (London: Forgotten Books, 2015; originally published in 1907), 91.

[440] Borgia, *Life in the World Unseen*, 120-123.

[441] Betty, *The Afterlife Unveiled*, 30-31 (citing Stringfellow, *Leslie's letters to his mother*).

[442] "The Charles Drayton Thomas séancc."

[443] Kelway-Bamber, *Claude's Book* , 20.

[444] Henry Thibault, *Letters from the Other Side* (London: John M. Watkins, 1919), 96.

[445] Austen, *The Teachings of Silver Birch*, 122.

[446] Kelway-Bamber, *Claude's Book*, 204.

[447] Sherwood, *The Country Beyond*, 71.

[448] Aber, *Beyond the Veil*, 354.

[449] Betty, *The Afterlife Unveiled*, 32.

[450] Heagerty, *Hereafter*, 75-76 (citing Randall, *Frontiers of the Afterlife*, 2010).

[451] Kardec, *The Spirits' Book*, 173.

[452] Allen, *The Realities of Heaven*, 125 (citing Stringfellow, *Leslie's letters to his mother*).

[453] Borgia, *Life in the World Unseen*, 15.

[454] Borgia, *Life in the World Unseen*, 12.

[455] Robert Hare, *Experimental Investigation of the Spirit Manifestations: Demonstrating the Existence of Spirits and Their Communion with Mortals. Doctrine of the spirit world respecting heaven, hell, morality, and God. Also, the influence of Scripture on the morals of Christians* (New York: Partridge & Brittan, 1855), 91.

[456] Heagerty, *Hereafter*, 98 (citing Randall, *Frontiers of the Afterlife*, 2010).

[457] Grace Rosher, *The Travelers Returned* (London: Psychic Press Ltd., 1968), 61.

[458] Borgia, *Life in the World Unseen*, 120.

[459] Heagerty, *The Hereafter*, 104 (citing Thomas Welton Stanford , *A Spirit Communication on the Death Experience*, Psychic Scientist, 1904).

[460] "The Ellen Terry séance."

[461] Borgia, *Life in the World Unseen*, 11-12.

[462] Heagerty, *Hereafter*, 89-90 (citing Randall, *Frontiers of the Afterlife*, 2010).

[463] Betty, *The Afterlife Unveiled*, 27.

[464] Augustus Henry Burbidge, *The Shadows Lifted from Death* (Stuart, FL: Roundtable Publishing, 2011), 78.

[465] Borgia, *Life in the World Unseen*, 61.

[466] Betty, *The Afterlife Unveiled*, 16.

[467] Taylor, *Witness from Beyond*, 8.

[468] Borgia, *Life in the World Unseen*, 46.

[469] Austen, *The Teachings of Silver Birch*, 117.

[470] Stringfellow, *Leslie's letters to his mother*, 83.

[471] Kelway-Bamber, *Claude's Book*, 17.

[472] Ruth Montgomery, *A World Beyond: A Startling Message from the Eminent Psychic Arthur Ford from Beyond the Grave* (New York: Coward, McCann & Geoghegan, 1971), 53.

[473] Eisen, *The Agashan Discourses*, 99.

[474] Charles Drayton Thomas, "Report re Lodge via Leonard," *Journal of the Society for Psychical Research* 33 (1945): 137-160.

[475] Thibault, *Letters from the Other Side*, 8.

[476] Betty, *The Afterlife Unveiled*, 29.

[477] Sherwood, *The Country Beyond*, 69.

[478] Heagerty, *The Hereafter*, 21.

[479] Borgia, *Life in the World Unseen*, 172.

[480] Betty, *The Afterlife Unveiled*, 33-34 (citing Stringfellow, *Leslie's letters to his mother*).

[481] Borgia, *Life in the World Unseen*, 138.

[482] Heagerty, *Hereafter,* 95 (citing Randall, *Frontiers of the Afterlife).*

[483] Borgia, *Life in the World Unseen,* 138.

[484] Heagerty, *The Hereafter,* 54-55.

[485] Thomas, "Report re Lodge via Leonard," 136, 138-160.

[486] Thomas, *Life Beyond Death with Evidence.*

[487] Stringfellow, *Leslie's letters to his mother,* 82.

[488] John Worth Edmonds and George T. Dexter, *Spiritualism* (New York: Partridge & Brittan, 1855), 89.

[489] "The George Harris séance," Leslie Flint Educational Trust, April 3, 1970, https://www.leslieflint.com/george-harris-april-1970.

[490] 'The Rose Hawkins séances," Leslie Flint Educational Trust, September 9, 1963, https://www.leslieflint.com/rose-hawkins.

[491] Crookall, *The Supreme Adventure,* 78.

[492] Michael Tymn, *The Afterlife Revealed,* 125 (citing Cummins, *The Road to Immortality,* 49).

[493] Taylor, *Witness from Beyond,* 64.

[494] Gilbert, *Philip in the Spheres,* 29.

[495] Ward, *Matthew, Tell Me about Heaven,* 111.

[496] "The George Harris séance," Leslie Flint Educational Trust, April 3, 1970, https://www.leslieflint.com/george-harris-april-1970.

[497] Betty, *The Afterlife Unveiled,* 30 (citing Stringfellow, *Leslie's letters to his mother).*

[498] White, *Letters from the Other Side,* 24.

[499] Heagerty, *Hereafter,* 89 (citing Randall, *Frontiers of the Afterlife,* 2010*).*

[500] Eliza B. Duffey, *Heaven Revised: A Narrative of Personal Experiences After the Change Called Death* (London: Forgotten Books, 2019; originally published in 1921), 60.

[501] Allen, *The Realities of Heaven,* 152.

[502] Betty, *The Afterlife Unveiled,* 92 (citing Taylor, *Witness from Beyond).*

[503] Borgia, *Life in the World Unseen,* 143.

[504] 'The Doctor Franke séance."

[505] Heagerty, *The Hereafter*, 54-55 (citing Lilian Walbrook, *The Case of Lester Coltman*, CreateSpace Independent Publishing Platform, 2013).

[506] Heagerty, *The Hereafter* (citing Walbrook, *The Case of Lester Coltman*).

[507] Kardec, *The Spirits' Book*, 255.

[508] Allen, *The Realities of Heaven*, 138 (citing Stringfellow, *Leslie's letters to his mother*, 49).

[509] Thomas, *Life Beyond Death with Evidence*, 116.

[510] Borgia, *Life in the World Unseen*, 52.

[511] Betty, *The Afterlife Unveiled*, 93 (citing Taylor, *Witness from Beyond*).

[512] "The Vic Scott Collection," including Marie Curie, Leslie Flint Educational Trust, séance recorded November 3, 1988.

[513] "Frédéric Chopin séance," Leslie Flint Educational Trust, July 7, 1955. https://www.leslieflint.com/chopin-july-7th-1955.

[514] "Frédéric Chopin séance," July 7, 1955.

[515] Borgia, *Life in the World Unseen*, 129.

[516] Ward, *Matthew, Tell Me about Heaven*, 108.

[517] Borgia, *Life in the World Unseen*, 100.

[518] "The Mary Ann Ross séance."

[519] Burbidge, *The Shadows Lifted from Death*, 134.

[520] Eisen, *The Agashan Discourses*, 99.

[521] Borgia, *Life in the World Unseen*, 182.

[522] Heagerty, *The Hereafter*, 54-55.

[523] Ward, *Matthew, Tell Me about Heaven*, 104.

[524] Borgia, *Life in the World Unseen*, 67.

[525] "The Ellen Terry séance."

[526] "The Terry Smith séance."

[527] "The Mary Ann Ross séance."

[528] "Mr. Wagstaff communicates," Leslie Flint Educational Trust, November 2, 1970, https://www.leslieflint.com/wagstaff-1970.

[529] Thomas, *Life Beyond Death with Evidence*, 149.

530 Allen, *The Realities of Heaven*, 157 (citing Randall, *Frontiers of the Afterlife*, 110).

531 Lodge, *Raymond or Life and Death*, 263.

532 Sherwood, *The Country Beyond*, 86.

533 "The Alice Green séance," Leslie Flint Educational Trust, December 18, 1967, Leslie Flint Educational Trust, https://www.leslieflint.com/alice-green-december-1967.

534 Thomas, *Life Beyond Death with Evidence*, 118.

535 Heagerty, *Hereafter*, 90-91 (citing Randall, *Frontiers of the Afterlife*, 2010*).*

536 Betty, *The Afterlife Unveiled*, 96 (citing Taylor, *Witness from Beyond*).

537 Borgia, *Life in the World Unseen*, 24.

538 Borgia, *Life in the World Unseen*, 25.

539 Thomas, *Life Beyond Death with Evidence*, 124.

540 Boulton, *Psychic Beam to Beyond*, 63.

541 "The Doctor Franke séance."

542 Stead, *After Death*, 4.

543 Kelway-Bamber, *Claude's Book*, 4.

544 James A. Pike and Diane Kennedy Pike, *The Other Side: An Account of My Experiences with Psychic Phenomena* (Eugene, OR: Wipf and Stock, 1968), 324.

545 Allen Putnam, *Flashes of Light from the Spirit-Land: Through the Mediumship of Mrs. J. H. Conant* (London: Forgotten Books, 2015; originally published in 1872), 58.

546 Betty, *The Afterlife Unveiled*, 30 (citing Geraldine Cummins, *Swan on a Black Sea*, Routledge and Kegan Paul, London, 1965).

547 Peebles, *Immortality and Our Employments Hereafter*, 151.

548 Ward, *Matthew, Tell Me about Heaven*, 61.

549 Borgia, *Life in the World Unseen*, 12.

550 Borgia, *Life in the World Unseen*, 119.

551 "The Lucillus séances," Leslie Flint Educational Trust, August 1, 1962, https://www.leslieflint.com/lucillus.

552 Stringfellow, *Leslie's letters to his mother*, 115.

[553] Betty, *The Afterlife Unveiled*, 42 (citing Barker, *Letters from a Living Dead Man*).

[554] "The Elizabeth Fry séance."

[555] Andrew Jackson Davis, *Death and the After Life* (Boston: Kobe and Rich, 1865), 95.

[556] Kardec, *The Spirits' Book*, 406.

[557] Borgia, *Life in the World Unseen*, 119.

[558] Jasper Swain, *On the Death of My Son* (London: Aquarian Press, 1974), 24.

[559] Suzanne Giesemann, *Awakening: Lessons from Beyond the Veil*, e-book, 2016, https://www.suzannegiesemann.com/books/.

[560] Ballard, *The Silver Birch Book of Questions & Answers*, 39.

[561] Tymn, *The Afterlife Revealed*, 113.

[562] "The Chinese Philosopher séance," Leslie Flint Educational Trust, July 30, 1959, https://www.leslieflint.com/confucius-july-1959.

[563] Nandor Fodor, "Chapter 3: The Voice of Confucius: Story of George Valiantine," *These Mysterious People* (London: Rider & Co. Ltd., 1934), 238.

[564] Crookall, *The Supreme Adventure*, 49.

[565] Betty, *The Afterlife Unveiled*, 2 (citing Barker, *Letters from a Living Dead Man*).

[566] Betty, *The Afterlife Unveiled*, 56-59 (citing Cummins, *Beyond Human Personality*).

[567] Betty, *The Afterlife Unveiled*, 58 (citing Cummins, *Beyond Human Personality*).

[568] Betty, *The Afterlife Unveiled*, 58 (citing Cummins, *Beyond Human Personality*).

[569] Betty, *The Afterlife Unveiled*, 59 (citing Cummins, *Beyond Human Personality*).

[570] Crookall, *The Supreme Adventure*, 49.

ISBN 978-0-9802111-3-9   US$24.95

9 780980 211139